The Batsford Encyclopaedia of

EMBROIDERY
TECHNIQUES

HEREWARD COLLEGE OF FURTHER EDUCATION
BRAMSTON CRESCENT
COVENTRY
CV4 9SW

The Batsford Encyclopaedia of
EMBROIDERY TECHNIQUES

Gay Swift

B T BATSFORD LTD · *LONDON*

For Harry

First published 1984
© Gay Swift 1984

All rights reserved. No part of this publication
may be reproduced in any form or by any means
without permission from the Publishers

ISBN 0 7134 3932 7

Photoset in Monophoto by
Servis Filmsetting Ltd, Manchester
Printed in Great Britain
by R.J. Acford
Chichester, Sussex
for the publishers,
B.T. Batsford Ltd,
4 Fitzhardinge Street,
London W1H 0AH

Contents

Acknowledgment

Grateful thanks are extended to all those people, museum staff and private individuals, who have offered time, space, assistance and advice to make this book possible, and to all the colleagues, students, teachers and young adults who have contributed both directly and indirectly: Abbot Hall Art Gallery. Nora Aitchison. The American Museum in Britain and Sheila Betterton. Jean Anderson. Margaret Armitage. The Ayrshire Branch of the Embroiderers' Guild. Belinda Baker. Bankfield Museum and Janet Pitman. Guy and Mary Barton and Joan Dutton. Di Bates. Bath Museum of Costume and Penelope Byrde. Beamish North of England Open Air Museum and Rosemary Allen. Bolton Museum and Art Gallery and R.J. Bradbury. Bowes Museum, Elizabeth Conran and Joanna Hashagen. The British Crafts Centre. British Needle Company Limited. Susan Butterworth. Cheltenham Art Gallery and Museum and Mary Greensted. Chipping Campden Church and Freddie Harrison. Colchester and Essex Museum and D. Clarke. Mrs Cowgill. Irene Coley. Lynda Colt. Cotehele House, Martin Briggs and Barbara Buttle. Amgueddfa Genedlaethol Cymru. Mattie Davidson. Lucienne Day. Beryl Dean, M.B.E. The Dean and Chapter Library, Durham, and Jill Ivy. Ard-Mhusaem na h'Eireann and Mairead Reynold. The Embroiderers' Guild, Rosemary Ewles, Ann Joyce and Lynette de Denne. Jeanette Fauvel. Fulneck Moravian Museum and Eunice Harrison. Gawthorpe Hall, Rachel Kay Shuttleworth, the Trustees, Eleanor Stewart, Pauline Gittens and Roger Dyson. Grace Glover. Joss Graham Oriental Textiles, London. Ann Green. Historic Deerfield Inc., Deerfield, Massachusetts, and Iona W. Lincoln. Gloucester Museum and Art Gallery and J.F. Rhodes. Mr Gray. Guildford Museum and Mary Alexander. Harris Museum and Art Gallery and Mrs A. Walker. Marianne Huber. June Irons. Jackson's Rugcraft Limited. Edith John. Lancaster Museum and The King's Own Royal Regimental Museum, Edith Tyson and Margaret Devlin. Leeds Museum, Barbara Woroncow and Helen. Leek Parish Church and D.A. Dawson. Estelle Lord, and Ken Lord for his patient and empathetic photography. Luton Museum and Doreen Fudge. Manchester Polytechnic, Judy Barry and Beryl Patten. Manila Cultural Centre, Philippines. West Nottinghamshire Society of Broderers, Chris Craggs and Grace Hewitt. Ann McNamara. Newstead Abbey, Pamela Wood and Iris Westbrook. Yasuzaemon Noguchi. Nottingham Museum of Costume and Textiles and Jeremy Farrell. Thelma M. Nye. Photo Precision, Huntingdon. Elizabeth Prickett. Richmond Brothers. Jean Roberts. Rhena Skinner. Margaret Smith. Stephen Simpson Limited and D. Ainsworth. Pauline Stride. Anne Stubbs. Belinda

Sufrin. Bessie Tapsell. Telford College, Meriel Tilling, Harriet Parker-Jervis, Mary Cross and Hilary Oberlander. Herta Puls. Textilmuseum St Gallen and M. Gachter-Weber. Phyllis Mary Thornber. Through the Flower Corporation, Santa Monica, and Judy Chicago. Traquair House and Mr P. Maxwell Stuart. The librarians at Settle, Yorkshire, and the Yorkshire and Humberside Libraries Joint Services. Simon Tuite. Whitbread and Company and J.F. Bartle. The Whitworth Art Gallery and Jennifer Harris. Celia and Claire Wilson. Evelyn Woodcock. York Museum, Elizabeth Hartley and Penelope Walton. Ann Young.

List of colour plates between pages 144 and 145

Introduction

Although this book is called an encyclopaedia it is only as objective, as definitive, and as final as one individual's attitude, selectivity and scope can make it. The writing of it has been an enrichment; as I learnt about their historical, geographical and economic backgrounds, techniques which once seemed tedious became fascinating. The romance of Ayrshire and Irish white work, for instance, assumed vital significance seen against a backdrop of famine, drudgery and exploitation. Pictorial images blossomed as wardrobe inventories or lists of Levant cargoes revealed a whole way of life, peopled by neatly braided women folding linens into oak kists, and sun-soaked workers packing spices, cochineal and elephant's teeth between layers of bright silks worked with pliant gold.

My primary aim has been to assemble essential information and provide a means of access to more detailed study. Discussion of historical background, representative pieces, and practical instruction is necessarily condensed, but the bibliography points the way to further study. The book is designed so that it can be used to recognize those techniques which constitute the traditions of embroidery, illustrated by typical examples and some variations.

Many embroideries defy definition and cannot be categorized since they are of mixed technique or have a unique style. Embroiderers may resent inclusions and omissions, emphasis and lack of it; but most techniques, sometimes dated or obscure, are included as points of reference for the non-expert. For instance, shisha work or abhla bharat is now well known in the West, but chikan, the delightful white floral embroidery from Lucknow, is little known despite its distinctive grace.

The acceptance of patchwork under the heading of embroidery is controversial. Several authors have made exhaustive and valuable studies of this exacting and often intricate technique. It includes quilting, appliqué and surface stitchery, involves an experienced understanding of the use and behaviour of fabrics, and possesses a long tradition of resourcefulness and creativity.

In the interests of clarity there has been no rigorous exclusion. Thus, although this is not a book about stitches, characteristic ones are illustrated and discussed; and, although some entries represent styles rather than techniques, their inclusion is valid in a proper study. Some subjects such as patchwork and quilting have been broken down into sub-species and entered separately so that they can be found more easily; but some areas, like transferring designs, should be understood as a whole, and are therefore dealt with as such and cross-referenced. Families common to many forms of open work, like picots, are grouped under a single entry. Names in brackets after the main entry heading are alternatives; *italics* in the text indicate cross references.

Professional workshop techniques are dealt with only briefly, and other entries merely give basic information rather than being concerned with technique, encouraging the reader to make full use of the bibliography. There is, for instance, no particular method common to samplers; but no enquiry should omit their study and so they appear as an individual entry. Gold and silver stitchery and the threads will be found under metal threads and metal thread work. Exceptions are made only where a particular technique has become universally known in an historical or geographical context, like or nué and underside couching.

The subject of lace is covered by brief definition and explanation under that entry. Any boundaries which divide lace and embroidery are a matter of convention and have no functional foundation. The needlemade laces employ techniques common in embroidery. Renaissance, Reticella and Venetian have separate entries because some authorities group them as embroidery, and because an understanding of their distinguishing features and construction is useful.

The plethora of names given to embroidery styles and methods through the Victorian period arose more often than not for commercial reasons. Where they are still known today or can be individually defined they are given as separate entries. The nineteenth century is admirably covered by Caulfeild and Saward.

One all-enveloping discovery which gradually became obvious as research progressed, was that the legacy of embroidery revivals over the last century or so has done much harm. Close examination of most forms of early stitchery, lovingly worked on hand weaves with hand–spun threads, made those recent copies of the style even more objectionable. Both Assisi work and Hedebo have been badly copied. Successful revivals include Ruskin work and Leek work. The only real solution is to become familiar with these early pieces and to try to understand how and why they were created. Nowadays embroiderers are diverging from the traditional techniques and using them more freely. This, and the wealth of new fabrics, are in turn imposing sophisticated values.

The feelings of guilt associated with copying are comparatively recent, not only in embroidery but in all creative fields. The early pattern books contained a rich source of starting points to be adapted for function, fabric and thread. Plagiarism is a necessary starting point, and however much it may be denied, every student is involved in its practice. Slavish representation of a historical piece is extremely difficult. In the attempt, a great deal can be learnt about the indigenous methods used before selective husbandry of flax, cotton and wool, before carding, combing and spinning mechanization, automated scouring and washing, loom manufacture and commercial weaving, control of dyeing and finishing processes, and modern marketing, communication and transport.

Nevertheless, some embroiderers still feel that too many rules can stifle creativity:

> Pens, pencils and brushes seem to paralyse the creative processes of the very people whose extensive knowledge of all kinds of embroidery should enable them to produce collectors' pieces. Even their knowledge is rarely used to the full, partly because these talented people are afraid to break down the barriers which, during the centuries, have been erected between different methods of embroidery, and partly because they are afraid to depart from the recognized rules upon which so much needlework seems to depend. It must be remembered that rules are made for

the guidance of beginners and they can be ignored quite safely by the embroiderer who has mastered all the basic skills, and who wishes to develop them.

EDITH JOHN

The large number of photographs of details may give the impression that all embroideries are obscure and intimate, but this is far from reality. Epic undertakings survive from the Dark Ages onwards, and huge ambitious projects are still successfully completed. Many of the familiar great works provoke such awe, and a sense that the dedication and time expended are unattainable achievements. I have tried to include some more modest examples to encourage practical involvement. Undated photographs are either recent, or their period is obvious from the accompanying text. Sizes of details are given in all instances except where scale is apparent. Where diagrams indicate the needle entering and leaving the ground on the right side in one movement, this is usually for the sake of clarity. For most stitchery worked in a frame, a vertical movement up and down through the ground is recommended.

The bibliography lists all useful books, even very general ones, although sometimes complete details cannot be given. They are intended to be of use to the worker and to the research student. Books other than those in English are given only where a comprehensive study necessitates their use. Those which proved impossible to locate either for reference or lending are omitted, as are those which offer no more detail than can be found here. The time lapse between compilation and publication means that very new books cannot appear. Victoria and Albert Museum publications and *Embroidery* magazines are indispensable. A few relevant articles are given in the bibliography, usually prefixed by authors' names. The individual bibliographies under the entries give only the author's name, and the date if that author has written more than one book; details of title, publisher etc. will be found in the main bibliography.

Small textiles are relatively easy to transport and hoard, and so there are few kinds of embroidery which are difficult to find. By prior appointment, the student will find a wealth of information within easy reach. The museum lists serve only as a casual introduction. Major textiles museums may well have little-known embroidery stores, and many less celebrated museums often reveal surprisingly comprehensive and rewarding collections.

AEROPHANE (areophane arophane)

A closely woven translucent fabric like soft muslin. In the tradition of *silk pictures* of the late eighteenth and early nineteenth centuries, aerophane was used together with areas of overlapping stitchery to create the illusion of receding planes. Later, during the Victorian period, aerophane was employed for raised decoration on costume and accessories to make

Aerophane: floss silk and chenille on cream silk. Probably Moravian, *c.* 1840. (*Bankfield Museum*)

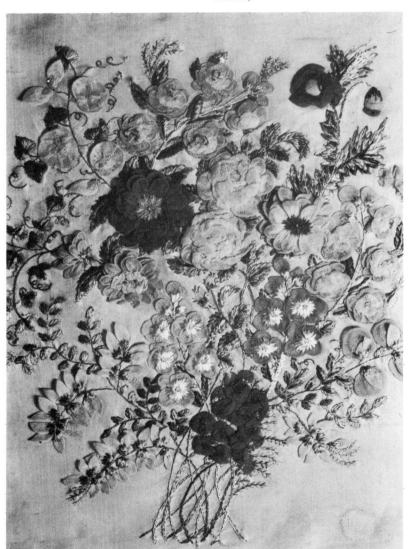

flowers and leaves, often in association with *ribbon work*. It was then described as crêpe work.

Collections
UK Gawthorpe Hall, Burnley; Bankfield Museum, Halifax

ALOE THREAD

The fibre of the aloe, lustrous and straw coloured, was used as a novelty embroidery thread in the late nineteenth century. It was worked over a wool padding on smooth materials, in formal, floral arrangements in satin stitch. Probably evolving from an earlier form of coarse lace, it may have flourished only in response to commercial promotion.

Bibliography
Caulfeild and Saward

AMAGER

Strictly disciplined cross-stitch panels from the Island of Amager between Denmark and Sweden. Most of the panels are dated, and fall between 1770 and 1852. They are worked in wool, silk or cotton on heavy linen, with opposing rows of birds, beasts, fruit and figures.
   Another type found on the Island consists of plaited stitch flettestingets, rows of long-legged cross stitch worked vertically with black silk on white linen.

Bibliography
Johnsen

Collection
UK Bankfield Museum, Halifax

AMELIA WORK

See *Dressed prints*

AMERICAN TAPESTRY

A silk needleweaving process worked on a 'broad, heavily marked, loosely woven fabric which would hold our precious stitches safely and show them to advantage' (Wheeler). The ground was entirely covered by long, horizontal needleweaving locked into the fine warp and catching the soft weft, changing colour in exactly the same way as true *tapestry*. It differs from Coptic *needleweaving* which is worked on a loom.

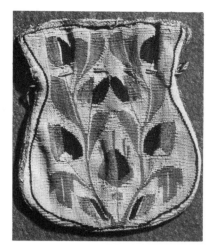

American tapestry: random-dyed pink, lilac and green silk, linen loosely twisted with fine metal plate. Baglet featuring wild pea flowers, needlewoven to the required shape. 13 cm (5 in.) long. (*Rachel Kay Shuttleworth Collection, Gawthorpe Hall*)

Introduced by Candace Wheeler in 1883, the work was produced by Associated Artists. Large figurative hangings were made to fulfil commissions, and then more commercially viable smaller pieces appeared as the work became known.

Bibliography
Wheeler

Collection
UK Gawthorpe Hall, Burnley

ANGLO-INDIAN EMBROIDERY

Popular during the late nineteenth and early twentieth centuries, Anglo-Indian embroidery was essentially an embellishment of the design on richly floral grounds. It closely resembled *brocade embroidery* and *Kashmir* of the same period, but Anglo-Indian is on a printed ground and brocade and cashmere are on woven patterns. The Indian prints featured the cone design. Silk thread was used in flat stitches, chain stitches and knots, with some loosely darned grounds, the stitchery often almost entirely covering the surface. Later, the print was voided, the main part of the design being surrounded with couched jap gold, sometimes with the addition of tamboured or machined chain stitch.

Machine and hand embroiderers frequently use printed grounds in a similar way, seeking direct cohesion between ground and stitchery. Satin stitch and straight stitch on the machine can give smooth, precise lines allied to the edges of printed colour.

The term Anglo-Indian may sometimes be used instead of *Indo-European*.

ANTICS (antiques)

Fantastic representations of animal and floral forms overlapping and encompassing one another, at the height of fashion on the vast expanses of Tudor petticoats revealed beneath the stomacher. Elizabethan portraits show linen stitched with dark lines or perhaps quilted with drawings of what were then mysterious and awe-inspiring monsters such as dolphins and elephants. They were not made to conform to repetitive pattern or conventional arrangement, but rampaged menacingly and most inappropriately across the fabric to great effect.

ANTIQUE SEAM

A simple *insertion* of faggoting stitch. Sometimes all insertion stitches are called antique seams, since they are most frequently found on old hand-spun and hand-woven textiles. Selvedges butted together decoratively avoid the loss of precious width lapped into a conventional seam.

APPLIED PATCHWORK (US: pressed quilts)

Some forms of patchwork, because of their characteristic geometry, cannot be pieced simply by sewing the patches together, but must be stitched to a backing or foundation. Traditionally the patches were often left unquilted, but they can be wadded in the usual way providing the fabric is fairly light and the piecing is smooth. Pressed forms are those which employ a running stitch to join each succeeding piece to the foundation. The first piece is stitched to the ground, the second piece faced on to it with right sides together, and a seam made through all three layers. The second piece is then turned and

pressed open with the fingers to receive the third piece in the same way.

All forms of applied patchwork are decorative contrivances which have little relevance to the original function of patchwork. They are ideal ways of exploring colour and tone relationships within the discipline of repetitive construction. *Patchwork* (pieced work, mosaic work) is dealt with as a separate entry, as is *applied work* where the patterns of applied fabric do not cover the ground completely. *Wadded quilting* is inseparable from all patchwork, and it is essential to consider both this and the whole area of quiltmaking collectively. This entry concentrates on log cabin, string and strip quilting so that basic method and the use of the machine may be explained. All other forms of applied patchwork will be found separately entered.

Log cabin patchwork and its variants, sometimes known as Canadian patchwork, are supposed to have their origins amongst those Settlers who moved to the Northern Territories following the American Revolution. The pattern is said to represent the structure of the roof of a cabin with its square central chimney and welcoming fire, and the strong shafts of snow-reflected light breaking the dark shadows of the interior. The affinity is undeniable when log cabin is seen on a whole quilt against a background of snowy linens and whitewashed walls.

The management of light and dark strips is the main design consideration. Sewing blocks together presents fascinating pattern possibilities. Blocks which are symmetrical on all four sides will give only one new set of patterns when they are joined together, but blocks which are not symmetrical have much more potential. Those symmetrical one either side of a central fold may be inverted and grouped differently. Blocks can also be set diagonally, with corners joined and alternating with plain blocks, or set in lattice strips. In this case, if straight edges are required for the patchwork, half blocks will be needed to complete the pattern at the edge.

Having decided on the look of the intended piece and its scale and

Applied patchwork: machine satin stitch reds and greens on green felt on the strippy principle, characteristic of Seminole Indian work. Cornely mossing and chain. 13 cm (5 in.) square. Made by Judy Barry and Beryl Patten

dimensions, collected together suitable fabrics in required quantities and found graph paper and drawing materials, the next stage is to make a scale drawing of the whole piece. Templates are not essential, but the preparation of some carefully measured paper or card ones will usually be helpful for arranging the cutting. These are not left in the work.

The material for the top may be of almost any kind. Early log cabin was probably made of cotton scraps, and the Victorians used ribbons and silks. Ancient applied strip patchworks from the Far East were constructed from silk samples. The technique has come to be associated with fabrics which are technically easy to handle and offer a wide range of colour with no textural variation. However, the proliferation of samples of furnishing fabrics has led to velvets, ribbed acetates and even brocades being used for patchwork, and experiments in suitings, tweeds and hessians are not unknown. The foundation cloth to which the pieces are stitched should be a firmly woven cotton. Substantial old sheeting is

suitable; new calico must be well washed and fully shrunk.

Cut a square of foundation cloth for each square of patchwork, making the cut strictly on the grain and leaving a generous seam allowance all round. The size of the square is determined by the number of strips of top fabric intended and by the scale of the work. The strips cut from ordinary cotton fabric will be between 1 cm ($\frac{3}{8}$ in.) and 2.5 cm (1 in.) wide, although working much smaller than this was once regarded as an admirable technical feat. Tape the foundation fabric to a flat surface and mark out, using a sharp pencil, a rule and a set square and compasses if the pattern needs them. Any of the log cabin family of patterns, with the exception of the pineapple variation, can be worked on this marked foundation cloth.

Cut out each piece for the top individually. It is very important to iron the fabrics quite smooth first. Take care to orientate each similar shape the same way on the fabric. Bias seams should be as few as possible. Transparent templates are useful for determining the exact position of any printed pattern on the cotton before the piece is cut out. On velvets, tacking and pinning should be done only on the turnings, which should be generous to allow for the fabric creeping whilst it is being sewn. Pieces

may be cut or torn without the aid of templates, but again it is essential that they are quite flat before piecing commences.

(It is possible to work the log cabin family of patterns without a foundation fabric, in which case they become patchwork rather than applied patchwork. However, it is impractical and difficult because it lacks stability. The only advantage is that each block can be stitched around its edge to a lining fabric, so forming pockets which can be wadded like *puff patchwork*.)

Apply the central square with tacking stitches right side up, overlapping the foundation fabric markings. Pin the first strip (piece 2 on the diagram) along one edge of the square with right sides together. The extended lines marked on the foundation cloth serve as a guide to the stitching line. Stitch, turn and baste. Lay piece 3 along the next edge of the square, covering both it and the short end of piece 2, with right sides facing. Stitch, turn and tack. Hand stitching is done with a small running stitch, and some workers prefer to incorporate regularly spaced back stitches as a reinforcement.

Machine stitch tension must be carefully adjusted so that a medium stitch length will keep the fabrics flat and easy to handle. After some practice basting can be dispensed with, but pins must lie with their points towards the machine needle so that they can be removed as stitching progresses along each strip. The use of a wide presser foot can be an invaluable guide for maintaining a regular seam width.

The pineapple pattern is marked and pieced differently. The construction of lines on the foundation cloth has diagonals. Working out from the extremities of the central square, each radiating line should be marked in equal divisions, irrespective of its square or diagonal nature. By using compasses these markings can be cross-checked for accuracy. The final division on each diagonal indicates the line for the corner triangle.

Tack on the central square. Pin the first straight strip (piece 2 on the diagram) along one edge of the square with right sides together. Using the extended lines marked on the foundation cloth, stitch, turn and tack. Position pieces 3, 4 and 5 similarly, allowing small overlaps at each corner, and turning and basting down each one as stitching is completed. The corner triangles are equilateral ones cut from a square.

The completed squares are carefully tacked together and joined with a simple seam according to their light-dark arrangement. Seams are often left exposed on the back of the work, but the squares may be quilted or lined.

Strippy quilting or string quilting seems to have come from Northumbria in England, although it is such a logical construction that it has a long history and many technical parallels throughout the world. The terms 'strip quilts' or 'stripey quilts' used for similar constructions are common throughout Britain and America.

Traditionally there is no difference between strippy and string, except that the blocks of the former could be halved alternately and inverted for chevron patterns. Amish patchwork (see *quilts*) is technically indistinguishable, though it was often made without a foundation.

The blocks are made individually with strips of top fabric cut on the straight grain and placed diagonally on the straight grain of the foundation lengths. There is a divergence of opinion concerning the direction of fabric grain. Some workers recommend that the diagonal strips of top fabric should be cut on the bias, thus returning all grains at right angles to one another on the finished top, but making all sewing on the bias. Since

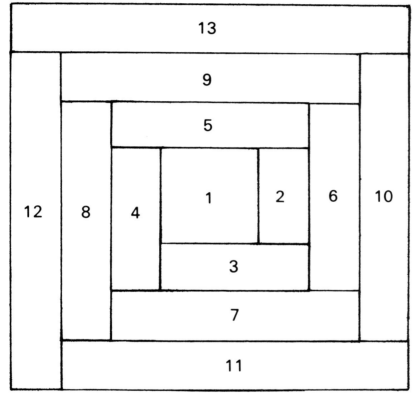

The card master template, marked out in order of joining, for log cabin. Unlike the foundation cloth, each piece has a seam allowance

Log cabin. The second piece is applied over the marked foundation cloth

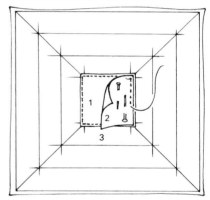

Courthouse steps

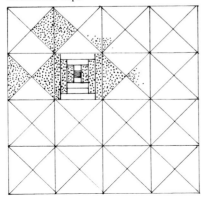

Diamonds

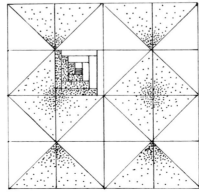

Straight furrow

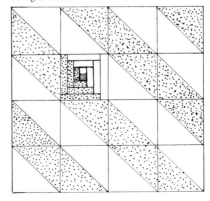

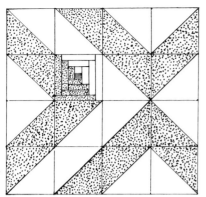

Barn raising

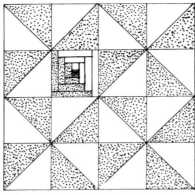

Windmill

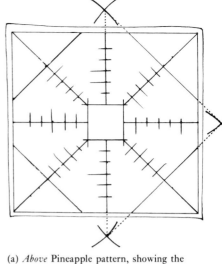

Pineapple

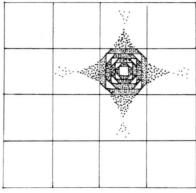

(a) *Above* Pineapple pattern, showing the foundation cloth marked; (b) *Below* Pineapple pattern with some pieces applied

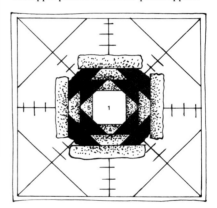

the strips are used diagonally, progressively smaller ones can be accommodated towards the corners. The sewing technique is the same as that for all applied patchwork. It is ideal for stitching by machine.

Once the base block is covered, a running stitch round the perimeter stabilizes the ends of the strips, which can be trimmed to conform to the block. Completed strips may be sewn to each other or alternated with plain strips. Pieced work of this kind applied to a foundation is often sufficiently heavy without a batting. However, it is easy to stitch, and can now be made direct onto a wadding or batting substituted for the foundation material. Some types of synthetic wadding have considerable stability and pass over the feed-dog as easily as a woven fabric.

Strippy blocks can be halved, quartered, cut into right-angled or isosceles triangles or into parallelograms, and rejoined to make simple or complex arrangements. They are at their best when made into new squares or rectangles and contrasted with areas of plain fabric in associated colours. All joining is better stitched by machine, but subsequent wadded quilting should be made by hand on a stretched backing.

Bibliography
Colby 1958, 1965; Davidson; Finley; Hall and Kretsinger; Osler

Collections
UK American Museum, Bath; Victoria and Albert Museum, London; Beamish North of England Open Air Museum, Stanley
USA Newark Museum, New Jersey

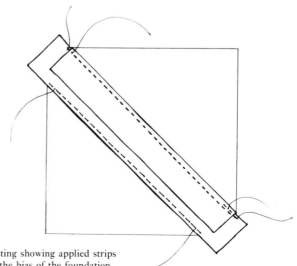

String quilting showing applied strips lapped on the bias of the foundation

APPLIED WORK (appliqué, onlay, laid work, laid on work, patched work)

The application, by means of close stitchery, of pieces of fabric to a flat ground of similar weight. Unlike appliqué, which is very variable, applied work is concerned with conventional forms in repetitive units, almost always cotton on cotton, and smoothly applied. It is used as an integral part of pieced quilts, and often the pieces are themselves composed of pieced work. This is the true patchwork (patches of fabric applied to an exposed ground which itself forms part of the surface pattern), as distinct from the generally known *patchwork* which is properly called pieced work in the USA. The entry on *applied patchwork* indicates another aspect, and all forms are dealt with collectively under *quilts. Hawaiian quilting* is an applied work form.

The technique flourished in both Britain and America from the early eighteenth century. Many traditional patterns and borders were common to both patchwork and applied work. Large and elaborate motifs were cut from printed cottons and carefully applied in complex border arrangements, or separate flowers and small features were reassembled into rich central medallions and floral swags. Scraps cut from sprigged prints were organized into blocks, often superimposed, and related to subsequent quilting patterns. Commemorative and narrative quilts demanded representational skills. The Pennsylvanian German quilts were often pictorial with social or political subject matter. There is still an enthusiasm for pictorial applied work in the USA.

Although the technique is the easiest to understand it does require time and dexterity. If a large-scale quilt is planned, applied work and quilting must be integrated. Decisions relating to size and construction must be made together with those about framing. Early applied work was almost

Applied work: cotton prints applied by machine through a synthetic wadding, 122 cm (48 in.) square. Made by Ann McNamara

certainly done without a large frame, although individual blocks or strips later to be joined together may well have been stitched on stretched fabric. For small shapes the grain of the applied fabric need not conform to that of the ground, but the rule must be obeyed for larger ones. Modern polyester-cottons with a cotton content of about 70 percent are ideal for both ground and applied shapes. Fabrics must be very closely matched in texture and weave, needles must be fine and easy to use, and threads must be firm and strong. The type of stitch and the colour of the working thread can emphasize or soften the pattern in relation to the ground. Tradition allows minimal surface stitchery, but stem, buttonhole, chain and herringbone are all permissible.

The applied fabrics are pressed completely flat and, working on a firm surface, they should be cut precisely with very sharp scissors, leaving narrow turnings. Shapes are of two distinct kinds: they may be regular and geometrical and determined by templates, or cut out freehand and determined by the outline of a print

on the fabric. Where necessary any drawn cutting lines should be made with a hard pencil on the back of the fabric. It was the practice for each piece to be backed with starched or dressed cotton fabric cut to the exact shape and stitched in with the tacking. There are a number of modern non-woven substitutes for this cotton, from which the correct weight can be selected. They make an excellent finish and are very easy to use, particularly the fine iron-on ones. This bonding fabric can be cut to the finished size of the applied piece and ironed on to the appliqué fabric so that the piece can be cut out around it with an allowance for turnings.

All the edges are turned and basted. Convex curves should be gathered first and concave ones snipped, and the tacking stitches used to produce a firm, flat edge. It is worth taking care to tack shapes to the ground fabric very precisely. Fabrics which will be damaged by pins can be held in place with double-sided adhesive tape, which is removed before the stitching journey around the shape is completed.

Finally, each piece is overcast with a

(a) Princess feather and sunburst; (b) Tea rose; (c) Dahlia wreath; (d) Whig rose

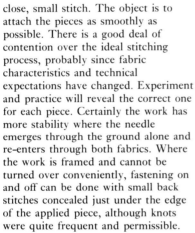

close, small stitch. The object is to attach the pieces as smoothly as possible. There is a good deal of contention over the ideal stitching process, probably since fabric characteristics and technical expectations have changed. Experiment and practice will reveal the correct one for each piece. Certainly the work has more stability where the needle emerges through the ground alone and re-enters through both fabrics. Where the work is framed and cannot be turned over conveniently, fastening on and off can be done with small back stitches concealed just under the edge of the applied piece, although knots were quite frequent and permissible.

The sensitivity of the modern sewing machine makes it ideal for most applied work. Using a carefully adjusted tension, appropriate presser-foot pressure and a short stitch, the machine can be guided slowly around curves and eased gently along the smoothest line. A straight stitch near the edge of the applied piece will leave a slightly raised rim of fabric. A satin stitch or open zigzag is more difficult to control precisely. The finish they give and the possibilities of line and colour offered make the sacrifice of perfect precision worthwhile. Ends of threads need careful finishing.

Subsequent quilting lines may be hand-stitched around the applied pieces, but often on old quilts the applied pattern was more or less ignored by the quilter, who built a second pattern over the whole surface. Machine quilting using the darning

foot is both speedy and accurate, and the resulting line is quite different from that done by hand. The working threads are continuous on both back and front of the quilting, and it is the threads which are under tension and not the fabrics. If the quilting is to be done by machine a synthetic wadding is preferable.

Bibliography
Carlisle; Finley; White

Collections
UK American Museum, Bath
USA Newark Museum, New Jersey

APPLIQUÉ (onlay, laying-on, poor man's embroidery)

All those embroidery and needlework techniques which include the application of one woven or non-woven material to another may be called appliqué. There is such variation that no specific method is typical, and reference must be made to many other entries for its extent to be appreciated.

Scraps and remnants of expensive fabrics have always been stitched to stronger and more serviceable materials for decorative purposes. Appliqué can be found in almost any culture, historical or ethnic, where personal or domestic coverings are used. It often imitates period-style embroidery, following conventional designs and outlines which would be occupied by stitchery on more expensive textiles. Equally, those rich embroideries may themselves fall from favour and be cut up and the pieces applied to more acceptable furnishings.

It was once a prerequisite of appliqué that it should lie flat on the ground fabric, match grain direction, and have edges turned or covered in some way. Since the 1930s, when exponents like Rebecca Crompton freed appliqué from its conventional

Appliqué: suitings, ticking and velvet on pieced union cloth. Detail of a room divider

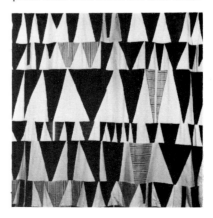

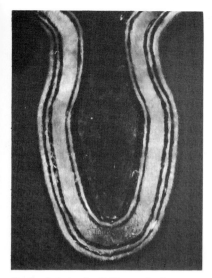

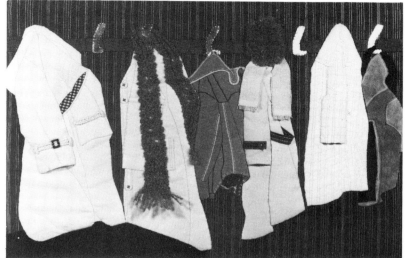

Appliqué: Labrador Eskimo, tail of a sealskin jacket deftly pieced with fine stitchery. (*Leeds Museum*)

strictures, it has become an accepted and integral part of embroidery.

Together with stitchery, appliqué has been enriched by a greater understanding of the creativity of other cultures. Hardwearing qualities must be a priority to the Eskimo and the North American Indian, and yet a considerable variety of immediately available natural materials are utilized,

Appliqué: North-western Indian bullock cart cover 122 × 107 cm (48 × 42 in.). Heavy slub cotton, primary colours. (*Leeds Museum*)

Appliqué: Alaskan Aleut Indian shaman ball, buff and natural sealskin. 20 cm (8 in.) diameter. (*Leeds Museum*)

Appliqué: imitative fabrics chosen for their textural scale. 61 × 43 cm (24 × 17 in.). Made by Harriet Parker-Jervis

with great skill in their decorative effect as well as their function. The Eskimos of northern Alaska made parkas from dyed translucent skins, the numerous seams decorated with stitchery and beading. Sometimes two layers were used, the top skin cut to reveal the one beneath. Narrow horizontal striping was constructed from intestines. The Northern and Canadian Indians made birchbark appliqué sewn with dyed spruce roots.

Bibliography
Crompton

ARABIAN EMBROIDERY

Madame Lucie d'Algiers founded a school in about 1840 for the purpose of providing some support to destitute Algerian women. Soft stitchery was done in floss silk on muslin, and laid work fillings and chained outlines were worked on firmer materials. Designs were derived entirely from local origins.

Bibliography
Caulfeild and Saward

ARI

See *Tambour work*

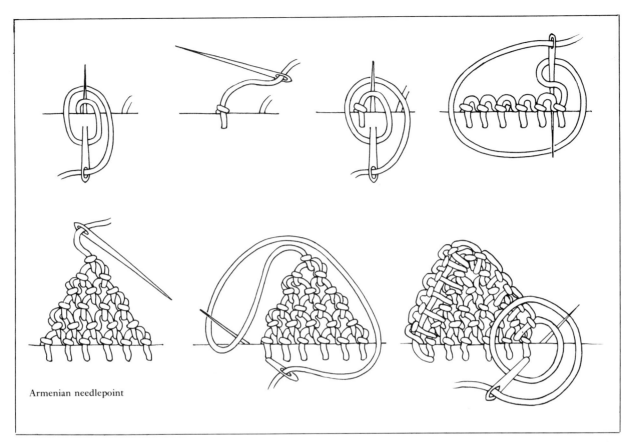

Armenian needlepoint

ARMENIAN NEEDLEPOINT (pyramid edging, dentelle de Smyrne)

Made by Mohammedan women, this is a favourite edging characterized by little knotted triangles, both coarse and fine, coloured and natural. There is a good deal of confusion between this and *bebilla*. Armenian is probably the relic, the remaining everyday edging, left from the period when bebilla was a status symbol. It may still have elaborations of rosettes and variable bands, but it seems that nevertheless it is classed as Armenian rather than bebilla. The little knotted lace stitch is worked directly onto the fold of the hem on many textiles. Simple padded buttons and tassels sometimes feature at corners. It is usually worked in black or white for edging scarves and yashmaks, and in primary colours for other domestic uses. The finest may be worked in ordinary sewing cotton, but European versions are often in crochet cotton on the edge of linen.

ASSISI

A term now applied very narrowly to simply constructed monochromatic borders of repeated animal motifs treated in reserve on a ground of cross stitch. The texture of the ground is accentuated by the voiding of the animal subjects which may or may not be outlined. It was usual to employ just one colour of working thread, a primary colour or a neutral. For some inexplicable reason, black with orange or yellow is preferred for recent pieces of Assisi type.

Historically, however, Assisi is exciting. Fifteenth-century Italian. pieces have Renaissance richness and Spanish ones of the same period have Moorish exactness. From the sixteenth century deep borders were stitched near the edge of linens, complementing open, geometrically based filet lace. These borders were often narrative, Biblical or legendary, with freely drawn, robust, heraldic animals bounding across them.

There are various theories for the origins of the voiding. It may have come from Egyptian ivory and pearl

Assisi: long legged, or long armed, cross stitch is worked from left to right

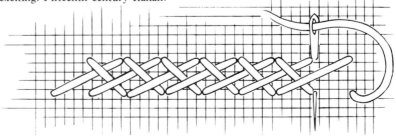

inlay on dark woods, or from contemporary woodcut illustrations, but many forms of open embroidery observe the same principle and it may be merely adventitious.

The association of Assisi with cross stitch is recent. Older pieces have outlines of angular back stitch, buttonholing or whipped running, and inside the voided subjects there are rosettes, stars and hearts, and sometimes the bird or beast itself repeated in miniature. The outlines of even running stitch which take up small picks of the ground are known as punto scritto. The grounds are often pulled with stitches which open the weave. Tent and single faggot are favourites, with plaited braid stitch, long-legged and double darning providing horizontal rows rather than the squared texture of cross stitch.

The style was revived in the town of Assisi in the nineteenth century. Copies of earlier designs were made on specially woven grounds, but the vitality and clarity was lost. Possibly it is the comparatively low standard of these tourist-trade copies which has caused Assisi embroidery to be neglected.

Collections
UK Victoria and Albert Museum, London; Nottingham Museum

AURIPHRYGIUM (aurifrigium)

The Phrygians brought embroideries to the Mediterranean from North Africa, and the imported metal thread work became known to the Romans, and therefore to the early Roman Church, as auriphrygium. Those who made the embroideries were called phrygiones. Written accounts as late as 1235 refer to a worker skilled in the use of metal threads as an 'aurifrigiaria'.

AYRSHIRE (Scottish sewed muslin, the Flowerin', tamboured muslin)

The fine, white, lacy stitchery on translucent cambric or muslin associated principally with baby robes and bonnets, which was produced mainly in Ireland and Scotland in the eighteenth and nineteenth centuries.

Assisi: sixteenth-century Italian voided border, red silk on natural linen, ground pulled with cross stitches, 6 cm (2½ in.) wide. (*Nottingham Museum*)

Assisi: sixteenth-century Italian borders, red silk on linen, double running, each band 4 cm (1½ in.) wide. (*Nottingham Museum*)

Early pieces are extremely fine and yet robust in design, and are mostly borders for flounces, caps and gowns. They tend to have contrasting areas of close and open stitching, giving an illusion of lace but with few worked fillings. They are not entirely floral, figures and animals suggesting associations with Italian point *lace*. Worked in a frame, Ayrshire was referred to as tamboured muslin, although there is no evidence that a tambour hook was ever used. Throughout its main commercial period the work is almost exclusively floral. Lively swags and sprays of flowers and ferns decorate panels and borders, liberally scattered with minutely worked needlepoint fillings. The work is all virtually reversible. Although the surface stitchery has

great textural richness, Ayrshire is intended to be seen against the skin or a shadowed undergarment, so displaying its translucent quality and the value of the fillings.

Northern peasant communities invariably have a tradition of white linen embroidery, and early Scandinavian and Celtic influences must have been strong in Scotland. Ayrshire has many similarities with old *Hedebo*. Amongst those legends concerning the beginnings of the Flowerin', the most romantic is probably that associated with Saint Kentigern (Saint Mungo), a monk who travelled throughout Northern Ireland, Cumberland and Scotland during the infancy of the Church in Britain. He is said to have found, in the recesses of a cave where he was resting, a 'Babe

Ayrshire: bodice of a baby robe, nineteenth-century. (*Rachel Kay Shuttleworth Collection, Gawthorpe Hall*)

Ayrshire: border, eighteenth-century, 6 cm (2½ in.) deep. (*Rachel Kay Shuttleworth Collection, Gawthorpe Hall*) ▼

clothed in a soft fair robe of exceeding fineness, glistening with a whiteness no earthly hands may compass' (Morris). The story cannot be authenticated, but it does complement Ann Macbeth's description: 'dream stitcheries . . . delicate traceries which told tales of an imaginative sentiment, . . . these Ayrshire embroideries rank perhaps higher, technically speaking, than any other needlework that the world has yet produced.'

Scotland has long been associated with the production of fine linens and delicate embroidery, both for domestic use and as a supplement to family income. The Treaty of Union in 1706 brought educational and financial encouragement. As the embroidery became increasingly commercial the demand for finer grounds led to the import of Indian muslin and cambric. By the late eighteenth century mechanical spinning in western Scotland was producing a fine cotton yarn. As machinery replaced home spinning labour became cheap, and both commercial and philanthropic efforts were made to advance workshops, training and trade. In 1786 Luigi Ruffini set up organized embroidery workrooms in Edinburgh, and more manufacturers and businessmen quickly followed.

Cottage industry and workshops alike were highly organized and highly exploited. Designers' drawings were transferred to wooden and metal blocks which were stamped on to the cloth or lithographed, with printed specifications for the workers such as contract delivery dates, types of stitches and fillings required, and payment related to technical standard achieved. Grounds were then parcelled into lots for local deliveries in both Scotland and Ireland (see *Carrickmacross*), where they were distributed to individual specialist workers. Most broderers had very restricted choice, no influence over design and little knowledge of the finished garment for which they were working. Samplers were made by the workshops both as teaching aids and as demonstration pieces for commissioned sales. By the 1850s skilled broderers worked a 17-hour day for 4d and children for ½d each day. There are records of between 20,000 and 30,000 employees working throughout Scotland and Ireland for one firm alone.

Mechanization, change in fashion, competition and economic stringencies brought Ayrshire work to a gradual decline by the middle of the nineteenth century. It was still practised as a more casual cottage industry into the twentieth century, but it became coarser and lost its lace fillings, growing more like *Madeira* work and *broderie anglaise*.

Crown centres of baby caps, often the only linen ground, were regarded as the masterpiece of the skilled

Ayrshire: front panel of a baby robe, mid-nineteenth-century. (*The Embroiders' Guild*)

Ayrshire: border, eighteenth-century, 5 cm (2 in.) deep. (*Rachel Kay Shuttleworth Collection, Gawthorpe Hall*)

Ayrshire: skirt panel of a baby robe, mid-nineteenth-century. (*The Embroiderers' Guild*)

worker. The cap band was worked in a border pattern, usually by the same worker. The main area of the crown was usually delicately sprigged or dotted, and gathered round the centre with tiny tucks. Christening gown shapes evolved from the French Napoleonic fashion, with a low neckline, puff sleeves, and a long, decorated centre front panel called a chemisette. The front bodice panel narrowed to an unattached point at the waist, with a small opening in the seam behind it, so that the point could be left out for boys or tucked in for girls.

All those characteristics which together constitute Ayrshire must be brought together in order to reproduce a recognizable piece. Close study of early examples is essential. A sheer linen lawn or fine, tightly spun, openly woven cambric must be bought from a specialist supplier. It must be meticulously stretched in a large slate frame which accommodates the whole panel to be worked (see *framing up*). Designs taken from historical examples, or closely adapted in relation to them, should be traced in blue with dressmaker's carbon, or drawn out with pale blue paint following the prick and pounce method of *transferring designs*. At least two weights of finest matt lace threads (140s) are needed for working, and the smallest needle sizes. Eyelets are always made with a stiletto.

Stitches have strong parallels with *Dresden work* and *Chikan*, consisting of satin, herringbone, overcasting and buttonholing, and chain. Tiny eyelets are unadorned. Larger point work may be overcast and then cut, or snipped, turned and overcast as in *broderie anglaise*. Most pieces have cutwork with lace fillings, but some have pulled or drawn fillings with tiny rows of double hemstitching.

Bibliography
Boyle; D.M.C.; Morris, J.A.; Swain 1955, 1970

Collections
UK Bowes Museum, Barnard Castle; Gawthorpe Hall, Burnley; The Moravian Museum, Fulneck; Guildford Museum; Nottingham Museum; Harris Museum and Art Gallery, Preston

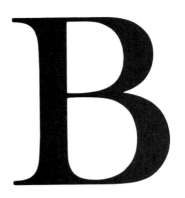

BACKING

The layer of material beneath ground or wadding which provides support and sometimes weight. Two kinds of embroidery necessitate backing: almost all metal thread embroidery is worked through both ground and backing, as are most kinds of quilting.

BADLA

An Indian *metal thread* of silver or silver gilt wire loosely coiled, and also the rather coarse, freely stitched embroidery which features it.

Collection
UK   Gawthorpe Hall, Burnley

BAGH

See *Phulkari*

BAKUBA (Kasai velvet)

A high pile *raffia* embroidery on woven raffia cloth made by the tribes of the Kasai region of Zaire. Traditionally the cloth is woven by the men and embroidered by the women. It is now limited to the Bakuba area on the Kasai river where it is used as clothing and blankets by people of status. A series of diagonal, chevron or key patterns, sometimes marked out but usually worked without guiding lines, are stitched with fine, softened raffia in a close pile in browns, yellows, pinks and purples, in cut pile stitch. The working thread is simply passed through the closely woven raffia cloth with an iron needle, leaving short ends which are cut individually. It is

sometimes used alone, sometimes complemented by flat stitchery, and often covers the ground completely.

The Babunda of Zaire embroider conventionally with raffia surface stitchery.

Collection
UK   Museum of Mankind, British Museum, London

BARGELLO

See *Florentine*

BARS (ties, brides)

Usually crossing an open area of the ground which has been drawn or cut, bars consist of one or several long stitches which can be reinforced or stabilized with further stitchery. They are traditionally associated with most forms of open white work and needlemade laces, but they need not be either white or delicate. The entries on Ayrshire, broderie anglaise, cutwork, drawn thread, Hardanger, Hedebo and lace describe how bars are used. They are frequently ornamented with *picots*.

The ordinary lockstitch on the machine can be used to imitate the bars of needlemade lace. Using a free needle and the ground stretched in a tambour frame, the machine stitch can

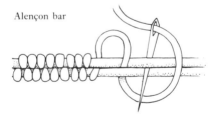

Alençon bar

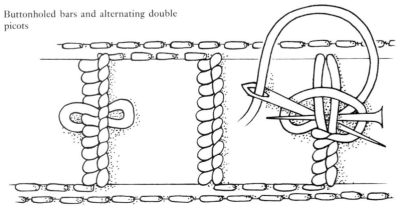

Buttonholed bars and alternating double picots

be formed across previously cut spaces, secured at either side by close darning. Careful adjustment of the tensions will provide an even twist between needle and spool threads. More freedom and useful exploration of ground fabric qualities is afforded by drawing yarns from openly woven linen and using a satin stitch or zigzag across the remaining yarns.

Bibliography
Benson 1946, 1952; de Dillmont; Gray 1973; Swift

BATUZ WORK (hammered-up gold, beten, bete)

A method of ornamenting silk embroidery by the addition of low relief plates representing animals, flowers or heraldic devices. It was often mentioned in ecclesiastical inventories and royal wills from the eleventh century to the fifteenth. Later it was known as bete or beten work, and was applied to gold decoration on woven grounds and incorporated in high relief metal thread embroidery.

Fairholt says batuz is an Old English term meaning embroidered, especially when applied to garments. According to Clabburn it means gold work of any sort applied to fabric.

Bibliography
Clabburn; Fairholt

BEADS

Beads are made from cumbersome stone, precious metal, amber and turquoise, delicately floral glass, lustrous pearls, plant and animal matter, all in many shapes and sizes.

The entry *beadwork* describes some of their functional and decorative uses. *North American Indian* beadwork, like that of Africa and many other cultures, may be stitched, woven or strung.

Beads are a fascinating material to work with; all kinds of pretty things can be done with them, either sewing them upon a ground, knitting or crocheting, or making use of a small bead loom. A good deal of the ready-made bought bead work, that only requires a monotonous ground to be filled in around an already worked pattern of sorts, is not at all suggestive of its possibilities. Beads of both paste and glass can be obtained in much greater variety than is usually known, from the most minute in size to large varieties of all kinds of shapes and patterns, the colours of most of them being particularly good. The larger ornamental beads are useful in many ways, sometimes taking the place of tassels or fringes.

CHRISTIE

Bibliography
Beck; Christie 1906

BEADWORK

The constructive and decorative uses of beads take many forms. Strictly, only those where beads are sewn to a ground can be classed as embroidery, although beads may frequently be supported by wire or thread constructions before being sewn down. Their use on very early textiles seems limited, but this may be because of difficulties involved with producing a sufficiently strong sewing thread to resist constant friction. Beads were perhaps not considered decorative enough to embellish rich textiles until small semi-precious stones could be pierced, or until small glass beads could be manufactured. In less restrained societies no doubt such inhibitions did not apply, and strong sinew and hair were used to thread beads made from any available material.

The bead networks from Egyptian tombs were made principally from faience with frequent additions of terracotta and turquoise. Beads of coral, pearl and semi-precious stones appear in profusion on medieval embroideries, particularly the mid-European ones. The Tudors and Stuarts used seed pearls and glass

Beadwork: Victorian teacosy, canvas totally beaded, partly worked, red, orange and white. 37 cm (14½ in.) wide

Beadwork: satin stitched and beaded landscape, varying greens dotted with poppy red. Made by Lynda Colt

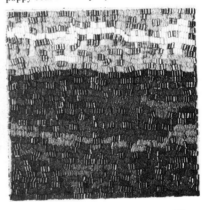

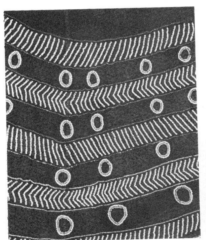

Beadwork: Xhosa skirt, South Africa, large turquoise and white glass beads on a red ochre brushed cotton. Detail. (*Leeds Museum*)

beads on costume and stumpwork, and constructed accessories and decorations from wired and supported beads. Seventeenth-century beading often features on wire constructions rather than woven grounds. Small rectangular baskets made of a heavy wire were decorated with wound coils of fine wire threaded with small beads. Interstices were occupied by figures, animals, flowers and fruit, sometimes constructed on card bases or worked

on additional wire constructions. The Victorians combined beads with many time-consuming crafts, and the use of very tiny beads in profusion or intricately arranged was a great conceit.

Rich beading on openly woven fabric and net can be achieved in *tambour work* with a hook. It is used extensively in fashion, either alone or combined with tamboured yarns, free machine stitchery or ribbon and braid work. Since the end of the nineteenth century it has been practicable with the *Cornely machine* chain stitch to sew small beads in dense or trailing linear patterns to almost any light material.

On ethnographic pieces it is often difficult to distinguish woven beadwork from that which has been couched in lines or stitched. Where strength is required the beads may be threaded in rows and then the working thread returned to stitch each bead individually, giving the appearance of bead weaving. Where the beads are applied in short couched rows as in some *North American Indian beadwork* they have a raised appearance. Eskimo beadwork was used mainly at the seams and hems of the soft birdskin clothing worn inside stronger garments. The Yoruba bead crowns and ceremonial pieces from Benin are creative achievements independent of their function.

Bibliography
Edwards 1966; Gunther; Hawthorn; Hunt and Burshears; Hurlburt; Wasley and Harris

Collections
UK Bankfield Museum, Halifax; Ipswich Museum; Horniman Museum, London; Museum of Mankind, British Museum, London; Victoria and Albert Museum, London; Pitt Rivers Museum, Oxford
USA Brooklyn Museum, New York
Canada Royal Ontario Museum, Toronto; Hudson Bay Company Museum, Winnipeg

BEBILLA (Greek lace, oyalar, oya)

A true lace in that it need not have a foundation fabric, although it may equally be argued that it is an embroidery, since the knotting technique employed is contrary to the

Bebilla: pink and white, 1 cm (½ in.) wide. (*Nottingham Museum*)

Bebilla: Turkish, nineteenth-century. Oya lace in coloured silks. (*The Embroiderers' Guild*)

buttonholing of needlepoint lace. Bebilla is a variable knotted edging construction belonging to the Middle East and the eastern Mediterranean, and copied in Europe. The Arabs claim that their lace is the ancestor of all laces (see *hollie point*). Confusion arises since *Ruskin work* is also called Greek lace, and the similarities may well reflect common origins or parallel influences. Bebilla is sometimes neutral and sometimes vividly coloured, in silks, cottons and sometimes hair. The simplest form is *Armenian edging* which can be extended and elaborated to form complex borders of flowers,

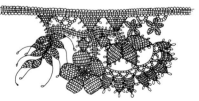

Bebilla: extended constructions

animals and figures supported on edgings of tussocks and mounds. These may overlap, and padding may be introduced to give the border another dimension. Motifs are frequently wired. Bebilla may be minutely delicate or comparatively coarse, and as much as 15 cm (6 in.) wide. It was used on textiles generally, but particularly to frame the face and decorate yashmaks. Very elaborate ones were reserved for special days, their width and complexity being a status symbol.

Ionides (*Embroidery* magazine) says that Mr Agop Mampre, an Armenian living in Turkey, stated that there was written information claiming an origin for bebilla in Syria, during the reign of Nebuchadnezzar (605–562 BC). There are more recent references, and Miss Ionides claims that when the article was originally written in 1937 bebilla was still being made for sale. Jones (*Embroidery* magazine) mentions oyalar being available for purchase in Turkey in 1975.

Besides its likeness to Ruskin work, it has both technical and design parallels with *stumpwork* and *Pre-Columbian* textiles, but theories of cross-fertilization may now be impossible to substantiate.

Bibliography
Caulfeild and Saward; Ionides

BED RUGGS (yarn sewn rugs)

Some authorities claim these as being peculiar to New England, and although they seem to be idiomatic to the USA as bed furnishings, as floor coverings they seem universal. Existing examples date from 1722 to 1833, and most of the lighter, softer kind for beds are initialled and dated. It has recently been discovered that they were worked almost exclusively with a needle rather than being hooked. There is debate as to whether the loops were worked over a quill as a

gauge to keep them even, but experiment proves this to be unnecessary for a practised worker. The ground was linen or jute, covered tightly with loops of homespun or mixtures of yarns following the curved contours of the simple floral pattern. Most rugs are softly multi-coloured, but occasionally there are monochromatic ones. The technique does not differ from that employed in simple looped *rag rugs*. Acadian rugs worked in the same way had a clipped and sculptured pile surface. They were made by the French in Quebec and Nova Scotia from the eighteenth century.

Bibliography
Bath 1979; *Bed Ruggs* (Wadsworth Atheneum)

Collection
USA Metropolitan Museum of Art, New York

BEESWAX

Used for smoothing and stiffening the working thread by drawing it through the wax. This is especially useful for metal thread work, for bead stringing, for some sewing and appliqué, and for leather work. Sometimes a thread may be waxed just at the working end, so as to pass more easily through a hole made with an awl or a hole through a bead. Special decorative containers and mounts for the wax were once fashionable. Often the edges of the wax were serrated so that the thread could be more easily pulled through it.

Bibliography
Whiting

BEETLEWINGS

The iridescent wings of dark beetles about 1 cm (⅜ in.) long were pierced with a small hole at either end and stitched to textiles, usually combined with embroidery. The technique was used in India, and in America and Britain in the nineteenth century. Spangles are still made in imitation, but for reasons of ease in manufacture their holes are at right angles to the ends, one at either side.

Collections
UK Gawthorpe Hall, Burnley; Bankfield Museum, Halifax

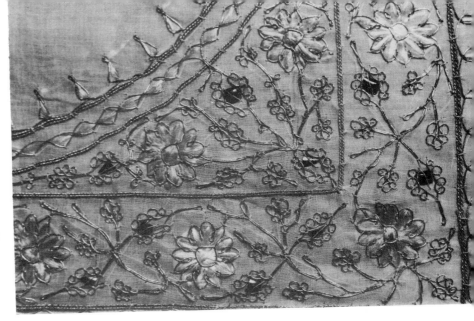

Beetlewings: Madras, loose jap gold and beetlewings on gauze. Detail 20 × 28 cm (8 × 11 in.). (*Bankfield Museum*)

BENEWAKA

A technique dating from around 1800 among the Pennsylvanian Dutch, benewaka was a type of darned network used on the end of pillow cases and show towels. It was worked on homespun linen, the drawn fabric borders overcast tightly so that they had the appearance of a coarse net. This network was then darned with a linen thread to make patterns of paired flower motifs. Tulips were a favourite subject.

Bibliography
Bath 1979

BERLIN WOOLWORK

The highly popular *canvas work* technique which enjoyed commercial success and occupied so much time in the nineteenth century. Patterns, prints and pictures were retailed in vast quantities and the specialized thread and grounds were numerous and often expensive. It was done almost entirely in tent stitch and converted to many ostensibly functional textiles, but a good deal was purely pictorial. It has its origins in the long tradition of counted, colourful, representational stitchery which first imitated tapestry. Vestiges of it remain today in printed pictorial canvas work, often sold as a kit complete with frame.

In 1804 Philipson, a Berlin print seller, published the first coloured prints on lined paper for embroidery. Then in 1810 Madame Wittich imported to Britain small numbers of patterns by Ackerman and others. By 1831 Mr Wilks of Regent Street in London was making large purchases, and the whole promotion gathered momentum and became a prominent industry. Berlin work owed its success both in Britain and the USA to the fact that counting stitches safely from a predetermined pattern offered more realism and apparent proficiency than could be achieved by working from a drawing.

Grounds were very varied but usually fine. Stitchery worked on coarser *canvas* with thicker thread was not referred to as Berlin work. Each commercial innovation promoted specific grounds and working threads appropriate to the pattern, many of which demanded considerable skill. Silk or wire grounds were very fine. The loosely twisted threads made from Saxony merino wool took dyes more brilliant than worsted crewels. In the days before aniline dyes, new mordants were developed for the old dyestuffs, and the fading which quickly muted textiles was slowed down. Anilines first came in the 1850s with Perkin's Mauvine and Magenta. (The original colours of most mounted embroidery on heavier materials can usually be appreciated by examining the back.)

There were numerous commercial

names for the working threads. Zephyr merino must have been the most sought after since this name became. almost a generic term for all fine Berlin wool. Merino has no lustre but it is an exceptionally fine fibre, allowing perfectly even spinning. The demand was for a soft wool with minimum twist, and so it had to be worked in short lengths to prevent undue wear as it passed through the canvas grounds. Zephyr was manufactured in a comprehensive colour range. Ombré was a shaded yarn in primary or muted tones, in long or short shades according to the gradation of tone over the length of thread. Partridge was similarly shaded but in soft browns and greys.

A form of Berlin work known as *raised woolwork* features in competent pieces from time to time. Canvas lace work consisted of a ground imitating that of lace, worked in black silk with the pattern in Berlin wool.

Bibliography
Proctor, M.G.

Collections
UK   Bowes Museum, Barnard Castle; Ipswich Museum; Leeds Industrial Museum; Harris Museum and Art Gallery, Preston

BISCUIT QUILTING

See *Puff quilting*

BLACKWORK (Holbein work, Spanish work)

A form of stitchery used largely on dress and at its most fashionable during the sixteenth century. Blackwork can be seen represented in minute detail on portraits by Holbein and other painters of Henry VIII's time. It takes many forms, but retains several important characteristics throughout, and work omitting these cannot strictly be described as blackwork. The distinctive feature is a regular, counted running stitch, which is completed by alternating stitches doubling it on the return journey, thus making the line exactly alike on both sides of the work. This idiosyncrasy can be found on early embroideries all around the Mediterranean, and probably paralleled the development of key and diaper patterns on stitched

Blackwork: sampler, sixteenth-century. (*Nottingham Museum. Photo: Layland-Ross*)

textiles generally.

Spain remained comparatively free of European influence for hundreds of years and instead assimilated Islamic designs. Much of the rural embroidery of Spain is either black on white or concerned with strong tone contrasts, and there are many similarities to the blackwork of the Holbein portraits in the distribution of patterns and arabesques. Linen textiles from the Salamancan area were often stitched with the natural chocolate brown local wool. Salamantine work was characterized by paired birds and flowers with strong Persian influences. The solidly worked birds sometimes had a fish or a tiny heart in red or blue set in their bodies, in the same way as the paired animals of early *Assisi* work.

There is, however, no real evidence that blackwork came from Spain. It was certainly known in England long before the Tudors. Katherine of Aragon came to Britain as a child

Blackwork: man's cap, *c.* 1600. Plaited braid stitch, working thread for fillings plied black and white. (*Nottingham Museum, Middleton Collection*)

bride in 1501. Her mother, Queen Isabella of Spain, was an enthusiastic needlewoman, and there is no doubt that Katherine's arrival, together with her entourage and their combined wardrobes and accoutrements, must have stimulated a revival of interest in embroidery in England. In 1536 her wardrobe list describes sheets 'wroughte with Spanysshe worke of blacke silke upon the edgies'.

The designs of the sixteenth century range from tiny understated borders on cuffs and bodices to powerful full-blown extravagances enriched with metal threads, beads and pearls. Many of the incuspated Holbein stitch borders consist of confined linear arrangements of angular divisions and rosettes. The early ones do not incorporate enclosed fillings but their patterns are obviously the precursors of the wealth of rich fillings which were to follow. The borders proceeded to open into billowing, all-over formal scroll arrangements of flowers, birds and beasts. The double running outline developed extensions and enrichments, and the fillings expanded Moorish diapers, squares and chevrons with inventive counted stitchery. Heavy outlines of braid and knotting stitches embellished with touches of red, green and gold replaced the Holbein stitch outline which became integrated with the fillings. Blackwork assumed prominence, ceasing to be a mere foil delicately complementing outer garments.

Blackwork need not always be black. There are a few very early examples worked in much lighter, but still neutral, colours, and close examination of the portraits will confirm this. It must be remembered, however, that

Blackwork: man's cap, *c.* 1600. (*Nottingham Museum, Middleton Collection*)

true black dye pigment was very fugitive, and that blackwork most frequently occurred on frills, sleeves and partlets which needed washing and were exposed to light. The famous Falkland cover in the Victoria and Albert Museum is a very beautiful example. Despite the fact that blackwork was usually made for wear it has survived well, and there are many other pieces in excellent condition.

The beauty of blackwork probably lies in accepting the limitations of counted stitchery on soft, evenly woven linen. The simplicity and understatement of the earlier period pieces is very appealing. When the technique becomes more complex the excitement of exploring and inventing fillings is a strong attraction, experimenting with the balance of lines and solids, dense and sparse patterns, vertical and diagonal directions. Blackwork is now used to explore variations of tone within a given context. It has surprising versatility, since it is accepted that the outline may be dispensed with, and patterns can overlap or interrupt one another, their juxtaposition being dictated by representational considerations rather than those of pattern. Density can be

Blackwork: traditional fillings used as a drawing. Panel 25 × 23 cm (10 × 8 in.). Made by Hilary Oberlander

varied by alterations of scale, complexity of pattern and thickness of working thread.

Evenweave fabric of linen or a luxurious mixture is essential. The traditional soft and rather delicate work needs a carefully chosen fabric. Very fine or very coarse work can be successful, providing material and working thread are satisfactory together. It is characteristic that the working thread should not stiffen, distort or pull the fabric, so preliminary experiments are necessary. The use of a frame is optional and preferred by most workers.

Stranded silks and cottons provide most textural variety because the number of strands used can be adjusted approximately to the textural density required in patterns and lines. Any threads which seem appropriate to the scale of the work may be used, but they must be lustrous rather than silky. Modern embroiderers often fail to appreciate that their work lacks the mellow qualities of old blackwork not simply because of the intervening years, but because of the differences between machine-made and hand-

Islamic Seljuk pattern common to both blackwork and Levkara

Blackwork pattern from a coif

Blackwork: man's shirt, seventeenth-century. (*Bath Museum of Costume*)

made materials. Whereas it may well be far too laborious for embroiderers to weave their own linen, it is worthwhile experimenting with yarn dyeing and random fading, or at least selecting deep browns, greens and blues to mix with a black working thread.

If the design is to be a Holbein stitch border, reference should be made to classical and traditional border patterns and consideration given to proportion and repeat in relation to the intended use of the embroidery and scale of the work. Blackwork with fillings must have outlines or unenclosed areas of a sufficient size to display the characteristics of each filling pattern. The balance of dark and light fillings, those with large patterns and those with small textures, and diagonal tendencies and vertical ones, must all be carefully organized. Outlines that are too hard and strict can cause the filling patterns to recede, as can disproportionately large areas of unworked ground. Stitchery experiments will reveal that too large a needle will upset the weave, and therefore the continuity of filling patterns, while too small a needle will damage the working thread and be

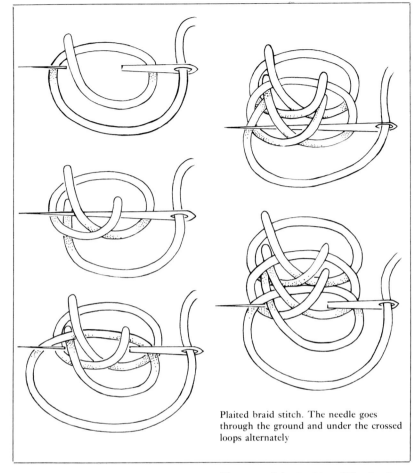

Plaited braid stitch. The needle goes through the ground and under the crossed loops alternately

difficult to handle. Blunt needles are best.

There are just three basic stitches, double running, back and cross, all counted by the yarn of the ground. Other linear stitches are permitted for outlines, and on some patterns little blocks of satin stitch may be used. Hundreds of filling stitches have been illustrated; many of them are interchangeable with *drawn fabric work*. Reference to contemporary portraits and sources of additional ornament will reveal more, and there can be further innovations and adaptations by addition or omission to vary density or direction.

Bibliography
Drysdale 1975; Geddes and McNeill
Collections
UK Museum of Costume, Bath; Gawthorpe Hall, Burnley; National

Museum of Antiquities of Scotland, Edinburgh; National Portrait Gallery, London; Nottingham Museum
Canada Royal Ontario Museum, Toronto

BLIND APPLIQUÉ

An ancient sewing process closely allied to *applied work* in technique, and to *Hawaiian quilts* and *San Blas appliqué* in design. Two layers of cotton are basted together, the design drawn out on the top layer, and this single layer cut, turned and hemmed to reveal the one beneath. The positive-negative designs are compartmented, usually with zigzag edges. It is called 'blind' either because the stitches are intended to be unobtrusive, or because it has no surface stitchery.

Blind appliqué may well have its

origins in the felt work of nomadic peoples in the Middle East and the coarse appliqués of the Himalayas, but it is now used largely in India for outer wear, animal trappings and canopies.

BLOCKING

Embroideries which have not been worked in a square frame often need straightening. This cannot be achieved with an iron, and in any case embroidery should never be ironed unless it is unavoidable.

Sew a tape round the edges with overcasting or long machine stitches. Make a flat, damp pad with soft, clean fabric on a clean board. Working from the centre outwards on each side of the embroidery pin it to the board, getting the grain of the ground quite straight. Tension is determined by the delicacy or otherwise of fabric stitchery. Closely stitched canvas work can be pulled quite hard. Cover it with clean, white, acid-free paper, then newsprint, and then a flat weight, and leave until quite dry. Drying could take as long as a fortnight and should not be hurried.

There are differing opinions about whether the right side of the embroidery should face the board or be uppermost. It may well be better to lay it face down simply to give it maximum protection.

BLUE AND WHITE WORK

The peasant embroidery of rural China, and particularly the remote northerly regions, is rather like stitched willow pattern. It is of white cotton and indigo thread, in cross stitch and double running. Except in some shared symbolism, it bears no relationship to court dress. It should not be confused with *Deerfield blue and white work*.

Bibliography
Baker and Lunt

BOKHARA

The Bokhara area of Uzbekistan has been well known for embroidery for hundreds of years. The beautiful designs are easily recognizable, but it

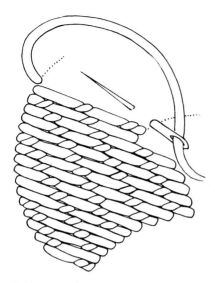

Bokhara couching

is the characteristic stitch (see diagram) which has always caused such interest.

BOLTON WORK

See *Candlewicking*

BOOKBINDINGS

Although some books with embroidered covers are in manuscript, the fashion in Europe for embroidered bookbindings probably closely followed the invention of printing. Embroidered gifts were very fashionable during the time of the Tudors. Bookbindings were made either by amateurs or by craftsmen attached to households. They were invariably stitched with metal purl, wire and spangles, and sometimes appliqué. The spangles were later imitated with stamps by bookbinders working on leather.

The covers made to contain the sacred texts of the Jains in Gujarat, India, were embroidered in metal threads and silks on satin or velvet, compartmented to accommodate figures and animals, or divided geometrically into continuous decorative fields with a wide border.

Bibliography
Davenport; Irwin and Hall

Collections
UK British Library, London; Victoria and Albert Museum, London;

Bodleian Library, Oxford
India Calico Museum of Textiles, Ahmedabad

BOXERS

Little opposing human figures, holding upraised emblems, commonly used throughout sixteenth to eighteenth-century embroideries, sometimes as part of a repeating border and sometimes as an independent motif. They are derived from earlier Italian and Spanish work and strongly connected with Renaissance putti. They are quite frequent on eighteenth-century *samplers*.

Bibliography
King 1961

BRAIDS

See *Cords and braids*

BROCADE EMBROIDERY

A general term covering those forms of stitchery which use the woven pattern of the ground fabric as a basis for the design. In the early eighteenth century, parts of the design were sometimes filled with beads, but in the late nineteenth century only the outlines and some of the details were worked. *Anglo-Indian embroidery*, *bugle work* and some *Leek work* are examples of brocade embroidery.

BRODERIE ANGLAISE (eyelet embroidery, eyelet ruffling)

An all-white, non-lustrous form of stitchery limited to eyelets, buttonholed borders and sparse surface stitchery, typical of Victorian underwear, nightwear and baby linen. Eyelets are either round or oval, borders wavy or scalloped. The confines of the technique dictate design limitations, and therefore simplicity is successful, but the work is repetitively laborious. Outlining, padding and buttonholing precede the final trimming away of the fabric from eyelets and borders. Properly done on best woven cambric, it was very strong, and a good deal has survived regular washing and ironing. Broderie anglaise probably developed simultaneously with *Ayrshire work*, retaining its characteristic simplicity as

a distinguishing feature. From the early nineteenth century white work was frequently trimmed with modest gathered flounces or deeper borders of *Moravian embroidery*. Whilst Ayrshire work was so fashionable, broderie anglaise was confined to these deep borders. As Ayrshire work declined, eyeletting was used more frequently on the whole body of the garment, taking over those areas previously occupied by Ayrshire work and absorbing some of its surface stitchery and fillings.

By the 1880s the simplicity was lost and floral motifs with padded satin stitch were introduced, and the work became known as Swiss work. *Madeira work* was a form of broderie anglaise produced for the tourist trade. The multiple machine could reproduce eyeletting and the later raised satin stitches remarkably well and with minute exactness. Modern single-head automatic machines make excellent eyelets, but the technique is rarely used since the manufactured trimmings are cheap and much more attractive.

The finest white cambric with a firm texture is the only suitable ground. Most broderie anglaise is worked in the hand. A small stiletto and some sharply pointed scissors are essential tools. All bars and buttonholing are worked with a tightly twisted thread which must be non-lustrous. A looser twist may be used for some surface stitchery. A looser, thicker twist may be used for some surface stitchery, often duplicating for the padding.

Designs were at first drawn or printed on paper and traced through onto the cambric. Eventually fabric borders could be purchased by the yard with the design already printed on them. When transfers became available they were an ideal medium for promoting eyeletting designs. The best way to transfer the design to the ground is by stretching the cambric over the drawing and tracing it through direct, using a fine brush point and pale poster paint. Sometimes a hard pencil has been recommended, but the lead inevitably soils the thread in working and, although the embroidery will need washing, it is not satisfying to persevere at discoloured work.

All the lines marking holes are outlined with a regular running stitch, single around tiny eyelets and double around larger ones. Each hole is cut as work progresses, the points being turned back with the needle and overcast. Any points not taken in with the overcasting must be carefully trimmed away beneath the work, preferably after washing the completed piece. Tiny eyelets are pierced with the stiletto rather than being cut, and overcast. Oval holes must have particularly well spaced stitches lying evenly around the curve and forming a neat point. Shaded holes, those with wider overcasting at one side, need padding with graduated running stitches. The overcasting must be worked at an even tension and carefully shaped. For extra emphasis the wide side may be buttonholed and the narrow one overcast. Beaded lines are usually worked on the straight grain and guided by withdrawing a ground thread to give upper and lower edges. For the cucumber-seed pattern and continuous lines of eyelets, both

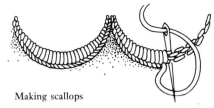

Making scallops

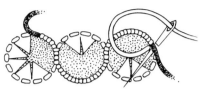

Clipped eyelets over a padding thread

running stitches and overcasting are worked in continuous undulating wave journeys so that the fabric is strengthened.

Edges are always wavy or scalloped and almost invariably buttonholed rather than overcast. Each process is continuous right across the work. Running stitch outlines are followed by padding in either running stitch or chain stitch or both. Edges are not turned and trimmed as eyelets are, but the buttonholing precedes the final trimming away of excess ground.

Where the buttonholing is all the same width the needle must always work vertically, keeping stitches touching one another. Where the buttonholing varies in width stitches must be accommodated accordingly, and even more care taken over tension. Shallow curves may be padded with running stitch alone but deeper ones will need the addition of chain stitches. Padding stitches should always run in the opposite direction to final buttonholing and should be considered as additional strengtheners. The working thread should be started and finished on the right side by running through previous stitching or taking up ground which is yet to be covered. A new thread is introduced into buttonholing by emerging through the purl loop at the edge of the previous stitch.

Surface stitchery does not occur on broderie anglaise in its early, purest

Broderie anglaise: nineteenth-century fine white cotton baby robe. Length of skirt 86 cm (34 in.)

form. It is acceptable if confined to trailing stem stitch, overcasting or overcast running, forming a very minor part of the design. The addition of round or oval padded dots seems to have been acceptable by the late Victorian and the Edwardian eras.

Bibliography
de Dillmont; *Weldon's*

BRODERIE PERSE (appliqué perse, Persian embroidery, cretonne work)

Motifs cut from printed chintz and cretonne, pasted and sewn to a plain ground. Both style and technique closely resemble *applied work* as used on quilts, but broderie perse was intended for use on small-scale household articles and it had surface stitchery and therefore more textural qualities. It probably dates from the first imports of printed cotton goods, when each little scrap was utilized.

Grounds match the tone of the darkest motifs and can be of any material except velvet. The applied motifs are selected for their subdued and harmonious qualities and black and white are excluded. They are arranged fairly closely over the ground. The pieces are pasted to the stretched ground and allowed to dry, and then the work is removed from the frame for stitchery. All the edges are buttonholed or feather-stitched with silk, and small details are added in linear stitches.

Bibliography
Caulfeild and Saward

BUGLE WORK

Embroidery having some major part covered completely with bugle beads individually stitched, or threaded on wire or a strong thread and couched. Bugle beads are small glass cylinders, either round or faceted in section, and usually in translucent pale colours. They are sometimes referred to as pipes. They tend to have more abrasive edges than round beads, and wear through the working thread, so that the Tudor pieces mentioned in inventories have not survived. There are, however, a few remaining examples dating from around 1700.

The five large panels which are an important feature of Victor Hugo's Hauteville House in Guernsey are good examples. Recently restored and cleaned, they feature birds and foliage in copper and gold thread and chenille on a heavy linen ground. The whole of the background is entirely covered with white bugle beads, threaded on wire and couched between each bead, forming a pattern of large waves.

Bugle beads feature on late Victorian costume stitched in close, flowing rows. They were also used in the same way on Edwardian costume and flapper dresses, applied with a tambour hook or the Cornely machine.

Collections
UK Hauteville House, Guernsey; Victoria and Albert Museum, London; Weston Favell Church, Northamptonshire

BULLION EMBROIDERY

Heavy and formal *metal thread work* is sometimes referred to as bullion embroidery. The metal threads themselves, particularly the larger purls, are known as bullion when described by mass or weight.

Buratto: interlocking silk weave with twisted weft, 10 cm (4 in.) wide. (*Nottingham Museum*)

BURATTO

Often mistaken for *lacis*, it is not on a netted foundation but darned on a woven gauze or leno, a very openly woven fabric with twisting pairs of warp yarns securing openings between the weft yarns. The technique was practised by the Peruvian Nazcas. Designs and instructions for it appear in sixteenth-century Italian publications, and the principle is still in use in the manufacture of nets and curtains.

The name also applies to a loosely woven translucent textile made from silk waste, probably because it was frequently used for this simple stitchery.

BURGUNDIAN EMBROIDERY

See *Or nué*

BUTTONS

The word 'button' was once used for any loose appendage on garments, usually what is now known as a tassel, and often purely decorative. Buttons as functional, rounded fastenings evolved in the sixth century as a necessary adjunct to shaped and fitted clothing.

For centuries, moulds made of a variety of substances have been covered with woven fabric to serve

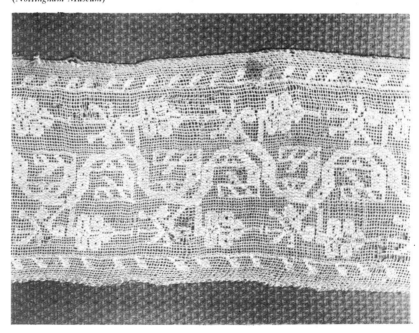

Buttons: Bosnia, tags and bodice front of a jelek, black and white couched cord, moulded buttons and wrapped ones. (*Bankfield Museum*)

Buttons: Ipek, Albania, Moslem jelek, maroon and gold, heavy twist and braiding completely covering the ground. Wood buttons wrapped in metal and silk with coral beads. Buttons 2.5 cm (1 in.) long. ▼ (*Bankfield Museum, Durham Collection*)

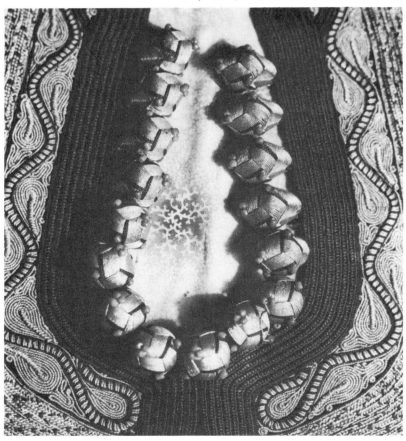

as buttons. These may be very sophisticated or quite primitive. They may be decorated with lace, needlewoven with silk thread, surface stitched with metal threads, encrusted with beads or ribbon work, or made with pulled stitchery and eyelets. The passementerie buttons of the seventeenth and eighteenth centuries were delicately decorated, and made for specific garments. On waistcoats and breeches they appear in close lines as a main feature of opulent decoration.

Dorset buttons and those made in Staffordshire, Scotland and elsewhere, were produced as a cottage industry in the eighteenth century. They were made of thread stitched over moulds or wire rings.

BUTTONS, APPLIED

The fastenings for garments and accessories often become a decorative feature in their own right, or a focal point of ornamental construction or extended surface pattern.

Buttons may also be used to decorate a surface independently of their function. The button blankets of the Kwakiutl American Indians are an example of this practice. The blankets, usually of dark blue wool, were imported. Military and pearl buttons, bells and thimbles were stitched with sinew in patterns and symbolic animal outlines.

Shell buttons are used exclusively to decorate the clothes of the London Pearly Kings and Queens, who have reigned over their individual districts of London since the late nineteenth century. A suit can weigh over 10 kg (22 lb) in buttons, carefully arranged in close patterns according to size and shape, white on black.

Bibliography
Gunther; Hawthorn

CADDOW QUILTS (Bolton work, boulton work)

Woven counterpanes in natural wool and later creamy cotton, with a raised pattern of knops. The hand-stitched ones are in imitation of the original woven ones. In Ireland a woollen counterpane was called a 'caddow', and there is a long tradition of white *knotted work* on domestic textiles in that country; but caddow quilts belong to Bolton in Lancashire where they were woven in quantity well before power looms. Traditional patterns developed, with names such as catstep border, hanging fir and peltering iron, and writers anxious to perpetuate these patterns recommend hand-stitched imitations. The method was taken to America by the early Settlers and developed into *candlewicking*.

Copies can be made on carefully chosen open weaves, but there are limitations in that a full width is required and heavy fabrics are not characteristic. Both working thread and ground must be non-reflective and natural or creamy in colour, the soft thread being much fatter than the yarn of the ground. Back stitch and open back stitch are the only two stitches needed to represent the horizontal weft knops.

CANADIAN PATCHWORK

See *Applied patchwork*

CANDLEWICKING (tufting, Bolton work)

Loops of cotton roving known as popcorns, grouped to form geometric

or formal floral designs and worked into a ground of softly woven cotton twill or bolton. Characteristically it is creamy-white or dyed a soft colour and used on a large scale for bedspreads.

The technique itself is ancient. It features on Coptic textiles quite extensively, sometimes used as long falling loops arranged in simple colour patterns, sometimes to make raised weft knops. Although candlewicking suddenly became popular in the first part of the nineteenth century in America with the large scale production of cotton, it almost certainly had its origins in *caddow quilts* and *knotted work*, and is closely related to *bed ruggs*. Workers used cotton wick intended for candlemaking, and formed the loops over turkey wing quills or small bones, which were removed as succeeding stitches were made. The rich texture, accentuated by concentrated light from a small window, was a perfect foil to simple interiors and warm wooden surfaces. Most examples are signed and dated. By the mid-nineteenth century candlewicking was elaborated by the introduction of surface stitches and the loops of roving were compacted and sheared to form raised outlines and spots.

The hand-stitched and the woven form are easily distinguishable. Although the hand-made one is rare now, the woven version where the roving loops are sheared is still thriving commercially. The thick, softly spun thread is quite unlike any produced for candle manufacture, and it forms a regular woven feature introduced approximately every 10 to 14 sheds. Individual picks are looped over a wire or wooden pin at intervals along the weft as required by the pattern, leaving the back smooth. In the hand-stitched version the design is not limited to the horizontal weft, and the roving can be introduced at any point on the ground and travel in any direction.

The design must be organized so that the popcorns are grouped to form two or three densities of texture on the same piece of work, varying from very close to quite open, and then used touching each other to make lines. Tufts, popcorns and flat running stitch

may occur together on one piece. The running stitch is best worked in geometric designs. Consideration has to be given to the extent of the worked areas otherwise the counterpane could become too heavy. The ground of unbleached calico must be one which will shrink on first washing to secure the popcorns or tufts in the fabric. The working thread is a thick, fluffy roving cotton with little twist, which is often worked double. A candlewick needle is a large one with a thick shaft flattened and curved at its point. Double-eyed ones are made to carry two lengths. Very sharp scissors are essential for clipping loops. The work is done without a frame.

Simple running stitch forms the loops, which are about 0.6 cm ($\frac{1}{4}$ in.) to 1.3 cm ($\frac{1}{2}$ in.) long. They are kept even by using a gauge, though practised workers soon dispense with this. The thread is started by leaving a tuft on the right side of the work and finished in the same way. Loops are cut only when all the stitchery is completed.

The finished piece is washed well to shrink the ground around the working thread and to cause the loops or tufts to expand above their holes, so that all the stitching is secured. Candlewicking must not be ironed; the crinkled calico ground is characteristic and will mellow with use.

Collection
USA Daughters of the American Revolution Museum, Washington DC

CANVAS GROUNDS

Any ground for embroidery which is even in weave and can be counted may be called canvas, but properly it is of cannabis origin, a strong, coarse vegetable fibre forming an open, stiff weave with single, double or multiple yarns. *Saint Cuthbert's vestments* have yarn-counted stitchery worked on a silk canvas with 64 yarns per linear inch, and at the other end of the scale stitchery can be counted on the coarsest rug canvas or on chicken wire.

Canvas is sold by weight, width, and number of holes per 2.5 cm (1 in.), colour and quality. The width of sixteenth-century seating, and hence the width of the woven canvas designed for making cushions, still influences both fabric manufacture and cushion-making today.

Berlin, silk or *coin net* is a hard, single canvas with a tightly spun round yarn, with from 22 to 40 yarns per 2.5 cm (1 in.). Now limited in availability, it was intended for fine Berlin wool work and was often coloured.

Binca, popular since the late 1930s, especially for simple stitchery at infant level, has both warp and weft yarns in groups of eight to ten, leaving sizeable holes between. It is usually in soft pastel colours, and it is not intended that the ground should be covered by the stitchery.

Cotton evenweaves, called canvas or fabric, may be matt or mercerised, with flattened or rounded yarn, with 16 to 25 yarns per 2.5 cm (1 in.). Doubles cottons are usually of 18 yarns per 2.5 cm (1 in.).

Crash, or Russian crash, is a pliable cotton linen union, usually of 25 to 28 yarns per 2.5 cm (1 in.), but it is variable in weave and weight. The yarn is slubby.

Evenweaves are normally of regularly spun linen, their distinctive features being that warp and weft yarns occupy the same space in either direction of the weave, and that they are sufficiently open for counting.

French canvas is of best, dark, unbleached linen. It was once of cotton but nevertheless of good quality.

Ida canvas is soft and loosely woven with a raised texture.

Java, Panama and Leviathan were all very similar. Of multiple weave, they were coarse and easy to stitch. They were used for furnishings and kneelers.

Jute is a fine quality, open, slubbed hessian in a double weave. Like Java, it can be in natural or softly dyed colours. Jute embroidery cloth or jute Panama has a double yarn and is comparatively small in count. It is used for finely knotted rugs.

Linen cambric is very fine, white and translucent, but may still be referred to as a canvas.

Locked weave canvas is like a heavy square-mesh net, two weft yarns twisting together at each intersection with the warp, forming a firm ground with minimal distortion.

Mono or congress canvas is plain and single meshed in medium counts.

Moskowa, railway (claret), net and graph were woven with regular coloured or metal warp and weft yarns which formed guiding squares over the whole ground. This could be left plain as a feature.

Pattern weave or Munster web canvas is a multiple with woven blocks of colour designed to guide geometric stitchery patterns.

Penelope or duo was the name given to the medium double-weave ground designed for cross stitch. It could be worked just over one yarn instead of two, where fine detail was required. In its unworked state it appears to have had cross stitch unpicked from it, and was thus named after Penelope the wife of Ulysses, who worked all day and unpicked each night.

Plastic, nylon and other synthetics are moulded to form a non-woven mesh, now easily available in several counts.

Rugs may be stitched on any strong,

Canvas overlays: circular insertions of cambric on a cream needlerun net lace parasol cover. The rose motif, 5 cm (2 in.) in diameter, is worked in strongly coloured silk cross stitch

coarse material, but regular knotted or looped-pile rugs are frequently made on canvas which is open and easier to control than closer hessian or jute grounds. The extent of the detail is determined by the canvas count. An American ground called miracle warp base could be tufted through floats on the weave, avoiding the regular weave of the backing. All those grounds coarser than seven yarns per 2.5 cm (1 in.) are suitable for heavier working threads, and may be referred to as thrums canvas.

Winchester canvas was produced specially for Louisa Pesel's embroiderers working for Winchester Cathedral before World War Two. It is a pleasant, slubby evenweave, still manufactured under its original name.

Wire mesh was popular for pole screens and face screens during the nineteenth century.

CANVAS LACE WORK

See *Berlin woolwork*

CANVAS OVERLAYS (drawn canvas work)

The practice of using a canvas overlay which could be counted and overstitched on a ground which could

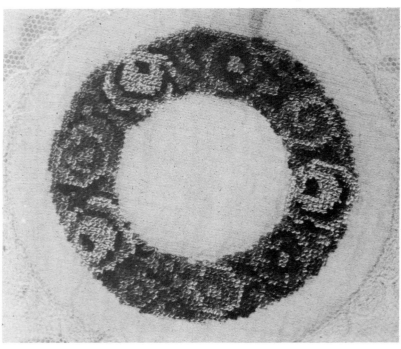

not be counted, seems to have been rare. Both fabrics were stitched through and then the overlay was withdrawn in individual yarns, exposing the ground and leaving the stitchery slightly raised. It was said to aid evenness, and help in transferring the design, but amateur results were often distorted and insensitive. There are commercial instances which are quite delicate. These appear to have been stitched over a fine, openly woven canvas, and it is suggested that both design and colour may have been printed on the overlay for speed and ease of working. It was sometimes called Gobelin, tapestry and tent stitched in one direction only over fine knitting needles.

Bibliography
Wilkie

CANVAS WORK (US: Needlepoint)

All those kinds of embroidery which are worked with counted stitches on an even, openly woven canvas are categorized under this heading. They are almost always coloured and the ground is usually completely covered in stitchery. Appearance, texture and scale are very variable, and the work may be confined to one stitch over the whole piece or may consist of many different stitches and several types of working threads. Canvas work is sometimes called *tapestry*.

The total filling of the ground with regular small stitches probably evolved through Coptic and Byzantine influences. It was known to the medieval church as *opus pulvinarium* and occurs in conjunction with metal thread work on vestments and furnishings. Much of it was worked in fine twisted silk for borders and orphreys. *Florentine* is a form of canvas work confined to undulating or chevron patterns making repeated sequences of colour.

The Tudors used a great deal of canvas work on domestic furnishings and decorative panels. Table carpets, screens, long cushions and pillows were entirely covered in stitches, wool or silk on linen and usually in tent stitch, the larger expanses imitating pictorial tapestries. Throughout the whole of the nineteenth century canvas

Canvas work: cross, long legged, satin and eyelet stitches on evenweave jute cloth. Kneeler, detail 25×30 cm (10×12 in.). (*Saint Alkelda's Church, Giggleswick*)

work was a fashionable pastime supporting thriving industries. It became known as *Berlin woolwork* with the introduction of fine worsted wools from Germany. This kind of stitchery is now used extensively by amateur workers for church kneelers and domestic furnishings. It is still very popular in kit form or as a means of translating stylized drawings or photographs. Interest in canvas work as an exploratory, expressive medium has undergone recent revival and subsequent decline.

Canvas work should be designed with attention to the use of the finished piece and consideration of scale of ground and stitchery. It is usually a functional textile subject to friction. Grounds should, therefore, be of good quality, and stitches should be short, covering the ground closely with an ample weight of working thread. There are hundreds of stitches to choose from, and study of some of them will lead to a more successful design. Where pictorial detail is required the stitchery will have to be quite fine, and it is practical to limit the variety of stitches used, perhaps choosing just tent or cross stitch. Areas of pattern needing less definition can benefit from more variety. Complex curves and linear parts of the design assume stepped and slightly

contorted characteristics when translated into stitchery, and these must be allowed for in the design process.

Canvas grounds are available in many forms, from fine silk coin net to coarse multiple-weave jute. The chosen ground must be quite stable; the yarn of which it is composed need not be smooth, but it must be strong. The count of the yarns over a given measurement will determine the scale of the stitchery and the ease of working. The weight must be appropriate to the purpose of the piece; a church kneeler may need a soft, heavy jute, but a picture or needlebook would be better worked on a stiff, light cotton or linen. The double-weave canvas known as duo or Penelope is designed for cross stitch, but the yarns can be divided on those areas where another stitch is required by the design. *Needlemade rugs* are normally worked on a coarse canvas of seven yarns or less per 2.5 cm (1 in.) with thrums or rug wool.

Working threads for canvas embroidery must be durable and able

Canvas work: panel of Elijah under the juniper tree. English, seventeenth-century. Wool and silk tent stitch on linen, 53 × 51 cm (21 × 20 in.). (*The Bowes Museum, Barnard Castle, Co. Durham*)

Canvas work: one of two fragments of a valance cut to make a chair seat and back, about 1570. Wool and silk tent stitch on linen, 53 cm (21 in.) deep. (*The Bowes Museum, Barnard Castle, Co. Durham*)

to withstand repeated journeys through the ground, friction at the eye of the needle and subsequent wear when the work is completed. Delicate threads may be used only in short lengths on pieces which are not functional. The finest silk coin net will accept just a silk or mercerised cotton twist, but a coarse canvas can be covered only with thick wool thrums. Most medium-weight stitchery is done with good quality worsted wools specially designed for the purpose. They are manufactured in large colour ranges. Each individual thread is quite fine, but they are intended to be used in multiples according to the scale of stitchery, the nature of individual stitches and their covering abilities. Experimental canvas work and the exploration of stitches and textures has led to the use of plastic raffia, nylon waste, acrylic strip, leather lacing and appliqué in various forms.

Needles are blunt with a long eye, and are sold as tapestry needles. For fine work it may be necessary to resort to small crewel or between *needles*, and for coarse work where outsize tapestry needles are unavailable a bodkin is a good substitute.

Work done in the hand will frequently become stretched diagonally because each stitch is pulled close to the ground in the same direction. Providing the stitchery is not too tight this stretching will be unnoticed on

smaller pieces, but larger ones will need *blocking*. Most canvas work is more satisfactorily worked in a frame, with the ground periodically readjusted to a sufficient tension as stitching progresses. Where the whole piece consists of *tent stitch*, stretching may be pronounced, a phenomenon well demonstrated by the Bradford Table Carpet in the Victoria and Albert Museum, London. This can be minimized but not entirely avoided by the proper diagonal use of the stitch wherever practicable.

Designs are normally transferred simply by taping the canvas ground over the full-size drawing on a hard surface and tracing through. Any medium other than waterproof felt-tip or Indian ink is liable to rub off and stain the stitchery. For more closely woven grounds either dressmakers' carbon or iron-on carbon are useful. Where designs are part of a series or set of embroideries it is possible to make calculated diagrammatic drawings on squared paper, and then

work direct from these drawings with the aid of matching grid lines in running stitch on the ground.

Stitchery done without a frame should be raised in the middle and worked progressively outwards. There are instances where this presents difficulties, such as pictorial or representational designs where the placing of stitches needs constant appraisal. Stitchery done in a frame should be started at the point farthest away from the worker so that it is always in front of the uppermost working hand on the frame. Work done should be covered to prevent wear and dust. The working thread is started with a running stitch where it will subsequently be covered, and finished under existing stitchery.

Bibliography

Dyer and Duthoit; Edwards 1967;

Gray; Kaufmann; Pesel 1929; Rhodes; Springall

Collections

UK Bowes Museum, Barnard Castle; Hardwick Hall; Traquair House, Innerleithen; Victoria and Albert Museum, London; William Morris Gallery, London; York Castle Museum
USA Metropolitan Museum of Art, New York

CARRICKMACROSS (the Flowerin', the sewings, the parcellings)

Described as the oldest Irish lace, Carrickmacross is really a form of appliqué with embroidery. A fine mull muslin is smoothed over a machine net and the main outlines of design are stitched through both of these and a backing, with a linen thread couched closely by means of another very fine one. The mull is then trimmed from the ground, leaving the net exposed to be further decorated. The edge is outlined and relieved with frequently spaced looped picots.

It was Mrs Grey Porter of Donaghmoyne and her sewing maid Anne Steadman who found that mull could be applied to machine net, at a time when Heathcote's invention of the bobbin net machine made fine nets readily available and cheap. Local women were interested, and the two ladies, together with some neighbours, formed a small school. During the famine years a number of schools were set up, dependent on that at Carrickmacross which supplied designs and dealt with orders. With charitable aid and public grants the manufacture of appliqué lace became extensive.

Carrickmacross soon became influenced by *Limerick* lace and fillings were added to enclosed areas. By 1850 it acquired guipure influence and the characteristic net was replaced by bars and picots forming areas of ground enclosed by delicate mull appliqué. A late version was worked on the mull alone, with the purity of *white work* satin stitch so typical of the best of Irish nineteenth-century embroidery. This had indented and foliate edges with heavily satin-stitched and buttonholed petals and leaves, the whole area applied to net for bodices

and blouses. A coarser variety was tamboured with quite thick soft cotton through muslin and net, with the muslin subsequently trimmed away from ground areas.

The industry fell into decline as more lucrative occupations took over at the end of the century and rural life became a little easier. However, the sewings are still practised in convents and in part-time schools, largely as commissions.

The outline of the floral design must be continuous and about half of the ground must be occupied with enclosed areas where the mull will be left covering the net. The drawing must be organized so that areas of mull form continuous irregular scallops along the edge of the piece. If the lace is intended as an edging the inside border must be finished with a rope of two twisting outline threads.

Square-mesh net is now difficult to find but this is unimportant, since the mesh was never really square but had additional short sides formed by the knots. The closely woven muslin is also an uncommon commodity. Both must be white or cream. Lace thread or fine crochet cotton of two weights

Carrickmacross: tamboured cotton on cambric and coarse net. Detail 33 × 25 cm (13 × 10 in.)

are needed for outlining, couching and fillings. Small between needles are ideal, and a pair of lace scissors with a very sharp point and a knobbed blade is necessary.

The design, including drawn positions for the picots at the edge, is printed or drawn out quite clearly with Indian ink on glazed calico or medium tracing paper, and then backed with a plain calico of the same size. The net is laid on top of the paper and the mull on top of the net, and all four layers tacked together along the right side and across the top. Small basting stitches are next made just outside the outline of the design, keeping within those areas which will eventually contain just the ground net. Where these stitches must cross an outline they should be taken beneath the calico rather than on top of the mull.

Taking the heavier working thread and couching it with the lighter one, the whole outline is now followed throughout, making close stitches at a slight diagonal across the heavier thread but with the needle ascending and descending directly beneath it. The needle lies flat across the ground at a slight angle to the couched line, taking up just a few muslin yarns and at least one strand of net at each stitch. The needle must not penetrate either drawing or backing. The

Carrickmacross: fine net, typical swags and scallops, with fillings and worked rings, bars and picots. Detail from a skirt designed by Alice Jacob of the Metropolitan School of Art, Dublin, 1901. (*Mhusaem na Éireann*)

Carrickmacross is the easiest form of delicate open net to make by machine. Some experiment is necessary to determine working method and scale so that the work does not become too stiff and heavy with stitchery. The design may be drawn on fine tissue to back the grounds and stitch through, but it is usually more practical to trace it directly. The mull can be taped over the drawn design on a flat, hard surface so that the lines can be traced through with a hard pencil or a fine brush and pale poster paint. With mull and net carefully basted together at frequent intervals the work can be eased into a tambour frame without pulling. A stitch tension should be selected which will provide a firm darned outline. The needle should be small and very sharp, and the working thread as fine as possible. Running the couched thread must be continuous.

The design will dictate that at some points the thread will have to be double, and at such return journeys it should be couched as one. Accuracy in following the design is essential, and different angles should be followed precisely. Where the outline reaches the outside edge of the piece the couched thread should be used to make regular picots. These are formed by a loop in the thread, secured against the edge line on the drawing by means of a pin through the loop. It is held in position with three close stitches over the doubled couched thread.

Once the outlining is completed net and mull are removed from the backing by snipping the basting stitches between the design and the calico backing. The work can now be held over the fingers whilst the mull is cut away from the net on the ground areas where the net must be exposed. Using the knobbed blade of the scissors between mull and net the outline is closely trimmed. At the edges both layers are cut, leaving the picots free. Adding selected areas of *net darning* or *lacis* fillings is appropriate and gives increased textural delicacy.

Cartisane: Germany, Osnabruck, cap, mid-nineteenth-century. Silver plate and wire wrapped and stitched, trimmed with wide braid. (*Bankfield Museum*)

Cartisane: Turkish purse of deep blue silk velvet stitched with gold wire in relief. Inside of red leather with cut-out decoration. 9 × 6 cm (3½ × 2½ in.) ▼

machine slowly and evenly, the whole outline should be followed with the darning stitch. The line can then be retraced with a whip stitch or a corded thread, depending on the scale of the work. The picots must be made by hand. If the finished lace would benefit from a slightly weighted edge the picots can be replaced by beads.

Bibliography
Boyle; Cole; Kay Shuttleworth; Pethebridge; Wardle

Collections
UK Gawthorpe Hall, Burnley; Moravian Museum, Leeds; Luton Museum; Ulster Folk and Transport Museum, Co. Down
EIRE National Folk Museum of Ireland, Dublin

CARTISANE

Thin parchment, vellum or card used beneath stitchery to produce hard edges, raised solids, or well defined shapes on a pile ground such as velvets. Cartisane is common in *metal thread work* and in *slips*. Some early laces consisted of vellum wrapped with metal or silk thread, and, together with wire, it still forms the support of costume headdresses and processional decoration. The pricking cards and backings for needlemade laces were frequently made of cartisane. In lace or fine translucent stitchery a gold or silver thread used as a cordonnet to outline a design is sometimes referred to as cartisane.

CASALGUIDI (Castelguidi)

A form of drawn fabric on linen, with four-sided stitch predominating and surface stitchery in high relief. Casalguidi is always worked in unbleached linen and made into small bags and purses. The subject matter is usually floral, but there are often figures and animals. It is peculiar to a few Italian regions and associated with convents.

The linen ground is drawn all over and opened with four-sided stitch. All the surface stitchery is raised and tightly padded, its solidity giving high relief. There are detached buttonhole petals, overcast scrolling stems, double buttonhole leaves, raised bars, and blocks of tagged detached buttonhole.

Casalguidi: buttonholed picot loops and knotted tassels. Bag 18 cm (7 in.). (*Rachel Kay Shuttleworth Collection, Gawthorpe Hall*)

Casalguidi: raised buttonholing and overcasting on drawn fabric ground. Bag, 15 cm (6 in.). (*Rachel Kay Shuttleworth Collection, Gawthorpe Hall*)

Edgings are elaborately worked with variations of buttonhole, half circles decorated with picots, rings supporting worked tassels, and balls suspended around the base.

Collection
UK Gawthorpe Hall, Burnley

CATHEDRAL WINDOW (Mayflower)

An elaborate form of *applied patchwork* and fabric construction which is not readily categorized since it does not have a backing nor does it produce a continuous flat surface like *patchwork*. Squares of cotton fabric are twice folded and joined together in rows, with smaller added squares concealing the seams. It is American or Canadian in origin, and despite stories of it being worked during the journey of the Mayflower it is probably comparatively recent in its present form.

Choose a fabric which is very easy to handle and sew; fairly closely woven cottons and cotton synthetic mixtures are best. The optimum size of the starting squares for this fabric is about 18 cm (7 in.). At least two different colours are needed. The constructed squares require about four and a half times the area of fabric of the finished piece, and the sewn-in squares about the same area of fabric as the finished piece.

Cut the large squares and turn in a 1 cm ($\frac{3}{8}$ in.) hem all round, mitreing the corners. With practice this can be done using an iron and without tacking, but little time is saved since accuracy is essential. Fold the corners of each square into the centre and pin them down. Sew along the edge of each fold through all layers by machine or by hand. These lines will show only on the back of the finished work. Fold the square again in the same way, bringing the sharp corners into the centre and, without penetrating the square underneath, sew them together very firmly. This joining must be made very neatly and in the same way each time.

Placing backs of squares facing, oversew together down one side in pairs and then rows. Cut the sewn-in squares slightly smaller than the finished size of each folded square. Place each sewn-in square diagonally over two seam lines and two stitched lines, across a pair of folded squares. Tack in place with a few bold central stitches. Roll and oversew the folded edges of the squares up over the sewn-in square, starting in the middle of one side with a width of about 6 mm ($\frac{1}{4}$ in.) and tapering to the pointed corners. It can be useful to turn in a tiny edge on the sewn-in square as the corner is reached, manipulating the fabric into even shapes and placing the stitches closer together. As rows of folded squares are joined to their

Cathedral window: Pieced block in cotton.
19 × 26 cm (7 × 10 in.). Made by Ethel
Mitchell

The construction of cathedral window
applied patchwork

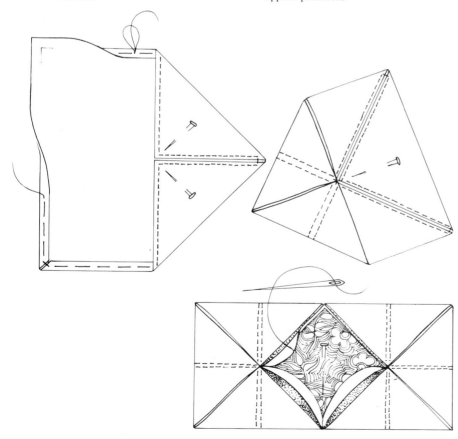

neighbours, succeeding sewn-in squares can be applied until all seam lines are covered. Those sewn-in squares which project at the edges of the finished piece can be folded inside a border strip, completed with triangles or left as a saw-tooth edge.

CHAIN STITCH

There are numerous kinds of embroidery from many parts of the world worked mainly or exclusively in chain stitch. The three kinds of technique involved in producing it may be difficult to separate without knowledge of the source of the textile.

Hand-worked stitching lacks total mechanical rhythm, but a practised worker can produce a line virtually indistinguishable from that formed by a hook. The line may be worked on less accessible areas like hems and turnings, and the needle will invariably return through a hole made slightly to one side of its emergence from the fabric.

Tambour work or hooked work is made by pulling the loop of the chain stitch back through the fabric with a small sharp hook. It can progress smoothly and speedily, can be made very fine on laces or very coarse on felted rugs, and the hook always returns the thread through the same hole.

The *Cornely* machine produces a chained line exactly like that made with a hook, but it can sometimes be distinguished, since the machine tends to flatten the line slightly and the twist on the thread remains constant. Starting and finishing is usually done by chaining under or over the same line.

CHENILLE

A very variable working thread or woven weft consisting of short tufts of fibre garnetted between the spun twist, looking rather like a caterpillar. It is made of cotton, silk or a synthetic. By the mid-eighteenth century it was fashionable in France and men's vests were embroidered with chenille in imitation of ermine. Chenille à broder is soft, fine and unwired, and can be worked to copy painting on velvet. Coarser ordinaire is used for couching, for working over open canvas or for

Chenille: Turkish towel-end with wide metal plate and blue and pink chenille. Detail 24 × 15 cm (9½ × 6 in.). (*Bankfield Museum*)

three-dimensional construction. Wired chenille rolio was used for many ornamental purposes by the Victorians. Chenille is now used mainly in weaving, and richly tufted versions are brightly dyed and shaped to form tiny birds and animals.

Bibliography
Caulfeild and Saward

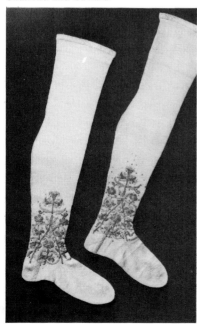

Chevenning: silk floss on white silk, samples. (*Rachel Kay Shuttleworth Collection, Gawthorpe Hall*)

Chevenning: boy's silk stockings, 1600–25. (*Nottingham Museum. Photograph: Layland-Ross*)

CHEVENING (clocks, coins)

The stitched, woven or knitted decoration extending from the ankle on stockings and socks. According to period, taste and cost it could take any form from elaborate metal thread scrollings covering much of the leg, to a few muted wheatear stitches immediately above the shoe. The term includes patterning on gloves, mittens and half hose.

Bibliography
Currey; Fairholt

Collections
UK Museum of Costume, Bath; Gawthorpe Hall, Burnley; Nottingham Museum

CHIKAN (chikankari, cikăn)

Delicate white work, soft muslin tanzeb with pulled fillings and shadow stitching, from Lucknow, Dacca and the Ganges plains of India. It is used mostly on garments and varies widely in quality, sometimes adding a little coarse stitched texture around the neckline for clothes in regular wear, sometimes worked with intricacy and delicacy in deep, rich bands on clothes, gifts and trousseau textiles. The earlier Bengali Dacca muslins are formal, and indicate Portuguese influences. Chikankari from Lucknow did not grow commercially until the middle of the nineteenth century. Although intended to satisfy a Western market it is essentially Indian, with butis and wide, flowing borders. The only white embroidery of the Indian Continent, chikan flourishes surrounded by vast geographical areas where highly colourful and often overtly glamorous embroidered textiles are so dominant. It may have connections with the symbolic purity of the Ganges.

There are several alternatives given for its origins. It is described as indigenous to the region around Lucknow, where the Kings of Oudh brought together the finest craftsmen and artists from the whole of India to work in their service; it is also reputed to have been introduced by Mohammedans trading with the Far East and encouraging industries to export suitable goods to Arabia. The Vedic scriptures and other written and

Chikan: nineteenth-century, white cotton on sheer muslin, pillow cover 61 cm (24 in.) square

visual evidence suggest that chikan is old and largely unaffected by recent influences. It was made professionally and as a cottage industry and much sought after during the period of British rule.

Chikankari designs are never geometric. They have flowing scrollings and bouquets of flowers, scattered with raised grain seeds of satin stitch. The stitched areas are often enclosed with more grain patterns making tight borders, sometimes with tiny powderings escaping onto the plain muslin.

Stem and back stitch (taipichi) make lines and outlines. Satin stitch represents grains of rice (murri) and millet (phanda). The pulled fillings (jali) are usually simple and kept quite flat. The characteristic stitch is the shadow herringbone, the bukhia. It is used to stitch the solid forms of flowers and leaves, always working on the wrong side, with the tiny stitches through the muslin forming the outlines. It is this technique, together with the consideration given to all the journeys of the working thread on the other side of the work, which gives chikan its misty appeal. Sometimes flowers and foliage are made with shadow appliqué using the same muslin as the ground; this is called khatwa. This is not considered true chikan although it is imitative of it.

Bibliography
Birdwood; Dongerkery; Irwin and Hall 1973; Watt

Collections
UK Victoria and Albert Museum, London
India Calico Museum of Textiles, Ahmedabad

CHINESE

The Chinese have never regarded embroidery as an inferior interpretative technique. Some of the written characters describing it are amongst the earliest pictograms in the Chinese language, and it seems certain that it has been an accomplished art for 4000 years. Technique, symbols and stylization have changed only very slowly. The characteristic couched metal thread, voided satin stitch, laid work and knot stitches persist throughout. Pekin knot was known as the forbidden stitch, since its practice over many years was believed to cause loss of eyesight.

Accounts of embroidery manufacture under the Regent Empress Tsu Hsi, who was appointed in 1861, indicate its cultural importance. The embroiderers lived and worked on the northern slopes of the Pekin Summer Palace. The year was divided into flower periods, and a fresh flower of the sort to be represented was set beside the pattern and the colours carefully matched.

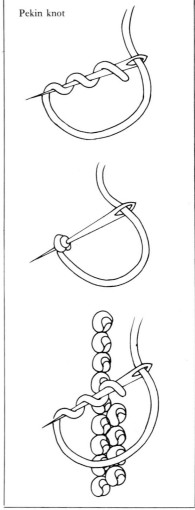

Pekin knot

Chinese: blue satin stitch on cream silk, partly worked band 15 × 8 cm (6 × 3 in.)

Chinese: multi-coloured Pekin knots on cream satin band 9 cm (3½ in.) wide. The metal thread is gilded paper wound over a silk core

Cultural influences and the Revolution have promoted forms of needlepainting and minutely shaded photographic realism which still reveal the traditional values. Thriving regional workshops, such as that at Soochow, produce satin stitch and darning pictures, often politically motivated or commissioned, and sometimes on an epic scale.

Bibliography
Ernst; Chung 1977, 1980; Mailey

Collections
UK Gawthorpe Hall, Burnley;

Victoria and Albert Museum, London
Canada Royal Ontario Museum, Toronto
China National Palace Museum, Taipei; National Museum of History, Taipei

CHINESE APPLIQUÉ
(buttonhole appliqué)

Usually small flower and leaf shapes cut from linen or cotton, their edges turned under and stitched to a ground of similar material by means of long radiating stitches surrounding each applied piece. A coarse version had larger applied flowers around the edge of the ground and some cut work. It belonged to the period immediately preceding World War Two, and much of it was produced in the Far East to satisfy the European market.

CLAMSHELL (shell, fish scale)

A peculiarity in the classification of patchwork, since it is now grouped with those which require a foundation fabric as an *applied patchwork* form, but Colby (1958) gives three methods of piecing it, none of which need a

Chinese appliqué: orange and green cotton buttonholed on linen. 15 × 20 cm (6 × 8 in.)

foundation fabric. Its chief technical characteristic is that it requires absolute accuracy at all stages.

The pattern consists of a tessellation, a single shape used exclusively; the shape results from discarding two equal elliptical segments meeting at the same point on the circumference of a circle. Joined in straight rows with their semicircles uppermost, they produce the visual effect of overlapping globes. There is no possibility of experiment with arrangement of the patterns, but great opportunity for the use of tone, colour and skill. Two templates are needed, one the actual size of the patches, one larger with seam allowances. All the patches should be cut on the straight grain exactly.

The first method leaves the inner shapes in the work and should therefore be used only where the added weight and stiffness are irrelevant. Taking the actual-size template, sufficient pieces are taken from a stiff, closely woven cambric or from bonding to complete the piece of work. The larger template, which has seam allowances, is then used to cut the shell pieces themselves. Each inner piece is then pinned or basted on the wrong side of each patch, and with the former uppermost the two are stitched together. The stitching must not pick up the face of the patch. Only the convex curve is turned, the extra fabric being accommodated in folds and never by gathering. The folds must be held flat by the stitching.

Clamshell: batik-dyed blue and lilac cotton on greens

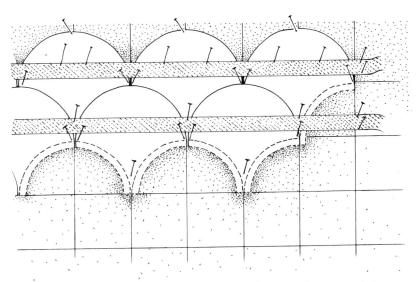

Clamshell: construction on a marked backing

Prepare a flat surface by ruling a grid of squares the same size as the diameter of the shells' full circle, and sufficiently long to extend slightly beyond the required row of patches. Sheet cork is by far the best for this purpose, but soft board or expanded polystyrene are suitable substitutes. The first row of prepared patches is laid touching the top line, with the corners of each template meeting the vertical ruled lines and just touching those of its immediate neighbours. A strong rubber band stretched over them and around the board will help to hold them loosely in position until each can be stabbed in place with pins. The second row of prepared patches is laid alternating with the first and covering their unhemmed edges. Template shapes must fit very snugly into each other, and the even, parallel placing must be maintained continuously. These two rows are tacked together so that there is no possibility of movement. They are then removed from the board and hemmed with tiny, even stitches on the right side. The tacking which basted together template and patch must remain, but the tacking which secured pieces one to another can now be removed and the two rows of shells returned to the board for the placing of the third row in the same way. By using iron-on bonding for the inner pieces all the tacking may be removed at this stage, but the stiff flatness of

the finished work is not always desirable.

The second method uses the inner pieces only as guides to be discarded, making it suitable for larger, softer pieces of work. A foundation fabric may be incorporated, but it is not essential. The template which has seam allowances is used to cut the pieces themselves. The actual-size template is used to cut a few inner papers, which for clamshell should be slightly stiff, about the thickness of a postcard. The card pattern is placed, oddly enough, on the right side of the piece, and basted. Using the card as a guide, the convex curve of the patch is turned, tacking to the wrong side of the patch face, without going through the card. The extra fabric must once more be accommodated in flat folds. The patches are set together as before, over a foundation fabric if this is practicable, using the card template as a guide continually. Each row is hemmed to its predecessor in turn, taking up the foundation fabric if it is present; all tacking stitches are removed as work progresses, and templates are snipped away and re-used for successive rows.

The third method again leaves the inner shapes in the work. Both convex and concave edges are turned, the convex ones pleated as before, the concave ones snipped at frequent intervals and tacked with small stitches. The shells are arranged with alternate ones interlocking at 90°.

The clamshell pattern can be produced by machine, using cottons previously stiffened with iron-on bonding and pieces cut to actual size. These can be stitched to a foundation using the darning foot and satin stitch or open zigzag.

Bibliography
Colby 1958, 1965

COGGESHALL

See *Limerick lace*

COIN NET

Very fine square-mesh silk canvas of an even weave. It occurs as the ground of *Saint Cuthbert's Vestments*, and as that of some Chinese embroidery. Canvas sold as coin net now is rarely of silk. It may be linen or synthetic, composed of a hard, rounded yarn, and often comparatively coarse.

Coin net: nineteenth-century bright floss silk, sometimes called Hankow work. A set of borders for court summer tunic on silk coin net. Each figure is 5 cm (2 in.) high

COLIFICHETS

Satin stitchery in floss silk on parchment or paper, often designed to be seen from both sides. It was probably taught in convents, since devotional subjects are frequent, with figure work and bouquets of flowers. Faces and hands were sometimes painted rather than stitched. Examples exist from the seventeenth to the nineteenth centuries in the West, but Chinese origins are likely. Those at Traquair House were 'brought from France by Ann and May Stuart in 1714'. A book of 22 colifichet pages, each with an inscription of a Chapel Office, belongs to the Museum of Fine Arts in Boston. The edges of the pages are reinforced and decorated with a looped silver wire.

Bibliography
De Farcy; Swain 1965, 1967

Collections
UK Gawthorpe Hall, Burnley; Traquair House, Innerleithen
USA Museum of Fine Arts, Boston; Metropolitan Museum, New York
Germany National Museum, Munich

Colifichets: eighteenth-century reliquary panel. Faded blues and lilac floss on perforated parchment, featuring Saint Aloysius Gonzaga. (*Rachel Kay Shuttleworth Collection, Gawthorpe Hall*)

CONSERVATION

The preservation of embroideries encompasses all those techniques common to textile conservation as a whole. It is a professional and sophisticated study constantly under revision, with new developments in many scientific fields playing their part. A number of national and international bodies are concerned, and qualifications such as those offered by the Textile Conservation Centre at Hampton Court are widely recognized. The aim of conservation is to ascertain the cause of deterioration and rectify it, with minimum disturbance to the textile as a document of history.

Although adhesives and bonding agents are now so varied and specialized, their long-term effects cannot be assessed accurately, and their use is gradually being replaced by careful simple stitchery which is reversible in the event of future development. Strong protective meshes are now available which support safely and indefinitely fragile textiles on display.

Bibliography
Finch; Kimmins; Putnam

CONSTRUCTION

See *Fabric manipulation*

Conservation: for restoration, a set of nineteenth-century curtains, metal thread on lined red silk. (*Newstead Abbey, Nottingham Museums*)

Conservation: stem stitching following the line of a dart, probably from a cap. Ninth to tenth-century. Silk on silk. From an excavation at Coppergate, York. (*The Yorkshire Museum, York*) ▼

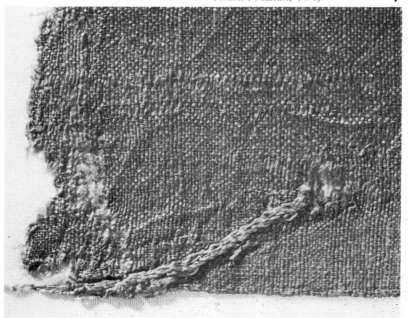

COPTIC EMBROIDERY

See *Needleweaving*

CORDED QUILTING

Two layers of fabric, a soft, fine one above and a more open weave for the backing, with stitchery forming enclosed floral motifs which are padded by introducing cotton roving through the backing. The flat areas of ground are closely ribbed in regular stitched parallel lines, chequered by cord divisions, or heavily encroached upon by contour outlines built out from the motifs. Unlike *trapunto* the backing was never cut to allow access to the shapes. The wadding was introduced through the loosely woven backing by means of a bodkin or stiletto.

The various techniques of quilting developed with enthusiasm in America, and adjusted to the availability or scarcity of materials. Corded quilting made use of linen or cotton weaves, but the wadding or stuffing was always cotton roving. There is no doubt that earlier quilts of this kind in England and Wales must have been stuffed with wool. Many American all-white quilts are beautifully planned, intricate and skilful.

Corded quilting is closely related to both *Italian* and trapunto.

Collections
UK American Museum, Bath

CORD QUILTING (Italian quilting)

Of the two defined methods of *Italian quilting*, that which is worked on only one layer of fabric is properly referred to as cord quilting. It achieves parallel lines of stitchery, without the use of a backing, with a herringbone stitch holding the cord in place beneath the ground. The herringbone forms two parallel lines of back stitch on the right side of the work. The resulting strongly defined line is harsher than Italian quilting. When the herringbone is used alone without the cord it is known as *flat quilting*. When the ground is translucent to allow the cord, which can be brightly coloured, to show through, it is known as *shadow quilting*. Both *trapunto* and cord quilting are referred to as stuffed work,

Corded quilting: English, eighteenth-century. Detail of a large linen bedcover. (*The Embroiderers' Guild*)

and often the word trapunto is also used for cord quilting. The earliest known examples are Sicilian, both techniques being called Italian quilting.

Many historical pieces have cord and trapunto quilting together. Trapunto necessitates the use of a backing through which the stuffing is introduced, and cord quilting does not. So an exceptionally light backing must be found which will serve the function of trapunto and still provide definition and relief when cording is worked under both layers. This combination of techniques is known in the American tradition as *corded quilting*.

Designing for cord quilting is specific. It is more conservative than Italian quilting, the single lines of herringbone being spaced regularly and seldom used as fillings.

Closely woven unbleached linen, sometimes glazed linen, is the traditional material, and a firm cord must be chosen matching the tone of the ground and appropriate to the scale of the design. The working thread must be strong. Buttonhole twist silk or linen are best, and beeswaxing the thread makes stitching easier and more regular. The needle should be very smooth with a large eye. A frame is essential. The ground should be loosely stretched, keeping

the grain at perfect right angles.

Most workers find a design transferred with a single guiding line more successful than attempts to provide parallel working lines for the stitchery. Experiments must be made to decide upon the best way of achieving a temporary line. On linen, a tacking line made through a tissue tracing is probably best. Chalk or pounce powder will adhere long

Cord quilting: sample of double-needle quilting and chain stitch, both Cornely adaptations. Coils of pink and blue on unbleached cotton. (*Manchester Polytechnic*)

Cord quilting: fine linen twill with no backing, partly worked showing design lines. Petticoat border fragment with several kinds of linen working thread. Early eighteenth-century, 23 × 41 cm (9 × 16 in.). (*Rachel Kay Shuttleworth Collection, Gawthorpe Hall*)

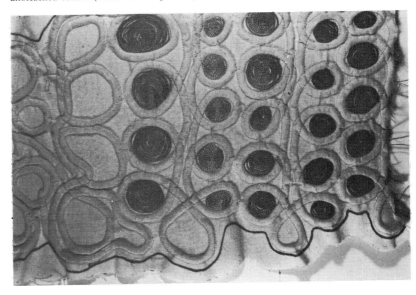

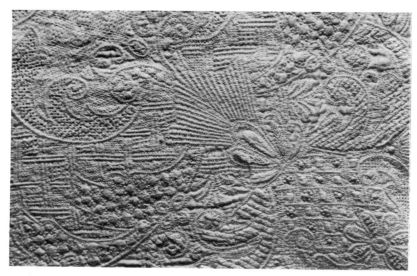

Cord quilting: German, early eighteenth-century quilting with drawn fabric and laid fillings. Detail 33 × 23 cm (13 × 9 in.). (*Bankfield Museum*)

CORDS AND BRAIDS

Generally, cords are round and braids are flattened. There are numerous uses for cords in embroidery, both functional and decorative. Those made of more expensive yarns are usually couched on the surface or used to form edgings. Raised fillings are worked over previously laid cord or string. In cord quilting the cord is held by stitching behind the ground.

Early references to laces may refer to cords and ribbons of silk or metal thread, useeto fasten and decorate garments. They ended in tags called poynts or ferrets. In regalia, lace means flat, figured metal braiding which may be quite wide. Russia braid is stitched to the ground between two raised ridges of metal, silk or rayon. Braid may be used to define borders, decorate edges, form fillings or interlaced to make elaborate and expansive *froggings*.

Bibliography
Bain; Barker

Cords and braids: brown and navy braid, lacet and leather, woven and couched. 15 cm (6 in.) square. Made by Karen Nichol, Manchester Polytechnic

enough to complete the stitchery providing they are drawn only on the immediate area to be worked. Tailors' chalk marks linen very firmly and on glazed linens can never be entirely removed.

Starting with a double back stitch to secure, the cord is held beneath the ground and the back stitch taken from side to side of it, evenly and firmly. Each stitch should encourage the cord up into the surface of the linen, forming a rounded line in relief. The cord should lie naturally and never be pulled. It may be necessary to slacken the ground in the frame from time to time, but if it is too slack uneven puckering will result. When the whole piece is finished and removed from the frame the tension of stitchery within the ground will adjust itself evenly.

Surface stitchery in combination with cord quilting provides a rich texture when it is limited to the characteristic unbleached colour. The intricate light and shade of stitchery complements the smooth rounded lines of quilting.

Collections
UK   Gawthorpe Hall, Burnley; Victoria and Albert Museum, London

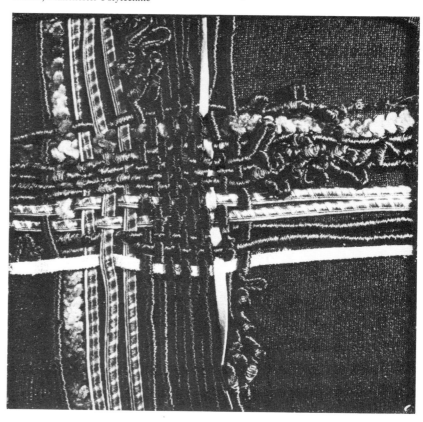

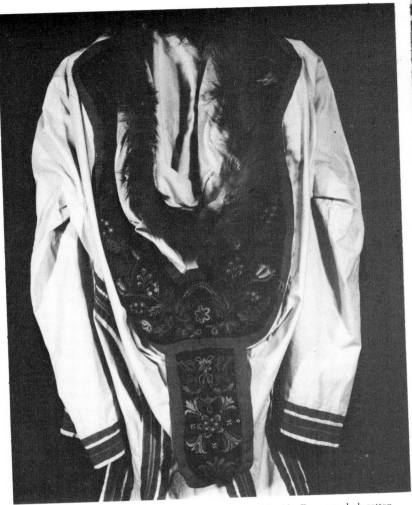

Cords and braids: Labrador Eskimo summer costume, white cotton and scarlet braid with a band of multi-coloured chain stitch on black. (*Leeds Museum*)

Cords and braids: Burmese, dark cotton twill cloth with red braiding and white seeds. Detail, seeds 1 cm ($\frac{1}{2}$ in.) long. (*Leeds Museum*)

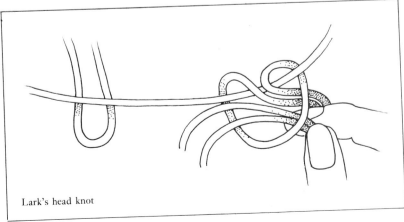

Lark's head knot

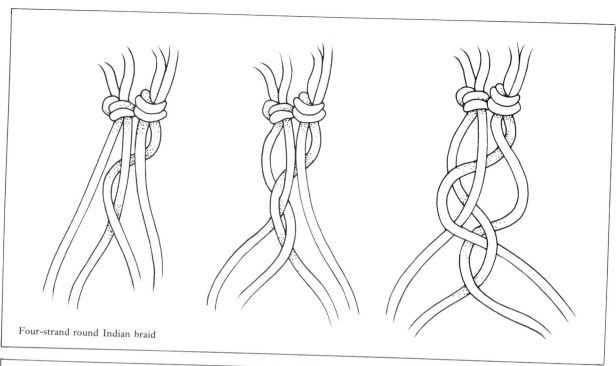

Four-strand round Indian braid

Six-strand round braid

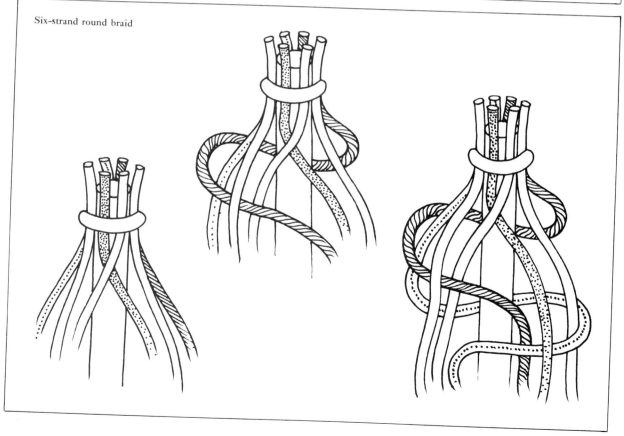

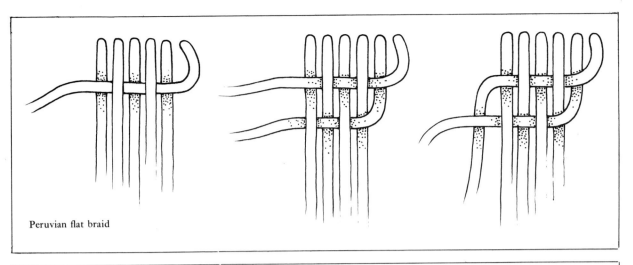

Peruvian flat braid

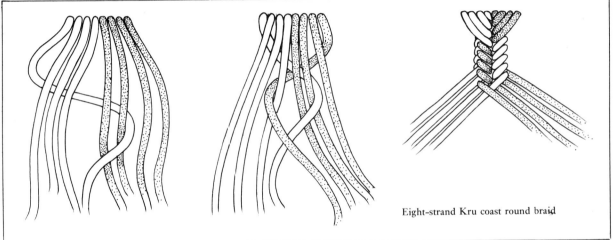

Eight-strand Kru coast round braid

CORNELY (US: Bonnaz)

A family of single-thread embroidery machines manufactured for various decorative purposes on a single continuous chain stitch principle. The hooked needle contacts a driving worm beneath the plate. The direction of the stitch is manually controlled. Each machine is capable of several adaptations. Cornelys can be made to chain, couch, cord, braid, and apply threaded beads and sequins. By changing tensions and stitch length they can make tufting and mossing textures.

The machine was invented in 1865 by Cornely, utilizing the idea of a self-looped thread and a universal feed, which had been rejected in the earliest days of the sewing machine. It was

Cornely: hessian, 15 cm (6 in.) square, satin stitched cerise chenille edged with the tufter in multicoloured rayon. Made by Rosemary Newdick, Manchester Polytechnic

very popular for extensive costume beading and braiding, and the flapper dresses of the 1920s brought it into wide use. The Cornely is still regularly used in fashion houses to make sumptuous textural decoration and areas of heavy beading.

Bibliography
Johnson, B.; Risley 1969

COTTON

Yarn or fabric made from the bols of fibre surrounding the cotton seed head. India was probably the earliest country to weave and trade cotton; it was woven there in the third millennium BC. The Greeks knew Indian muslins as gangetika and the Romans were particularly fond of them. The

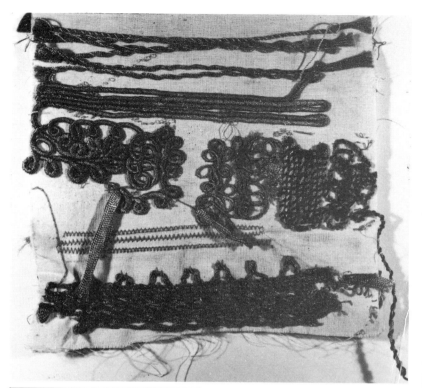

Cornely: braiding sampler, pinks, greens and reds on unbleached cotton. 19 cm (7½ in.) long. (*Manchester Polytechnic*)

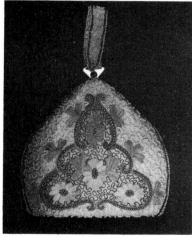

Cornely: tiny pearl beads, fine passing and pastel silks, cream aerophane over linen, 14 cm (5½ in.) wide

excellence of the cottons was judged on their fineness. Trade with Europe became very profitable and by the eighteenth century the western world was flooded with muslins, calico and chintz. The popularity of fine cottons reached its peak in Napoleonic fashion, and flowered embroidery was much in demand. Western industrialization reversed the traffic and destroyed India's trade in fabric but not in embroidery.

There are many varieties of plants in the family Gossypium suited to cultivation in various parts of the world. Cotton fibres are smooth and taper to a closed tip, each attached to an individual seed on the fruit bol. The ripe fibre is oval in section and hollow with a corkscrew twist, making it soft and absorbent when spun and woven.

The six-stranded silks or floss manufactured for embroidery are in fact mercerised cotton. They vary a good deal in quality and in the range of colours available. Some particularly pliable and lustrous ones are marketed as floss cotton rather than stranded cotton because of their superior quality and suitability for use on precious grounds. The six strands can be separated.

Among other cotton threads there are tightly spun perl ones which retain their lustre and are retailed in varying weights and limited colour ranges. There are thick lustrous ones and thick matt ones, and a number of single strand fine threads used mainly for neutral or white embroideries.

Bibliography
Hodges; Marks

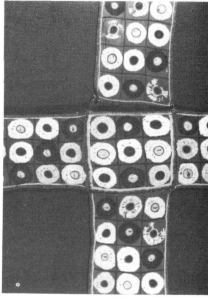

Cotton: cruciform Indian gaming board from Banni in Kutch, each arm 41 cm (16 in.) long, bound in red cotton. The game, champat, is played by Muslim herders. The central pouch stored the counters. (*Leeds Museum*)

COUCHÉ RENTRÉ

See *Underside couching*

COUCHING

A universal stitch with many variations both in technique and appearance. It consists of fastening one working thread to the ground with another by making stitches over it as a separate journey.

COUNTED THREAD (by the thread)

Stitchery which is planned according to counting the weave of the ground rather than measuring or estimating distances. It always has, therefore, some geometric element. Grounds may

Cotton: Turkish nineteenth-century towel border, gold passing, pink and green silks on soft, open cotton ground. Detail, 8 × 9 cm (7 × 3½ in.)

be extremely fine as in *Ayrshire work* or coarse like that used for *needlemade rugs.*

CRACKLESTITCH MESH

See *Tape lace*

CRAZY PATCHWORK (puzzle patchwork, crazy quilting)

An *Applied patchwork* method which was probably used originally as an economic expedient. It is usually rich in colour, top stitched rather than being oversewn or hemmed, and often has surface stitchery with herringbone, chain and feather predominating.

By the nineteenth century it had become a favourite pastime, utilizing scraps of silk, satin and velvet, ribbons and lace. Later pieces had monograms, names and mottoes, with applied 'objets trouvés', epitomizing the fashion for memorabilia. Caulfeild and Seward distinguish crazy from puzzle. They describe the former as being quite flat, the overlapping edges secured and decorated with surface stitchery, and the latter as being hemmed and turned with no decoration.

Crazy patchwork tends to be regarded as flippant, but to do it well does demand care and skill, since the range of fabrics characteristic to it vary in weight and behaviour, and the choice of colour is crucial. There is no standard method of construction, but it must be well planned. Scraps must be used selectively. Traditionally, if a whole top is to be made in joined blocks, these should number nine large or 20 small ones, divided by a framework of plain strips. All applied pieces and the foundation must be strong and carefully pressed. Iron-on bonding may be used to strengthen fine or unstable weaves.

Cut the foundation cloth either to block sizes or to the full size of the intended piece of work, leaving seam allowances. Pin the first patch either centrally or to the top right-hand corner. Succeeding pieces can be applied with a turned seam or by top stitching or with a mixture of both. If turned seams are to be used each piece

Cotton: mercerised cotton on linen scrim, each wheel 2.5 cm (1 in.)

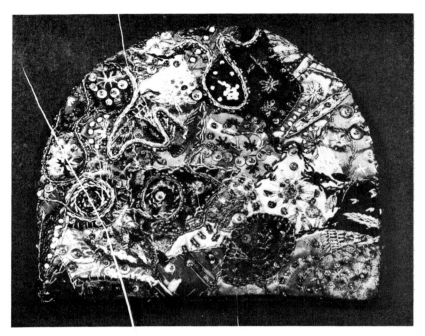

Crazy patchwork: small teacosy, mid-nineteenth-century, silks, plush, beads, silk stitching and sequins. (*Nottingham Museum*)

Crazy patchwork: green cottons and velvet cut in the form of a map to represent precise field patterns ▼

must be tacked right sides together with the previous piece, and both joined to the foundation with a running stitch. The tacking is removed, the piece turned down, and the next piece begun. If top stitching is used pieces can be applied one after another, their leading edges folded under and tacked ready for subsequent all-over top stitching of the whole piece of work.

Crazy patchwork is easy to do by machine, although in a few difficult corners stitching may need hand-finishing.

Bibliography
Caulfeild and Saward

Collection
UK Nottingham Museum

CRÊPE WORK

See *Flowers, Aerophane*

CREWEL POINT

Canvas work is generally known in the USA as needlepoint, and so a term was needed to distinguish the restrictive regularity of needlepoint from the freer use of bold stitchery on canvas or coarsely woven fabric. The word crewel employed by the Elizabethans always referred both to the wool and to the stitching. The word point has been used even more loosely to describe almost any needlemade decoration. Vertical and horizontal satin stitch are most favoured in crewel point, with the introduction of long-and-short for larger areas. Stem and back stitches form any lines, and raised areas of French knots or pile stitches are permissible. The small proportion of canvas ground remaining is often left unworked.

CREWEL WORK

Probably once described *Jacobean* work, but the term is now used for any worsted wool stitchery on a large scale. It is associated with free working rather than counted stitchery.

Bibliography
Baker, M.L.; Edwards 1975; Hedhind; Jones, M.E. 1974; Turner, Miss

Crewel work: fine coloured wool chain stitch on linen. Eighteenth-century pockets, 36 cm (14 in.) long. (*Rachel Kay Shuttleworth Collection, Gawthorpe Hall*)

Crewel work: blue wools on linen, stool top 25 cm (10 in.) in diameter. Made by Nora Aitchison

Cross stitch: Russian, red, green and blue goats' hair on heavy plain linen. Sleeve ends, detail 15 × 25 cm (6 × 10 in.)

Collections

UK American Museum, Bath; Gawthorpe Hall, Burnley; Guildford Museum; Victoria and Albert Museum, London; William Morris Gallery, London; Platt Hall, Manchester; Cotehele House, Saltash
USA Museum of Fine Arts, Boston; Metropolitan Museum, New York
Canada Royal Ontario Museum, Toronto

CROSS STITCH (gros point, sampler stitch, cushion style)

Describing two diagonals crossing a square of ground yarns, cross stitch is virtually two opposing lines of *petit point*, one over the other. (Some authorities give gros point as merely a coarser version of petit point, the diagonals in one direction only.) One of the oldest and simplest of embroidery stitches, it was used by the Phrygians, the Egyptians and the Hebrews. In medieval times it featured extensively, used in the same way as it is today, for ecclesiastical furnishings and cushions (see *opus pulvinarium*). The Moroccan version is called straight and diagonal stitch, since classically it formed straight lines on the other side of the work. During the nineteenth century cross stitch was so popular for samplers that it became identified with them.

Bibliography

Agutter; Bengtsson; Kiewe 1950; Nye; Priscilla 1899; Wilkie

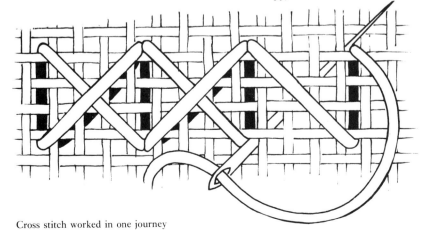

Cross stitch worked in one journey

Cross stitch: Greek, eighteenth-century,
heavy silk in dark colours arranged to catch
the light in horizontal and vertical blocks.
Rhodian sperveri, each border square 10 cm
(4 in.). (*Leeds Museum*)

Cross stitch: eighteenth-century sampler,
Morocco. Moorish diagonal and straight
stitch is worked in two journeys to produce
a cross stitch on the right side. This is the
reverse.

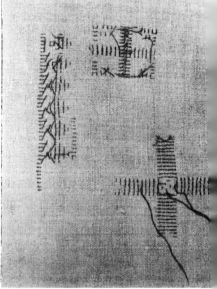

CUTWORK

A general term embracing all those
methods of construction where areas of
ground are cut away, leaving the
motifs supported either by bars or by
continuous lines of stitchery combining
their edges. Cutwork differs from lace
only in that it is coarser and less
decorated. There are many coloured
variations amongst regional
embroideries, domestic textiles and
costume, but cutwork is usually
associated with white or natural linens
and cottons because of its affinity with
lace.

Bibliography
Ashton; Cave 1962, 1964; de Dillmont;
Lewis; Minter; Shorleyker; Thomas
1936; *Weldon's*

Cross stitch: Palestinian robe, applied yoke
in strong colours, silk on linen. (*Leeds
Museum*)

Cutwork: orange and white linen, overcasting and chain stitch. Hungarian sleeve top, detail 13 × 19 cm (5 × 7½ in.)

Overcast bars with the ground clipped ready to turn

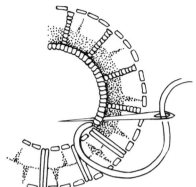
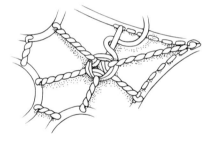

Cutwork: the sequence of working edges and darning bars

Twisted bars

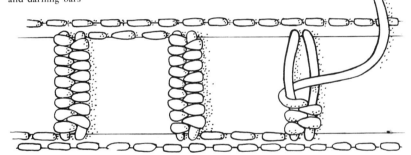

Collections
UK Guildford Museum; London Museum; Nottingham Museum
USA Metropolitan Museum of Art, New York
Italy Industrie Femminili Italiano, Florence
Switzerland Textilmuseum, St Gallen

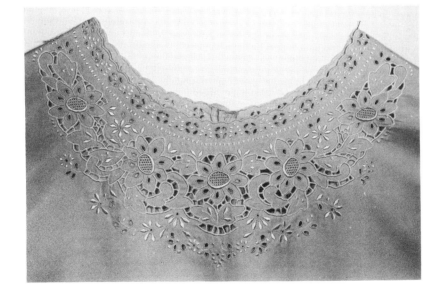

Cutwork: blouse, white floss on blue shantung.

Early cutwork. (*Ilké and Jacoby Collection, Textilmuseum, St Gallen*)

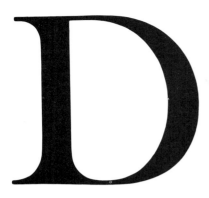

DACCA MUSLINS

See *Chikan*

DARNED NET

See *Net embroidery*, *Filet*

DARNING

A simple running stitch with inexhaustible variations in its use, found on textiles from most cultures where weaving has been dominant or sophisticated. Darning may be used to form outlines or fillings, open the ground with pattern or close it with added opacity, describe geometric patterns or draw representationally. All darning is reversible. In its simplest form it is a running stitch, and distinguishable from satin stitch in that it always progresses with the needle facing the same way throughout any single journey. In *free machine embroidery* the term darning refers to the ordinary even lockstitch achieved with equal tensions. There are eight hand embroidery variations, although not all darning can be strictly categorized.

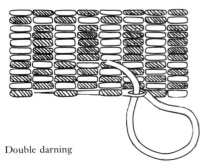

Double darning

Damask darning is a filling worked both vertically and horizontally with stitches of equal length, travelling first one way and then the other. Both sides of the work are alike. It is usually counted and regular, adding density without textural depth. It is the same as cloth stitch in filet and lace, and frequently resembles woven damask fillings. Occasionally stitches travel in one direction only on selected fillings.

Double darning, also known as pessanté darning, is a filling. Used as a single line it is known as Holbein stitch or double running and is characteristic of *blackwork*. It is closest to pattern darning but worked in two movements, the second row returning to fill in the spaces left by the first, using the same stitch holes. Regularly alternating spaces and colours will produce vertical columns of colour, and diagonal or chevron patterns can be made by staggering the colour repeat. A Roman textile from Verulamium (St Albans) has an edging of overcast stitches with six working threads darned through them, and a Coptic cloth in the Ashmolean Museum, Oxford is similarly finished, with red and green alternating working threads. The early sixteenth-century Fetternear banner, although contemporary with the fashion for double darning or Holbein stitch used

as a line, shows the stitch used as it was in Islamic and Greek textiles, as a filling. The close darning is carefully disciplined into chevron and diagonal blocks of pattern. Chamba rumals, the narrative embroideries of the Punjab, also have double darning used as a filling, but it has a fine irregular texture.

Honeycomb darning or surface darning is normally used as a line. It is distinguished from huckaback only by its ground of specially made honeycomb weave. A continuous running stitch in overlapping and interlacing journeys across the fabric makes symmetrical pattern sequences which take up only the long floats provided on the surface of the ground.

Huckaback, also known as huck weaving, is a very similar linear technique to honeycomb. Huckaback may be done on any ground which has regularly spaced groups of long float yarns, or on any fabric where small groups of yarns can be taken up by the needle at regular intervals.

Irregular or reversible darning consists of single stitches which travel from one side of a defined shape to the

Darning: four darned fillings surrounding laid work. Green, blue and orange, cotton on linen sampler, the central square 8 cm (3 in.). Made by G.T. Glover

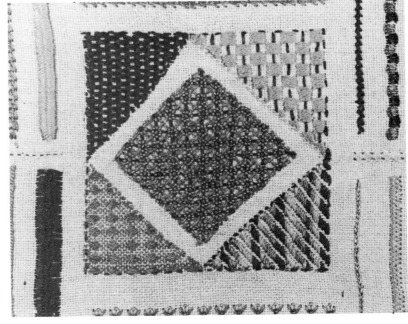

other, the stitch re-emerging to cross succeeding shapes in its path, and voiding outlines. Stitches are usually quite close together, often mistaken for satin stitch until the reverse side is examined, showing a neat, muted outline of small stitches. The needle can travel in any direction, but only in one direction in one shape. The emphasis is on rich coverage of the ground, exploiting the lustre of the working thread by adjacent changes in direction. The *heer bharat* stitchery of India is a sophisticated example.

Pattern darning differs from irregular darning only in that the stitches must follow the weave of the ground. Once more, outlines are usually voided, and so the stitches are accommodated within geometric shapes, taking up one or more ground yarns with each stitch, depending on the density of colour required. It occurs frequently on European and Scandinavian peasant embroideries.

Surface darning is a covering filling stitch, entering the ground only at the

Darning: heavy wool curtains with pattern darning in greens and orange. Detail 152 × 66 cm (60 × 26 in.)

Darning: Indian pillow cover, 46 cm (18 in.) square, running stitch in primary colours on unbleached calico. (*Leeds Museum*)

extremities of each shape. It may be worked with a satin stitch with lengths of working thread beneath the shape or as a darned filling. The laid threads are darned over in the opposite direction, still only entering the ground at the edges. The opposing darning threads may be laid in groups or woven in patterns.

Swedish darning can be grouped with huckaback and honeycomb. It has the same continuous running stitch, but the regular detours in pattern sequence form more complex clusters of long stitches on the surface, contrasting with interspersed groups of small picks of ground.

Bibliography
Bird and Bellinger; D'Harcourt; Wild

Collections
UK Gawthorpe Hall, Burnley; National Museum of Antiquities of Scotland, Edinburgh; Ashmolean Museum, Oxford

Huckaback, a two-colour darning pattern

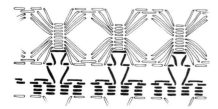

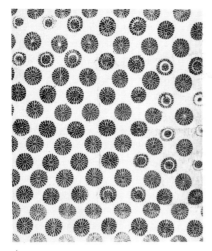

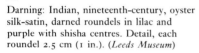

Darning: Indian, nineteenth-century, oyster silk-satin, darned roundels in lilac and purple with shisha centres. Detail, each roundel 2.5 cm (1 in.). (*Leeds Museum*)

Darning: Indian, early nineteenth-century, chamba rumal. Multi-coloured silk on cotton. 56 × 91 cm (22 × 36 in.). (*Rachel Kay Shuttleworth Collection, Gawthorpe Hall*)

Darning: cotton, 18 × 14 cm (7 × 5½ in.). ▶ Made by Kenneth Dow Barker (*By permission of Lanercost Abbey Mill and Ceolfrith Press*, 1979)

DÉCOUPÉ

See *Reverse appliqué*

DEERFIELD BLUE AND WHITE WORK

Worsted crewel threads were too expensive for the early American Settlers to import, and so they spun and dyed their own yarns and working threads. The native vegetable dyes were considered inferior to precious indigo, and so blue threads tended to be reserved for more important decorations. Attempts were made to match the blues of Canton china, and the style of *Jacobean* crewel work was married to more direct Oriental influences. The attraction of pale indigo over-dyed with native dyestuffs sometimes proved too much, and other soft colours appeared in the work.

In about 1895 two Deerfield ladies, Miss Miller and Miss Whiting, collected early pieces and designs and set up the Deerfield Society of Blue and White Work in Massachusetts.

Collections
UK   American Museum, Bath
USA   Memorial Hall Museum, Deerfield, Massachusetts

DESIGN

Frequently in embroidery the word design is used as a noun and has come to mean the finished plan or cartoon or full-scale diagrammatic drawing which is transferred directly on to the fabric. This is more properly called a pattern, especially where it is to be repeated.

The verb 'to design' implies the overall process of planning a piece of work, both visually and in functional terms.

Before pattern books, designs were copied from indigenous or imported sources. Representational drawing was stylized and adapted to conform to the medium and scale. Further adjustments through generations of copying and enriching influences often resulted in the forms being no longer clearly understood, and they became vehicles for decorative expression and the mystical rules and rituals which

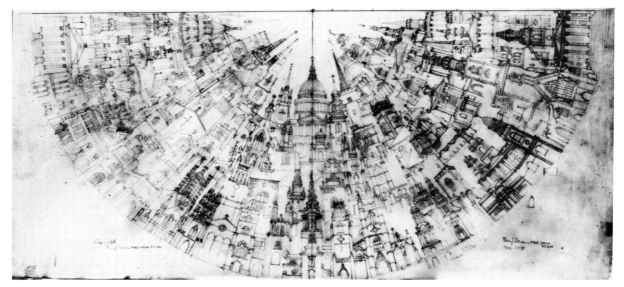

Design: cartoon for the Jubilee Cope. Made by Beryl Dean, M.B.E. (*Photograph: Millar and Harris*)

Design: the Greek Glastra motif. Several symbolic origins are suggested. It has evolved to total abstraction. (*Rachel Kay Shuttleworth Collection, Gawthorpe Hall*)

Design: stumpwork motifs from entirely different locations indicate common sources

governed the appropriate use of colour, stitch and space. Early samplers were, in effect, dictionaries of pattern and stitches for secular use, to supplement natural observation and references to illustrated herbals. Professional embroidery had a system of apprenticeship, and designs were frequently drawn direct onto the fabric

by painters. Mary Queen of Scots was allowed her 'imbroderers' to draw out designs, many of which clearly came from Conrad Gesner's *Historiae Animalium* published in 1551. The woodcuts from Pierre Belon's naturalist books published in 1555 appear worked in tent stitch on the Oxburgh hangings.

The Venetian Vinciolo published his book of cutwork and needlemade lace patterns at Turin in 1589. Shorleyker's *Schole-howse for the Needle*, published in 1624, is well known, though some of

his drawings must have been printed considerably earlier, since they appeared on textiles at the end of the sixteenth century. In 1640 John Taylor's little book *The Needle's Excellency* appeared, copies of which can be examined in the British Library and in the Rylands Library, Manchester. Designs stamped or block printed direct on to the fabric probably became available early in the seventeenth century.

As voyagers recorded tropical plants, birds and beasts, and brought home exotic pattern and decoration, a wealth of material offered new impetus. Audubon, the artist perhaps most

Design: spot sampler, seventeenth-century. (*Nottingham Museum. Photograph: Layland-Ross*)

Design: the use of derivative design, neutral colours on white. Made by Betty Prothero. (*Photograph: Chris Locke*)

▼

Design: pattern dictated entirely by ritualistic symbolism. Maya priest's costume, which must be worked entirely by men. Quiche Indians, Chichicastenango. Chain stitch in various pinks on heavy black twill. (*Leeds Museum*)

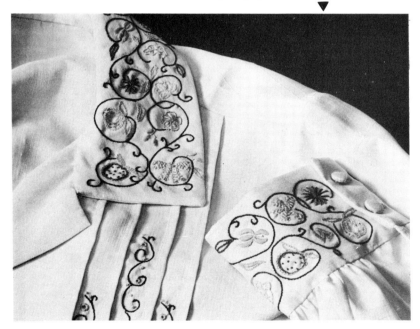

famous for his *Birds of America*, published between 1827 and 1838, was notable for his backgrounds as well as his birds. They appear frequently on embroidery from that date onwards.

Coloured prints on lined paper for needlework were first sold by Philipson in Berlin in 1804. These enabled the amateur needleworker to count stitches rather than copy drawings. The achievement of detail and realism led to the craze for wool work on canvas which swept Europe and America.

The technique of block printing extended from commercial embroidery such as Ayrshire, through itinerant professionals planning quilts, to the amateur intent on white work linens and flounces. Block prints on paper could be purchased and transferred by means of prick and pounce.

Iron-on transfers were invented by William Briggs in 1875. Commercial designs can still be bought in many forms, widely ranging in quality and subject matter. The art school training of embroiderers has done little to alter demand, but has recently made some inroads on awareness and on the general standard of printed designs.

Bibliography
Blunt 1950; Blunt and Raphael 1979; Cabot 1941 and 1946; Dance; Daniels; Delamote; Nevinson; Ricci; Swain 1980; Taylor; Walpole

Collections
UK British Library, London; Victoria and Albert Museum, London; Rylands Library, Manchester
USA Valentine Museum, Richmond, Virginia

DICTAL LACE

See *Tape lace*

DOMETTE (US: outing flannel)

A knitted wool, wool and cotton, or wool and synthetic fabric brushed into a high pile, used for wadded quilting.

Originally a wool and cotton interlining woven by Josiah Domett in Manchester, it was luxuriously soft and light. Recent versions are often knitted for increased pliability.

Domette is at its best as a batting between fine fabrics for quilting on the machine. Using the darning foot without the feed dog the three layers may be delicately drawn over with free stitchery. A fine working thread is ideal, and the occasional use of blocks of narrow satin stitch or zigzag adds depth and variety.

DORSET BUTTONS

The cottage industry centred on Dorset probably as early as the mid-seventeenth century, producing linen- or thread-covered buttons, usually white. They were stitched over horn or felted wool moulds or buttonholed over wire rings. Staffordshire Leek buttons and those made on the west coast of Scotland were more frequently coloured, using silk over hard moulds.

Bird's Eye buttons were buttonholed over a wooden dome with a central perforation, its ridge of buttonhole loops framing the outside of the flat base.

Dorset Knobs were needlewoven over a tiny wooden hemisphere then pressed and polished.

High Tops were as small as 3 mm ($\frac{1}{8}$ in.), a spider's web needlewoven over a high cone then pressed and polished.

Honeycombs were woven on rings, sometimes just filled with radiating threads, sometimes overworked with weaving or spider's webs.

White Singleton's were tiny rings covered with white glazed cotton, padded and gathered to the back and secured there with radiating stitches forming a line inside the ring on the top side.

Sorted into sets and sizes, they were sewn to cards for sale. Jaffrey's invention in 1841 of the linen-covered button-making machine caused decline and hardship.

Collections
UK Gawthorpe Hall, Burnley; Dorset County Museum, Dorchester; Leeds Industrial Museum; Harris Museum and Art Gallery, Preston

DORSET FEATHER STITCHERY

An enthusiasm developed in the 1950s for feather-stitched patterns loosely based on traditional smock patterns. A firmly woven satinized cotton is a frequent ground with well twisted, round cotton working threads. Close shades and tints of related colours are characteristic. Stitches are usually confined to varieties of chain and feather regularly spaced with an easy tension. Ric rac braid is used to support spirals and robust trailing stems.

Bibliography
Armes; Pass

DOUBLE RUNNING

See *Blackwork*

DRAWN CANVAS WORK

See *Canvas overlays*

Dorset feather stitchery: typical pattern distribution with ric rac braid

DRAWN FABRIC (pulled fabric, pulled work, punch work, punto a giorno, à jour embroidery)

Worked mainly on loosely woven linens and sometimes on extremely fine ones, drawn fabric depends entirely on the displacement and bunching of ground yarns by the tension of repetitive stitchery. The ground is never withdrawn as in *drawn thread*. On fine work pulled grounds can be difficult to distinguish from drawn thread ones.

Drawn fabric is one of the techniques which involve changing the structure of the ground and thus exploiting the natural beauty of yarn and weave rather than merely complementing it with surface stitchery. It is probably as old as man's ability to weave an openly textured material. It can be found on most embroidered linen from the earliest examples, alongside drawn

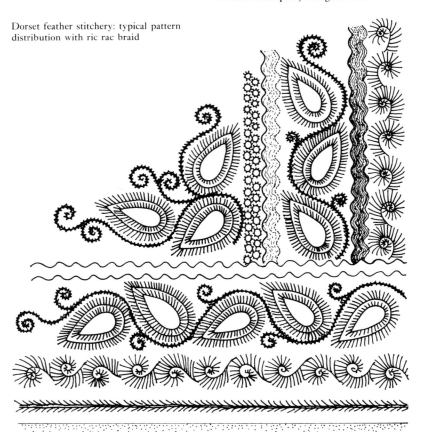

thread work, padded white work, quilting, and counted stitchery of all kinds. The wealth of fillings available resulted in extensive fine linen samplers preserving the vocabulary for succeeding generations. This has led to a preference amongst amateurs for working within rectangular confines, although most pulled work was used on fillings inside floral motifs as all-over grounds. It is conventional and indicative of proficiency to work a variety of fillings on one piece of work.

The earliest surviving examples, dating from around 1200 AD, come from Peru, the Middle East and Mamluk Egypt. Double running and drawn fabric were worked in coloured silk and metal threads on geometric borders. The increase in trade in the sixteenth and seventeenth centuries brought fine linen embroidery and soft muslins, rich in white, coloured and metal stitchery, and stimulated interest in delicate openwork. Embroideries from the Greek islands and the east Mediterranean were multi-coloured and interspersed with metal threads. Turkish and Persian pieces utilized more softly coloured threads and expertly handled metal plate. Italian ones were often without

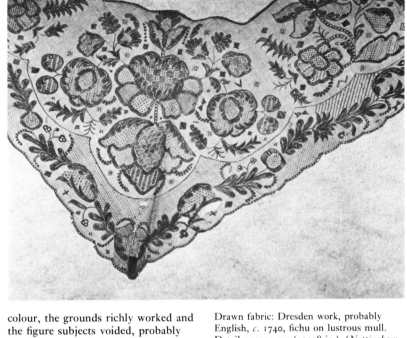

colour, the grounds richly worked and the figure subjects voided, probably the forerunner of *Assisi* work. German linen work of this period and earlier, *opus teutonicum*, contains many drawn fabric stitches.

European work of the eighteenth century became fine and sophisticated, approaching needlepoint lace in texture and appearance. With the availability

Drawn fabric: linen on scrim, 14 × 15 cm (5½ × 6 in.)

Drawn fabric: Dresden work, probably English, *c.* 1740, fichu on lustrous mull. Detail 25 × 20 cm (10 × 8 in.). (*Nottingham Museum*)

of fine cambric the stitches became tiny and very varied, and the resulting style became known as *Dresden work*. The gossamer-fine variations of drawn fabric are often classed as lace, and certainly were for the purposes of duty, taxes making them prohibitive for all but the very wealthy.

In contrast to the lace-like techniques, drawn fabric was extensively used on coarser and heavier natural linen grounds for panels, coverlets, waistcoats and petticoats. Eighteenth-century linen work is often thick with pulled grounds, intricately padded and quilted, and all available space lavishly filled with surface stitchery and eyelet patterns. It now seems to be established that grounds were not cut to expose more loosely woven linings for drawn work, but that the fillings were worked directly on the ground, sometimes aided by the regular withdrawing of yarn, making it technically drawn thread work rather than drawn fabric.

Mass-production caused a decline in interest throughout much of the nineteenth century. In the early twentieth century Mrs Newall revived

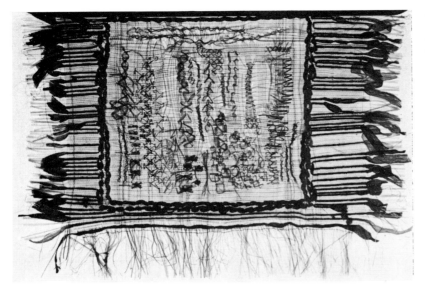

Drawn fabric: plastic sacking, 41 × 28 cm (16 × 11 in.). Pulled work with ravellings, and bright ribbon weaving. Made by Harriet Parker-Jervis

drawn fabric rather in the Tudor and Stewart style as part of a cottage industry at *Fisherton-de-la-Mere*.

Open ground materials on any scale have been used, from hessian to the finest muslins, and so characteristics are found in the stitchery rather than the general visual effect. The usual material for pulled fabric work is an open-weave linen or linen scrim with round, easily separated yarn which has not been beetled smooth. Some workers are becoming interested in the very fine techniques on muslin and organdie, probably as a reaction against the coarse surface stitchery which has recently dominated embroidery.

Working threads should not be dominant, since it is the pattern of holes they make rather than the stitches themselves which are important. The thread must be well twisted since soft threads are liable to fluff and destroy the sharpness of the technique. If the thread is exactly like the ground throughout there is a risk that the work will seem to be of all one texture. Early *Hedebo* overcame this by incorporating rich surface stitchery. Sharp changes in tone or in the introduction of colour need careful consideration, and reference to

historical pieces with colour and metal threads is advised.

Needles must be appropriate to the fabric. Although blunt tapestry needles are normally recommended this is always on the assumption that the ground is coarse evenweave linen. For work on fine fabrics the needle must be fine, beautifully polished, and with an eye large enough to travel through the fabric with minimal damage to the working thread and the ground yarn.

A sharp needle will definitely be required from time to time to finish ends and hems. Small samples can be worked in the hand, but a tambour frame or a square frame will make the work far easier, since tensions are better controlled and loosely woven linens are not liable to distortion.

There is no specific order in which the ground is prepared for working. Decisions about transferring the design and marking the fabric can be made only for each individual embroidery and worker, and it may well be that several processes are taking place at the same time. Since drawn fabric has convenient outlines they can be marked out with coloured threads so that alterations are easy and harmless. Prick and pounce reinforced with pale poster paint is often most successful on linens. Tailors' chalk should be used only where lines are certain. Agnes Leach suggests the use of transparent templates to assist the final planning of the design on the ground. It was traditional, on some fine translucent grounds where outlines

Many drawn fabric fillings are worked in diagonal journeys. Single faggot stitch, shown here with horizontals and verticals on the right side, and reversed, with diagonals on the right side

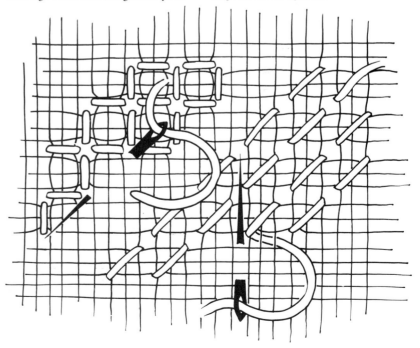

were tiny or absent, to transfer the design to the reverse side and work fillings from the back. Drawn fabric laces were often transferred by tacking a parchment pattern beneath the ground and following the outlines with a tiny stem stitch.

It is tempting, especially on small table linens, to complete the hem before the main body of the work is begun. However, the edge is best left overcast to prevent fraying, and worked last. Turning and tacking a temporary hem leaves a bruised and soiled fold which is difficult to remove.

The fillings divide conveniently into two groups, those worked horizontally and vertically and those worked diagonally. Some are completed in one working journey and others only half done and completed on the way back. Some may be worked in blocks or added to in successive rows. Where there is choice in working procedure there will also be inevitable variation in the finished texture.

The selection of a filling is influenced not only by its density, direction, weight and texture, but by the practical application to the shape it is to occupy. The possibility of mixing fillings should not be overlooked. Larger expanses of ground where the pattern of a filling is better understood visually, may well benefit from alternating diagonals of dense and light

Indian drawn ground

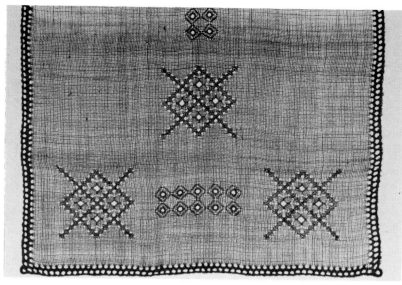

Drawn fabric: open evenweave with hemstitching, 31 cm (12 in.) wide. Made by Susan Butterworth.

bands, for instance. Both the working and the finished embroidery are more satisfying if fillings have been chosen very selectively, and adapted and varied within the confines of that selection.

Outlines normally come from the chain, stem and knot families, ordinary chain and double knot being favourites. The all-important factor in drawn fabric embroidery is the proper handling of stitch tension. Most stitches can be greatly varied by changes in tension, to the extent that they become unrecognizable. Working

threads should be used in short lengths wherever possible, starting off and finishing beneath outlines and never inside a filling. In working, the proper twist of the thread must be maintained.

Free drawn fabric stitchery with the machine can be achieved on most open weaves by stretching the fabric in a tambour frame and using a zigzag stitch to bunch the ground yarns. With care, and precise adjustment of thread tensions, repetitive pattern is a practical possibility, but the textural richness and variable densities of free stitching are usually more rewarding.

Bibliography
de Dillmont; Fangel; Leach; Lofthouse; McNeill 1971; Ramazanoglu; Wark

Collections
UK Museum of Costume, Bath; Gawthorpe Hall, Burnley; Fitzwilliam Museum, Cambridge

DRAWN IN DRAWN THREAD
See *Threading*

DRAWN THREAD (punto tagliato)

Worked mainly on linen and sometimes on remarkably fine cotton,

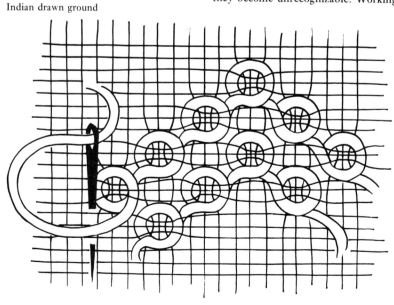

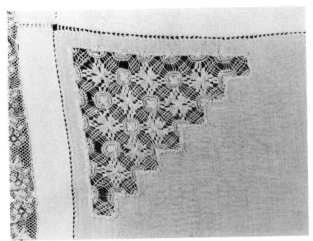

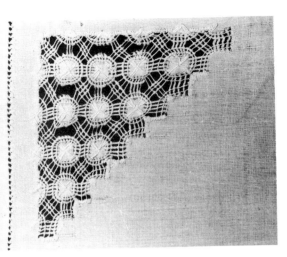

Drawn thread: white linen mat openly drawn. Wear damage shows the vulnerable areas

the varieties of drawn thread all depend on the cutting and withdrawing of yarn from the fabric. Although hemstitching, needleweaving, Hedebo and Hardanger and the laces are dealt with separately they are interrelated and share many characteristic stitches. Drawn thread is an extension of the clustering methods of hemstitching. The elaborate wheels and webs of Tenerife lace and the bars and picots of Richelieu and Renaissance can all be incorporated in drawn thread. It is often confused with *drawn fabric* or pulled work, where yarn is displaced but not removed. On fine work, drawn grounds can be difficult to distinguish from pulled ones. Drawn grounds and the stitchery worked over them are frequently imitative of *filet* and may be given as filet work or lacis work. Whilst *cutwork* requires the whole filling to be composed of stitchery, drawn thread work leaves a mesh of ground yarns to be grouped and elaborated. Unlike drawn fabric it weakens the structure of the ground and is more subject to friction and wear. It is traditionally in white or self colours, a strictly limited use of colour accentuating its textural richness, but national costumes sometimes include bright primary colours.

Drawn thread work is certainly a logical embellishment to lovingly spun, loosely woven linens of the kind that were frequently used by the wealthy long before the Birth of Christ. The oldest surviving pieces of drawn thread are often worked with their own ravellings, a trait arising from both the urge to integrate stitchery with the weaving process and the necessity to utilize fully hand-spun yarn. Drawn thread is often associated with fringing, and fringes came to be grouped and knotted like the working thread on withdrawn areas of the body of the fabric.

Coptic fragments, indicating developments from the superb *needleweaving* roundels, are ascribed to the sixth century, and coarse work was prevalent a little later in Spain and Sicily. Many named versions have evolved and confusions have arisen where publications categorized them according to geographical locations or commercially promoted patterns. In Spain, Italy, Sicily and Cyprus, styles were often given names of religious significance. The general breaking up of the ground fabric became more and more elaborate and open, sometimes appropriately known as frost work, until, hastened by improvements in the regularity of yarns, the ground fabric disappeared altogether and the delicate stitching became needlepoint lace.

There are three categories of drawn thread which have as their basis a ground of open squares.

The version described as filet drawn thread is so called because it produces an open texture of squares over the ground like filet network. The main motifs are left voided and undrawn, the design outlined by a running thread which is then overcast or chain stitched, thus slightly raising the outline. It is sometimes buttonholed with the knot towards the voided cloth. Equal numbers of ground yarns are withdrawn and left, alternately, in both directions. The drawn ground is then overcast, either in both directions or transversely, becoming exactly the same as *Russian drawn ground*.

Blocks of ground yarns withdrawn in one direction only and grouped with needleweaving are known as 'al pasado'. Fine work, where the blocks are needlewoven with a yarn closely resembling the ground, is known as 'zurcindo'.

Work where yarns are withdrawn in both directions, leaving larger squares than filet, seems to come under the category of Mexican drawn work. *Tenerife* drawn thread is worked in exactly the same way as Mexican but later bears the characteristic, separately made sols.

The disciplines of drawn thread are those of all counted stitchery. If the embroidery is to withstand wear, the stitchery must stabilize remaining ground yarns and strengthen the structure. There are arguably two basic alternatives in considering the choice of a design. The embroidery may form an extension of the hem, developing as a border or relating to it as a central feature. In this case, it relies entirely on the relationship of open and closed areas and surface texture for its appeal, and the exact placing of the drawn areas on the ground is determined by counting. Secondly, it may be outlined independent of the weave enclosing voided areas and forming drawn grounds adjacent to them. This kind is often floral or representational in some way, and the design must be transferred to the ground in outlines before counting begins.

The choice of ground in relationship to working thread is critical. It requires care and sampling before a decision is made. Drawn thread is traditionally worked on cambric, lawn, muslin or on evenweave linen which can be counted. The ground yarn must be sufficiently smooth to be withdrawn with ease, and sufficiently stable to withstand withdrawal of yarn until it can be replaced by stitchery. The ground of traditional pieces varies in scale from lawn with over 100 picks to 2.5 cm (1 in.) to coarsely spun hand-made linen with less than ten.

In practice the working thread should be slightly coarser than the ground yarn for surface stitchery. Oversewing, hemstitching and clustering, and sometimes the fillings, can be completed in a finer thread, perhaps the ravellings. The texture of ravellings is quite different. Even slight differences in tone or lustre of the thread and the ground yarn will influence the finished embroidery. Whether it is sewing silk for silk fabric, linen lace thread for muslin or lawn, or linen twist for evenweave, the working thread must be strong and smooth.

Although blunt tapestry needles are normally recommended, this is always on the assumption that the ground is coarse. For work on fine fabrics the needle must be fine, well polished, and with an eye large enough to travel through the fabric with minimal damage to the working thread or the ground yarn. Fine pins and sharply pointed scissors are essential. Small samples can be worked in the hand, but a tambour frame on a stand or a square frame will make the work far easier, since tension can be maintained and both hands can be used to manipulate the threads.

There is no specific order in which the ground is prepared for working. Each individual must make the

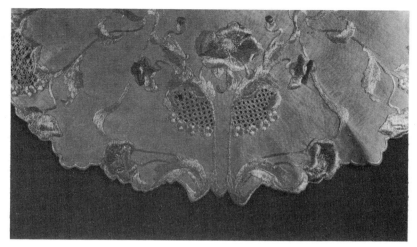

decisions about counting out, transferring the design, working from squared paper, withdrawing yarn, and marking the fabric. It may well be that several processes are taking place concurrently. Some workers prefer to transfer the design only with coloured thread, so that alterations are easy and harmless. Prick and pounce reinforced with pale poster paint is often most successful on linens. Tailors' chalk should only be used if lines are certain. Agnes Leach suggests that transparent templates could be used for planning the design on the ground. According to the extent of the work, it may well be worth taking up a good deal of preparation time counting and marking the ground. Find the centre and tack four arms of a cross in each direction to each edge, using a coloured thread. Quarter these divisions as seems appropriate to the distribution of the design. The tacking stitches themselves are more useful if they are regular. Having decided the base-number of most of the clustering to be used, which will probably be two, three or four, the basting stitch can alternate over and under that number.

Where yarns are to be withdrawn in short lengths this can be done in the frame, but complex areas involving long stretches of counting must be done with the ground free, or with the whole piece stretched out fully in a square frame. If yarns are to be withdrawn completely throughout the piece consideration must be given to the edge. Withdrawn blocks will

Drawn thread: nineteenth-century floss silk on linen, pinks and creams, sinuous forms with isolated drawn fillings. Height of poppy 18 cm (7 in.)

extend through fringing or hem, and if this is not desirable the blocks must stop short of the edge, and yarns must be either overcast or woven in. Attempts to dispose of yarn ends inside a hem are not successful and lead to distortion, especially after washing. It is tempting, especially on small table linens, to complete the hemming before the main body of the work is begun. This often leads to counting difficulties at a later stage. The ground is best left overcast to prevent fraying, so that the edge can be worked last. Turning and tacking a temporary hem can leave a bruised and soiled fold.

Withdrawing trials on a spare piece are advisable, especially if the ground is fine. The first yarn of a block is always reluctant, but the rest follow

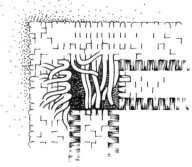

Drawing a corner

easily. The remaining fabric may be less disturbed by drawing several yarns one by one in small blocks rather than pulling out right across the ground with each yarn. However, if the yarn is to be used for subsequent stitchery, comparatively long lengths will be needed. There are three ways of treating the ends of blocks of drawn yarn. The first is to overcast. This can be done in the appropriate position before the yarn is withdrawn, or after the ends have been cut; the latter is more usual. The second is to reserve short ends of yarn tacked underneath the work which can later be secured beneath surface stitchery, incorporated into couched or padded outlines, or developed as a textural feature. The third is to turn each yarn separately and needleweave back into the ground. This is very strong, but small opaque blocks appear which must be considered as part of the design.

Working threads should be used in short lengths wherever possible. The

Clustering the edges

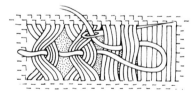

Single crossing

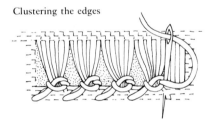

The central securing thread is followed by two trailing knotted ones

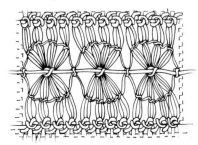

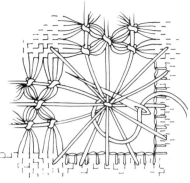

The open square, 15 spokes

friction imposed by crossing and overcasting will not destroy their lustre so quickly as that involved in needleweaving and knotting. Experience will determine the optimum length to complete a row without having to finish off an old thread and start a new one awkwardly. Starting and finishing methods must be consistent since they have a direct effect on the pattern of the stitchery. The thread can be started a little way into the work so that the first few stitches will cover it, making tiny back or whip stitches where it turns, piercing the yarn of the ground and the working thread with the securing stitches. Renewing the working thread on an open ground is achieved by running the old thread on into the linen in the direction of working, and starting the new thread well behind completed stitchery, introducing it to the continuation of the work at the point where the old thread left off. Starting and finishing may involve changing temporarily to a sharp needle.

Tension of stitchery and direction of smooth hand movements must be consistent throughout. The needle is always pulled towards the worker and towards completed stitchery.

The work is finished by taping upside down over a soft pad and spray-damping, then very lightly pressing, not ironing. Finally the hem is worked.

Free drawn thread stitchery with the machine can be achieved on most open weaves by stretching the fabric in a tambour frame and then withdrawing areas of yarn before stitchery begins.

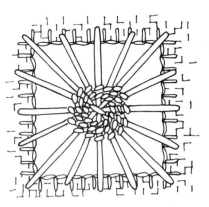

Overcast, any number of spokes. Spiralling back stitches start with a knot in the centre and finish by running through beneath

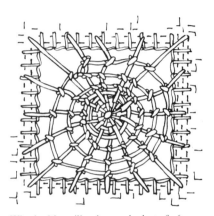

Wheel with trailing knots, the last of 16 spokes coming to the centre and beginning the woven spiral

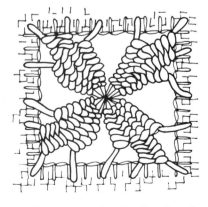

The Calado wheel: 16 spokes. Start from the top right corner and work over two, introducing the two adjacent spokes and gradually narrowing to the middle

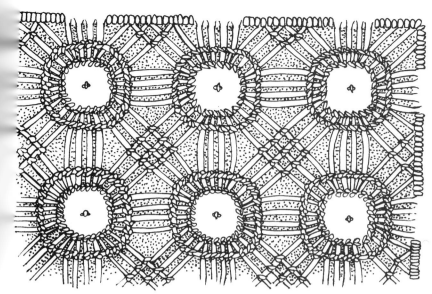

Yarns drawn in both directions and spaces reinforced with diagonal threads

Ground yarns can be bunched with close satin stitch or open zigzag. The needle tension should be considerably slacker than the spool so that the stitch loop is concealed and the satin stitch is smooth. Repetitive pattern is impractical, but there is scope for plenty of experiment with fillings, raised stitchery over cords and the use of metallic threads.

Bibliography
Butterick; D.M.C.; de Dillmont; Leach; *Needlecraft Magazine*; Priscilla 1909; Thomas 1936

Collections
UK   Museum of Costume, Bath; Gawthorpe Hall, Burnley; Nottingham Museum

DRESDEN WORK (point de Saxe, point de Dinante, Flemish work, toile de mousseline)

A fine white form of drawn embroidery which emerged during the eighteenth century as a substitute for lace. It was worked on cambric or muslin with floral motifs often outlined with shadow herringbone. Fillings were contained in the leaves and flowers, their versatility a salient feature. Dresden work occurred throughout Denmark, Germany, and Saxony, both professionally made and as a necessary accomplishment for gentlewomen. With commercial success it became variable, and by the mid-nineteenth century all fine, floral European white work with a cambric ground was known as Dresden work. It was often designed to be mounted onto net for blouses and collars, and in this style adapted readily to manufacture by machine.

Bibliography
Fangel

Collections
UK   Gawthorpe Hall, Burnley; Bankfield Museum, Halifax; Harris Museum and Art Gallery, Preston
Denmark   Industrial Arts and Crafts Museum, Copenhagen

DRESSED PRINTS (Amelia work)

A form of appliqué employing bright prints and lustrous fabrics to figures cut from stiff paper specially printed for the purpose. Fabrics were snipped and turned under the paper and applied to a ground by means of stitching or adhesive. Named after the invalid woman who popularized it, it was a pastime only for the dextrous. It probably evolved from raised figures on Chinese screens (see *stumpwork*). The Chinese examples are conceived within the traditional stylization of pictorial representation, the figures padded, with painted faces and real hair, the landscapes or interiors worked in flat stitchery and decorated

Dresden work: shadow stitched darning and herringbone with a profusion of drawn fabric patterns. Each buta is 9 cm (3½ in.) long. *c.* 1760. (*Rachel Kay Shuttleworth Collection, Gawthorpe Hall*)

with miniature ornaments. The late Victorian and Edwardian versions imitated the style, influenced by contemporary Western illustrations.

Bibliography
Smith

Collections
UK Gawthorpe Hall, Burnley; Leeds Museum

DRESSING A FRAME

See *Framing up*

DRIZZLING

See *Parfilage*

DURHAM QUILTING

See *Wadded quilting*

Dressed prints: Chinese, detail 31 × 36 cm (12 × 14 in.) of panels for a screen. Painted and printed silk supported by padded card

Dressed prints: coloured paper prints, cut out and retouched, the figures in cotton and silk, raised from the ground. Framed in an arrangement of shells. (*Rachel Kay Shuttleworth Collection, Gawthorpe Hall*)

E

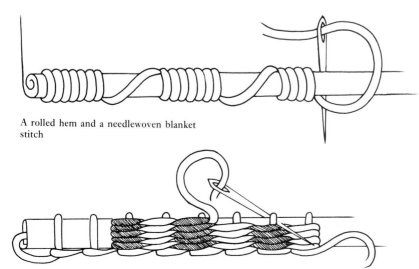

EDGINGS

On most embroideries, except those made specially for fitted costume, the treatment of the edge of the textile or ground material is integral and characteristic. In many instances the end of the weave, the extension of the border or the decoration of the hem is the main, or perhaps the only, feature

North American Indian edging. Thong needlewoven with hairs to the edge of the skin ground

A rolled hem and a needlewoven blanket stitch

Edgings: Persian scarf border, bright silks on linen, hemstitched, with bullion knots, picots, and black darning representing tiny scallops. Detail 19 × 11 cm (7½ × 4½ in.)

of embellishment. Hems may be elaborately constructed from pieces of the fabric like those quilts with sawtooth edges, or the ground may be scalloped and eyeletted to form a feature like *broderie anglaise*. The extremities of the fabric may be intricately contoured and dotted with picots as they are in laces, or rigidly overcast and bound as they are on camel trappings and ceremonial saddlery. *Casalguidi* is encrusted with separately made buttonholed appendages, and *Tenerife* work has its sol circles added by means of

needleweaving. Delicate bebilla flowers are knotted as flat shapes growing from little tussocks constructed along a hem, and robust Pre-Columbian Nazca borders of knit-stem stitch figures and animals are padded like small rag dolls.

EMBOSSING

Needlework in relief, achieved by padding with moulds, felt, packed wadding or layers of close stitchery. Although the technique occurs in many kinds of embroidery, the term is applied mainly to religious and ceremonial textiles, and particularly to military dress uniform where areas covered by metal threads are often highly raised and formal in treatment. *Stumpwork* shares many similarities.

ENGLISH QUILTING

See *Wadded quilting*

ETCHING EMBROIDERY

See *Silk pictures*

EYELET WORK

Broderie anglaise may be found referred to as eyelet embroidery since it consists predominantly of two kinds of overcast eyelets, those formed around cut shapes and those constructed around holes made by a stiletto. Both buttonholed and overcast eyelets are a common feature in many forms of white work and linen embroidery. On coarse or open weaves eyelets may be evenly spaced and

counted. In this form they appear as drawn fabric fillings or continuous borders, and in Icelandic eyeletting as an all over ground allowing gradations of colour.

There is an attachment for making eyelets by machine, producing close satin stitch circles with small stiletto holes. Drawn fabric ones can be made with the straight stitch by controlling the machine very slowly, so that the tambour frame can be moved back and forth placing the needle alternately into the stiletto hole and out to the perimeter of the eyelet all around the circumference.

Eyelet work: square from a hausa robe, white cotton with exhaust indigo stitchery in wool. 51 cm (20 in.). (*Leeds Museum*)

Eyelet work: eyelets with chain stitch, wool, ribbon and braid on an open wool ground. Red, purple and maroon waistcoat. Detail 20 × 23 cm (8 × 9 in.). Made by Margaret Smith

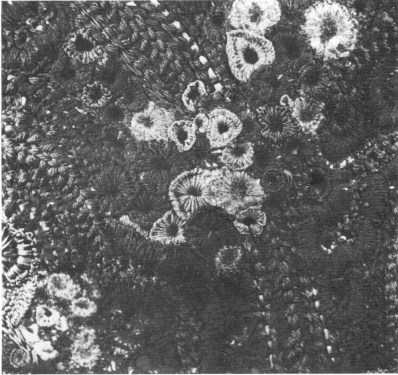

FABRIC MANIPULATION

A recent term embracing all those
traditional techniques in which the
fabric is folded, pleated, gathered,
bound, wrapped, ruched, shirred and
tucked. It includes many areas where
fabric is used as a three-dimensional
construction material, with or without
the support of padding and stiffening.
In that it has become a creative
alternative to pure stitchery it may be
categorized as needlework rather than
embroidery, but the two often appear
together. Old needlework manuals,
containing many manipulative
techniques now neglected by
dressmaking, prove useful sources.

Bibliography
Beetons; de Dillmont; Frew; Lemon;
Weldon's; Odhams

Variations on a construction common to
buttonhole edge on garments, sawtooth
edge on quilts, star patchwork, and tags

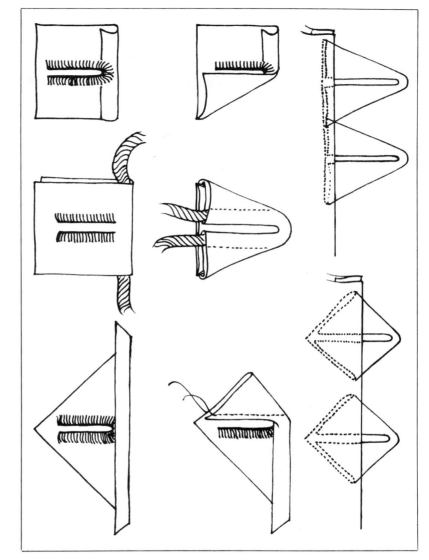

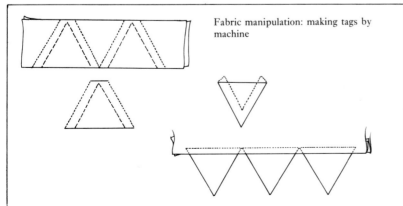

Fabric manipulation: making tags by
machine

FAÇON D'ANGLETERRE

Much of the skill of *opus anglicanum*
was lost with the Black Death around
1349. With the disappearance of
underside couching a wider stitch
vocabulary took over, stitchery was less
detailed, and it became known as façon
d'Angleterre.

FAGGOTING
See *Insertions*

FALSE EMBROIDERY

A North American Indian weaving
technique which resembles lines of

Fabric manipulation: furnishing weave on a felt ground; red, pink and orange chevrons of machine satin stitch cut into strips and hand pleated. (*Manchester Polytechnic*)

tightly worked bullion knots. As each shed brings another section of warp to the front of the weaving, selected warp yarns are bound with a few coils of moose hair. The length of hair continues at the back from one coil to another.

Bibliography
Turner, Geoffrey

FALSE QUILTING

See *Flat quilting*

FEATHERING

In embroidery and textile construction the term is an ambiguous one. It is used for both the clipping of curves and the outline stitch occasionally used in *applied work*. As a quilting term it loosely describes edges, outlines and

Fabric manipulation: pin tucking, machined folds of green felt on bright green cotton, featuring frayed cotton prints and machine satin stitch seeding. 10 × 13 cm (4 × 5 in.). Made by Amanda Rudolph, Manchester Polytechnic

grounds broken by lines of stitchery, as well as those areas occupied by feather patterns.

The more authoritative use of the term, however, is as a general one applicable to all expansive uses of long flat stitches or directional fillings on professional embroideries. As *opus plumarium* this definition has probably been used since the earliest Roman influences.

FEATHERWORK (feather appliqué, feather mosaic)

The application of feathers to textiles or skins by stitching, weaving, knotting or gluing in patterns of colour, size or texture. It occurs in many areas of the world and is not confined to tropical regions. The Victorians adapted the technique to collages, hats and fans.

Bird skins were a recognized trade commodity for China in 2205 BC. The use of feathers in textiles and ornamental accessories was once widespread amongst many cultures, both sophisticated and tribal, but their application in embroidery is restricted. A historical study is impossible because feather textiles can only survive under the most ideal conditions.

Aztec and Mayan chiefs' ceremonial capes were made of red, green and blue feathers. The Spaniards brought home fabulous feather textiles from Mexico, Yucatan, Brazil, Guatemala

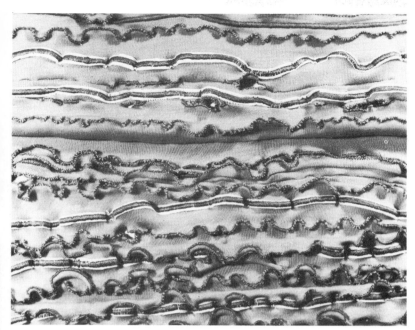

Fabric manipulation: red stretch fabric distorted by green close satin stitch zigzag over strips of bonding. 18 × 23 cm (7 × 9 in.). Made by Rosemary Newdick, Manchester Polytechnic

Featherwork: Peru, pre-1533, Chimu garment piece, yellow, red, blue and black macaw feathers stitched over a holding cord on coarse cotton. (*Whitworth Art Gallery*)

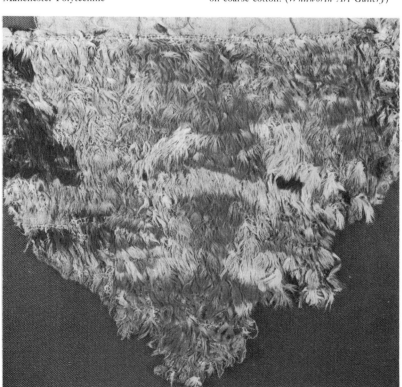

and Peru in the sixteenth century. Their name for artists in feathers was amantecas. Mexican scarlet feather fabric was particularly prized. Very soon the South Americans were producing featherwork to please their Catholic conquerors, and a number of ecclesiastical pieces are in existence. The crown given by Montezuma to Cortez still survives.

Harmsworth's *Natural History*, published in 1910, illustrates the mamo, exclusive to Hawaii, and gives it as extinct, since its feathers were used inside the great cloaks of the chieftains in the time of Captain Cook.

Featherwork is still practised by the Maoris in New Zealand.

Collections
UK British Museum, Museum of Mankind, London; Whitworth Art Gallery, Manchester
Austria Museum für Volkerkunde, Vienna
France Cluny Museum, Paris
Peru Museo Nacional de Anthropologia y Arqueologia, Lima

FELT

A non-woven or sometimes a knitted material which is traditionally all wool but not definitively so. It can be cut and applied in quite small pieces because it does not fray, and is often dyed in a wide range of flat, clear colours. Felts are made by subjecting combed wool, sometimes laid in simple coloured patterns, to friction and compression, or by shrinking and rubbing knitted yarn.

Examples of felting and of felt appliqué occur from the western territories of Russia and from northern China from almost 2000 years ago. The Russians and Mongolians practised felting and felt appliqué extensively, and it is strongly associated with Near Eastern nomadic peoples. The Turcoman of Iran make many felt bags decorated with appliqué and chain stitch, and the work extends to large covers and trappings for animals.

Indian *namdhas* have a felt ground.

Bibliography
Fairholt; Fél

FELTWORK PICTURES

Relief pictorial representations of flower pieces or bowls of fruit worked in felt or velvet with some surface stitchery. Influenced by *stumpwork* and contemporary Pontypool enamelled tin goods which were so fashionable, felt pictures belong to the end of the eighteenth-century. Descriptions of examples invariably suggest a muted range of colours, but the pictures were enclosed in box frames and glazed, and would probably be subjected to light for a long period of time. A basket worked over padding in silk or chenille contained padded fruit or moss roses and auriculas, their petals tinted and curved into relief, with highlights and shadings worked in surface stitchery.

FILET (lacis, netted work, squared netting)

A darned pattern worked on a ground of square-mesh net, making use of simple stitches often extended to form complex, meandering, maze-like patterns. Now considered a white work or monochromatic technique, filet was once multi-coloured, sometimes incorporating metal threads, rich beading and lavish appliqué. Its scale can vary from the finest net it is possible to hand-knot to that suitable for coarsely worked hangings. *Guipure d'art* is a specialized form.

There are two quite differently constructed nets, one with squares, appropriate for contrasting fillings and

Filet: eighteenth-century Persian nakshe. Red, green and orange silk on black with metal thread, 10 cm (4 in.) wide. (*Nottingham Museum*)

Filet: coarse white linen filet mat. Detail 38 × 25 cm (15 × 10 in.)

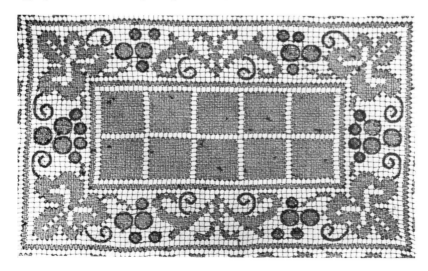

open areas, and the other with a hexagonal construction suitable for outlines enclosing fillings. The first technique is called filet and the second *net embroidery*.

Medieval *opus araneum* was probably largely unornamented, but netted silk veils, cauls and caps embroidered with silk are recorded as early as 1092. As a popular lace form filet was used throughout Europe at least from the thirteenth century. A crespin or caul to contain the hair became an important fashion item, and it is likely that cryppen work referred to the white stitchery, beading or metal thread embroidery which enhanced those nets.

German and Italian pattern books of the sixteenth century feature designs for network. The Italian Vinciolo dedicated his book of designs to Catherine de Medici. Mary Queen of Scots, her daughter-in-law, was supplied with gauges and needles for netting during her captivity on the Island of Lochleven.

The Venetians made maglia quadrata, squared net filled with darned patterns. Borders, squares and insertions of filet often alternated or combined with cutwork or lace. It was fashionable to add filet to green silk fabrics, and enrichment with metal threads was frequent. Styles, subjects and materials changed, bringing numerous variations. Renaissance examples developed from simple geometry to representations of figures and animals.

Square netting declined when both bobbin net and lace could be made by machine. However, it continued to be popular in association with cutwork, set in alternating squares. There were many magazine promotions, with netting workers offering their services to the embroiderer. Netting was exported from France to make borders, insertions and mats throughout the nineteenth century. A few kinds remained popular in their own localities, like the diamond net pinnspets in northern Sweden. Edwardian crochet patterns were copied from earlier filet lace.

There is a tendency to regard the filet tradition as being concerned entirely with symmetrical pattern, scrollwork and formal borders, but

Filet: eighteenth-century Persian work known as shabkeh duzee, 13 cm (5 in.) wide. (*Nottingham Museum*)

several early pieces survive which are pictorial narratives. Filet lace, the technique of stitching on the net, traditionally employs very few stitches, since the limitations imposed by the ground can be fully explored to give great textural and pattern variety. The journey of the working thread must complete all stitched areas logically without encroaching on clear ones. The doubling of the thread occurring at intersections must be incorporated as a definitive detail of the design, since it produces opaque lines. The quality of any outlining is determined by the direction it follows on the work. Straight lines worked with the same thread and stitch may be thick or thin, tessellated or wavy. The use of squared paper may have advantages for the beginner, but, once the potential of the technique is grasped, designing on anything other than the most modest scale will have much more vitality without it.

A few machine-made, square-mesh nets are available commercially but most are woven or twisted rather than knotted. Workers are immediately at a disadvantage, since this weave is usually insufficiently stable. Some theatrical nets stiff with dressing offer possibilities, and these are attractively coloured. Net containers and mesh bags of all kinds are well worth investigating as potential ground fabrics. All must be framed before stitchery begins. Hand made netting using a needle or shuttle and a mesh or gauge is fully described by both Knight and Melen.

The needle for stitching must be blunt-ended with a good, wide eye.

Working threads are slightly twisted and soft rather than hard and resilient.

The net ground is stiffened before it is worked, and stitching is done on a frame. The net should be soaked in a strong gelatine solution. Small pieces can be immersed before they are stretched, and large pieces may be painted with the gelatine solution after they are put in a frame. Small pieces to be worked in the hand must be prepared by soaking and draining and then pinning to a previously measured and marked board to drip and stiffen. Spray starch may be substituted but only where the working process is short.

Ideally, filet should be worked in a square, metal frame made from a firm, unyielding wire which will not bend to the stretching of the ground. Small

Weaver's knot

wooden frames are efficient substitutes. In either case the frame should be sparsely padded and then bound with diagonally-wound cotton tape. Time spent on preparing an evenly bound frame will be repaid by later efficiency, and the frame can be re-used indefinitely. Another method, once common in use for all reseau and many needlemade laces, was that of totally covering the wire frame with a wrapping of soft cotton yarn, and then folding over it a firm ribbon, overcasting the edges of the ribbon together on the inside of the frame. The net must be laced to previously measured and marked points on the frame binding. It should be tied firmly to each inside corner, allowing a short distance between frame and net. The tying thread should be stitched to the binding. The sides of the net can then be sewn to the frame, the needle

Filet: sixteenth-century Italian filet with diagonal network, 5 cm (2 in.) wide. (*Nottingham Museum*)

Filet: eighteenth-century Persian. Blue and white on black, 10 cm (4 in.) wide. (*Nottingham Museum*)

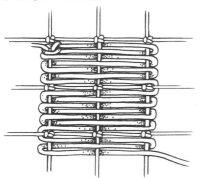

Reprise, the basic darning stitch

adjacent square when all four corners and sides bear a loop. It can be extended and elaborated over a set of holes, or worked again over the same journey for density.

Definitions of pattern within areas of toile or reprise are often achieved by the repetition of single-square open interstices surrounded by an interlaced working thread. These apparently complex movements become methodical with a little experience and the establishment of rhythm and regular tension.

Outlines, usually prominently worked with a thick thread, are made in two journeys with a form of couching. The needle twists around the junctions of the mesh clockwise, returning over itself with anti-clockwise movements. Edging stitches may be adapted to fill the extremities of the pattern and pass from one area to another with cohesion. Further stitches such as loop (point d'esprit), stars, circles and woven wheels are permissible, but belong rather to *guipure d'art* and to *lace*.

Careful treatment of the finished work will restore its crisp quality. The net should be taken from the frame and laid on a cloth pad. Using a layer of thin white cotton over the wrong

the knot worked in. With experience the knot can be appropriately concealed on the wrong side.

Reprise stitch (punto a rammendo), the ordinary darning stitch which passes the thread over and under the mesh either vertically or horizontally, is often worked in a considerably coarser thread than that of the mesh. Stitched close, it can make an almost opaque texture.

Toile or linen stitch (punto a tela), also known as cloth stitch, fills an interstice by looping a corner and then a side alternately, moving on to the

Toile extended

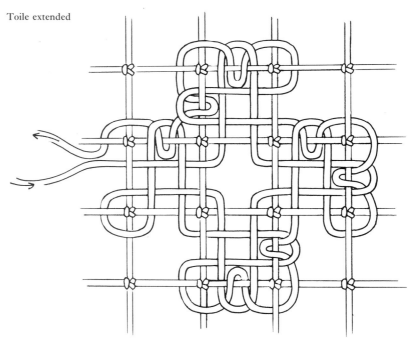

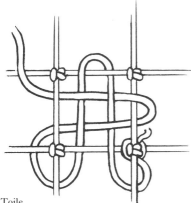

Toile

taking both yarns at the edge of the net and pulling it parallel and fairly taut.

Fastening on and off is achieved with a lacemaker's knot. Sufficient thread must remain to pull the knot tight before the ends are cut close and

side of the work it should be lightly sprayed with water and pressed gently with a warm iron.

Bibliography

Bain; Carita; de Dillmont; Goubard; Hald; Knight; Melen 1977; Vinciolo; Waller; *Weldon's*

Collections

UK   Royal Scottish Museum, Edinburgh; Bankfield Museum, Halifax; Victoria and Albert Museum, London; Nottingham Museum
USA   Metropolitan Museum of Art, New York

FILLINGS

All those repetitive patterns and areas of close stitchery limited by outlines or defined by voiding are called fillings in embroidery. They may form open, lacy textures or dense, heavy colour.
Pattern may be loose and irregular or tightly measured and counted.

FISHERTON-DE-LA-MERE

In the 1890s Josephine Newall founded a group working with the disabled which continued for some 30 years. Based on an appreciation of Italian seventeenth and eighteenth-century work, Fisherton-de-la-Mere embroideries were usually natural or cream linen worked in pulled or drawn thread to a high technical standard. There was a postal service to workers and the embroideries were widely exhibited. See p. 85.

Bibliography

Howard 1981

Fillings: Afghan, twentieth-century. Heavily gathered bright satin stitch in brilliant reds and oranges with white beads. (*Leeds Museum*)

Fillings: The Dinner Party. Elizabeth R place setting, 46 cm (18 in.) wide, part of a 49′ triangular table. (© *Judy Chicago 1982. Photograph: Michael Alexander*)

Fillings: detail of centre roundel 6 cm (2½ in.). (*Photograph: Michael Alexander*)

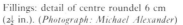

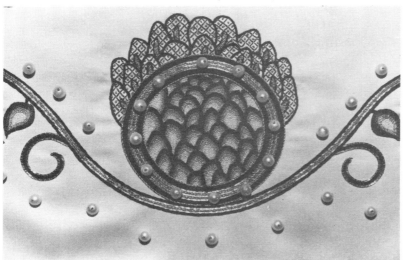

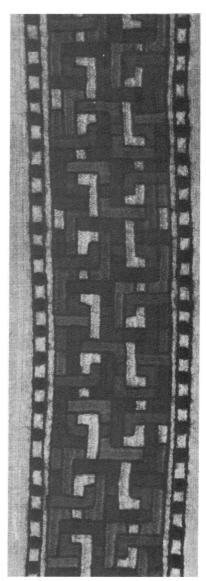

Fillings: Turkish, twentieth-century, wool in strong colours and black outlines. Roumanian stitch on unbleached linen. Width of border 10 cm (4 in.)

FISH SCALE EMBROIDERY

A popular Victorian diversion utilising the decorative versatility of the scales of coarse fish to produce floral sprays or bird forms on silk, satin or velvet. The scales were arranged in curves or rounds, selected according to size and type, to form flower heads or overlapping areas of feathers, in conjunction with silk surface stitchery or chenille. They were particularly appropriate for representing maidenhair fern. Designs were often surprisingly ordered and even classical. The technique was considered suitable for a number of household articles which were essentially concerned with adornment and would not normally be washed. It probably arose from the surge of interest in imported ethnic artifacts and the novelty of employing durable animal remains. Scraps cut from shell were, and still are, used in the same way. A number of modern forms of sequins and sew-on celluloid or pressed acetate shapes are reminiscent of fish scales in texture and colour. See p. 86.

Bibliography
Caulfeild and Saward

Collections
UK Gawthorpe Hall, Burnley

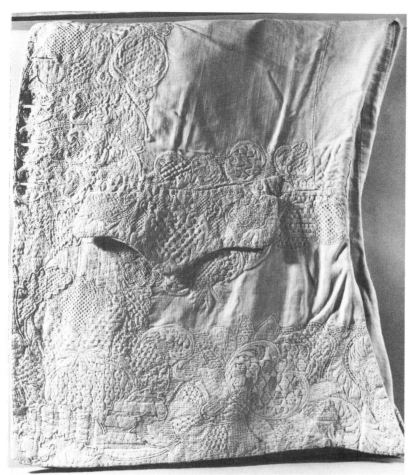

Fillings: English, 1720–40. White linen waistcoat, drawn fabric, drawn thread, darning, satin stitch and knotted fillings. (*Nottingham Museum. Middleton Collection*)

FISHSKIN APPLIQUÉ

An accomplished and sophisticated technique practised until recently by the Aleuts and other Eskimo groups. Translucent strips of dried seal intestine are, in fact, the most common material, substituted away from coastal areas by bear and deer intestine. The material is worked with precision and care into panels and decorative bindings, together with beads, fringes and fur. Most of the strips are decorated with small braided and couched chevrons and triangles in hair. (See *Quillwork and hairwork*, and *North American Indian beadwork*.)

Bibliography
Gunther; Hawthorn; Turner 1955

Collections
UK British Museum, London; Horniman Museum, London; Pitt Rivers Museum, Oxford
USA Museum of the American Indian, New York
Canada Hudson Bay Company Museum, Winnipeg

Fisherton de la Mere: Linen on close linen, drawn fabric using Elizabethan stitchery. Motif 33 cm (13 in.) long

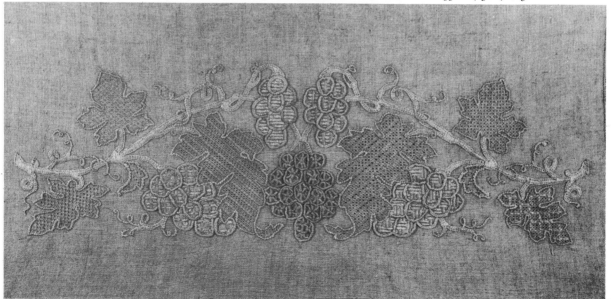

warmth, and beautiful fabrics needed lining for durability, but with the advent of more comfortable domestic surroundings heavy petticoats became an encumbrance. Although interlinings were gradually dispensed with, backings kept costume fabrics crisp and luxurious, and the embroidery styles were retained. Stitchery was still evenly distributed over the whole ground, and silk stuffs had more substance with chained or herringboned scroll work. Late seventeenth-century and early eighteenth-century flat quilting was almost always saffron yellow on yellow or white linen and frequently worked in chain stitch.

Designing for flat quilting must follow the historical convention, otherwise it becomes just surface stitchery. Ground fabric may be fine opaque linen quite closely woven, or substantial plain silk, yellow, natural or white in colour. The working thread should be yellow silk. Prick and pounce transfer methods are best, worked over with poster paint and a fine brush. Alternatively a tacking line made through a tissue tracing may be sufficient for less detailed work.

Stitching should be under sufficient tension to raise the ground very slightly.

Fishscale embroidery: velvet bag, nineteenth-century, worked in fishscales, chenille and purl. Each scale 6 mm ($\frac{1}{4}$ in.). (*Rachel Kay Shuttleworth Collection, Gawthorpe Hall*)

FLAT QUILTING

This is the only quilting method which does not incorporate some form of padding. It may have only one layer of ground but more usually has two, the slightly raised appearance being achieved by double lines of chain or back stitch enclosures formed under tension, or herringbone stitch worked across the back.

Wadded quilting was essential for

Flat quilting: English 1800–50. Detail of a pillow sham. Yellow silk chain and back stitches on two layers of white linen. (*Embroiderers' Guild*)

FLORENTINE (Bargello, flame stitch, Hungarian point, zickzack stitch)

Perhaps the best known of all embroidery forms. Florentine consists of counted stitchery on an even ground, the stitches arranged in a continuous solid pattern of regular divisions containing repeated sequences of colour. Theoretically, it should be possible to work Florentine patterns in most canvas stitches, but the simpler ones such as tent and cross stitch are preferable, and the accepted 4/2 Florentine is best of all. It is usual to employ one stitch exclusively, emphasis being on the juxtaposition of colour rather than on textural interest.

The tales connected with its origins are romantic ones. Hungary was invaded by the Magyars under Arpad in 895, and they brought with them the Eastern Steppe designs. After the Mongolian withdrawal in the thirteenth century Hungary became populated by the Siebenbuergen peoples, renowned for their needlework.

Many forms of embroidery have been exported and imported over the centuries by royal marriage, by princesses and their entourages and trousseaux, by favours encouraged and sought in their countries of origin and their marital homes. In 1383 King Vladislav V of Poland married Princess Jadwiga of Hungary. She was just 13, very fond of embroidery, and later an accomplished needlewoman. He was a member of the Jagiello family, and it seems likely that her origins and his family name together gave rise to both terms, Hungarian point and Bargello.

Corvinus I spent much of his time in Renaissance Florence, married an Italian, and started a cultural centre in Ofen, later to be called Budapest. Both there and in other parts of Hungary he established Italian artists, encouraging them to combine Hungarian tradition with Italian technique. Florence's cultural importance during the fifteenth century under the Medici involved the flowering of the textile arts. The burgeoning of pattern and design, the developing sophistication of spinning, dyeing, weaving and embroidery, and the change of emphasis from the purely ecclesiastical to mainly secular brought brilliance and vitality. Beautiful, shimmering silks could be stitched or woven into fabulous auroras of glowing colour, and it was here that Florentine work was firmly established.

The Museo Nazionale in Florence, which houses a set of seven seventeenth-century Florentine work chairs, was once the Bargello prison (giving rise to more conjecture on the name), and the story has it that this form of needlework was introduced to the prisoners there in the fourteenth century as a form of therapy. In view of the usual prison conditions at that time this seems unlikely, although it must be remembered that political prisoners may have experienced conditions more conducive to needlework. The chairs are described by the Museo as having backs and seats worked in punto unghero silk.

Florentine work has been used in Britain since the sixteenth century. Several writers insist that colours then were soft and muted, but most of the stitchery was done on pillows and furnishings and so would be constantly exposed to light. An inventory of 1600 describes the colours as being 'Carnacon pinks, Marigolde-colour, Purples, Blews, Straw-colour, Murrey, Ladie-blush, poundecythrone-colour.'

A recent upsurge of interest in Florentine embroidery has led to many pattern forms and colour sequences being offered in pictorial and diagrammatic form, and further investigations by interested textile artists. Although radiating Bargello is not new, there are several publications exploring the possibilities of Four-way or Kaleidoscope Bargello as a novelty.

Designs can be derivative but should normally be regarded as geometric. There are three patterns which form the basis of all developments. The Puzta or Feathered Carnation probably came through Byzantium, influenced by the Magyars and Finnish counterchange designs. Alternating diamond ogees represent ragged carnations, the tones of colour ranging from light at the apex to dark at the edges of the petals, or vice versa. The V motif, variously described in context as Blitz Troellakan, the Burning Mountain pattern, the Lightning motif and Thunder and Lightning stitch, has horizontal lines of exaggerated

Florentine: pale greens and greys, late nineteenth-century. A worked corner 15 cm (6 in.) square. (*Rachel Kay Shuttleworth Collection, Gawthorpe Hall*)

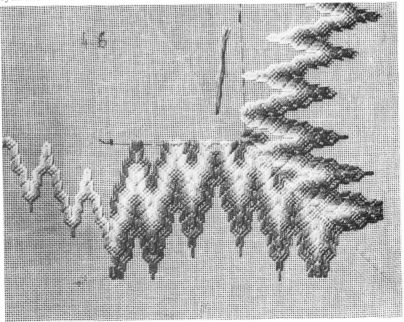

peaks and valleys, often complex in outline, with the light colours usually at the top. The Wave pattern is constructed like the V motif but it is curved, sometimes with complex outlines, and with elaborately graded colours.

It is often simplest to plan the design by experiment on a spare piece of canvas, working out the scale in relationship to the whole piece. Unless the pattern is to have variable edges, in which case guide lines must be drawn on the canvas with waterproof ink, it is unnecessary to transfer the design in any way. The pattern is achieved by counting.

Modern Florentine is almost always stitched on single-mesh canvas or soft jute, the scale being determined entirely by the matching of yarn in terms of complete coverage. By using more or less strands of the fine wools retailed in wide colour ranges, canvas in the 10–18 yarns per 2.5 cm (1 in.) range is suitable. Experiments with working threads, length of stitch and stitch tension are advisable. The Florentines and the Elizabethans used silk, the Scots later used tartan wools, and mercerised cottons were favourites when they were first marketed in good colour ranges. Needles should be of the tapestry type. Florentine need not be worked in a frame since it does not warp easily, but one may be preferable for larger pieces. On soft grounds the edge must be either turned or oversewn. On hard canvas the yarns protruding at the edges interfere with working and damage threads;

a tape binding tacked around them is well worth while.

Stitchery should begin at the point furthest away from the worker. However, it is sometimes more comfortable to turn the work so that the stitching line is always towards the hands, in which case starting at the centre is better. Always bring the needle up through unworked ground and return it through the hole already occupied by the working thread of the previous row.

Four-way, Radial and Kaleidoscope Bargello is an adaptation which makes use of both vertical and horizontal stitches to make patterns which radiate from a central point and repeat on all four sides by means of mirror images.

Canvas mesh is never square. Non-woven substitutes should be, but must be checked. Designing for Four-way starts by establishing the centre of the pattern on the canvas by folding, and then counting out both horizontally and vertically from that point to establish the extremities of the intended shape. Counting should be done with a regular tacked line. Measurement of the resulting rectangle will show that it is slightly longer in one direction than in the other. It may be more satisfactory to accept this discrepancy in Kaleidoscope Bargello than to attempt to adjust the pattern to fit an exact measured square. Mark the rectangle with a tacked line or with a waterproof ink and cut at least 5 cm (2 in.) outside it to allow for turnings.

Using the regular, counted basting line once more, the diagonals must be indicated. The canvas must be flattened on a table where it can be placed at horizontal eye level. By moving the canvas very slightly, diagonals created by the tabby weave will become clear and a ruler can be placed alongside the appropriate one. This line should be ruled with a hard pencil. It will not meet the corners exactly but must bisect the other lines at the centre. Squaring-up lines corresponding to both design and working canvas are essential, and should be used appropriately to the

Florentine: English, dated 1747. Pocket book of bright silks on linen bound with green ribbon. (*Embroiderers' Guild*)

scale and size of the work.

In order to display the pattern at its best it may be a good idea in Four-way either to introduce small areas of tent stitch or to vary the half-step of the Florentine. The total pattern shapes will dictate variations in the steps at the meeting corners. Many proportional variations of the simplest gradations of colour can be achieved by changing the number of stitches in each horizontal block.

Florentine stitch

Florentine may need *blocking* but pressing is unadvisable and unnecessary.

Bibliography
Barnes and Blake; Christensen and Ashner; Coats; Fischer and Lasker; *Golden Hands*; Hall and Riley; Kaestner 1973, 1974; Silverstein

Collections
UK   Gawthorpe Hall, Burnley;
Italy   Museo Nazionale, Florence

FLOWERIN'

All the white work and laces produced commercially throughout the eighteenth and nineteenth centuries in Scotland and Ireland were known collectively as the Flowerin', although the term is more narrowly applied to *Ayrshire* work alone.

Bibliography
Swain 1955

FLOWERS

Three-dimensional flowers have been made from fabric and thread to decorate costume, domestic artifacts and animal trappings wherever woven textiles occur. They are frequently used in conjunction with embroidery, and *bebilla* and *stumpwork* ones are stitchery constructions. The Victorians made them from *ribbon work*, *aerophane* and a variety of threads and materials.

Despite the realism achieved with plastics the traditions of flower making persist in many countries and the techniques are little changed.

Bibliography
Caulfeild and Seward; *McCalls'*

FLUTED EMBROIDERY
(orné wool work)

An extraordinary nineteenth-century technique whereby pictorial subject matter was represented on canvas by dyeing or printing the working thread in accurately measured lengths of colour which occupied the necessary distance on the ground. Wools, cord, canvas and accompanying paper picture serving as a guide were retailed in kit form. The wool was called orné, although this term was used for other variably dyed yarns. It was wound onto balls in successive lengths each of which formed a complete horizontal row of stitchery across the picture. The cord was laid between stitches and ground, forming a trammed, raised line. Railway canvas, marked with red threads at regular intervals to assist with proper distribution of tension, determined the accuracy of the design.

FOUR-WAY BARGELLO

See *Florentine*

FRAMES

The assumption that professional embroidery is worked in a frame and that amateur work is done in the hand is misleading. Appliqué needs a stretched ground, and time-consuming metal thread work, particularly if it is to meet high standards, must be framed. Those forms of stitchery close to needlemade laces are worked on a stiff backing rather than a frame. The minutely accurate eighteenth- and nineteenth-century white work techniques were done over the hand, each portion stretched between the fingers. All tambouring needs a frame and so does most free machine embroidery. Filet is worked on its own special wire support.

Small round frames vary from those tiny ones which are a sewing machine accessory to ones 30 cm (12 in.) or more in diameter. They are called tambour, hoop, hand hoop or ring frames and may be made in wood, plastic or aluminium. Modern ones are all adjustable, but older ones either had a simple sprung split to the outside ring or could be used only on medium-weight weaves. It is customary to bind the inside ring with cotton tape, or, in the case of a metal one, the outside round wire. Table clamps are available for round frames, and some may be screwed to a table stand or a floor stand. The fanny frame is a version of the tambour frame. It is attached to a stand and a flat base held down by the worker's own weight between body and seat. Oval rings are still made. They are considered suitable for fine, thin quilting.

Square or tent frames are of four kinds and vary from about 30 cm (12 in.) to 91 cm (36 in.) wide. All have two opposing bars with tapes to which the ground or backing may be stitched. The tapestry frame has round stretchers with screw threads and adjustable blocks or stops. The hand frame has flat stretchers and cotter pins with wing nuts. The slate frame, sometimes called leader or star, has flat stretchers with variable positions for its pins and nuts. The stretcher frame has flat stretchers but round bars, with the cotter pins to the ends of the round bars. All may be attached to table or floor stands.

Every embroiderer should possess a tambour frame, but other kinds are not essential. Simply made rectangular stretchers or even old picture frames may be used. The wood must be clean and smooth, and sometimes binding with cotton tape is helpful. Ambitious pieces of embroidery, and particularly those where several workers will be employed together on the same ground, may need purpose-built frames. Quilts may be worked on peg rug frames, but *quiltmaking* in any quantity requires a special working frame with ratchets.

FRAMING UP

Many kinds of embroidery need the support of a working frame and for some it is essential that the fabric should be quite taut. Depending on the size and scope of the work all types of *frames* have their uses. Specialized framing methods like those for *quiltmaking* and *Limerick lace* are discussed under their entries.

It is helpful to measure and mark the centre of each webbing on the bars. Only the backing is framed, the ground being stitched

Straight grain in a round hoop

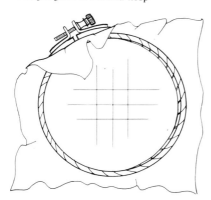

to this afterwards. The backing is usually linen, close or open, coarse or fine, according to the work. It must be washed and shrunk before use. All backing and ground material must be cut with the selvedge vertical. To mark the straight grain vertically and horizontally make a running stitch cross on that portion of the backing which will be framed first.

With the frame unassembled, cut a piece of backing exactly on the straight grain, just 10 cm ($\frac{3}{8}$ in.) larger than the total size of the design. (Often the area to be embroidered is much larger than can be accommodated in a frame. In this case three sides of the backing material are stitched to the webbing in the usual way. For the fourth, place the right side of the backing to the right side of the webbing, pinning and overcasting on the wrong side. The ground is then stitched to the backing on three sides as before, but the fourth is secured with upright basting. Excess ground and backing must be carefully rolled between wadding or old blanket, held in place with loose tacking stitches, and covered against friction and marking.) Fold a length of string into each side and knot the ends. Stitch this into the fold with a strong thread through both layers of backing. Fold the top and bottom of the backing and match the centre of it with the centre of the webbing on the bars. Working from the middle of each edge, butt the backing fold carefully on to the webbing, using

the pins vertically and taking care over the straight grain. Starting from the middle of each edge, oversew or double stitch linen to webbing with a strong thread, strengthening each end.

Assemble the frame, rolling extra backing onto the bars and inserting the pegs on the stretchers. The linen will be straight but not taut. Using a packing needle pull a length of string from the ball without cutting it, and thread quite loosely alternately through the sides of the backing (over the string edge previously sewn in) and over the stretcher of the frame, right across each one. Cut the ground material on the straight grain leaving at least 3 cm (1$\frac{1}{4}$ in.) all round the design, and place this on the backing. Match the centres and pin. Using a sewing thread of similar colour to the ground, start with a knot at the middle of one edge and oversew ground to backing, beginning in the

Stitching the string into the edge of the backing

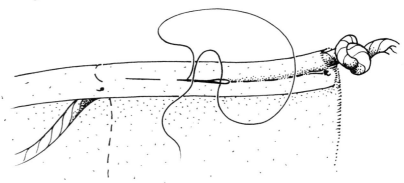

Stitching backing to tapes

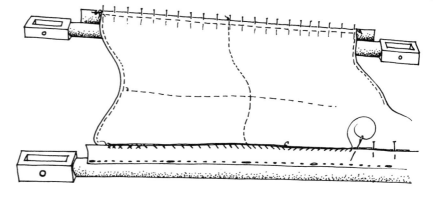

middle of each side each time. The stitches should be less than 1 cm ($\frac{3}{8}$ in.) apart and vary in length, spreading the tension over a wider margin, and should extend across the backing for firmness. Strings on the stretchers and pegs holding the bars can now both be adjusted until the backing is quite straight and taut. Cut the string generously from the ball and secure each end with a temporary knot.

When working on a frame, old soft cloths should be tacked around the sides of the work for protection, and that part of the ground fabric which is immediately beneath the hand and arm of the worker should be especially protected. Whenever the work is left it should be covered.

Working with one hand on top and the other underneath soon becomes easiest, with thimbles used appropriately.

During an extensive piece of work it is likely that several embroiderers will be seated around

The corner of a completed square frame mounting

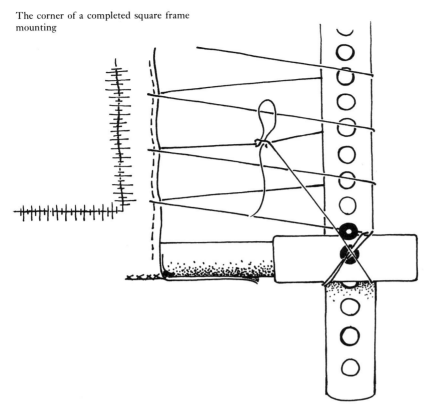

fabric in any direction. Experiments without the frame have been made, but it is usual to work with the ground stretched in a tambour frame. Varieties of line can be achieved by varying speed and thread tensions, and by using the zigzag stitch.

Free stitching probably began in the 1870s. It was developed as a mending and finishing process on machine-made laces and multiple embroidery, and at the turn of the century it was used to reproduce landscape paintings. The creative development of single-head machine embroidery was not possible until there was domestic electricity supply, and a break with the limitations of hand embroidery reproduction.

Although the straight-stitch machine had been used to make a wide satin stitch for many years previously, the *Irish machine* came into industrial use in the early 1900s. It was not until the 1960s that the swing needle domestic machine made its popular debut. The *Cornely* chain stitch machine has just one thread and can be used for beading, cording and braiding. It is rarely used domestically, but children's toy sewing machines employ the same principle.

By the twenties the whole area of possibilities was being explored by Dorothy Benson as promotional material for Singers. Rebecca

the frame at the same time. In any case, whether the work is large or small, it is traditional and expedient to avoid turning the frame over, and so the worker must learn to begin and finish each working thread from the right side. With a single knot to stop the end of the thread pulling through, begin from underneath and make one small stitch overlap another in a position where it will eventually be covered with stitchery. The knots on the back may be trimmed or sewn in collectively when the embroidery is completed. Fastening off is a reversal of the process, but the end is brought to the right side and trimmed away.

Bibliography
Dawson 1968; Dean 1958

FREE MACHINE EMBROIDERY

With the presser foot removed and the feed dog lowered, the sewing machine stitch can be run freely over a ground

Free machine embroidery: vibrant greens and blues, tiny patches of applied prints on the domestic machine. 10 × 13 cm (4 × 5 in.). Printed and stitched by Diane Gomrey, Manchester Polytechnic

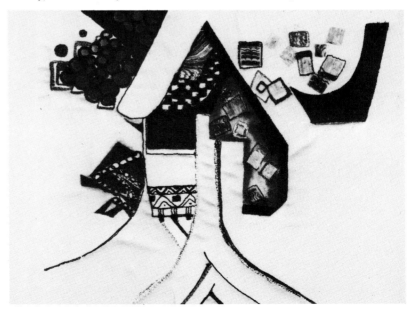

Free machine embroidery: mechanically embroidered lace flowers applied beneath chiffon, blocks of satin stitch, hand-stitched beads and french knots. Detail 8 × 5 cm (3 × 2 in.)

Crompton used the machine as a drawing medium in conjunction with Dorothy Benson's detailed decoration. Machine embroidery was included in the national examination syllabus for the first time in 1957 and has since then been gradually accepted as an additional technique of construction and surface enrichment, bringing a strong new influence into textile decoration.

The machine embroiderer moves the surface to be decorated appropriately to the fixed position of the needle. The machine should be regarded as a free drawing medium with a continuous line. An electrically driven machine is essential. It should have a smooth, unhurried start and be controllable at very slow speeds. There are many decorative possibilities with an ordinary straight-stitch machine. The addition of a zigzag stitch is a distinct advantage, but fully automatic patterns are unnecessary.

The choice of a method of design transfer depends on the nature of the whole embroidery. It is a mistake to attempt to draw all the lines in advance. The machine must be allowed its role as an independent medium and too much planning denies its essential characteristics.

The ideal ground is a fairly open, fine one, but almost any woven or non-woven material offers interesting possibilities. Only very close weaves are impractical. Specially manufactured machine embroidery threads are finer and more pliable than sewing threads. Thicker yarns can be used in the spool for cable stitch, and there is a metallic yarn which can be used in the needle. It is well worth hunting for any fine machine threads and experimenting with fabrics, stitches and tensions. Needle size is governed by both fabric and thread, but delicate stitchery will require a fine needle.

Raise the presser foot lever and remove the presser foot. Lower the feed dog or cover it with a plate. Stretch the ground material evenly and tightly in a tambour frame with the grain quite straight. This is made easier by placing both frame and fabric on an uncluttered, flat surface. Raise the needle to its highest point and carefully slip the stretched fabric beneath it. Lower the presser foot lever to engage top tension and take one stitch through the fabric with the hand wheel to bring up the spool thread. Holding the ends of both threads between fingers and frame, and controlling the frame lightly with thumb and second finger on either side, commence stitching. Once the feel of moving the surface under the needle has been experienced another start will produce more controlled results.

Machine embroidery has only four stitches. The ordinary sewing stitch which causes both threads to interlock within the thickness of the fabric is called darning stitch. For whip stitch the lower tension must be loosened so that the spool thread is pulled up onto the surface of the fabric. This is capable of considerable variation by reducing or increasing the tension contrast and varying the speed of the machine and the distance between the stitches. In an exaggerated form long loops may be pulled in circular movements, in which case whip stitch becomes feather stitch. Some thicker threads can only be accommodated in the spool, and so the tensions must be reversed and the stitchery done upside down with the right side of the ground in contact with the throat plate. This is called cable stitch. The needle thread is slackened and the heavy spool thread is couched by loops from the needle.

Zigzag stitchery may be wide or narrow, close or spaced. Usually the needle tension is slacker than the spool one, giving a smoothly rounded stitch on top, but by putting another colour in the spool and varying the tension dual colour lines result.

The restrictions of the tambour frame may be overcome in several ways. When the embroidery is larger than the frame the work cannot be seen as a whole whilst stitchery is in

Free machine embroidery

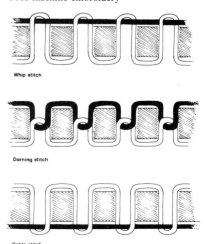

Whip stitch

Darning stitch

Cable stitch

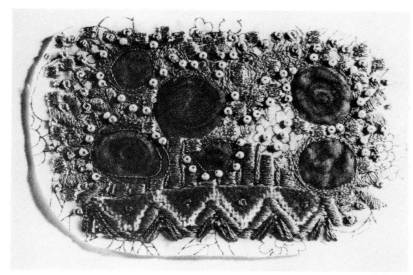

Free machine embroidery: fine cottons, silk and muslin applied with darning and zigzag, hand stitchery and beading. Green, white and silver. 8 × 10 cm (3 × 4 in.)

progress, so sometimes the work must be lifted away and spread out for re-appraisal. The frame can be moved about the fabric without removing the whole piece from the machine and without constant re-adjustment of the outer ring. Expansive areas of free stitchery can be done without the frame, using the presser foot with or without the feed dog. More control is possible using the darning foot alone, a method particularly suitable for quilting fine fabrics. All the fabrics are tacked together loosely but at frequent intervals before stitchery begins. Control is not precise and the approach should be towards flow and continuity.

Bibliography

Benson 1946, 1952; Gray 1973; Risley 1973; Swift

FRINGES AND KNOTS

The logical decoration of any textile edge, especially where fraying warp threads occur. The simplest is made by unravelling a straight edge, leaving the woven part natural where it has sufficient stability, or stitching it where

Fringes: finest cream silk scarf, satin stitch floss in bright pink, white and green. Added looped and knotted fringe 20 cm (8 in.) long

progressive fraying is likely. Grouping with introduced threads or knotting and tasselling the yarn itself produce infinite variation. Wrapping, binding and beading techniques provide many possibilities for further enrichment. Separately made tassels, leather or metal objects contribute weight and ornamentation.

Bibliography

Ashley; Bain; Graumont and Hensel; Harvey

FROGGINGS AND BRANDENBURGS

The braided ornament surrounding garment fastenings where a loop slips over a button or toggle. Normally associated with military uniform and

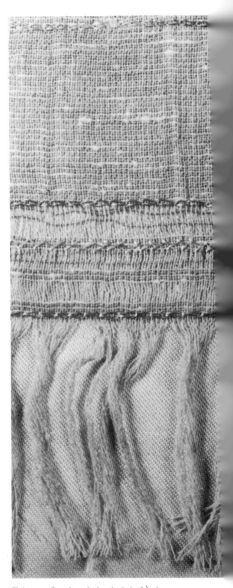

Fringes: fine hand-dyed slub fabric, bunched with stitchery and frayed. Made by Anne Stubbs

Fringes: hand-spun woven hanging with tassels of wrapped natural fleece. Length 61 cm (24 in.)

metal thread work, froggings do occur elsewhere, ranging from the utilitarian and conventional fastenings on duffle coats to complex interlaced strapwork extending over wide areas of jackets and coats. The two braids most commonly used are the flat, nine-plait military braid and soutache (Russia) braid, which consists of plaiting over two parallel round cords. The term brandenburgs derives from the association with Prussian army uniform.

Soutache is attached with small invisible running stitches starting at a place where the join will be least noticeable. It should be carried over design lines from start to finish without a break. When intersections are reached, a gap is left in the running stitches on the first journey, and on returning to this point the braid is threaded through the gap.

Bibliography
Bain; Skaney; Walker

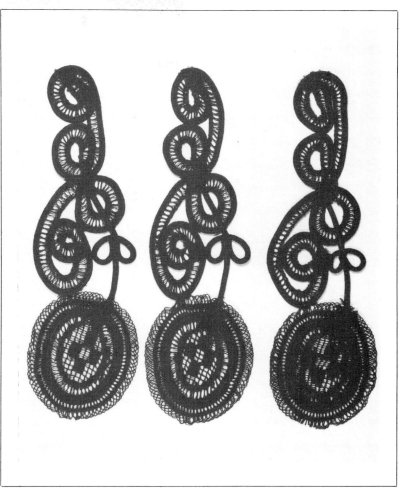

Froggings: Victorian black silk, separately
made. 13 cm (5 in.) long

GOLD WORK

See *Metal thread work*

GREEK LACE

See *Ruskin work*

GRISAILLE BEADWORK

A particular form of nineteenth-century *Berlin woolwork*, the subject of the design worked in monochrome beads and the ground worked in wool or silk. Beads were clear or opaque or sometimes metal. Designs were published specifically for grisaille to be made up into firescreens and tea cosies. The beading was heavy and produced uneven weight on the ground, but the classic sculptural effect was sought after.

GROS POINT

Properly, highly raised modelled lace with bars, but the term has come to be used for most coarse tent stitch or cross stitch canvas work, especially that of a pictorial kind. The term *petit point* probably once distinguished all delicate white work from heavier stitchery, gros point. Thus, anything other than the finest silk tent stitch also became gros point.

GROUND

The main area of material which is either directly stitched or bears previously stitched appliqué. Usually woven fabric, it can be bark, felt, leather or paper.

In design terminology it is the whole field unoccupied by the main component features. *Voiding* leaves the subject or outline in reserve whilst the background is decorated with stitchery.

GUIPURE

An interchangeable term, the only common feature being that it usually describes open edgings or accessories. It may refer to open, raised lace, to heavy, wired, metal lace, to net and filet net work, to rouleau edges bound with metal thread, and to continuous lace fabric.

Bibliography
Fairholt; Marshall

GUIPURE D'ART

A form of *filet* belonging to the nineteenth and early twentieth century, divergent because some of the stitchery was not strictly interwoven with the square mesh but built up on top of it like surface embroidery on more closely woven material. Much of the stitchery of necessity still travelled parallel to the mesh, so the typical curvilinear floral patterns and scrolling of large-scale filet gave way to geometric arrangements in the coarser guipure. Lace stitches such as point d'esprit, point de feston and point de Bruxelles featured with numerous star forms and wheels. Sometimes the mesh was hand-knotted, but more

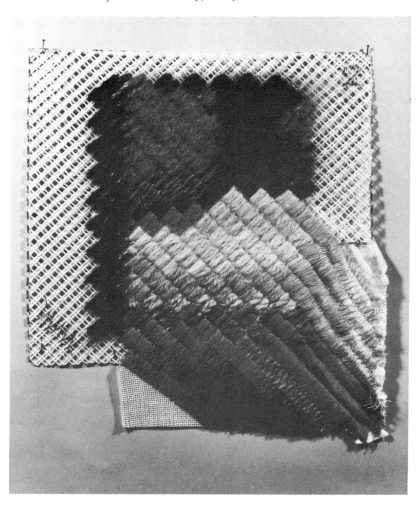

Gros point: soft mohair hand stitchery to hard Irish machine diagonals. Small canvas superimposed on coarse penelope, greys, beiges and greens, 13×15 cm (5×6 in.). Made by April Moseley, Manchester Polytechnic

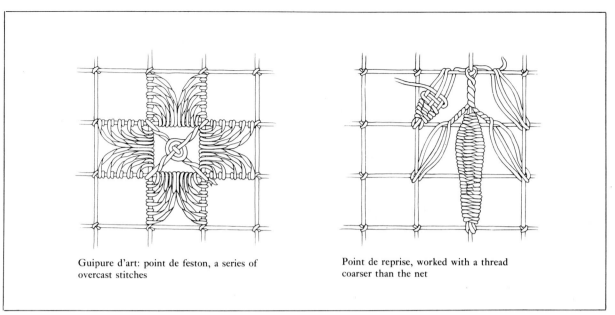

Guipure d'art: point de feston, a series of overcast stitches

Point de reprise, worked with a thread coarser than the net

often it was produced commercially. Guipure d'art appeared mainly on household furnishings as inserted bands or pieced squares. Seams between woven fabric and knotted mesh were a constant technical problem.

Bibliography
Goubard; *Weldon's*

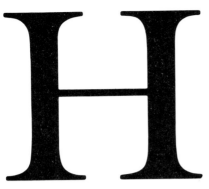

HAIRWORK

See *Quillwork and hairwork, Silk pictures*

HARDANGER

Named after the district surrounding the Hardanger fiord on the west coast of Norway, it consists of soft cotton or linen thread on heavy, evenly woven linen, white or natural in colour throughout. 'Kloster' blocks of satin stitch, worked before the threads are cut and removed, protect the sides of the cut squares. Both blocks and square holes are almost always uniform and constant throughout the piece of work, but fillings and treatments of overcast bars, sometimes with picots and loops, are rich and variable. The kloster blocks make an indented stitches, probably because of some ancient numerical symbolism, but there is no strong rule, sevens and twelves being quite common. They can be varied in height as well as in width. Some formal surface stitchery is traditionally permissible. It decorates gala costumes, and the collars, cuffs and neckbands of more everyday wear. Its popularity has spread widely, but outside Norway it is used largely for table linen.

The origins of Hardanger are lost in a plethora of influences. Numerous conflicting claims are made. There is evidence of both style and technical association with early Persian textiles, and obvious links with Renaissance white work and lace, and *opus teutonicum*.

Planning the pattern should be done on squared paper. Hardanger always has strict geometric forms, sometimes isolated, sometimes overlapping. The kloster blocks made an indented outline to each shape, usually further broken by rows of more blocks set outside the line. The heads of the stitches in the blocks always face what will eventually be a cut space. It will be found that these potential cut spaces inside the shape will leave rows of grouped loose yarns. These, too, are characteristic, and will be overcast. The kloster blocks consist of an irregular number of working threads over a regular number of ground yarns. The pattern is transferred to the ground by means of tacking and then detailed counting.

The Scandinavians wove their own linen yarns and produced a beautiful

Sequence of diagonal working of needlewoven bars

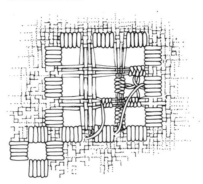

fabric for Hardanger. Modern specialized versions, often with a double yarn, may be easy to work, but they are lifeless and weighty and bear little resemblance to real Hardanger. A linen ground should be chosen which has a fairly soft yarn, with little lustre and a rather closed weave, so that the edges of the blocks will not fray. There are two working threads, cotton or linen, a thicker one for making the blocks and a finer one for the fillings. The thicker one should closely cover the ground and both should match exactly in tone and colour. Blunt-ended needles are usually best. The eye should be as large as the fabric will allow, so that the soft working thread is better protected. Hardanger may be worked in the hand or in a frame.

There is a strict order of working. All the kloster blocks are completed first. Fastening on and off must be done securely inside them. The working thread is quickly used. An ideal length is that which will minimize thread damage and allow enough to avoid frequent re-loading of the needle. Next, all the additional surface stitchery is completed. Groups of chevroned satin stitch are appropriate, together with eyelets, back and chain, but all are worked within a strict geometric format.

The work is removed from the

Hardanger: sample showing characteristic features. 11 × 16 cm (6½ × 4½ in.)

Hardanger: Norwegian, nineteenth-century. (*Embroiderers' Guild*)

frame for cutting and withdrawing of the ground yarns. The number of yarns cut is always one less than the number of stitches in the kloster block. Using a pair of very sharp small scissors, cut all the vertical yarns first and then all the horizontal ones within a given enclosed shape. This will leave a series of open squares surrounded on all sides by either a kloster block or a group of unwoven ground yarns. It is necessary at this stage to decide if the work is to have *lace* stitch fillings, since many of them need to be incorporated in the overcasting.

Always worked diagonally across the embroidery, close overcasting passes alternately from a vertical group to a horizontal one. The thread is fastened securely inside the blocks which outline the shape, passing beneath the interstices. There must always be enough thread in the needle to complete the diagonal journey. The groups of yarns may be finished with *needleweaving* rather than overcasting, but the two methods should not be used together on the same piece of work. If lace fillings are to be dispensed with it is usual to decorate the bars modestly with *picots*. Hardanger is finished with mitred hemstitching.

Bibliography
Anchor; Bright; de Dillmont; Howard 1966; Liley; Priscilla 1909; Snook; Thomas 1936; *Weldon's*

HAUSA ROBES

The Hausa of North Africa, and Nigeria in particular, have a long tradition of embroidery. Designs are predominantly Islamic in influence, but it is clear that the working interlacing patterns and circles were in general use long before Islam. Each component is named, and although they now appear quite abstract, most still have magical lizard associations. Sometimes the colours are muted, sometimes brilliant. The riga has embroidery concentrated on the large front pocket and the left shoulder, and the shabka mai yanka is decorated all over both front and back. Stitchery is usually confined to open chain stitch and some couching, with a long triangle of needleweaving at the neck, and circles of open insertion stitchery incorporated in the main circles of the design.

Bibliography
Heathcote

Hausa: the distribution of pattern on a full length robe

Hausa: robe detail, cotton strip weaving, white on indigo, open chain and eyelets. (*Leeds Museum*)

Collections
UK   Leeds Museum
USA   Field Museum of Natural History, Chicago; American Museum of Natural History, New York; Museum of Primitive Art, New York

HAWAIIAN QUILTS

Square applied work quilts consisting of top, batting and lining, peculiar to the Hawaiian Islands in their four-way symmetrical design and contour quilting stitchery. The designs are silhouettes of flat colour achieved by the complex cutting of folded fabric, and often the whole quilt is decorated with one extensive piece. Early quilting patterns, until about 1850, were strongly influenced by New England ones, but gradually contour quilting developed. Parallel lines of stitching follow the perimeter of the applied shapes inside and out, working progressively outwards from them, until they cover the whole ground and the whole of the shape. Hawaiian quilts are usually filled with a layer of flannel since warmth is not a priority. This makes them flatter than most.

The quilting tradition was taken to Hawaii by the New England missionary women. On 3 April 1820, aboard the brig Thaddeus off the Sandwich Islands, seven American wives and four Hawaiian ladies held their first sewing circle. The Hawaiians knew little of needlework with woven fabrics. They were experts at weaving and construction with vegetable fibres and at making garments from felts, but they had no pieces to patch and no grounds to quilt, so everything had to be imported to the Islands. The New England ladies taught them to stitch and sew, and, in using quilting as a missionary vehicle, brought new status and fashionable zeal to those Hawaiian ladies who had quilts to display.

Designs probably came directly from the simple stamp printing of the Islanders although there are many legends about the origins of the patterns. Women often worked secretly on personal designs which became their property, and copies were frowned upon. Characteristic named designs have mythological, environmental and symbolic origins. Ka ua Kani Lehua is the Rain That Rustles Lehua Blossoms, and Na Molkama is a pattern which relates to the Hanalei waterfalls. Quilt tops and linings are of cotton, but batting varies. Most tops are calico, usually white or unbleached, but occasionally the applied shape is white on a coloured ground. Early quilts were frequently of turkey red on white. Because the fabrics were first washed to pre-shrink and remove excess dye, even the brightest colours often have a softly variable tone.

The techniques involved are similar to those employed in all *quiltmaking*. All fabrics must be meticulously ironed but folded creases must be made only with the hands. The cotton to be applied is normally folded three times. Vertical and horizontal folds alone are not typical. The final fold of the fabric should be diagonal to form a triangle of eight layers, making four folds on the bias. Tack the paper pattern through all eight layers firmly, taking care that the bias edge is correctly placed and that the indented centre of the pattern matches the piko, the centre of the piece. Cut the fabric around the pattern one layer at a time. Although it may be necessary to use small scissors with sharp points to enter a fold, the main cutting is best done with very sharp shears.

With the ground fabric on a smooth surface, centre the piko and unfold the applied piece, using a straight edge to check the position of all fold marks in relation to the ground. Starting from the piko each time, baste both fabrics together, then run a tacking line around the whole of the applied piece about 2 cm ($\frac{3}{4}$ in.) from its edge. Using a matching thread begin oversewing from a position near the piko, turning the edge under a little way ahead as the stitching proceeds. Snipping of curves and indentations should be kept

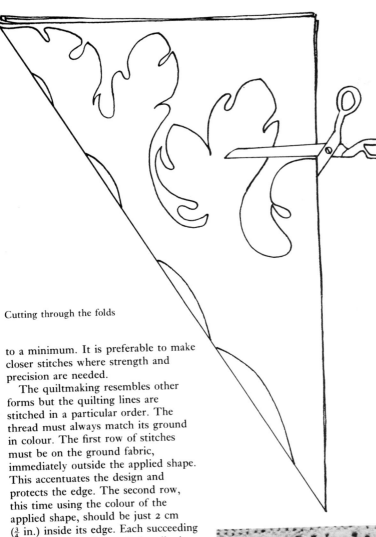

Cutting through the folds

to a minimum. It is preferable to make closer stitches where strength and precision are needed.

The quiltmaking resembles other forms but the quilting lines are stitched in a particular order. The thread must always match its ground in colour. The first row of stitches must be on the ground fabric, immediately outside the applied shape. This accentuates the design and protects the edge. The second row, this time using the colour of the applied shape, should be just 2 cm ($\frac{3}{4}$ in.) inside its edge. Each succeeding row follows parallel until the piko is reached. Changing to the thread which matches the ground fabric, the same order is followed, concentric to the first row of quilting but spreading outwards, until the edge of the quilt is adequately secured.

Bibliography
Bath 1979; Gahran; Jones, S.M.

Collections
USA Honolulu Academy of Arts; Shelburne Museum, Shelburne, Massachusetts

HEDEBO (Hebeo, Danish work)

Because its appearance varies so widely according to period, Hedebo syning

can be difficult to identify. It is native to Denmark and always white on linen, but since the nineteenth century it has undergone popular and commercial exploitations which have changed its essential characteristics. Accounts of its historical tradition vary widely.

It seems to have been in the first instance symmetrical and floral, a robust form of surface stitchery with drawn fillings. Eighteenth-century Hedebo was spun, woven and embroidered by the heath people. Girls prepared elaborate trousseaux and shirts for their men on closely woven linen with a soft working thread. The *drawn thread* fillings called Dragvaerk, worked with overcasting and needleweaving, were pulled tight and close to form richly raised textures. All fillings were outlined with Hvidsoem, close rows of chain stitches, single chain stitch forming tendrils and stems. Leaves were worked in chevrons of satin stitch and smaller flower forms in buttonholing.

The later type reveals parallels with Reticella, Mediterranean forms of white work such as Levkara and Greek lace, and with Hardanger. The drawn fillings and their flowers formed part of a geometric border consisting of square groups of cut squares. Working methods were similar.

Hedebo: Danish, late eighteenth-century, cotton on linen. Detail 11 × 20 cm (4 × 8 in.). (*Bankfield Museum*)

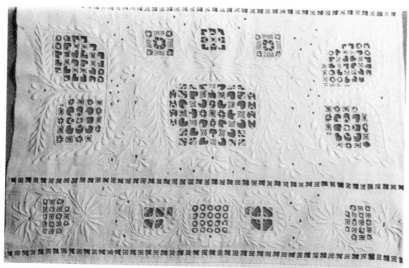

Hedebo: Danish, Island of Sjaelland, 1849. Cotton on linen. Detail 23 × 33 cm (9 × 13 in.). (*Bankfield Museum*)

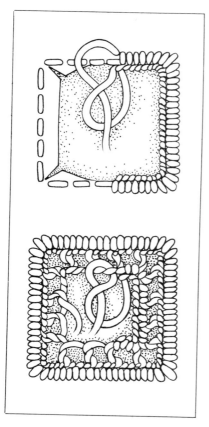

Working a cut square. The filling must be completed without joins. Renewing the thread is done during the buttonholing

Finally, Hedebo became an amalgam of *cutwork* and coarse *lace* fillings with heavily decorated buttonholed edgings, the surface stitchery merely presenting a foil to the open areas. The extensive cutwork necessitated the use of a fine closely woven linen or cotton ground and lace thread. Surface embroidery was still worked in thicker, soft thread, but the work became white throughout rather than cream in colour. Elaborate lace fillings include buttonholed rings, woven wheels and *Armenian needlepoint*, and edges were finished with deep scallops heavily decorated with needlepoint loops and picots.

Bibliography
Clabburn; de Dillmont; Dreesman; John 1961; Liley; Snook 1972; Thomas 1936

Collections
UK   Bankfield Museum, Halifax
Denmark   Kunstindustrimuseet, Copenhagen

HEER BHARAT

The collective term, with geographical variations, for Indian embroidery which consists of floss silk used in long stitches. These are arranged for maximum deflected light across the silk. It applies particularly to the geometrically based *Phulkari*.

Collections
UK   Victoria and Albert Museum, London

India   Calico Museum of Textiles, Ahmedabad

HEMSTITCHING (drawn thread work)

The drawing out of a few ground yarns inside a turning, with the hem incorporated into the drawn portion by means of counted overcasting and bunching of the ground yarns. Hemstitching and *drawn thread* work are synonymous. Drawn thread work is usually referred to as such when it occupies an important and expansive area of the piece of work. As a subordinate border or occupying a small percentage of the total ground, it is called hemstitching. It can also be used to decorate a straight seam. Some textbooks treat hemstitching as a functional extra, but it is often elaborated to include many stitches typical of counted thread embroidery, and can play an important part in the design of the textile as a whole, as it does in *Ruskin work*.

If there are corners to be turned on the work the exact position of these must be determined before any withdrawal of yarns is done, so that the weave on the hemmed corner itself can remain intact. Depending on the depth of hemstitching required, two or more threads are withdrawn from the fabric throughout its length, leaving a short piece to tuck under the hem at the corners, about 2 cm ($\frac{3}{4}$ in.) from the raw edge, or wherever it is intended that the fold is to be stitched down. The hem is then turned and tacked, *mitreing corners* as they are reached.

Alternating stem stitch

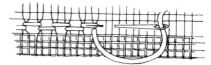

One yarn withdrawn

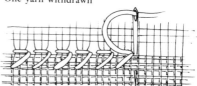

The withdrawn ground can be used as the working thread, but in this case extra yarns must be withdrawn before the hem is measured and tacked, so that there is sufficient yarn to complete the piece. Introducing variable threads which do not resemble the ground is part of the tradition. Wide hemstitching, especially that which is overcast, may have alternating coloured threads in wool or silk.

Bibliography
de Dillmont; Liley; Snook 1972

HOLBEIN

See *Blackwork*

HOLLIE POINT

A needlemade *lace* characterized by simple voided designs and the fact that traditionally it is made as an *insertion*. Strictly, it consists of just one stitch, a looped buttonhole encroached over laid

Hollie point: English, eighteenth-century. A child's cuff edged with Valenciennes bobbin lace. (*Embroiderers' Guild*)

threads in successive rows. The stitch bears the same name.

It has been suggested that the voided holes in the buttonholing resemble holly berries, but Hollie point and holly tree probably share a common origin in the word 'holy'. Hollie point is historically associated with religious houses and probably has its ancestry in *bebilla* and other Arab laces brought back from the Holy Land during the Crusades. It has

Hollie point: second half of the eighteenth century. Baby's bonnet, crown and insertion. (*Embroiderers' Guild*)

Hollie point: the basic lace filling and edging

parallels with early Sicilian and Italian *drawn fabric*, and was an acceptable part of Puritan dress. As a favourite embellishment to baby clothes it thrived until the nineteenth century.

Bibliography
Caulfeild and Saward; Christie 1920; de Dillmont

HONEYCOMB DARNING

See *Darning*

HONEYCOMB QUILTS

Another name for traditional English *patchwork* which was often exclusively of hexagonal patterns such as Grandmother's Flower Garden, or rosettes forming border swags, or alternating diamonds.

HORSETAIL

See *Maltese silk*

HUCKABACK DARNING

See *Darning*

ICELANDIC EYELETTING

Called augnsaumur stitch; some eighteenth- and nineteenth-century linen textiles from Iceland have borders and grounds worked over completely with square eyelets tightly packed, so that their edges share the gap formed in the weave by neighbouring eyelets. The subject matter is often representational, with colour changes occurring without rigid definition, rather in the manner of pointillism in painting.

INDO-EUROPEAN EMBROIDERY

The seventeenth-century interchange of textile influences between Asia, the Far East and Europe resulted in amalgams of styles, and workshops were set up in India to satisfy European tastes. The best known style was perhaps the Portuguese-influenced Bengal or Goa embroidery, which consisted of quilts and wall-hangings richly worked with fine chain stitches in yellow Tussur silk. Pictorial, hunting, and wild life scenes happily combine Iberian and Indian styles with Chinese formalization.

Bibliography
Irwin 1959; Irwin and Hall

Collections
UK Hardwick Hall

INLAY

The fabric forming the pattern or design is placed on top of the ground and both are cut simultaneously with a sharp blade. In this way the pattern pieces can be inlaid in the ground exactly and oversewn together to form a smooth, continuous fabric. Obviously, the remains of the first fabric now act as a ground to the remains of the second, and the whole piece of work may be produced in reverse colours. Counterchange designs are, therefore, characteristic.

INSERTIONS (openwork seams, faggoting)

A term used generally for all those stitches, braids, laces and fillings which occupy the space between two edges of fabric, whether for functional or decorative purposes. The space may be at a seam, constructed as part of a border, allowed between a decorated area and the main body of the textile, or cut or drawn from the ground to accommodate the insertion. Hemstitched borders are often referred to as insertions, probably because their appearance resembles that of a lace sewn in. Some authorities use the term faggoting as synonymous with insertions, whilst others reserve it for the slim drawn thread or hemstitched border sometimes associated with an insertion-joined seam. Rarely, wide bands of needleweaving where the yarns of the ground are bunched by the stitchery are described as faggoting.

There are a great many insertion stitches, most of which are related to *lace* fillings. Some are very modest, a series of twists and loops joining two edges of fabric held slightly apart over the fingers. Others are elaborate, and may incorporate braids or laces together with complex stitch repetition. These are worked with the edges firmly tacked to a stiff backing, so that the width of the insertion cannot vary.

An idiosyncrasy of buttonhole insertions is that they are frequently

Antique seam

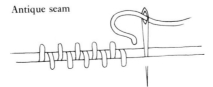

Twisted insertion

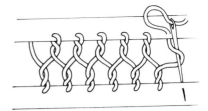

Knotted insertion. Many variations include separately constructed edgings butted and whipped

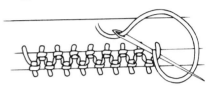

worked in blocks of colours matching the rest of the embroidery, a needle-full for each block, so that the seam is multi-coloured.

Many insertion stitches are worked separately on the opposing sides and then connected with knots or lacing.

An 'entre deux' is a separately made braid or lace which has a sewing edge on both sides to stitch to either side of the seam.

Bibliography
Clabburn; de Dillmont; Minter

IRISH MACHINE

An industrial embroidery machine with a 1.3 cm ($\frac{1}{2}$ in.) wide zigzag stitch, designed originally for mending and finishing laces made on multiple machines. Workers in many cases did not use a tambour frame, despite the fact that the machine has no presser foot and no feed dog. The use of a tambour frame is, however, considered advisable. The knee lever can be used to control the width of the zigzag stitch continuously as the machine is stitching, so allowing smooth curves and precision. The stitch can be locked to a pre-selected width or set either side of a central line.

Bibliography
Johnson; Risley 1969

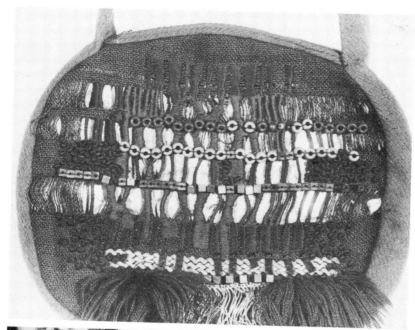

ITALIAN QUILTING (cord quilting)

There are two clearly defined methods of *cord quilting*. Both are sometimes referred to as Italian quilting, but only that which has a yarn introduced between two layers of fabric can properly be so described without controversy. It is often used with trapunto (which has yarn or wadding introduced through the back after stitching) on the same piece. Parallel lines of stitching are made through two fabrics, the stuffing introduced in yarn between them from behind, making raised edges on an otherwise flat ground. Although earlier designs

Irish machine: brown and navy drawn thread work on a blue hessian bag. 30 × 25 cm (12 × 10 in.)

Irish machine: satin stitch variations on acetate silk, padded and set in a type box

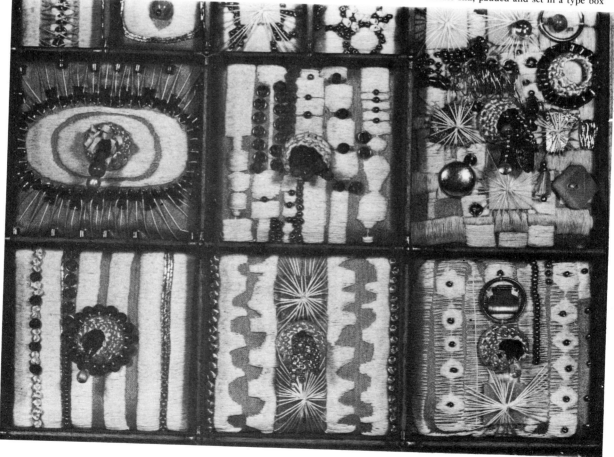

often consist of elaborate linear interlacings, filled areas are achieved by using consecutive parallel or contour lines. The technique is frequently used in association with pulled work and eyeletting. Where the ground is translucent to allow the yarn, which can be brightly coloured, to show through, it is known as *shadow quilting*.

It would seem likely that Italian quilting was introduced in the Renaissance as a direct result of the trade in rich silks and satins, and so the technique and the fabrics are closely associated. Certainly the visual appeal of quilting is enhanced by lustrous fabrics, but a great deal was still done on linens for coverlets and undergarments, and for accessories and warm outerwear. Throughout the seventeenth century and well into the eighteenth the technique was widely practised throughout Europe and was highly fashionable. It is mainly the linen pieces which have survived, but the design of many of the most beautiful silk and satin ones can be studied on period portraits.

Italian quilting gives a softer line with lighter shadows than cord quilting. For intricate or repeat patterns reference must be made to typical historical pieces so that the technique can be properly translated into designs which have characteristic values. Contrasting interlaced, undulating or parallel textures are helpful. It must be remembered that areas of quilting add more weight and density to the ground than does lightly sprinkled surface stitchery. The distance between the stitched lines must be previously calculated to accommodate the chosen yarn.

Almost any closely woven fabric may be used, with a very soft, open weave as the backing. For traditional work it is still possible to obtain Italian quilting wool to thread between the lines of stitching, but any soft bulky yarn is suitable. The working thread must be strong; buttonhole twist silk or linen are best, and beeswaxing the thread makes stitching easier and more regular. The needle should be very smooth with a large

Italian quilting: inset Italian quilting by machine on silk. Made by Lynda Colt

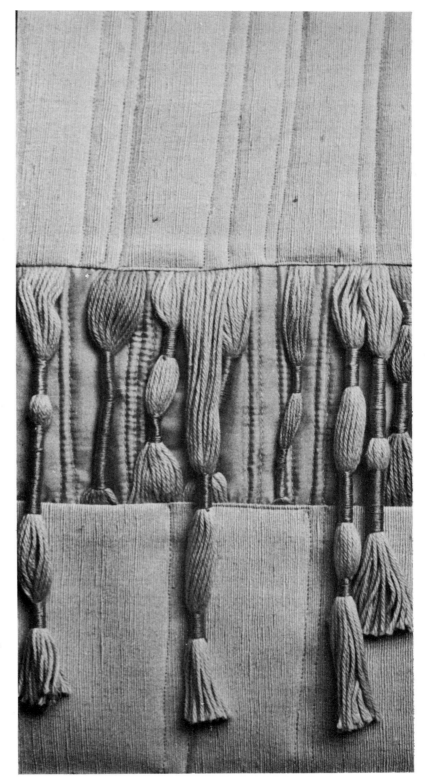

eye. A frame is essential. The ground should be loosely stretched, keeping the grain at perfect right angles.

Most workers find a design transferred with a single guiding line more successful than attempts to provide parallel working lines for the stitchery. Experiments must be made to decide upon the best way of achieving a temporary line. On linen a tacked line made through a tissue tracing is probably the best. Chalk or pounce powder will adhere long enough to complete the stitchery providing they are drawn only on the immediate area to be worked. Tailors' chalk marks linen very firmly and on glazed linens can never be entirely removed.

The back stitches must be regular and absolutely smooth, not so tight as to pull the ground but tight enough to control the quilting yarn evenly. Starting and finishing ends are run under lines to be worked or under

those which are already worked. Where the quilting yarns intersect, the working thread is taken beneath the channel. Close study of early pieces reveals that outside curves often have slightly closer stitches with the occasional double back stitch to secure.

Using a yarn needle, bodkin, or heavy tapestry needle, introduce the wool between the layers of fabric into the channel made by the stitched lines. Start at an end or corner, leaving a short tail of wool and run the yarn through for a little way before bringing the needle out. The distance will probably be dictated by the length

Working the filling from the back

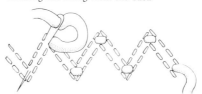

of the needle or the extent of the curve on the line. Re-insert the needle at the same point, leaving a minimal loop of wool at each hole. This prevents stretching the yarn and so distorting the fabric. Where it is necessary to move to a point in the design which is not immediately adjacent, bring the needle out and leave a short length of yarn at the end and at the new beginning.

Collections
UK   Gawthorpe Hall, Burnley; Guildford Museum

ITALIAN SMOCKING

A form of smocking in reverse, not only found in Italy. Rows of firm smocking stitches are worked on the back of the fabric to control the gathers. Surface stitchery may then be worked over the pleats on the right side without needing to perform the dual role of function and decoration.

JACOBEAN

Worsted wool or crewel embroidery in formal, floral scrolling arrangements on linen or cotton twill. It varies in scale from quite delicate borders and valances to full length tester curtains, heavy with vigorous stitchery. Using the Tree of Life and the language of symbolism, hillocks, birds and beasts fill any available space. As the flowers and leaves became more ponderous they were charged with stylized botanical detail and lavish decorative stitchery.

Spun wool dyed in natural colours and woven linen have been available

Jacobean: seventeenth-century fine wool on linen, partly worked. Width of piece 17 cm (6½ in.)

since pre-history for the most humble dwellings. Larger houses and castles were provided with isolated areas of comfort by their bed hangings, door curtains and pillows. These textiles co-existed happily with tapestries and imported velvets, brocades and damasks. They provided a fertile field for the Celtic and Byzantine strapwork and scrolling designs and soon succumbed to the enveloping influences from the Middle East and India. By the Stuart period they had developed into a distinct form, strongly related to other textiles in design and subject matter, but strictly reserved in technique, materials and stitchery. Although during the early seventeenth century many other forms of embroidery and lace were being produced, the Jacobean period has become synonymous with this particular style of *crewel work*. It has many predecessors and antecedents, and it is difficult to detect to what extent development is influenced or related. American *Deerfield Blue and White work* is one example.

Wool colours were selected and carefully graded so that pinks and reds or blues and blue-greens predominated. Vegetable dyes, so frequently subject to light, gradually faded, and so the soft colours now associated with Jacobean wool work are not necessarily those intended by the original designers. Rarely, the embroidery was monochromatic.

The fashion for delicately printed Indian cottons brought a return to light, graceful arrangements, but with the Georgian revival flowers and leaves were thick and powerful once more. Interest in crewel embroidery survived the nineteenth century in rural America and re-emerged in Britain in needlework magazines offering designs for antimacassars and fire screens. The vigour of Jacobean design was absent, and these promotions contributed little to an appreciation of a valuable tradition.

It is essential to make a thorough study of typical and soundly worked historical pieces before attempting an interpretation. The distribution of shape and pattern, colour and detail, developed logically and rationally and need to be understood.

Bibliography
Davis; Fitzwilliam and Hands; Jones, M.E. 1974; Kiewe 1957; *Penelope*

JANINA EMBROIDERY (Joannina, Yannina work)

A term used loosely and variably by a number of writers, now accepted to refer specifically to the characteristic embroidery from the chief town of Epirus on the north-west mainland of Greece. Janina belongs to the group of freely worked Greek embroideries with Turkish influence. The patterns are always floral, with stylized rose, leaf and cone motifs worked on softly spun

Janina embroidery: silk floss Cretan stitch in red, blue, green and cream on open linen. Detail of 28 cm (11 in.) wide band. (*Rachel Kay Shuttleworth Collection, Gawthorpe Hall*)

cream linen in double running and fine *darning* in muted primary colours. The marriage cushion covers show the bridal pair and their parents and attendants, often on horseback, surrounded by vases of flowers.

Bibliography
Bart; Currey 1950; Johnstone 1954, 1961; Petrakis

Collections
UK   Gawthorpe Hall, Burnley; Fitzwilliam Museum, Cambridge
Greece   Benaki Museum, Athens; The Museum of Greek Folk Art, Athens

JAP GOLD

See *Metal threads, Metal thread work*

JAVA CANVAS WORK

Java canvas is very stiff, a brownish, multiple weave intended to be stitched with simple geometric and repetitive patterns. There is evidence that coarse weaves of this kind have a long history, but the technique of embroidery upon them emerged as a category during the mid-nineteenth century. The articles made from java canvas were serviceable and domestic, on the same scale as those made from *Leviathan work* and coarse huckaback *darning*. Colours were softly contrasting, leaving considerable areas of ground. The working thread was wool, wool thrums or soft cotton. Edges were characteristically braided or bound rather than being hemmed.

JEWELS

Precious stones have been used on textiles probably as long as they have been part of jewellery. Methods of drilling were extremely time-consuming even on the softest minerals, so most were set into pierced metal mounts or settings equipped with loops to accommodate a strong thread. Ceremonial and ecclesiastical vestments were frequently encrusted with precious cabochon stones, but because they were subject to *parfilage*, misappropriation and friction, few of the garments survive intact. Secular accessories such as hawking gloves have survived, however, and give some indication of the lavish decoration displayed, particularly on Byzantine and Elizabethan textiles.

Collection
Austria   Imperial Schatzkammer, Vienna

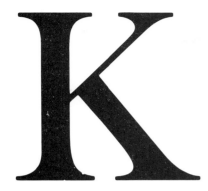

KALEIDOSCOPE BARGELLO
See *Florentine*

KASAI VELVET
See *Bakuba*

KASHMIR

Embroidered shawls were not made at all in Kashmir until after 1800, when they were introduced by the Armenian, Khawäja Yüsuf, who trained workers to make them in imitation of the more expensive woven ones. By 1840 the embroiderers had begun to specialize in illustrating the stories and romances of Indian and Persian history and these designs became preferred in the West. Amli map shawls, showing a pictorial plan of Srinagar, were produced in the second half of the nineteenth century. The export of both pattern-woven and stitched shawls was eventually supplanted by other embroidered goods as fashions changed, but Kashmir was long recognized as an imitative style.

Bibliography
Birdwood; Dhamija; Dongerkery; Irwin 1973

Collections
UK Bankfield Museum, Halifax; Victoria and Albert Museum, London
India Calico Museum of Textiles, Ahmedabad

Kashmir: shawl, multi-coloured simple stitchery on locally woven pashm wool. Pre-1838. Detail 16 × 18 cm (6½ × 7 in.). (*Bankfield Museum*)

KATHIAWAR

Lavish and glamorous surface stitchery decorating delicate garments and veils, domestic textiles and cattle trappings, from the Kathiawar district of western India. Characteristic features are *shisha* glass and long, close darning stitches influenced by *Phulkari* from the Punjab. Used on the often translucent skirts, blouses and veils of women and children, the embroidery offers dense textural areas of opacity in contrast, and the mirror glass gives moving weight and flow. It is customary for a Kathiawar girl to wrap her trousseau in a square of embroidery known as a chakla, which later hangs in the house. For superstitious reasons all pieces of Kathiawar embroidery have a tiny corner unfinished.

Bibliography
Birdwood; Dhamija; Dongerkery; Irwin and Hall 1973

Collections
India Calico Museum of Textiles, Ahmedabad

KELLS EMBROIDERY

The desperate plight of the Donegal Irish in the 1880s led to the introduction of textile crafts of several kinds intended for sale. Celtic serpentine designs based on the Book of Kells were introduced by Mrs Ernest Hart. Patterns known as O'Neill and Tyrconnell were popular in England. The stitchery was worked on vegetable-dyed Galway flannel, linen or wool with a glossy linen thread. More ambitious pieces such as curtains were undertaken from time to time.

Bibliography
Boyle; Morris 1965

KIMONO

The word used in the West to describe

Kimono: crepe silk with print, rice paste resist and silk and metal embroidery, blue-grey with a scarlet lining. Detail. (*Leeds Museum*)

Kimono: soft pinks and greens, silk and gold thread. Detail. (*Collection, Yasuzaemon Noguchi*)

a garment means in its native Japan the whole professional art of kimono, an art which views the human body as a shape upon which to display a sophisticated expertise, a culmination of thousands of years of design and technical development. Each craftsman at every stage in the production of kimono works in close liaison and symbolic unity with his fellows. Designs are sensitively stylized, with carefully observed realism, in an extraordinary economy of line and form. Each contribution, from the

Kimono: naturalistic colour and detail, tie-dye, silk and gold. (*Collection, Yasuzaemon Noguchi*)

efforts of the silk worm, through sorting, selecting and processing, spinning, weaving, finishing, tie-dye and rice-paste resist, painting, silk embroidery and metal thread work, has equal importance on the finished work.

KINCOBS (kimkhwābs)

Rich brocades of costly weaves, dyes and embroidery, native to Benares and used for robes and hangings. Most of the opulent textiles widely exported from India and Persia for hundreds of years were described as kincobs. Their design has undergone continuous change and cross-fertilization.

Collection

India Calico Museum of Textiles, Ahmedabad

KITS

Since the explosion of early Berlin woolwork on to the market, ready prepared grounds, complete with instructions, threads and sometimes even basic tools, have been available for those workers reluctant to exercise choice or decision except in their initial purchase. Designs to be carboned through, or grounds with printed or photographically reproduced designs already on them are still remarkably popular. The means for enlarging and transferring a favourite photograph or portrait mechanically onto canvas are now readily available.

KNOTTED WORK

There are two technical varieties, one composed of French, Pekin or coral stitch, the other of couched lines of thread which have been previously knotted. Both are done on similar pieces and frequently occur together.

Kits: printed in seven colours on dressed linen, stretched ready to work and frame. 10 × 18 cm (4 × 7 in.)

There is a long tradition of white counterpanes, either surface stitched or quilted, throughout the Mediterranean countries, Britain and Ireland, and, through the influence of the Portuguese, in India and Pakistan.

A cover made in Northern Ireland in 1738 is worked almost entirely with a creamy hand-knotted linen thread closely couched on a gently bleached linen. There is contemporary and earlier European and Hispanic work of a similar kind where the knots are made as part of the stitchery and combined with chain and raised

Knotted work: North American Indian moose hair knot for surface stitchery

composite stitches. This may well have been a prototype of *Mountmellick*, and of the *candlewicking* tradition in America.

Cotehele House has a suite of furniture dated around 1725, which is upholstered in Queen Anne knobbed woolwork, or Queen Anne's tatting. The closely knotted wool is couched between the knots in a design of coloured flowers and foliage.

Bibliography
Pesel (*Embroideress* no. 16); Rolleston

Collections
UK Victoria and Albert Museum, London; Cotehele House, Saltash

KUNA INDIAN

See *San Blas appliqué*

LACE

An infinite variety of open, usually fine, exquisite textiles which have fascinated for many centuries. Embroidery and lace making are so close that it is not possible to discuss the one without overlapping the other. The ancient names opus filatorium and *opus araneum* seem to have applied

loosely to any textile construction which was mainly open, in particular fine *drawn thread* and *filet*. Numerous distinctions defining embroidery and lace have been offered, but so many exceptions prove the rule. Primarily thought of as white and delicate, there are many coloured and coarse laces within the classification.

Although some are identified by their place of origin, laces are best understood from the technical way in which they are made and the tools used. Needlepoint is made entirely with a needle; bobbin laces are very varied, but all are constructed using bobbins to plait the threads between pins arranged on a cushion; mixed laces employ both needle and bobbins at some stage during their making; net laces like filet are hand-netted and then decorated, and bobbin or machine-made net is hand-worked with needle darning or *tambour* in the manner of *Carrickmacross* and *Limerick*. Knitted laces, tatting, crochet and macramé are grouped as

laces, and a number of embroidery forms such as *Tenerife* and *Ruskin* are also defined as laces by some authorities.

Since most lace techniques have developed from open embroidery, stitches and patterns are shared. Ayrshire, Chikan and Hedebo are recognized as embroidery, but Renaissance, Reticella and Richelieu are all classed as laces. Bebilla and Hollie Point are exclusively buttonholed. Reference should be made, too, to those entries concerning edgings and picots.

The development of white, open embroidery together with sophisticated spinning skills brought into being the intricate laces of the sixteenth century. Sometimes open spaces were cut away in the ground to accommodate subsequent stitchery, but often warp and weft threads were reserved at

Lace: early cutwork and needlepoint. (*Ilké and Jacoby Collection, Textilmuseum, St Gallen*)

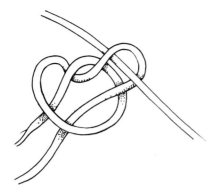

Lacemaker's knot

intervals forming an open trellis for needleweaving and buttonholing. Having mutilated the ground in this way it was easier to work with a supporting parchment stitched behind it. From that stage it was logical to add increasingly elaborate edgings, until the ground became the embroidery in its own right. However, fine white embroidery continued to develop, and seventeenth-century excise duties and taxes restricting the lace trade brought to the forefront quantities of exquisitely stitched muslins from Bohemia, Belgium and

Germany, known collectively as *Dresden work*.

Needlemade laces have grounds of two kinds, consisting either of bars or of net patterns called reseau. Laid or reserved constructions of threads are worked with buttonhole, overcasting or needleweaving. Outlines may be heavily padded with stitching or flat and understated. Solid fillings may be constructed by rows of stitches closely worked into preceding rows, and open ones by laid parallel threads worked over in subsequent journeys. Picots of various kinds are incorporated and tiny decorated rings or buttonholed wheels may be applied. Some laces are formed around a basis of laid braids and some have a picot braid applied as an edging.

Bibliography
Bath 1974; Caulfeild and Saward; Collier; de Dillmont; Earnshaw; Freiherr; Hald; Lefébure; Lewis; Nordfors; Palliser; Pfannschmidt; Simeon; *Weldon's*

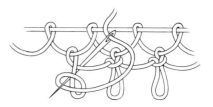

Purls

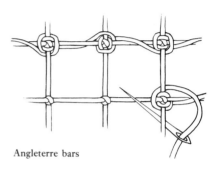

Angleterre bars

Point d'Esprit

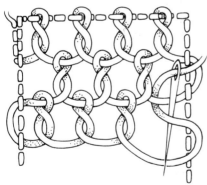

There are many variations of the basic lace stitch filling

Point de Sorrento

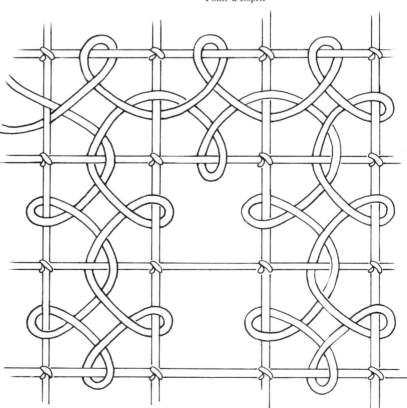

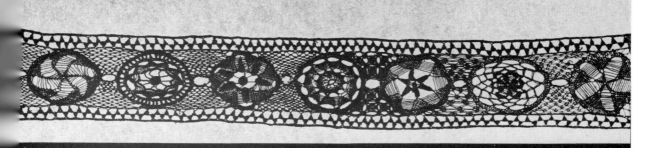

Lace: Russian lace stitch sampler in heavy linen thread. Detail 46 cm (18 in.) long

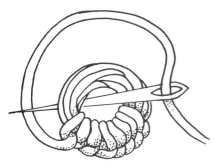

Buttonhole ring characteristic of drawn thread, Hedebo and tape lace

LACE FILLINGS BY MACHINE

This kind of machine embroidery probably owes more than any other to the tradition of lace and fine stitchery and can only be imitative. It consists of free straight stitchery across circular holes cut in a finely woven ground, the edges overworked with a padded satin stitch made by moving the tambour frame from side to side.

The ground must be fine and firmly woven, easy to stitch through but retaining its shape. Thread and needle must be very fine, with the tensions delicately adjusted to form the needle thread loop on the wrong side of the ground. The material must be carefully and firmly stretched in the tambour frame.

Using slow and deliberate movements double circles of close stitches are made on the ground fabric. The space between the double lines should be minimal and they should never overlap. In some instances it may be necessary at this stage to remove the ground from the frame, but if the circles can be trimmed with sharp-pointed scissors whilst still in the frame this is preferable. The ground is returned to the machine, and the fillings are begun by stitching slowly across the circles to make bars, stepping back and forth over the edges to reach the point for successive ones. Where lines intersect a single stitch backwards keeps the junction in place. Radiating fillings with an inner circle may be achieved by splitting a diagonal bar with single stitches reaching from the circumference. The needle returns to the centre and makes single stitches within each radial angle for woven wheels, travelling in a spiralling motion. Spider's webs are made in the same way but secured at each junction with a single reverse stitch. When the fillings are completed a thicker thread is couched around each circumference with close there-and-back straight stitches. This helps to strengthen the circle and builds a slightly deeper texture to conform with the scale of any hand stitchery, which may be added when the machining is finished. The embroidery must be kept carefully trimmed and finished at the back.

LACIS

See *Filet*

LAID ON WORK

See *Applied work*

LAIDWORK (honeycombing)

All those solid or open fillings which consist of working threads couched down by patterned tying stitchery are known as laidwork. The technique occurs very widely. Many Byzantine and medieval embroideries, whether religious or secular, consist mainly of laid fillings. The technique evolved to accommodate working threads which would otherwise be spoiled by frequently passing through the ground. Laid work should not be confused with lead or lerd works, which are the fillings of laces.

Solid fillings, with the ground covered by close threads overstitched with lattice patterns, scrolling or veining may be seen on *opus anglicanum*, on the Bayeux tapestry and on many forms of *metal thread work*. The Norwegian and Icelandic form is refilsaum. *Or nué* is a specialized form. Open fillings, where the ground appears as the base of the couched pattern, are typical of *Jacobean* and traditional *crewel work*. Many are combinations of simple stitches, sometimes worked in several colours.

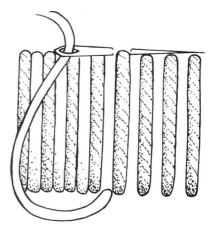

Laidwork: laying the basis, the second journey

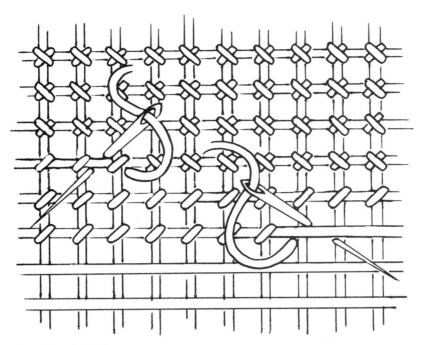

Crossed couched filling

Some laidwork couching patterns

Buttonhole filling over surface satin stitch

Oriental, Roumanian and Bokhara couching are all similar laid fillings in which the needle returns along each thread to couch it down before the next is laid. The laid threads no longer have parallel precision, and assume the appearance of rows of stem stitch. Much Greek and eastern Mediterranean embroidery is dominated by variations of this stitch.

Bibliography
Christie 1920, 1938; Davis; Johnstone; Fitzwilliam and Hands

LAMINAE (lama, paillons, spangles)

Originally of thin metal sheet, usually gold or silver, they are flat or raised shapes used to enrich textiles, either incorporated in the ground or as edgings and appendages. Early references associate them with the Phrygians, but there is evidence of them in many societies where precious metals were worked. In the Middle Ages they were fashionable on vestments and clothing as stars, moons, crescents, leaves and rings, and simple gold spangles or *sequins*. Many became jewellery within the embroidery, enamelled or set with cabochon stones. Their use on ecclesiastical vestments declined with the Reformation, but they remained in understated form in many kinds of formal embroidery.

Laminae made of precious metals are now rare. Hand-cutting is still practised for those on some regional embroidery, particularly in the Middle East and India, but most are made mechanically. Metals have been largely replaced by synthetics, but shapes and colours remain remarkably traditional. Some are punched into facets or curves to break or bend the light, and some are made in representational

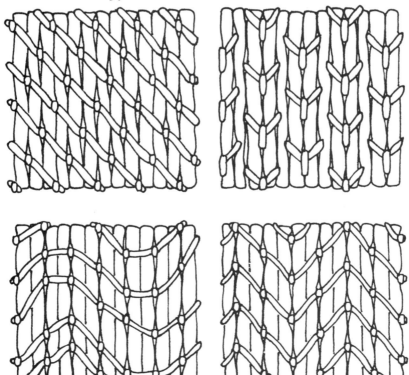

Laidwork: Italian, seventeenth-century. Coarse linen ground completely covered in laid floss silk couched with fine gold passing. The design is professionally drawn on both ground and slips. Panel 43 × 58 cm (17 × 23 in.). (*Private collection*)

form like fish or daisies. All have at least one hole so that they can be sewn on.

LA PALMA LINEN

See *Tenerife embroidery*

LAWN

A fine fabric once of linen and now usually of cotton. It is associated with *Ayrshire* work and *Dresden work* and other forms of fine white stitchery.

LEATHER APPLIQUÉ

The application of soft leather to a woven or leather ground for decorative purposes. Leather is pliable and accommodating and cannot fray, and so it may easily be padded and is suitable for *inlay*. Exactly the same technique is used in a variety of circumstances. Siberian and Alaskan peoples were expert, and several North American Indian tribes until recently deftly applied many forms of animal skin, gut and sinew one to another. (See *Fishskin appliqué*.) In India the Great Rann of Kutch and neighbouring Gujarat have for centuries had the reputation for producing the most beautiful embroidery, much of it leather appliqué. At the end of the thirteenth century Marco Polo said that their sleeping mats were 'of red leather depicting birds and beasts in gold and silver thread, sewn very subtly.'

The use of foil-coated kid on ecclesiastical work has become popular, padded areas being incorporated amongst the purls and passings.

Probably the most well established forms of leather appliqué still practised are those on professionally made sheepskin garments and outer clothing of the Hungarian peoples. The style of

Laidwork: Persian, eighteenth-century, couched gold and pink and blue silk on cream satin. Corner of a mat. Width of gold braid 1 cm ($\frac{1}{3}$ in.)

ornament is closely allied to early linen work, and certainly preceded the coarse satin stitch virágosás embroidery, although by the eighteenth century both techniques appear together on the same garments. The ködmön, a leather jacket still worn by women and once part of the dowry, was almost always decorated with leather appliqué and some surface stitchery. Colour and ornament have regional characteristics but the main area of pattern was the enclosed back panel of the ködmön. The leather was carefully prepared and very simply oversewn to the ground with firm, regular stitches. Because all the applied shapes are rounded and leather stretches, the technique often provides a quilted appearance. The more elaborate ködmöns are further embellished with free-standing leather tags and intricately cut ornament. On some, small rounds of leather previously embossed over heat are stitched on rather like large-scale sequins.

Bibliography
Fél; Turner

Leather appliqué: Hungarian waistcoat, primary colours, polished leather appliqué with cut outs, the fur remaining as a lining. (*Leeds Museum*)

Leatherwork: brightly coloured chain and eyelets in silk which penetrates only the top layer of the skin. Manitoba, probably Chipewyan. (*Leeds Museum*)

Collection
UK Victoria and Albert Museum, London

LEEK WORK

A form of floss silk stitchery with jap gold outlines worked on plain or printed silks or velvets. Close scrollwork of flowers and leaves almost covers the ground. The colour is rich and soft. It has strong parallels with both *Anglo-Indian* and *brocade embroidery* and is not always easy to identify.

The Leek Embroidery Society in Staffordshire arose with a number of other organizations in reaction to Berlin woolwork, as part of the Arts and Crafts Movement. Well known artists contributed designs, and architects commissioned pieces of work. Leek work was used on ecclesiastical furnishings and its influence may still be seen on traditional pieces. The Society made a copy of the Bayeux tapestry which is now in Reading Museum. It was formed in 1879 by Elizabeth Wardle, wife of Thomas Wardle, President of the Silk Association of Great Britain and Ireland. Leek produced the silk

Leek work: stitchery following print on silk, richly coloured silk, and metal thread outlines. (*Rachel Kay Shuttleworth Collection, Gawthorpe Hall*)

Leviathan work: cotton and jute with wool stitchery. Detail 30 × 20 cm (12 × 8 in.)

threads and yarns, wove threads and trimmings, and ran the dye houses and printing works. Mr Wardle worked with natural dyes, concentrating on deep colours for wild silk.

Bibliography
Howard 1981; Parker

Collections
UK Leek Art Gallery; Reading Museum and Art Gallery

LEVIATHAN

Coarse canvas work belonging to the late nineteenth and early twentieth century. Heavy wool stitchery, with Leviathan stitch predominating, was produced for rugs and mats on a specially made doubles jute cloth. It was treated as surface stitchery rather than covering the ground completely. Similar canvas called jute Panama is still produced for canvas work church kneelers. It is pleasant to work and very durable.

Bibliography
Caulfeild and Saward

LEVKARA WORK (Cyprus embroidery)

White cutwork and geometric fillings of satin stitch, with deep fringes of knotted ravellings, associated principally with the village of Levkara outside Nicosia in Cyprus. Linen and mercerised cotton threads were imported during the nineteenth century, and Levkara work developed into a commercial success. It was called 'tagiadhes', from the Italian punto tagliato or drawn thread, and designs indicate strong Middle Eastern influences. Patterns are almost all based on the characteristic long diamonds, with little flourishes decorating the blocks. The Islamic Seljuk chevrons which make up a row

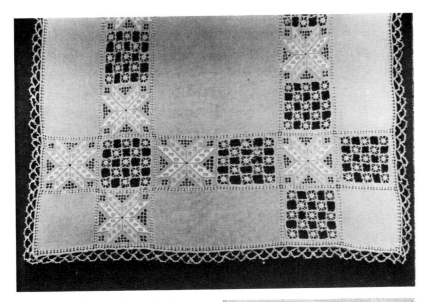

Levkara work: linen on linen, all white mat, 30 cm (12 in.) wide

Levkara work: buttonholed bars and hemstitching. The tasselled edging is worked separately. (*Rachel Kay Shuttleworth Collection, Gawthorpe Hall*)

of diamonds (see *Blackwork*) are called 'the river', and half diamonds used as a pattern are called 'the arch'.

Bibliography
Johnstone

Collection
UK   Gawthorpe Hall, Burnley

LIMERICK LACE

There are three kinds of Limerick lace, the needlerun, the tambour and the appliqué, all worked on a net foundation and all technically embroidery. They are softly delicate, light and very open in texture, and always white or cream. Only the needlerun net is reasonably durable, and it is this original form which has the wealth of filling stitches and the characteristic curves of adjoining eyelets.

Machine-made bobbin net was manufactured at Coggeshall in Essex from around the year 1820. It was embroidered or tamboured with wild flower sprigs and trailings. Charles Walker, at that time training for the Church, involved himself with the designing and technicalities of

lacemaking, and later with the net manufacturer's daughter. They took a number of lacemakers with them to Limerick in 1829 and founded the industry there for both philanthropic and commercial motives. The enterprise was no doubt of some value in relieving famine and poverty like most *white work* of the period. The original needlerun lace assumed some of the aspects of *Carrickmacross* with the addition of appliqué. At a later stage speedier *tambour work* took over and the fillings disappeared.

Limerick lace is open and trailing and may occupy quite a large area, such as the full length of a skirt or the largest wedding veil. The border consists of long shallow scallops formed by a picot edging, each curve

containing five or six smaller scallops, often formed with a second journey of the edging. The simpler designs are concentrated along the edge of the lace, trailing out amongst sprigs and isolated flowers. Richer patterns have central sprays and devices, with spreading blooms. There are more swags and scallops forming undulating enclosures. The scale of the pattern and its repeat will be dependent on the size of of working frame available.

It is not essential to use square-mesh net as a ground, but if a hexagonal net is used it must be soft and very fine. Lace thread or fine crochet cotton of two weights are needed, one for outlining and one for fillings. A little picot edging should be chosen which has one straight edge and one with long loops closely spaced. Small crewel needles are ideal, and a bone stiletto is necessary for the eyeletting. All the outlining is worked with the net in a large frame, and the fillings with a tambour frame.

Old manuals state that the design is printed or drawn out with Indian ink on glazed calico. The most suitable available equivalents seem to be dressmaker's carbon on a closely woven stiff cotton or poplin. Vinyls are too heavy for the net and paper backings irritating to work over in a frame. Lines must be drawn firmly and clearly.

Framing up the net must be done without stretching. It can be oversewn direct to the webbing on the bars, but the other two sides are held taut with a wide tape taken over the bars at each end, and held there with a few stitches. The net is basted to these side tapes which are in turn laced gently to the frame. Any spare net reserved at the top or bottom of the frame should be carefully rolled in soft fabric and loosely tacked to the webbing. Finally, the design is basted beneath the net.

Using the heavier working thread, begin outlining, running over and under the bars of the net. The thread is secured with a single loop pulled tight, and ended in the same way, running the tail a little way along the outline. The line is continuous, so starting and finishing ends can secure each other. Small curves and undulations in the design should be fully rounded and clearly defined. The line should be run outside the outline rather than inside it. Where the design dictates doubling of the thread, the return journey should overcast the first. The runs of little buttonholed or overcast eyelets are part of the outlining journey. The stiletto must be used gently to open the net for the stitching. Thread tension should always be carefully controlled throughout, so that the finished textile has soft drape and grace.

With outlining completed all tacking stitches are carefully snipped and the net is removed from the frame. *Net darning* or *filet* fillings are added with the aid of a tambour frame. The picot edging is added by oversewing it to the last scallops with the heavier outline thread. The net is trimmed away from the edge as the stitching progresses.

Limerick cannot be imitated by machine since its softness and delicacy and characteristic outlining are inappropriate. However, darning on net by machine is attractive, and reference to typical Limerick designs may well be worthwhile. The design may be drawn on fine tissue to back the net in the tambour frame or it may be worked free-hand. The needle should be fine and very sharp. A darned outline is usual, but whip stitch produces a variable texture, and cable stitch can be controlled to produce a comparatively smooth outline. The tissue drawing is torn away or washed out after the stitching is done.

Bibliography
Boyle; Cole; Lovesey; Pethebridge; Wardle

Collections
UK Gawthorpe Hall, Burnley; Colchester and Essex Museum; Moravian Museum, Leeds; Victoria and Albert Museum, London; Luton Museum; Ulster Folk and Transport Museum
Eire National Museum of Ireland, Dublin

LINEN

Yarn, thread or fabric made from flax, plants of the linum family. The cultivation of flax was staple to the economies of several great civilizations, especially that of Egypt, which traded linen products in exchange for cedar from Tyre and Sidon. Animal fibres were considered unclean and religiously undesirable, and so linen was needed for all ceremonial and expensive textiles, and worn by priests and by the dead.

Linen was once grown in most countries and was the earliest vegetable fibre to be used commercially for yarn. It is obtained by a lengthy process from the stem of the plant, giving long lustrous fibres which lack elasticity but

Linen: Russian tablecloth, nineteenth-century. Blues on grey. The pulled border is 4 cm (1½ in.) wide

Linen: sleeve of Croatian hemp blouse with rich pleating and panels of pulled and overcast fillings enclosed by scalloped buttonholing. Lace stitch fillings occupy the main panels. (*Bankfield Museum*) ▼

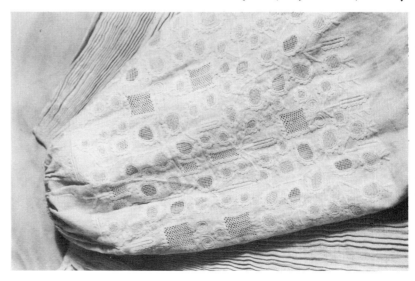

are extremely strong, hardwearing even when quite loosely spun. It is said that weight for weight it is stronger than steel and much more durable. Woven linens made over 5000 years ago are still in existence, and linens made hundreds of years ago are still quite serviceable. Individual fibres are brittle and wiry and less even than other natural ones. They conduct heat and absorb moisture, but accept dye with reluctance. Combined with synthetic yarns they have great advantages, particularly for wear, and the traditional admixture with silk produces fabric of a most attractive quality. The finest line fibres are selected from the short tow ones, and it is these which are spun for the best fabrics. Good flax comes from Egypt, France, Holland and Ireland. It is not easily grown in England. In 1791 an Act allowed a subsidy of four pence for every stone of home-grown flax. The Earl of Strafford, Lord Lieutenant of Ireland, introduced flax there in 1633.

Always the most widely used ground for embroidery throughout the western world, the cloth is texturally satisfying and invites decoration. Those which are closely woven for maximum endurance are too difficult to work on, and those which are attractively slubbed must be avoided for even, repetitive stitchery. All linen stretches, especially in wear. Historical garments are usually layered, and stitched with all-over patterns or quilting, and modern ones are lined. Many linen embroidery fabrics are specially woven to fulfil counted thread stitching purposes of various kinds. The finest linen fabric was perhaps that produced for the making of babies' bonnets during the height of *Ayrshire work*. Many mixtures and synthetics are sold as embroidery linens and so the term linen has come to include them in that context. It must also be remembered that the term can be used to describe household textiles collectively, as table linens, undergarments, trousseaux and dowries. For this reason misconceptions arise in translations and transcriptions.

Bibliography
Bellinger; Campbell; Hodges; Marks; Moore

LINEN GROUNDS AND WORKING THREADS

Most counted stitchery requires a smoothly spun single tabby weave of open texture known as evenweave. There are many varieties of finish, lustre, yarn, colour and count. Some, loosely described as Celtic cloth, crash and linen embroidery cloth are too variable for strict definition.

Aida is a white, polished linen or jute evenweave, usually with both warp and weft tabby woven in groups of four, the weft interlocking in pairs to produce a texture like fine huckaback or binca. It is fairly easy to count since the interstices are well defined, with nine to 2.5 cm (1 in.).

Cambric is a white, soft, translucent, openly woven linen with a fine, uneven yarn, numbering about 60 to 2.5 cm (1 in.). Fine white and coloured linens differ from cambric in that they have a heavier yarn and therefore more body. They are distinguished from fine cottons only in their lustre.

The term canvas is used for those fabrics of any fibre which are tightly spun and firmly woven with space between the yarns. Linen canvas are usually referred to as *coin net* or congress fabric. They are grey, unbleached or sometimes coloured. Congress has bias stretch and must be carefully framed. Winchester canvas is softer, coarser and more like jute, designed especially for making church kneelers, with 18 yarns per 2.5 cm (1 in.).

Ducks, drills and druggets, once known collectively as Barnsley linens, are closely woven, unbleached and lustrous. They were used for *smocking* and, together with twill, crash and softer Celtic cloth, are the reminders of hand-loom weaving and the embroidery of ordinary people.

Glamis and Glenshee are lustrous, coarse, quality linens with 16 to 29 yarns per 2.5 cm (1 in.), in natural and some colours. They are usually evenly woven and easy to count, the most popular of linen grounds.

Hardanger is a flat linen or jute evenweave with warp and weft tabby woven in pairs. It is the finest of the mutiple weaves. Despite its name, it really bears little relationship to the traditions of *Hardanger* work.

A form of huckaback is still manufactured and made up into household linens, but it is not easy to buy by the length. It is a softly woven, loosely spun ground, with regular floats of single yarns in both directions which can be picked up individually by the needle in *darning* patterns.

Heavy scrims closely resemble Glamis but they are more slubby. Very open, fine scrims are multifarious; one of the most pleasant to use and also the cheapest is the naturally coloured medium-weight one sold for polishing windows. Many scrims, particularly the heavier ones, are dressed to make them stiff, and it will be necessary to wash the dressing out before drawn thread or drawn fabric can be worked. They are unbleached, white or coloured.

Working threads in linen are limited to a few ranges of very similar softly spun two-ply or single ply, usually Danish, linen lace threads, and a few specialized ones such as tailor's buttonholing. Colour ranges are limited but lustrous and very beautiful. Some were once called 'flourishing thread' or 'lin floche'. Finer lace threads, suitable for many forms of white work, are sold in a range of weights with some variation in twist.

LINEN LACE WORK

See *Ruskin work*

LINSEY-WOOLSEY (lynsy wolsye)

A colonial American household staple fabric spun and woven at home. It was stiff, serviceable, hard-wearing and versatile. It responded to the indigo dye so popular in eighteenth-century America, and was frequently used for quilts, bed covers and valances, either pieced or patterned with blue resist. It was often embroidered with crewels. Several authorities claim origins for it in the Lindsey area of South Humberside in England or in a similarly named village in Suffolk, and it is described as being all wool, wool and silk, a wool weft on a cotton warp and a wool weft on a linen one.

LOG CABIN

See *Applied patchwork*

worked in manageable sections which are joined later. The presser foot or the darning foot can be used to quilt expansive areas and varieties of *applied patchwork* can be successfully adapted to machine stitchery. Ribbons and braids can be stitched to a ground by guiding them beneath the presser foot. *Raised appliqué* and applied *flowers* are more possibilities.

Bibliography

Benson 1946, 1952; Butler; Clucas; Cooper; Crompton; Gray; Higgins; Osler; Swift

MADEIRA

The technique of *broderie anglaise* was developed to satisfy the tourist trade in Madeira around the 1870s. It was worked on fine linen, crêpe de chine, lawn and heavy Japanese silk for blouses and costume accessories. The only change it underwent was the slightly more extensive use of surface stitchery than that which was gradually being added in Britain. In Madeira, the working thread was often of a pale greenish-blue rather than white. The style is virtually indistinguishable from what was known as Swiss work, but it tends to be more modest, the floral

MACHINE EMBROIDERY

Machine embroidery began as an imitation of hand embroidery and designs were indistinguishable. The machine could successfully copy oversewing, satin stitch and linear surface stitchery, but it could neither knot nor loop, so needlepoint techniques had to be achieved with netting, and buttonholing and needleweaving with narrow bands of satin stitch. Multiple machines still almost entirely imitate hand embroidery. A great deal of tourist trade embroidery is now done by machine. Even the superbly formal naturalism of Japanese kimono stitchery is now frequently copied by machine at all but the most expensive end of the market.

Free machine embroidery is discussed as a separate entry.

Single-head machine embroidery is now widely recognized as an additional technique of construction and surface enrichment, neither imitative of nor competitive with hand embroidery. Using simple sewing techniques, materials can be applied one to another on an elaborate scale and large areas can be worked with comparative ease. Non-fraying materials can be stitched down with a straight stitch, others can be backed with bonding, bound with braids, or formed into separate constructions with their own turned hems. Large areas can be

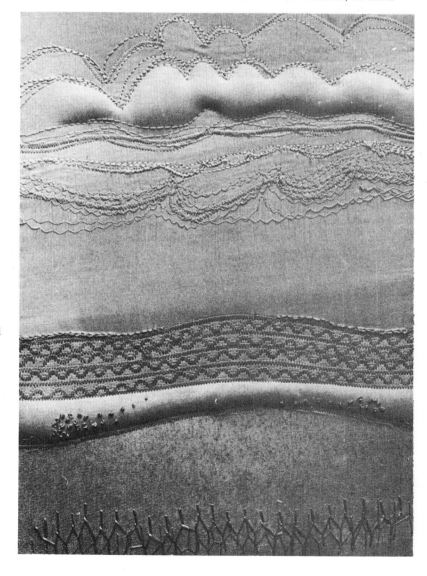

Machine embroidery: sprayed ground with free and automatic patterns and some hand stitchery. Made by Lynda Colt

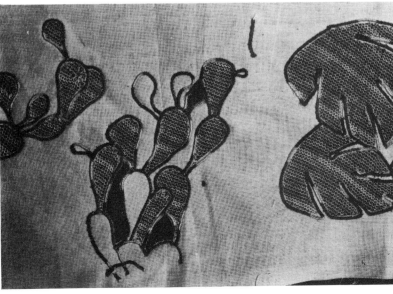

Machine embroidery: Singer touch-and-sew chain stitch. Deep pink, blue and grey on white sail-cloth. 25 × 18 cm (10 × 7 in.). (*Manchester Polytechnic*)

forms comparatively sparse and conservative. The *Home Lovers' Encyclopaedia* says Madeira had groups of round eyelets only whereas broderie anglaise had ovals and rounds.

MALTESE EMBROIDERY

Small tufted tassels formed of a thick soft cotton thread, tied into a strong ground to form simple patterns. The Island of Malta produced a variety of textiles to satisfy the tourist trade in the late nineteenth century. This spaced tufting technique occurs in early Coptic weaving.

Bibliography
de Dillmont

MALTESE SILK (horsetail, sewings)

A heavily twisted, fine silk thread used conventionally to couch jap gold or silver. It must be waxed.

MANILA WORK

See *Piña cloth embroidery*

MARSEILLES QUILTS

All-white corded quilts made without continuous filling. A filling was introduced after stitching had been completed by forcing cotton yarn or wadding through the muslin backing into selected areas of the pattern. The term Marseilles quilts probably did not apply until the importation of machine-woven copies began to satisfy the fashion for *corded quilting*.

MELON SEED EMBROIDERY

Not to be confused with cucumber seed pattern which belongs to *broderie anglaise*. Several embroideries survive from around 1880 which employ small

Machine embroidery: multi-coloured thread on white cotton, cut away to show knitted backing. The 121 allows radiating stitches to be controlled so that they always lie in a horizontal position to the direction of the stitched line. Sample detail 20 × 15 cm (8 × 6 in.). (*Manchester Polytechnic*)

METAL THREADS

The techniques of *metal thread work* are discussed under that entry.

The use of metal threads is as old as the arts of the goldsmith and the weaver. Virtually pure gold beaten into thin sheets, known as aurum battatum, was pared in extremely thin strips. It was sufficiently malleable to work into warps, stitch through open weaves and wind around a silk core to couch on to the fabric.

Threads of beaten gold found in the Taplow Barrow (Buckinghamshire) belong to the late sixth or early seventh century, and there are parallels from several other sites of the same period. They are 2.5 mm ($\frac{1}{10}$ in.) wide. Later, solid gold strips beaten much thinner were wound round a silk core to form the kind of thread from which *Saint Cuthbert's vestments* were made. The gold sheet for the thread on these vestments is just 0.25 mm ($\frac{1}{100}$ in.) thick and cut into strips which are between 2 mm ($\frac{1}{12}$ in.) and 3 mm ($\frac{1}{10}$ in.) wide. It is clear that both cutting

Machine embroidery: spray-dyed green and gold appliqué, wide satin stitch and tufting. Detail 33 × 25 cm (13 × 10 in.). (*Manchester Polytechnic*)

Machine embroidery: Schiffli multiple and Cornely chain stitch. Blue jubilee spots on blue cotton. 25 × 20 cm (10 × 8 in.). Made by Christine Hall, Manchester Polytechnic

seeds as the main feature. Seeds of many kinds are used in tribal costume and body decoration, and feature from time to time on free surface stitchery.

Vegetable material cannot be pierced once it has dried. Seeds must be strung on a waxed linen thread, washed if they are sticky, and dried before use. If it is intended to dye pale ones, partial drying before being simmered in a hot dye bath will assist saturation of the colour. Polishing or waxing helps to preserve them and makes them pleasant to use. Because of their shape, variable directional patterns can be achieved by threading melon seeds on to attractive yarns and using them for continuous couching, looped stitchery or knitting. Dried without perforations, they can be applied to a ground by *free machine embroidery* under translucent fabrics.

Metal threads: bodice, raised work on black silk, 1670–80 (*Nottingham Museum. Photograph: Layland-Ross*)

Metal threads: purl, twist and jap on black velvet. Panel detail 13 × 16 cm (5 × 6½ in.). (*Collection P.M. Thornber*)

knew it as Venice gold.

Little is known about how gold thread was made. Wire can be drawn, beaten and cut, just as plate can be reworked into other forms, and the process may not always be deduced from examination of the products. With or without the use of mechanical aids the craftsmanship has always been just as precise as that of contemporary jewellers. Modern gold wire is formed by first moulding, annealing and forging a silver bar about 75 cm (29 in.) in length. The bar is drawn to about 150 cm (59 in.) and polished to accept the gold foil which is wrapped around it. After burnishing, the bar is drawn through progressively smaller holes until the required gauge of wire is produced. Very fine wire is formed and polished at high speeds on diamond dies. That intended to make jap or other wound threads is flatted through rollers and then spun onto silk or synthetic yarn core. The metal content is carefully controlled for maximum beauty and strength.

Jap gold, the modern equivalent of aurum battatum, once had a higher percentage of precious metal than controlled Admiralty requirements, but it has been largely overtaken by plated alloys and by synthetics. Its colour varies from pale, almost greenish hues

and winding the metal was entirely done by hand, since the distribution of the spirals varies to accommodate the width of the strip. The completed thread is just over 1 mm ($\frac{1}{20}$ in.) thick.

The alternative to aurum battatum was burnished gold. The gold leaf was reduced in thickness by being beaten between pieces of thin vellum, the interleaved layers heaped together for final thinning. This was then burnished on to animal membrane which was in turn cut into thin strips. Both this and the wound plate were known to medieval Europe as Cyprus gold, although they were probably made in several countries and merely traded from Cyprus. The Tudors

to rich deep oranges and reds. The tone is largely influenced by the colour of the silk or rayon core. It should always be couched, but even from the purely traditional aspects contrasting couchings are richly variable. Early users turned the gold at any drawn line, so producing gleaming ridges of curved gold at either side of the linear stitches. Later workers laid the gold continuously and worked lines over it, giving a glossy smoothness. The medieval craftsmen usually couched their gold vertically, producing a rich play of light by superimposed horizontals and contrasting areas of curved couching.

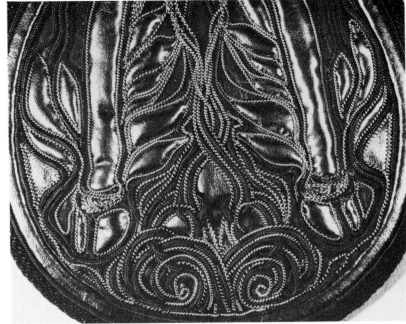

Metal threads: shaped panel, raised and overlapped coppered leather, copper purl and black braid. Detail 15 × 18 cm (6 × 7 in.). Made by Di Bates

Metal threads: nineteenth-century slipper shape. Pearl, smooth, rough and chequered purls, all silver on cream silk satin

Plate is a flat strip of metal with harsh reflecting qualities. Although on some historical pieces, especially those from Persia and Turkey, it is readily worked through various grounds, its use is now normally confined to surface couching. It occurs frequently on historical military uniform where it is expertly handled to cover moulds or *stamps*. The flat gold plate used on accessories during the latter part of the nineteenth century was known as clinquant. Plate can be textured according to the worker's needs by pressing on to a hard, indented surface. It is not attractive used alone, but is at its best combined with other threads in richly raised and textured areas.

Purls or canetilles are fine wire spiralled into a hollow spring. They are available in many varieties and sizes and under various names. Modern ones contain only a small percentage of precious metal, and so remain bright for many years. The term purl embroidery was commonly used for much metal thread work of the seventeenth century, and it also refers to some picot edgings on braiding and lace. The word bullion is used collectively for the bulky purls, and the fine ones are still occasionally called minikin. Bead, badge, Jaceron and pearl purl variously describe the thread which resembles a string of close, very glossy beads. Bright, smooth, or shine purl is a highly burnished bright wire coil, complemented by rough (or dead) which is the dullest, since its reflecting areas are very small. Bright check, or chequered purl is formed by winding the wire onto a square, sectioned bar making it flattened and crimped, so that adjacent facets along the spiral sparkle radiating lights. The wider type of purl known as frizé or frizure is made in this way, but it is usually of flattened wire. Badla is an Indian silver or silver gilt wire resembling coarse chequered purl. Check purl is made in the same way as the bright, but the reflecting areas are smaller, so breaking up the light more. Lizardine is a crimped pearly purl used to define prominences.

Passings are round and fine, durable and pliable, easy to work, with a minutely broken gleam. Their name indicates that they are intended to pass through and over the ground easily,

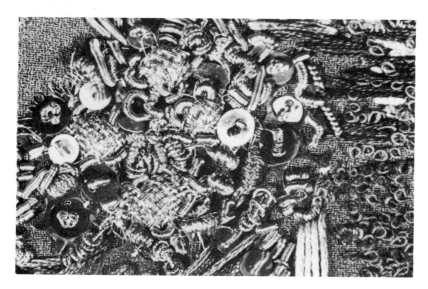

Metal threads: browns and gold, mossing, sequins, bullion knots and purls. 5 cm (2 in.). Made by Pam Pickering, Manchester Polytechnic

and they are at their best used on flatter, quieter areas for darning or perhaps drawn textures. Wavy passings have slight indentations and closely resemble a fully extended coil.

Tambours and passings are interchangeable in use. There are fine synthetic metal threads so precisely manufactured that they can be used through a sewing machine needle, so luxurious that they are indistinguishable from precious metal. Tambours were developed to be used in the tambour hook and so they possess similar qualities to passings, but are often softer.

Crinkles, twists and cords also have overlapping definitions. Crinkles tend to be fatter, exaggerated examples of wavy passings, stamped or rolled with regular indentations. Twist is a finer cord of two plys or more. They are usually couched for linear work rather than being used for fillings. Cords can be very heavy, and some are suitable only for accessories rather than the embroidery itself. They are couched by slipping a thread between the twists, and their weight will often need firm back stitches, especially at turnings. All plied thread may be untwisted for the separate use of individual strands.

Gimp or guimp consists of flattened spirals of wire traditionally used for edging. Crimped gimp gives a miniature undulating line. Some finer metal edgings are still manufactured under the name of gimp.

Flat metal braidings and ribbons are known as lace, and sometimes as orris lace. They may be wide or narrow and are often elaborately woven with complex Jacquard patterning. Russia braid and soutache are also available in many weights and kinds. They can be couched down in interlacing or linear patterns, used as outlines, or sewn as a foundation for decorative stitchery.

Metal threads are available in many finishes. The introduction of synthetics, coatings and platings has improved them and made them more versatile. The content and manufacture of imported threads is not controlled and they should be used only where durability is not important. Synthetic twists bonded with coloured rayons or coils around stiffened wire cores offer fresh possibilities.

Bibliography
Battiscombe; Birdwood; Christie 1938; Dawson; Dean 1968, 1977; Glover; Hodges; Lambert; Simpson; Whiting; Wild

Collection
USA   Metropolitan Museum of Art, New York

METAL THREAD WORK

The use of precious metal alloys or synthetic equivalents, either alone or with other working threads. It occurs almost universally, and throughout the history of leather, felt and textile decoration. There are many kinds of *metal threads* and endless ways in which they can be used.

Precious metals are an expression of wealth and opulence. Rich textiles are reserved for leisure and festive occasions, and costly metals occur on everyday garments only where society demands that status is noted or substance reflected in dress. In many civilizations there were court embroidery workshops and incumbent designers and broderers attached to larger households, either wholly maintained by them or partly commercially based. In communities where heavily decorated garments were fashionable, thriving workshops continued well into the twentieth century. These were ideal conditions in which to master the skills of working with gold and silver, and so the elaborate use of metals on clothing, animal trappings and ceremonial textiles has come to be regarded as professional and specialized.

Archaeological records demonstrate the sophisticated working of metal threads from the earliest Byzantine influences. *Saint Cuthbert's vestments* are indicative of the standard which existed in Europe and the Mediterranean countries during the Dark Ages. By the twelfth-century *opus anglicanum* was becoming dominant, and many pieces of importance are contained in major collections. With the Reformation and the advance of humanistic thought embroidery became secular rather than religious. Lavish gold grounds providing heavenly settings gave way to landscape and representations of the natural world.

Metal thread embroidery now offers a rich and expressive medium, and a wealth of suitable grounds and threads. It extends throughout religious and ceremonial embroidery both professional and amateur, through military and heraldic regalia, and into expensive fashion and ethnic costume. The technology applied to metal threads has made them even more beautiful and durable. The multiple reflection of light amongst their

Metal thread work: Jubilee cope, appliqué, surface stitchery and metal threads. Made by Beryl Dean, M.B.E. (*Photograph: Millar and Harris*)

Metal thread work: Persian, eighteenth-century, cream silk ground, pattern-couched fillings of fine passings, and red and blue silk. Mat 33 × 46 cm (13 × 18 in.)

surfaces can be compounded by both simple and intricate uses, and varying depth and directional flow. Skill in the handling and use of the threads is essential, and this takes time and practice.

Initial decisions about design will include the general organization of an extensive piece and the making-up methods involved. Design making for ecclesiastical work may be largely dictated by function and setting, and the obligatory use of specific symbols. Since gold work is so time consuming, design should be precisely organised, although some details such as graded fillings or colour changes may be determined as work progresses. Allowance must be made for the fact that the weight of metal thread work, especially where it is padded, will affect the shape and movement of the ground fabric. Positioning should be considered in relation to function and wear. The prick and pounce method of *transferring designs* is usually the most appropriate.

raising thread made specially for the purpose can sometimes still be found. String can be bought coloured, but some workers prefer to dye their own with acid-free dyes. Paddings used beneath purling on regalia vary from thin yellow kersey to dense unbleached felt. Motifs are further raised when completed by mounting over thick, rag-waste felting on to a final backing, using linen lacing stitches across the back.

Several kinds of *needles* are useful, particularly crewel for sewing, chenille for threading ends through, and a packing needle. Those a little too large are preferable to those which damage the working thread by dragging it through too restrictive a hole. Purls are threaded with long egg-eyed needles. A mellore, a short metal tool with one pointed end and one spatula-shaped end, is used to manipulate the

Metal thread work: gold purls and pearl beads on cream satin. Bag 18 cm (7 in.)

Metal thread work: sampler on linen, appliqué and slips. Detail 30 × 23 cm (12 × 9 in.). (*Lancaster Museum*)

Almost all metal thread embroidery is worked through both ground and backing to give support and sometimes weight. Linen, or a firm substitute, of the correct weight for the embroidery, is the usual choice for a backing. Badges and emblems are worked on black flax specially prepared with gum. Experiments with hanging and draping the backing with the ground, together with experience and handling of finished embroideries will help to make the correct choice.

Many grounds and applied materials have their uses and it would be limiting to be specific. Consideration must be given to the life expectancy of the finished embroidery, particularly if it is intended for wear, in relationship to the expense of the metal and the working time involved. This consideration should lead to the use of strong, fast-dyed materials which do not easily attract dust. Complex weaves or patterns need care from the design point of view and knits or stretch fabrics, even if applied only in small surface areas, may well present considerable difficulty.

Modern synthetic threads are now

in common use for couching, although the traditional choice is Maltese silk. Beeswaxing also seems to have been dispensed with, although those who prefer silk still prepare each length by waxing. Varying thicknesses of hard cotton string may be needed for padding metal threads and embroidery yarns. Other, softer yarns can be used for padding to give quite different undulations. A yarn called yellow

metal thread, and tweezers are useful. Some workers use two thimbles, one for each middle finger. A pair of straight scissors with strong, sharp points will be needed for the stitchery. To contain the purls, a compartmented tray with very shallow sides and depressions can be constructed from a slim piece of natural, smooth wood. The tray should be lined with substantial baize, velvet or felt glued

achieve a smoothly manipulated curve is best. The jap should be wound double onto a spindle or reel made specially for the purpose, or on to a firm roll of felt.

Start a working length of thread with a small knot and two tiny stitches, using a crewel needle, in a position where it will be covered by subsequent work. Leaving about 2 cm ($\frac{3}{4}$ in.) of jap, hold the ends in place and take a stitch over both. The distance between stitches will be determined by the texture or quality of the line required, and the function of the embroidery as a durable piece. The habit of twisting the gold spiral with each stitch will soon be acquired, so that it is completely closed against the core, which should show as little as possible. The couching should always be at right angles to the jap, firm, but not so tight that it pinches the gold.

There are many ways to turn corners and angles, but the couching pattern must be maintained. A diagonal stitch is sometimes needed,

Metal thread work: King's Own Royal Lancaster Regiment dress jacket. Detail of the black cloth collar. Silver passing, rough purl and plate. (*Lancaster Museum*)

Metal thread work: King's Own Royal Lancaster Regiment gold epaulette. Several purls including wavy, wrapped passing, plate and heavy gold wire. (*Lancaster Museum*)

to it. A flat area of wood should be reserved unlined as a cutting surface. Fine pins are useful for holding small pieces of appliqué. Acid-free tissue should be used for covering worked areas of the embroidery and for storing metal threads.

Square or slate *frames* are preferred. *Framing up* must be done accurately and carefully. There are many alternatives to trestles, but comfort, a good light and an adequate surrounding surface are essentials. The same criteria apply to the use of a circular frame, which can be weighted by its edge to overhang a table.

The convention of using jap or passing in double rows has advantages and the technical skills of handling it in this way are well worth mastering. Even where a single fine line is required the use of two threads to

A bout taking down the end of couched jap. The jap is introduced singly but couched double

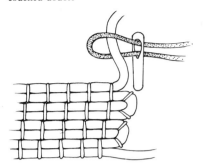

Couching metal over string. Jap gold introduced as a loop and worked double

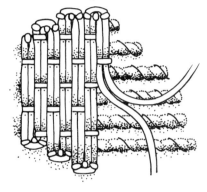

and the tension on the working thread may be such that a small back stitch is necessary to secure it before resuming the couching pattern. The mellore is used to persuade the gold into position. A similar method can be used for larger areas, the essential difference being in the starting process. The gold is couched double to the end of the row, the lower thread cut and the upper one turned. A new, single thread is introduced and couched double in company with the turned one. When the opposite end is reached the first gold is cut and the second one turned to be stitched double with a third, and so on. On very small areas the turn is made by a couching stitch over one thread of gold, and the silk is taken underneath to emerge on the opposite side where it secures the gold again so that both lines can be couched together.

The ends of the couched jap should be left on top of the work as long as possible. If they are in the way they can be tidied with tacking stitches. It

may at some point become necessary to take them through to the back before the couching is completed, in which case they can be temporarily tacked beneath finished areas (or secured with adhesive tape), so that they do not become entangled with succeeding stitchery. To take the ends through to the back of the work, use a chenille needle sufficiently large to accommodate the jap into the eye of the needle leaving a loop, and give a sharp tug to the needle from beneath the work to pull the jap through. Metal threads which are too large to be pulled through without damaging the fabric can be separated and taken down piece by piece. Another ploy which proves useful is to form a bout with a strong thread in the needle, so that the metal thread need not go through the eye at all.

The method known as bricking is commonly used for rows of filling. The couching stitches are made alternating with those in the preceding row. The needle must emerge a row's width away from the first and return angled just beneath it so that the gold is kept close. Simple patterns using straight lines and diagonals are

Metal thread work: Silver Jubilee 1977. Blue velvet ground, raised kid and satin, various purls, twists and cords, edged with heavy blue cord. 43 cm (17 in.). Made by Di Bates

achieved by the distribution of the couching threads, and colour can be introduced. The gold must be flat, and the couching stitches careful and regular. Large areas of pattern, especially where these are more complex, need guiding lines stitched or drawn on the ground. An extension of bricking, where the technique is used exclusively, is known as or nué.

Tight curves and circles are always worked from the outer edge to preserve the smoothness of the line or circumference. The gold threads can be started separately, leaving a short space between. For the first row stitches alternate, one being taken over both gold threads, the next taken over the inner thread alone. Adjustments to spacing must be considered as the inside of a curve or the centre of a circle is approached. No two stitches should coincide.

Pointed shapes or solid couching are achieved by dovetailing the gold. Only

Metal thread work: Silver Jubilee 1977.
Detail 18 × 20 cm (7 × 8 in.)

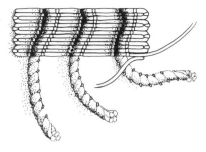

Couching metal over string. Jap gold introduced single and worked single, in two journey lengths

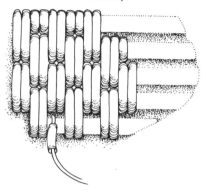

Purl couched over felt strips

the outer thread describes the point, the inner one being cut and taken down later very close to the angle of the outer one. The inner one is reintroduced for the other side, leaving an end. Succeeding rows are treated in the same way until the shape is filled. The ends are then taken down one by one, starting at the point, with a single thread filling the centre piece.

String is very versatile as a foundation for padding jap or purling. A smooth cotton one is best, in varying thicknesses. Leaving a short end, it should be sewn down in place under very slight tension, without causing the ground to pucker. The needle must come up through the ground and down through the string from side to side. Thick yarns other than string are worth trying. Spaces can be left between the rows of gold, and other metals, yarns and beads introduced to cover the string.

Basket pattern is made over a string foundation. The string is sewn down firmly in regular rows, each spaced its own width from the last. Double rows of jap travelling in the other direction are fastened with a double stitch and passed over two strings, secured very firmly in each second valley until the end of the area is reached. This double row is repeated. Then, starting with a third row, the gold passes over one string only, and then over two, so that couching stitches are in alternating valleys. Lengths of purl may be used in the same way. Variable spacing and slight changes in treatment produce their own richness.

Purls are at their most suitable used over curved areas where their reflective qualities are at best advantage. Most ceremonial embroidery is purled by cutting the metal to the required length and using it like long beads picked up onto the working thread. The felted area of the cutting board is used for this purpose to support both purl and scissors, and the cut lengths are then easier to retrieve with a needle. They are placed parallel with one another across the shape to be covered. Very short lengths can be used like bullion knots, clustering a filling or powdering a ground. A smooth egg-eyed needle is necessary

for purl threading. Sometimes purl is couched across rather than being threaded, the wire coil being opened just sufficiently to allow the couching thread to slip down and disappear.

Traditionally, burden stitch consisted of just one kind of purl or jap worked alternately over rows of evenly spaced laid string. Now even richer textures are obtainable because variety is encouraged. The laid threads can vary in type, thickness, colour and spacing, as can the stitches worked over them. Purls alone are versatile, but the introduction of linen yarns, silks and synthetics has endless possibilities of colour and texture. Long stitches laid over several rows of padding can be contrasted with short ones which tightly wrap a string, intervening hollows being filled with surface stitchery. Beads can be introduced to change light qualities and depth.

The highly raised work characteristic of ceremonial military or court dress features padding over wooden or card stamps with purls.

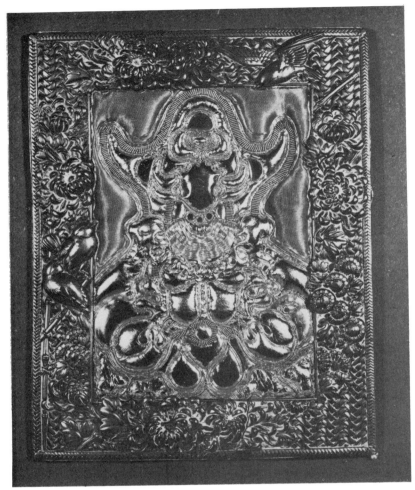

and laid work stitched into the leather. It can be padded in several ways common to the metal stitchery, and can be couched down in strips. There are synthetic alternatives.

Bibliography

Aber; Child and Colles; Cutts; Dawson; Dean 1968, 1977; de Dillmont; DeFarcy; Dirsztay; Dolby; Ellwood; Freehof and King; Henze and Filthaut; Johnstone 1967; Lawson; Norris; Roeder; Symonds and Preece

Collections

UK Bowes Museum, Barnard Castle; Museum of Costume, Bath; Durham Cathedral; Bankfield Museum, Halifax; Lancaster City Council Museum; Imperial War Museum, London; Jewish Museum in London; National Army Museum, London; St Paul's Cathedral Treasury, London; Victoria and Albert Museum, London; Whitworth Art Gallery, Manchester;

Metal thread work: Steel Queen. Silvers on gun metal with a steel frame. Raised purl, passing, kid and miralon. 18 × 23 cm (7 × 9 in.). Made by Di Bates

Metal thread work: Indian slippers, twentieth-century, passing on leather

Formal, and appropriate to this function, it does not readily lend itself to less stereotyped embroidery. Experiments using linen-covered wooden supports are a useful practice in the manipulation of thread, and may contribute valuable ideas. *Raised appliqué* offers another range of subtleties. Small card cuttings can be pasted or sewn to the ground, and purl laid from side to side to make a precise raised plateau. Lettering is traditionally done in this way. Exciting surfaces can be constructed by taking very long lines of couching over repetitive shapes of varying thicknesses to form a laid area. This process, sometimes confused with *or nué*, is occasionally called Italian work.

Traditionally, applied pieces were mounted on card and pasted, with severe couched lines around them.

Whilst this kind of formal treatment may sometimes be appropriate, greater freedom and richness are achieved with broken edges, particularly on velvet grounds. Where a difficult ground fabric is encountered it is often necessary to make *slips* matching the grains, cutting them out and applying them to the ground without causing distortion. The position of the slip to be applied must be marked on the stretched ground. The frame containing it must be slackened and the piece cut out, allowing turnings. Applying the embroidery in position, the slip should be pinned and then tacked, and finally oversewn or slip stitched closely.

Metallic kid should be used in small areas only, unless a dominant reflective field is needed. Its harsh, glassy quality can be softened with couched

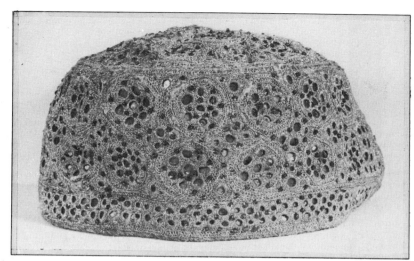

Metal thread work: hat from Afghanistan. Shisha pieces revealed by eyelets. Pale gold and pink beads. (*Leeds Museum*)

Nottingham Museum
USA   Jewish Museum, New York; Metropolitan Museum of Art, New York
Hungary   Hungarian National Museum, Budapest
India   Calico Museum of Textiles, Ahmedabad
Israel   Israel Museum, Jerusalem

MEXICAN DRAWN WORK

See *Tenerife embroidery*

MICA

Crudely trimmed pieces of mica, a transparent, flexible mirror-like mineral laminate, were used to decorate Tudor and Stuart *stump work* gloves and bookbindings, and in the eighteenth century were a favourite decoration on men's waistcoats. They appear on Eastern embroideries until the twentieth century, but were eventually overtaken entirely by *shisha*.

MIRRORGLASS

See *Shisha*

MITREING CORNERS

The proper folding and finishing of right-angled corners of the ground, associated particularly with counted work such as *drawn fabric, drawn thread* and *hemstitching*. Mitreing is

designed to form a flat, regular, clearly defined right-angle turned onto the right side of the work. The exact turn of the hem and the position of any hemstitching will have been determined previously in preparation for the worked embroidery. The hem may already be overcast to prevent fraying, and this can in most cases be left in.

Turn the folds of the hem and crease them, following the yarn of the ground. Unfold the hem and fold over the corner to form a right-angled triangle, with the actual corner of the finished hem falling exactly mid-way on the hypotenuse. Unfold the triangle and cut away the unwanted ground just outside this last creased line, allowing for fraying but sufficiently

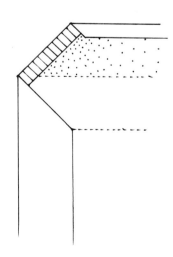

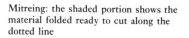

Mitreing: the shaded portion shows the material folded ready to cut along the dotted line

trimmed to avoid bulk in the hem. Fold the corner diagonally, opposing the direction of the previous line, with the actual corner of the finished hem on the fold. Back stitch down the fold from the corner, leaving unstitched the final portion for the first turning of the hem. Unfold, open out the seam and reverse the corner. Tuck under and crease the first turning of the hem and tack carefully in place, conforming to any drawn border.

Corners are sometimes mitred without the preparatory line of stitching, but this method is less able to withstand wear and washing.

MIXED MEDIA

The accomplishment of skills peripheral to the central discipline has lately been a teaching objective. Art generally has encompassed the man-made as well as the natural world and explored new and urban sensitivities. Embroidery has become one of the areas subject to the art/craft conflict. As attitudes have broadened it is no longer considered valuable or essential to devote thousands of hours to painstaking stitchery. Techniques such as integral drawing, printing, photography and collage have become acceptable. The use of mixed techniques is now commonly accepted, too, so that quilting and cutwork, for example, can happily be used on one piece. Exploration and exploitation of embroidery methods together with the combined use of other expressive techniques has led to a refreshing spontaneity in an otherwise very deliberate medium.

Bibliography
Newland; Proud; Seyd

MOLA WORK

See *San Blas appliqué*

MORAVIAN EMBROIDERY

The Moravian Church was founded in Bohemia in 1457 and spread to other European countries and to America. A feature of Moravian communities was their ability to organize craftsmanship and expertise not only for their own use but to satisfy commercial markets. The girls and married women lived together and were educated in the crafts, bringing their national influences and integrating them with local ones wherever they settled. Thus the sect has become identified with a number of forms of embroidery.

In America the settlement at Bethlehem was one of the earliest, and it became so influential that a great deal of eighteenth- and nineteenth-century embroidery in the United States is known as Moravian work. *Aerophane* and ribbon work, romantic and Biblical crewel pictures, and family portraiture and mourning pieces were made in abundance. Ayrshire and white work, known generally as French work, also flourished. 'Everything was embroidered; gowns, from the belt to the lower hem, finished with scalloped and sprigged ruffles in the same delicate workmanship, were everyday summer wear. . . . Small articles, like collars, capes and pelerines, were almost entirely covered with the most exquisite tracery of leaf and flower, a perfect frostwork of delicate stitchery'. (Wheeler).

Many Moravians settled in Ireland in the eighteenth-century, contributing their expertise to the development of *Carrickmacross*, *Limerick* and *Mountmellick*. The Gracehill settlement at Ballymena in Northern Ireland made Ayrshire work in a wide variety of designs.

The settlement at Fulneck in Yorkshire was begun in 1743. The sisters there had numerous commercially viable crafts among their accomplishments, including button making, and many forms of lace and white work.

A fine, white, nine-stranded cotton was once manufactured under the name of Moravian.

Bibliography
Nylander; Ring; Wheeler

Collection
UK   The Moravian Museum, Fulneck

Moravian: embroidery from Vlčor district, Uher Brod. Orange with edges of black hearts, and plate beneath the needleweaving. 8 cm (3 in.) wide (*Bankfield Museum*)

MOUNTMELLICK

A coarse and durable form of raised surface stitchery done with white knitting cotton on white satin jean. Mountmellick is the only form of Irish white work which has no open areas. It is characterized by a slightly lustrous ground encrusted with non-lustrous stitch textures and surrounded by a heavy knotted fringe of the same thread. It has raised satin stitch flowers, French knot blackberries, bullion knot ears of wheat, passion flowers, acorns and ferns.

Mountmellick is in Queen's County near Waterford. At the time of mechanization new work had to be found for those women and children who had previously been employed in the cotton and woollen industries. One account states that Mountmellick was introduced by the Society of Friends and spread to neighbouring convent schools, and it was certainly adapted by the Moravians and used for finer work on children's clothes. Mrs Johanna Carter is said to have invented it, and it was she who set up a school and organized the production of household goods, particularly bedspreads. White and creamy counterpanes in satin stitchery and *knotted work* are strongly associated with the Irish tradition.

As a style, Mountmellick became popular with Victorian needlewomen, and gradually became sprawling in

design and debased by the introduction of pale colour. It reappeared as part of the promotion of art needlework towards the end of the nineteenth century, but probably had no commercial significance.

Bibliography
Leach and Cartwright; Thomas 1936

Mountmellick: nineteenth-century soft white cotton on white satin jean, with a knotted and twisted fringe. 25 × 30 cm (10 × 12 in.)

MUSLIN

A fine, translucent, openly spun cotton. Marco Polo said that 'mosolins' were made of gold and silver and came from Mosul in Turkey. The Arab peoples used the term 'maucilli' for fine, openly spun cotton weaves, and many of these may well have had metal threads incorporated in the weft or embroidered as darned or drawn fabric borders. By the Middle Ages a strong cotton cloth was made at Mosul, but indications are that this was heavy and durable.

Muslin was manufactured in Europe and America from the late eighteenth century. It was probably at its height of fashion in the West during the Georgian period for dresses and accessories and for *Ayrshire*.

Chamber's Cyclopaedia of 1788 gives varieties of muslin as betelles, tarnatans, mulmuls, tanjeebs, terrindams and doreas. *Chikan* and Dacca muslins from India have poetic names like evening dew, running water and woven air.

Bibliography
Fairholt

Collections
UK Museum of Costume, Bath; Platt Hall, Manchester

NACRE WORK (mother-of-pearl work)

A Victorian innovation whereby pieces of mother-of-pearl, probably from buttonmaker's waste, were trimmed into small shapes and perforated to sew onto rich grounds. Small linear details were often added, with metal threads or silks.

Ecaille, or stamped quillwork, was in imitation of nacre work, using opened out birds' quills.

Bibliography
Caulfeild and Saward; Lambert

NAMDHAS

Wool *felt* mats with coarse wool chain stitch in characteristic curved designs produced in large quantities in Kashmir for both home and export trade. Although these felts are now associated with Indian manufacture they were probably originally imported there from more northerly territories. The word 'namdha' applied to felts with incorporated felted decoration, but has come to include those which are chain stitched. The natural coloured wool or mixture felts are produced both mechanically and by hand, then passed out to home workers or small workshops where the embroidery is done, often by children. The stereotyped sinuous foliage designs continued to command a wide market until the 1950s, when more vital animal and bird motifs and colourways were introduced by new designers. Forms are treated as solids, usually with darker outlines, the

emphasis being on spatial relationships. The work is essentially coarse and technically very simple.

Gabha rugs are similarly embroidered, but composed of shaped woollen pieces fitted together to serve as a ground.

The chain stitch technique has been extended to use on hessians with the ground almost covered, in designs resembling Gabha rugs, and the namdha designs are now used on thick cottons. Both adaptations are for export.

Bibliography
Dongerkery

NEEDLEMADE LACE

See *Lace*

NEEDLEMADE RUGS

Coarse knotting or stitchery worked in the hand with a needle, completely covering a woven foundation, usually in imitation of Oriental rugs and carpets. The knotted pile type is sometimes called Turkey work, especially when combined with areas of smooth stitchery. The smooth-faced kind is a form of *canvas work*. *Bed ruggs* or yarn sewn rugs (sometimes known as Acadian rugs since they were made in the eighteenth century by the French settlers in that area of Nova Scotia) are small coverings worked on linen in looped running stitches in homespun wools. Needlemade rugs can be made much finer than hooked or latchet-made rugs, and so offer far more opportunity for detailed pattern.

The process of stitching rugs on a felt or woven ground is ancient, and each culture, particularly those in colder climates, has its own variations. As tapestries and wall hangings were imported to Europe they were imitated in canvas work table covers and furnishings. Turkish and Middle Eastern rugs were similarly copied in looped and cut pile stitchery on woven grounds. The less wealthy, resourcefully utilizing all woven waste, used similar techniques, and developed styles appropriate to their homespun grounds and strips and scraps. By the eighteenth century these are documented both in Europe and

America as variations of *rag rugs* and bed ruggs.

Rugs take a long time to make, and the satisfying textures and glowing colours of a well designed rug made of properly considered materials make the time involved worthwhile. This does not preclude the use of synthetics and mixed yarns, but the comfortable bulk of wool, and the subtlety of even the strongest colours it absorbs from the dye bath, make its continuity of tradition difficult to deny. The matching of yarn to ground is particularly important for rug making. If the yarn is too thin for the ground, flat stitchery will not adequately cover it and tufted knotting will quickly flatten, fray and wear; if the yarn is too thick it will distort the ground and create progressive working difficulties and a misshapen finished rug. Inferior materials, either ground or yarn, are a false economy.

Open mesh canvases in linen, jute or cotton, giving $3\frac{1}{2}$ or more holes per 2.5 cm (1 in.), should be of a double weave. Plastic and nylon moulded foundations are coming into use, but their unaccommodating properties may cause friction, and therefore more wear on the working thread. Jutes, cloths which are sometimes known as Patterdale or Winchester canvases, have a closed single or double weave which is pleasant to handle but more difficult to count. It is generally advisable to work smooth-faced rugs on openly woven canvas. The jutes are excellent for pile rugs. Widths vary from 61 cm (24 in.) to 114 cm (45 in.).

There are no rules governing the thickness or weight of working threads and it is essential to experiment before estimating quantities for the whole rug. It is traditional to introduce small breaks of colour within areas of pattern, so the purchase of perfect dye-bath repeats is unimportant providing the distribution throughout the rug is uniform. On old textiles, hand-dyed yarns and threads are often uneven in colour, a feature which might be imitated to advantage. Heavy yarns are usually referred to as thrums, medium ones as Brussels thrums, and fine ones as crewel wool. It is much easier and more efficient to use several strands of thread in the needle rather than attempt to untwist

Needlemade rugs: Surrey stitched rug on
evenweave jute 91 × 61 cm (36 × 24 in.).
Glowing colours on a dark ground. Made
by Ann McNamara

threads which are too thick. Even
those of identical manufacture from
the same spinner can vary in thickness
and it may be necessary to introduce
another strand at regular intervals
along the knots or stitches to maintain
an even weight. For smooth-faced
rugs, canvas with 5 holes per 2.5 cm
(1 in.), or jute cloth with 8, will need
about 150 g (5 oz) of working thread
per 30 cm by 30 cm (per square foot).
For pile rugs, the same foundation will
need about 250 g (9 oz).

The greatest wear and tear on a rug
is at its edges. The foundation material
must, therefore, be carefully prepared.
Jute cloth is best stitched immediately
on the sewing machine through one
thickness only, with a wide zigzag and
firm tensions. Before any work is
begun on open canvas the end edges
must be dealt with to prevent fraying.
On the edge where work is to start the
canvas must be creased between the
double bars, making a hem of between
6.4 cm (2½ in.) and 2.5 cm (1 in.),
depending on the coarseness of the
canvas. The turned edge must not
interfere with the mesh, both layers
coinciding. It is secured with a
horizontal cross stitch using a waxed
linen thread, over a pair of weft yarns
of the ground. The opposite end of the
canvas should be temporarily oversewn
so that the extent of the pattern can be
judged as the work approaches it, and
the edge then turned appropriately in
its permanent position. If the raw
points of the canvas prove irritating
they can be folded inside a wide cotton
tape stitched loosely in place. For pile
rugs the fold-over should be on the
front of the rug so that the ends of
canvas are lost in the tufts. The stitch
which produces the most successful
edge is plaited edging stitch. It is
begun at the top right of the work,
travelling three on and two back, the
needle always passing from the back to
front. The ends of jute cloth rugs are
overstitched in the same way, or
turned under and hemmed, or finished
with applied *fringes* or ravellings.

Needles should be blunt, long and
large, and the thread should slip easily
through the eye to avoid wear.

Although any canvas stitches can be
used, most workers select from
traditional ones for smooth faced rugs.
Cross stitch, French stitch, interlocking

Surrey stitch

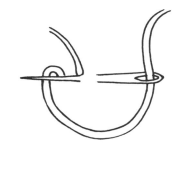
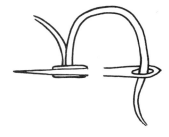
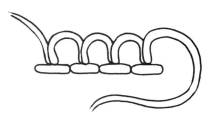

Turkey or Ghiordes knot stitch

Soumak stitch

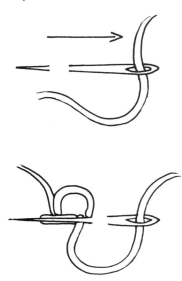
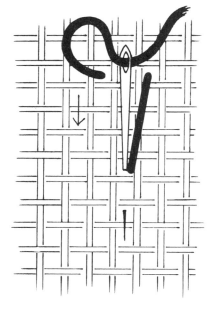
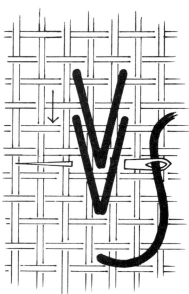

Gobelin stitch, rice stitch, *tent stitch* and Soumak stitch predominate. Soumak, used to imitate Caucasian woven rugs, is also known as Kelim, Ottoman, Spanish plait and knitting stitch. There are two stitches which produce tuft or pile, Ghiordes or Turkey knot, and Surrey stitch. Their texture is exactly the same and preference can be decided only by practice. Both produce a much shorter pile than that made with a latchet hook. The stitches must be worked closely so that when the threads are cut they support each other vertically. The pile can be trimmed and shaped if this is considered necessary, but normally minimal trimming with long, sharp shears used flat across the tufts will be sufficient.

Bibliography
Bath 1979; de Dillmont; Matthews

Collections
UK   The American Museum, Bath; Clandon Park, Dorking; Hardwick Hall, Mansfield; Norwich Cathedral; Knole House, Sevenoaks
USA   Henry Francis du Pont Winterthur Museum, Delaware; Metropolitan Museum of Art, New York

NEEDLEPAINTING (acupictura, peinture à l'aiguille)

The representation of painting in style, subject matter, composition and brush-stroke technique, whether aspiring to close resemblance of existing paintings or substantially imitating contemporary idiom.

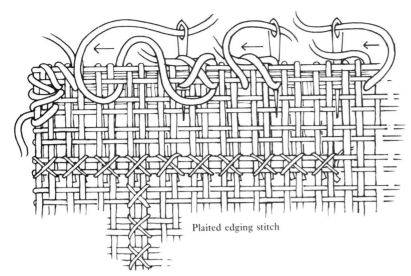
Plaited edging stitch

Like most representational and figurative media, embroidery has always had affinities with, and parallels to, the formal painting and painterly mannerisms of its day. Under patronage it was part of the function of a painter not only to design for the embroideries of the Church or the household but in many cases to draw the design out on the ground and instruct the stitchers in its proper execution.

Embroideries which are directly concerned with the balance of dense pattern against empty ground, and forms flattened in the interests of decoration, are largely uncontroversial. The expression of form in light and shade and the use of vanishing point perspective are now not only acceptable but encouraged. Since the boundaries of what is permissible in painting no longer exist, areas of textile creativity have taken over many of the conventions of naturalistic painting. Embroidery now embraces not only brush-stroke virtuosities but also the harsh linear qualities and soft spray technology associated with graphics. Attitudes fluctuate, but it is the protesters who are most articulate:

About the middle of the last century, several ladies, notably Miss Linwood, Miss Morritt of Rokeby, and Mrs Delany, copied pictures in worsteds. Some of these are wonderfully clever and even very pretty, but they are rather a painful effort of pictorial art under difficulties, than legitimate embroideries.
ALFORD 1886

The wrong method of going to work is to imitate the effect sought after by the painter. . . . Such things as perspective, light and shade or modelling of form, should all be very much simplified if not avoided, for embroidery conforms to the requirements of decoration and must not falsify the surface that it ornaments.
CHRISTIE 1928

In any case, whatever its evolution, wherever its origin, the true intention of embroidery is adventitious ornament. And, I would go so far as to say that, the moment such ornament is not adventitious, then it is not true embroidery. Due to the peculiar qualities of its media, embroidery is limited, and therefore must be kept within its limitations. In no way must it aim at effects legitimate only in other arts. It is an art which should render in the abstract natural forms, and thus find the secret of its power in presenting ornament. The very instant it attempts to actually realise or compete with nature, it loses that power, for, from the very nature of its technique it can never be pre-eminently successful as a picture, in fact, it loses in decorative effect far more than it gains in realistic representation.
CARTER 1932

NEEDLEPOINT

An indeterminate word used in widely differing contexts. It can mean embroidery as a whole or counted stitchery in particular, all fine white work with a lacy texture or needlepoint lace specifically. In America it is used to describe canvas work, crewel work, and pictorial or

decorative stitchery on a coarse scale with large stitches.

Bibliography
Ambuter; Borssuck; Fisher 1972; Hanley; Lanz and Lane 1973; Rhodes 1975; Roth

NEEDLES

The Arms of the Worshipful Company of Needlemakers have Adam and Eve as bearers: 'And the eyes of them both were opened, and they knew that they were naked; and they sewed fig leaves together, and made themselves aprons.'
GENESIS III 7

Needles of wood, bone, quill and even thorns are still in use in some societies. It seems likely that steel needles were first made in Spain, and that Continental traders brought Spanish, and later German ones to Britain. Wire drawing and needlemaking was practised in monasteries until the Reformation, after which there are records of workshops and retail shops in London, with the centre of production on Old London Bridge, which was destroyed by the Great Fire. A number of the needlemaking families moved to Warwickshire, including the Morralls, and later the Shewards. Cromwell granted a Charter in 1656, and even today most of the world's supply of needles comes from Redditch. In 1700 a horse-mill for scouring and pointing needles began at Studley.

Modern needles are made from Sheffield crucible-cast steel of various kinds, alloys being introduced for some purposes. The steel is rolled and cold-drawn, then straightened and cut into double lengths. The lengths are reheated and rotated over plates for absolute uniformity. Points are formed at each end by turning and grinding the wires. A press makes the groove and the eye, and finally separates the two needles. They are then ground, hardened and tempered, and finally scoured and polished.

In common with most skills, needlework demands a selection of good and varied tools. Betweens and the similar but larger sharps are the needles in most common use. As different kinds of embroidery are embarked upon a store of needles is built up, and the worker learns to acquire more unusual ones speculatively. Serviceable large needles of wood or bone can be made easily with an electrically driven drill and band saw.

The diameter of a needle is described by its size number, which is a standard measurement throughout, but lengths vary from the smallest betweens and beaders at 2.5 cm (1 in.) to the longest yarn darner at 8.9 cm (3½ in.). Specialist needles such as packing, sail and mattress needles may be even longer.

Ball-point needles are manufactured for both machine and hand sewing on knitted synthetics and jerseys.

Barnsley needles were once recognized as superior in quality. There is considerable evidence of steel needles being made there and in nearby Sheffield in quantity by the late sixteenth century.

Beading needles are hair-fine with long eyes and made only in the smallest diameters. They may be quite long to allow a number of beads or bugles to be threaded together. A strong thread should be chosen which can be flattened to go through the eye. Sablé (a grain of sand) bead needles were used for stitching minute Venetian beads.

Betweens, quilting needles or tailors' needles are like sharps but shorter. They encourage small, even sewing stitches and are normally available in sizes one to ten.

Blunts are even shorter than betweens with stouter points than sharps.

Calyx-eyed needles or self-threading needles are made of soft metal at the double eye which has sufficient pliability to open and close and allow a thread to be passed through.

Candlewicking needles have a thick shaft and a large eye. They may be curved or slightly widened at the point. Double-eyed needles are used for two-thread tufting.

A casing needle is like a bodkin, yarn or tape needle, and is designed to turn cording right side out.

Chenille needles, originally intended only for stitching delicate garnetted threads through open weaves, are short with very large eyes. They are available in the same sizes as tapestry needles, but have sharp points.

Crewels are like sharps and are made in similar lengths, but have a longer eye for thicker threads.

Darners are very long with large eyes for taking wool and thicker threads. The additional length enables a large hole or thinning area of fabric to be spanned before the working thread is drawn through. Most are available in alternate sizes only. Long darners are of the same diameters as darners. Wider ones are described as large yarn darners. A variation in the smaller sizes has a blunt point.

The glover's leather needle has an extra-sharp point and a three-sided shaft to cut rather than tear. It is made in small sizes for fine leather.

Mattress needles have an eye at one end and points at both. They are about 18 cm (7 in.) long and are used for stitching through thick layers of padding for attaching buttons to mattresses. They can be used for *stobbed quilts*.

Netting needles are often waisted, with a split or forked eye at either end. A long thread is wound in a figure-of-eight motion from one end to the other.

Pearl needles are probably no longer available in their original form of a pliable and very fine brass wire about 7.6 cm (3 in.) long. Tiny oyster seed pearls were drilled with a very small perforation. Imitation ones also need a fine needle and thin sewing thread.

A quilting needle is a short sharp in size seven or eight.

Sharps are ordinary sewing needles, longer than betweens but in the same sizes. Those larger than betweens may be referred to as sadlers' quilting needles. They are designed for use through several layers, like furnishing construction and outerwear tailoring.

Straws or milliners' needles are slightly longer than sharps, with round eyes. They are particularly useful for smocking. There are wider ones with blunt points called harness needles.

Tapestry or rug needles have a large eye, and a blunt point that does not split ground yarns or working threads.

Whitechapel (or Chapple, 1738) needles seem to have been much sought after for their quality and resistance to rust.

The yarn needle or bodkin is always large but very variable. Bodkins may

be round or flat, and may have two eyes, a large and a small, for adequate control of varying thicknesses of thread. The yarn needle is like a long tapestry, but it may have a shaped, flattened or curved point which is sometimes quite sharp.

Bibliography
British Needles; Whiting

NEEDLEWEAVING

The decorative replacement, in the form of a working thread, of yarns withdrawn in one direction from a woven fabric. Lewis Day defined it as '. . . a sort of tapestry with the needle, just as . . . tapestry itself may be described as a sort of embroidery with the shuttle.' Widely regarded as a white or self-coloured technique suitable for table linen, it is still used

Needleweaving: green and blue mercerised cotton on orange linen. Drawn border 2.5 cm (1 in.) wide

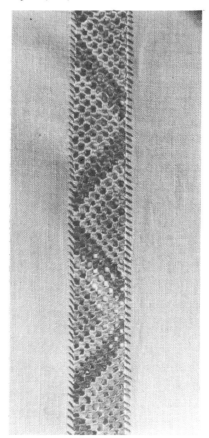

Above: Collapsible box decorated throughout with mirrors, shisha, beading and tassels. Made by Belinda Sufrin. *(Photo: David Pimlott)*

Above right: Romania, sleeve cuff. Close silk and couched metal on thick cotton

Right: Bokhara, portion of a curtain. Twisted silk on fine linen. 40 x 38 cm (16 x 15 in.)

Leek work, nineteenth century. Detail of *Prayer of Thanks* by Mrs Warren. *(The Parish Church of All Saints, Leek)*

us Anglicanum, detail of frontal. *(By permission of Chipping Campden*
urch and Photo Precision Limited, Huntingdon)

North-west Indian phulkari work wedding shawl, *c.* 1850. *(Photo: Joss Graham Oriental Textiles, London)*

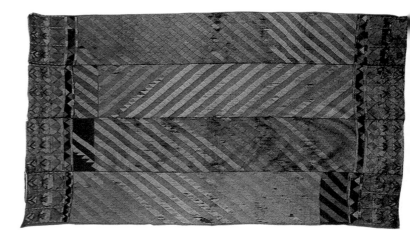

Indian, from Sindh. Late nineteenth-century buttonhole and chain stitch. Detail of all-over stitchery, 51 x 36 mm (20 x 14 in.)

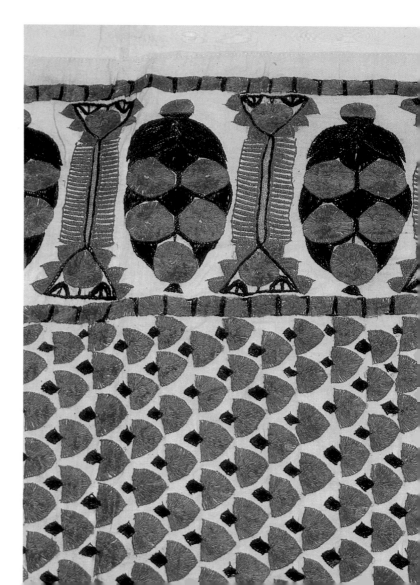

Opposite: Saint Cuthbert's vestments. Tenth-century maniple, John the Evangelist. *(By permission of the Dean and Chapter of Durham)*

Above: Panel II of the Overlord Embroidery,
showing the British 3rd Division and the 27th
Armoured Brigade awaiting the order to sail.
The Embroidery is 82.9 metres (272 feet) long,
consisting of 34 panels each 2.43 metres (8 feet)
long. Designed by Sandra Lawrence and made
by the Royal School of Needlework, it is housed
in the Overlord Gallery at Whitbread and
Company in Chiswell Street, London EC1

Right: Woman's doublet, 1610–20. (*Bath
Museum of Costume*)

Opposite: Sampler with boxers, *c.* 1800. Wool
on soft open linen. 30 x 27 cm (12 x 10½in.)

Wire-wrapped silk and velvet coils and amethyst pebbles, glass, fabric and maiolica flowers, copper and plastic purls, copper wire cones and metal pendants. 18 x 20 cm (7 x 8 in.)

Encroach. Joined fabric strips bleached and stitched. Detail, 12 x 17 cm (5 x 7 in.) Made by Anne Young

on European costume in primary colours.

The weave may be withdrawn in regular blocks or asymmetrical solids and holes. The distribution of the stitchery may be in any position across the shape to be woven, holes being achieved by turns in the working thread. Stitched weaving may be in tabby and twill, in counted chevrons and blocks, or in laced clusters made with whipping or single overcasting stitches which interlock one with another. Yarns need not be withdrawn in regular borders; they can be staggered or withdrawn in groups or over an irregular form. Needleweaving can be worked over wide satin stitch floats as a surface stitch without withdrawing yarn from the ground. The stitches occur in many other forms of open work and almost all *lace*. It is an excellent technique for experiment since stitchery of textural value may be produced on almost any woven or non-woven ground, and with almost any material adapted as a working thread.

The history of needleweaving is long and universal. Much of it was worked as an integral part of the weaving process, groups of picks being reserved from the action of the shuttle, leaving all warp yarns intact but unwoven, ready for subsequent embroidery. The Coptic loom embroideries, intricate roundels or medallions, colourful and often pictorial, were stitched in this way. Needleweaving occurs in peasant and national costume throughout Europe, the Mediterranean and northern Asia, usually in bright colours on coarse cotton or linen. It has a vibrant, richly textural quality. Subrikolás, the Hungarian needleweaving consisting of tied bundles of yarn with a finished woven

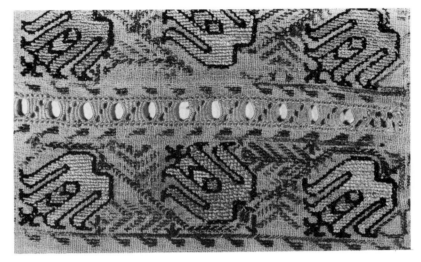

Needleweaving: Turkish, cross stitch and needlewoven band, silk on linen. Eighteenth-century, detail of a dress, 18×11 cm ($7 \times 4\frac{1}{2}$ in.)

appearance, is in the same technical tradition. It sometimes has details represented by contrasting surface stitchery. Danish *Hedebo* is a form of needleweaving, and so is *American tapestry*.

Traditional grounds are variable, but must be openly woven with a yarn which is easily withdrawn in one direction. The choice of a ground material will be governed by the purpose of the finished piece and by the kind of needleweaving intended. A smooth, twisted working thread, slightly thicker than the yarn of the ground, is important for conventional work, and especially for that which is to be washed frequently. It is often necessary to work with long lengths of thread which must be durable throughout the stitching process. Experiments may include anything from the finest lace thread to thick string; the thread may be hard or soft, lustrous or non-reflective, smooth or hairy, even or knopped. Leather thongs, paper and fabric strips, ribbon

and vegetable fibres, all have viable possibilities. Even metal purls, previously threaded in long lengths or taken up individually, may be overcast and woven through groups of bars. Single threads are always preferable in all cases.

Tapestry needles with a blunt point will be suitable for most work, and bodkins or yarn needles for weaving with coarse threads. Needles may be dispensed with altogether where bulky threads are woven through an open ground. Where ground yarns are to be withdrawn extensively the use of a frame is advised, but modest borders are often easier worked in the hand. If the work is to be done on a hard canvas, a metal ground or a prepared peg board, all rough edges or protuberances must be taped over or masked with waste fabric to prevent damage to the working threads.

The distribution of withdrawn areas and patterns across the ground is marked with a tacking thread. As yarns are withdrawn the ends are normally woven back or turned and fastened with small back stitches. Subsequent surface stitchery will secure them, and any loose lengths should be trimmed. The tied bundles which are often a feature of edges may be made with *hemstitching* or almost any looped stitch.

Early Italian drawn border

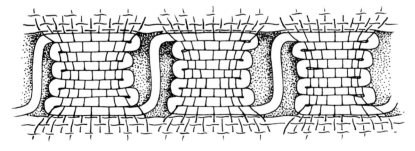

Needleweaving: Coptic medallion from Panopolis. Red and blue. 10 cm (4 in.) wide. (*Bankfield Museum*)

The general appearance of needleweaving can be imitated by machine. Linen scrim offers a wide range of possibilities. Yarns may be withdrawn either before or after the ground is stretched in the tambour frame. Stitch tension should be adjusted to produce a zigzag, with a tighter tension on the spool than on the needle thread, so that the latter lies smoothly around grouped yarns. With steady vertical movements of the frame the needle will take up regular groups of yarns. Sudden horizontal movements will join bars. By withdrawing larger areas of ground, free stitchery has more scope, and complex interlaced surfaces can

Overcast bars

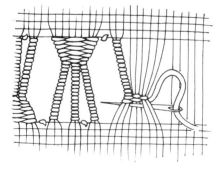

develop. Discarded ground ravellings can be used to pad the zigzag stitch over the bars, form new diagonals or areas of tufting. Completed bars may themselves be cut from the ground and used as part of an applied surface on another embroidery. Fine metal threads designed for machine use provide rich lustre and extend the possibilities.

Bibliography
Fél; John 1970; Day; de Dillmont; Nordfors; Risley; Swift

Collections
UK   Bankfield Museum, London; British Museum, London; Victoria and Albert Museum, London; Whitworth Art Gallery, Manchester; Ashmolean Museum, Oxford

NET EMBROIDERY (hexagonal net embroidery, tulle embroidery, hand-run net, needlerun net, embroidered net lace)

Simple darned linear stitchery on fine net, usually self-coloured. It occurs from the early nineteenth century on fine gowns and veils, imitative of soft, flat lace. Generally, that with a fine darned thread is called embroidered net, and that with small patterns worked in a much heavier thread than the ground is called net lace. Later

examples are creamy or beige and incorporate finely woven silk braids applied in scrolling patterns, and small blocks of satin stitches and sometimes eyelets. It is still produced on veiling, often by working with rayon or other synthetic threads on the machine, either stitched in a tambour frame or by using the darning foot. Net with a hexagonal construction is quite differently embroidered from that with a square construction, which is called *filet*.

In 1809 John Heathcote produced a machine which could make hexagonal net. This fine, silky fabric became known as bobbinet, usurping the lacemakers' monopoly. Lace was in many households more profitable than farming, but the machine survived inevitable antagonism, and with the addition of delicate hand stitchery a form of needlemade lace on bobbinet

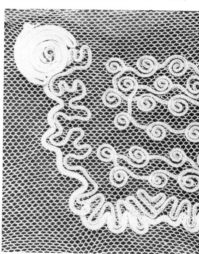

Net embroidery: Russia and lacet braids, Cornely stitching on soft net in blues and pinks. 10 cm (4 in.) square. Made by Christine Hall, Manchester Polytechnic

could be produced far more cheaply than conventional lace. Machine-made net was embroidered in workshops, commercially in homes, and by women for their own use. Limerick (see *Limerick lace*), Coggeshall and *Carrickmacross* became famous as commercial centres for net laces. Working threads were usually of the same colour as the net ground, but sometimes varying tones, colours and even metal thread were used. Pale beige-gold silk net was worked with a thread of the same colour imported from China by the French.

Traditionally, continuous lavish borders have a large repeating motif, central areas being filled with spots or powderings. Despite its delicacy the designs for net embroidery must be bold and positive. Intricate details will look mean and crabbed. Lines are continuous, so there-and-back journeys must be contrived. Of the two approaches, the first kind has fillings producing a variety of open or closed textures surrounded by firm outlines; the second is entirely linear without fillings. The treatment of the edge is crucial to the weight and behaviour of the net. It may be buttonholed or finished with a tiny picot braid, or it may be totally ignored.

Instruction books of the nineteenth century indicate that the design should be printed or drawn out with Indian ink on blue drawing linen or glazed

Net embroidery: Carickmacross, *c.* 1890. Detail of bertha collar with fillings and cutwork. (*Embroiderers' Guild*)

calico. A closely woven stiff cotton or poplin bearing the design traced through dressmakers' carbon is a suitable substitute. Lines must be drawn sharply. This backing is cut into working parts which are tacked individually in appropriate positions beneath the net. *Framing up* the ground must be done without stretching or distortion. Instructions will be found under *Limerick lace.* Alternatively, the ground can be merely basted to the stiff backing bearing the design, which is sufficient to keep it taut. A tambour frame is adequate for trials or small pieces.

Net should be chosen which is fine, soft and strong. Terylenes and strong synthetics are ideal, providing their mesh is clear, regular and hexagonal. Well twisted working threads in two or more thicknesses are required, since it is usual to work patterns fine and outlines bold. The stitching may be worked in any threads appropriate in lustre and colour, whether matching or contrasting. Lustrous working threads on an opalescent net are equally beautiful, as well as milky threads on a sparkling one. There is a wider straw needle with a blunt point called a harness needle which is ideal. Substitutes must be long, blunt and not so wide that the mesh of the net is disturbed.

First work outlines in a running stitch with an easy tension. Fine fillings may also be in running stitch, or patterned fillings may be used. There should be strong textural

Net embroidery: four fillings

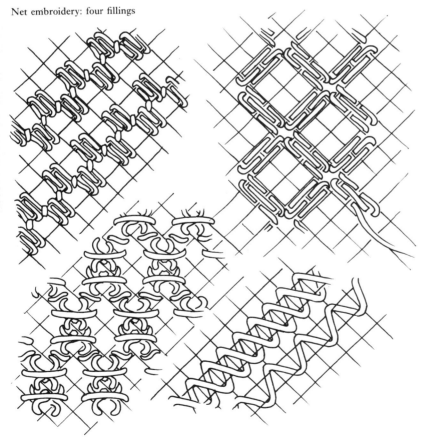

movement between territories advanced, stimulated by the influences of missionaries and commerce, styles of usage and decoration fluctuated. The Eskimo had once decorated his inner bird-skin garments with beadwork and the Plains Indian wore luxurious belts and garments with bead borders. With the introduction of horses, trappings and harness were lavishly ornamented. By the mid nineteenth century artifacts were sought after on the European market, beadwork and quillwork being perhaps the most popular.

Early beadwork was constructed according to a symbolic language of colour and pattern which became submerged by commercial factors. Patterns and isolated shapes are based on square and triangular geometry, and repeated linear patterns form parallel straight or chevron lines. The Mic mac double curve motif was used extensively, and by the 1850s distinctive stylized floral arrangements reflected French and Dutch influence.

The ground for beadwork may be either skin or cloth. Army uniform cloth was often utilized. The sinew was prepared while still moist, lengths being scraped clean and rubbed soft so that fibres could be stripped away.

North American Indian beadwork: nineteenth-century Penobscot, the Algonquin Federation. Seed beads couched on black cloth. 25 × 20 cm (10 × 8 in.)

contrast between outlines and fillings. Care must be taken in starting and finishing threads. Where thick and thin threads contact each other advantage may be taken of their juxtaposition, one being used to secure the ends of the other. Outlines can be made more precise by working loose buttonhole or feather stitches over thick threads with thin ones.

Basic instructions for machine embroidery on net are given under *Carrickmacross*.

Bibliography
Boyle; de Dillmont; Pethebridge; Thomas 1936; Wardle; *Weldon's*

Collection
UK Nottingham Museum

NORTH AMERICAN INDIAN BEADWORK

Before the traders and settlers brought glass and porcelain beads, Indians used natural ones extensively to decorate

Net embroidery: white cotton on fine white silk net, one of a set of 14 identical 25 cm (10 in.) mats

garments, treasured belongings and ceremonial articles. They were made from minerals, seeds and wood, carved bone and teeth, and worked shell. Many had religious significance and were family or tribal heirlooms. The famous wampum, which was exchanged at festivals and gatherings and later traded with the Dutch and English, consisted of smooth sections of purple and white shell strung in lengths or stitched to wide belts. The beadwork made with coloured glass beads was in many ways a substitute for *quillwork and hairwork*, which was more time consuming and exacting, and the design and technique of both have marked similarities.

Glass beads reached the eastern seaboard around the 1660s but were not used by western and northern tribes until about 1800. As trade and

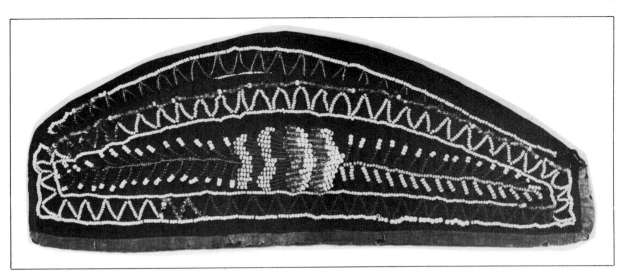

North American Indian beadwork: Glengarry, pre-1870, Woodlands Iroquois. Fine black velvet, white, pink and green beads

These were twisted by rubbing them against the knee with a quick motion, keeping them elastic with saliva. They were stored loosely plaited and wrapped. While sewing, the length was continually moistened by applying saliva with the fingertips. The working end was formed into a hard point which had to be kept stiff and dry. The beads were sewn only through the top layer of skin, the sinew never penetrating entirely through the ground. Animal sinew was so successful that it was only reluctantly superseded by linen thread, which occurs mainly on cloth grounds.

There were several characteristic stitches. Beads could be sewn individually or threaded a few at a time. Lazy squaw stitch consisted of

Spot or overlay beading

Lazy squaw stitch

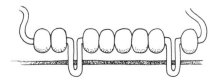

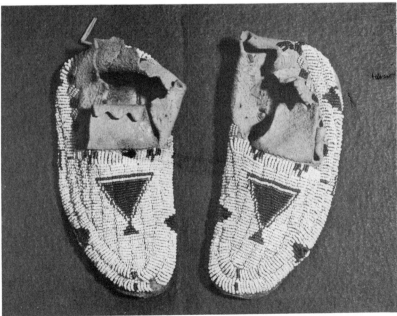

North American Indian beadwork: Moccasins, late nineteenth-century. Mainly white beads, lazy squaw stitch and sinew thread. (*Rachel Kay Shuttleworth Collection, Gawthorpe Hall*)

taking up a row of beads with each stitch and covering the ground in areas of parallel lines. These lines were packed quite closely so that the weight and displacement of the beads caused them to form loops. Alternatively, the beads could be strung on a continuous second thread which was then couched to the ground between each. This could be worked in close lines or in the curvilinear designs.

Bibliography
Bath 1979; Ewers; Gunther; Hawthorn; Hunt and Burshears; Wood

Collections
UK British Museum, London; Horniman Museum, London
USA Denver Art Museum; Indian Service Museum, Browning, Montana; Brooklyn Museum, New York; Museum of the American Indian, New York; University of Pennsylvania Museum in Philadelphia

ONLAY

See *Applied work*

OPUS ANGLICANUM (opus anglicum, de opere anglicano)

The famous English *metal thread embroidery* of the Middle Ages. From the sixth century the Church became established in Britain. The sophisticated technique and stylized design of Byzantine textiles was imported and began to flourish. The few remaining fragments, represented chiefly by *Saint Cuthbert's vestments,* show that by the time of AElfflaeda in the tenth century this influence was developing into a professional tradition in its own right.

After the Conquest needlework continued to develop alongside the building of the great abbeys, monasteries and churches. European ecclesiastical embroidery was all of a high standard in both design and technique, but English work in particular was much sought after, and even now the phrase opus anglicanum refers only to embroidery. There were many profitable workshops in London and the men and women employed there were subject to a seven-year apprenticeship. The number of mentions in the Vatican inventories suggest that opus anglicanum reached its peak at the end of the thirteenth century. Although it must surely have extended widely into secular work most of this has been destroyed. By the mid-fourteenth century opus anglicanum became known as Façon d'Angleterre.

The standard attained by English technique, in silk as well as in gold embroidery, was so high that exquisite craftsmanship must be included amongst the features of opus Anglicanum: it is almost invariably – to use the term frequently met with in inventories – optimé operata, bene breudata, subtilis operis. The finely drawn lines constantly exhibited by the delicate silk stitching are truly marvellous, and without the aid of such masterly execution the grandly conceived designs could not have attained the distinction that gave English embroidery in the thirteenth and fourteenth centuries such widespread reputation.

CHRISTIE, 1938

Frescoes, mosaics and embroideries alike show that workers were content with the mode of expression appropriate to their chosen medium. Design was nearly always narrative rather than purely decorative. Embroidery workshops would be stocked with drawings, and versatile artist-craftsmen would adapt these and draw them out on the grounds, together with written or verbal instructions for their interpretation.

The vast semicircular field of the cope presented an interesting design challenge solved by a number of progressing arrangements and divisions. This aesthetic value may be one of the reasons why copes have survived from the opus anglicanum period rather than other vestments and furnishings, or it may be simply that they were stored sensibly in flat cope chests, not subject to folding and continuous friction. Another factor in their preservation is that, apart from a brief period during the Reformation, they have stayed in fashion. Some chasubles remain, offering just as much proof of the quality of the embroidery of the period, but chasuble shapes changed and many were mutilated. All the Pre-Reformation embroidery now preserved was hidden or taken abroad during periods of religious persecution.

The Salzburg cope, and the Jesse cope in the Victoria and Albert Museum, have the Tree of Jesse arrangement, with his figure lying at the centre back hem and the Tree branching from him in a scrolling design. The Ascoli Piceno and the Agnani copes have a regular grid of roundels over the whole ground. The

Syon cope in the Victoria and Albert Museum, the Steeple Ashton, and the Saint Bertrand-de-Cumminges copes have all-over quatrefoils. The Toledo, Pienza, and the Butler Bowden copes have an arcading arrangement in the perpendicular style, with decorated spandrels. (Christie gives a comprehensive survey of vestments and their whereabouts).

The ground for the embroideries of the period consisted of a coarse linen overlaid with a fine one, and this was completely covered with silk stitching and metal thread. Where velvet was used this was backed with linen and covered with a fine linen. The embroidery was worked through all three layers and the surface linen trimmed away afterwards to expose areas of velvet. This fine linen supported the stitchery on the velvet pile (see *opus consuetum*). The faces of figures were spirally stitched, especially on the cheeks, the intention being that the reflected light from the thread would indicate roundness. The whorls of gold were sometimes pressed and moulded to accentuate this reflection. Most vestments, frontals and dossals were liberally stitched in silk and Cyprus gold. The metal was almost always a very fine, flat strip of silver gilt twisted on a silk core. Occasionally thin plate was couched direct in woven or diaper patterns, and some plain surface couching persisted throughout the period for linear work. The process of *underside couching* was one of the main technical features in the success of opus anglicanum.

Bibliography
Broderie religieuse; Christie 1938; Dean 1958, 1980; Johnstone 1967; Kendrick 1937; King; Marshall; Symonds and Preece; V & A Museum booklets

Collections
UK Victoria and Albert Museum, London
USA Metropolitan Museum of Art, New York; Museum of Art, Philadelphia

OPUS ARANEUM

The ancient process of decorating networks, now referred to as *filet.* Complex netting techniques, both functional and decorative, occur in archaeological finds associated with Iron Age settlements. Ornamentation often took the form of interlaced metal threads or spangles. The medieval name for the working of the netting itself was opus filatorium.

Bibliography
Hald

OPUS CONSUETUM (opus conservatum)

A term used indiscriminately, and variously attributed to several techniques, inventors and writers. It seems appropriate in many references to regard it as synonymous with *appliqué*, and therefore equally suitable for describing the use of slips and the practice of cutting out precious pieces from worn textiles and remounting them. On the large Tudor hangings referred to as hallings, the hard-edged figures are often represented in appliqué, with features worked in narrow lines of silk or even painted. The technique has been attributed to Sandro Botticelli who was also associated with the promotion of thought work (Armenian appliqué) but it was an accomplished textile form long before his time. The practice of applying heavily outlined figures with painted features and details enjoyed a brief revival in the nineteenth century.

Bibliography
Marshall

OPUS PHRYGIONIUM

See *Auriphrigium*

OPUS PLUMARIUM

All surface stitchery which was not metal thread, outlining, or counted on open weaves was once known as opus plumarium. Embroidery was often referred to in the ancient world as feathering, and most flat surface stitches can allude directly to the textural qualities and patterns of feathers. The plumarii mentioned by Pliny were craftsmen in the art of acupingere (see *needlepainting*). Links have been suggested with the Arab practice of breaking grounds with tiny rich patterns, and with the fondness for birds in early Spanish textiles.

Bibliography
Alford

OPUS PULVINARIUM (cushion work, shrine work)

The regular canvas and cross stitches; all those which occupy small square spaces counted by the yarns of the ground.

Bibliography
Alford

OPUS TEUTONICUM

A masterly attainment of comparatively coarse white work with drawn and pulled grounds, belonging to Germany and Saxony in the Middle Ages. Flourishing alongside the monumental metal thread embroideries, it makes use of Biblical subjects and epic narratives not unlike cartoon sequences. Large pieces were made of durable linen, less valued and easier to store than the gold work, so that the few which survived constant use and the ravages of the Reformation remain intact.

Distinctive characteristics are the soft contrasts of opaque and translucent grounds, with the stitchery an integral part of the weave, and the juxtaposition of open, patterned and more solid areas handled with careful consideration. The drawing is often superb. In fact, opus teutonicum is rarely white. Even lovingly cared-for linens darken with age, and mellow beiges and cool browns are a feature. Accents of colour are particularly frequent in darned fillings. There are occasional touches of metal thread.

Opus teutonicum was abandoned in the fifteenth century in favour of coloured stitchery, but survived in a similar form until the mid-seventeenth century in German-speaking Switzerland.

Bibliography
Schuette and Muller-Christensen

OPUS TIRATUM

Drawn thread and *drawn fabric* on open grounds, an early lace form consisting of grouped horizontal and vertical yarns overcast to make net-like

Or nué (p. 152): representation is achieved by the spacing of the couching stitches

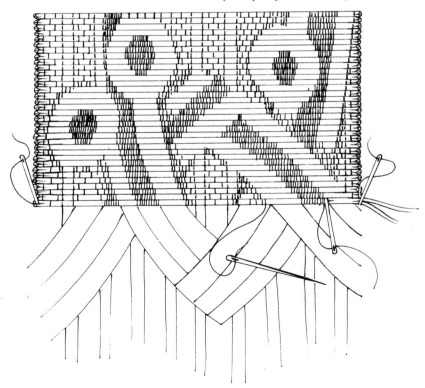

structures. The earliest references to it are in the twelfth century.

Bibliography
Lovesey

OR NUÉ (Burgundian embroidery, Italian shading, glaze stitch)

A method of couching closed lines of metal thread to form a continuous laid area over the ground. It developed from the Middle Ages into the seventeenth century, the best examples being produced in Burgundy in the fourteenth and fifteenth centuries. Subjects are usually Biblical and figurative, treated with disarming detail and realism. Or nué represents the disciplined facility of the Renaissance succeeding the formal closed areas of pattern so characteristic of *opus anglicanum*. It is a tedious and expensive technique associated with the depth of translucent colours in enamelling and painting, but relying almost entirely on reflected light for its own colour. It produces the richest and most rewarding of all metal thread surfaces.

The gold is laid from side to side, usually double. The waxed silk couching stitches are completed on each journey, so that a design involving several couching colours will employ an equal number of needles at any one time, each threaded with its own colour. The spacing of the couching stitches produces varying densities of tone, and the colours of the silk define the elements of the design.

The use of coloured couching threads to obtain small geometric patterns over laid gold is not or nué.

Bibliography
Dean 1958, 1980

Collections
Austria Imperial Schatzkammer, Vienna
Italy Museo delle Opere del Duomo, Florence

PADDING

Several embroidery techniques such as quilting and stumpwork include padding, as do those which involve constructing padded shapes previous to their being applied to the ground. Separately stuffed soft forms may be stitched to the ground or may function as free-standing sculpture. Padded appliqué may be turned over a stiff backing before it is stitched down, accentuating the contours and forming a hard edge. Experiment with dressmaking and upholstery techniques, especially by machine, in widely varying fabrics, is a rewarding exercise.

Bibliography
Ladbury

PALLS

The Guild embroideries made during and after the *opus anglicanum* period are often richly decorated. The funeral palls of the Guild of Fishmongers of the fourteenth century, the Merchant Taylors, the Saddlers, and the Vintners of the fifteenth century are superb examples. Perhaps the best known is that of the Brewsters of the late fifteenth century.

PAPER

Apart from its obvious preparatory functions paper is used as a ground for embroidery and as a backing. *Colifichets* were stitched on paper and the Victorians made framed mottoes and small items such as bookmarks from *perforated card work*. Another

nineteenth-century pastime was the stitching of mats on brown card with silks and worked edgings, in imitation of leather.

Paper and thin card has been used as a backing material on many forms of embroidery, especially where close stitchery or beading can be carried over pre-cut shapes from edge to edge. Writing or printing on the paper can often assist in dating the work.

During the 1960s embroidery began to be used as a direct drawing medium and therefore, conversely, it was once more acceptable to stitch on paper. Machine stitching and perforating on paper has potential.

PAPER CUTS

A favourite method of evolving flowing repetitive and symmetrical designs for embroidery. In central Europe, and particularly the Slovak countries, folding and cutting has many decorative uses including textile decoration. Folded and cut paper also forms the basis of a number of patterns traditional to American applied patchwork, and Hawaiian quilts are designed in the same idiom.

Bibliography
Pranda; Rubi

PARFILAGE (drizzling, unravelling)

After the Reformation all the metal thread was unpicked from most old ecclesiastical embroideries and melted down. Pearls and gems, too, were torn away from vestments and church furnishings. In time this was to become a craze, with tool cases made especially for the occupation and social gatherings arranged for the purpose. Its extensive use in the court of Marie Antoinette led to many comments by contemporary writers.

PATCHWORK (mosaic work, US: Pieced work)

The practice of joining by means of stitchery one fabric to another to form a continuous geometric surface. True patchwork is sometimes referred to as mosaic patchwork, and in the American tradition, pieced work, to distinguish it from *applied patchwork*

and from *applied work*. Confusingly, applied work is also called patched work in the United States. *Wadded quilting* is another method inseparable from patchwork, and it is essential to consider all four methods collectively. *Inlay* resembles patchwork, but the circumstances in which it is used are different. The term quilting is sometimes used to describe patchwork. Quilts and quiltmaking are dealt with as separate entries, as are all the forms of applied patchwork.

Many kinds can be done equally well by machine, and although accuracy may sometimes be sacrificed for speed, this is not so for an experienced worker. Since it came into domestic use the machine has led to the development of forms of patchwork, quilting and appliqué which offer new characteristics.

Geometric logic and repetitive precision are the main fascinations of patchwork. There is great satisfaction in the manipulation of one or more shapes to produce exciting juxtapositions and three-dimensional illusions. Progressively repeated and combined, shapes can be used to construct extensive permutations on either flat or undulating surfaces, or to complete enclosed spheres and cubes.

Some authorities distinguish between patchwork quilts and thrift quilts; the former consisting of left-over fabric from dressmaking, samples and piece ends, the latter being made from used fabric, the least worn areas of garments and linens.

Leather and skin mosaic work is at least 3000 years old, but the earliest surviving woven pieced work belongs among silk finds in the Caves of a Thousand Buddhas along sixth-century trade routes in Serinda.

The flood of calicoes and chintzes exported to the Western world not only stimulated the interest in decorative patchwork but also influenced design in associated appliqué and quilting patterns. In America the early imports were prized even more because the Hanoverian government severely restricted trade to the new colonies. When embargoes were lifted and eventually Independence came, patchwork and applied work blossomed almost as a celebration, and developed into a

Patchwork: cotton prints pieced by machine through a synthetic wadding. 122 cm (48 in.) square. Made by Ann McNamara

highly inventive folk art.

In Britain by the eighteenth century fashion demanded extensive wardrobes amongst the upper classes and dressmakers' pieces were plentiful. Whole families occupied winter hours making and sewing pieces. It was traditional for quiltmakers to collect pattern ideas from neighbours, visitors and pedlars, in the form of pieced single blocks. These were kept as reference material and handed down the family like samplers. Most time and expertise was lavished on the best quilts, and because they were treasured they have survived. They can only be approximately dated by their materials and paper backings because scraps were hoarded from one generation to another.

For early patchwork neither templates nor papers were used. The simple shapes could be cut on the grain by folding, and paper was an expensive commodity. It was not until about 1845 that templates became an accepted part of the patchworker's equipment. Papers, however, remained part of the economical resource of the craft, and they were normally carefully removed for another quilt. As basic shapes became more complex and greater accuracy was needed, templates were made from a variety of metals, wood and ivory. Double or window templates were not invented until the early part of the twentieth century.

Early quilts were designed as a single unit rather than being treated as an all-over repeating pattern. Some were as much as 366 cm (12 feet) wide, so much of the stitchery, particularly central areas of appliqué, must have been very difficult to handle. Applied work, appliqué or onlay flourished at its best in both Britain and America during the latter half of the eighteenth century and the first half of the nineteenth.

Pattern names in the British tradition are few and regional differences minimal, but clearly they were the forerunners of the great American tradition, where the romance of symbolic language and superstitions grew quickly. By the nineteenth century, arrangements of pieces, borders, bands and blocks, traditional to the northern countries of Europe, soon acquired regional names which changed as contact and trade grew in the New World. They were influenced by political events, religion and folklore. With Independence the practice spread to Canada, where it was fully explored and extended and in turn richly influenced American and English work. Although the superb technique of the eighteenth and nineteenth centuries is rarely matched, traditional patchwork is still widely practised. Its valuable place in Canadian and American history is recognized by private and public collections.

In British patchwork most mosaic patterns were made from hexagons and diamonds or hexagons exclusively. Used alone, hexagon patterns were referred to as honeycomb work. Equilateral hexagons were also known as squares, sixes or sextains. Six of these arranged around a central one form a rosette. Star patterns and diamond blocks made from hexagons were popular. Variants of the equilateral hexagon, the church window, which is elongated with two opposing points on a central axis, and the coffin, which is also elongated but has opposing sides top and bottom, were used alone or combined with squares and diamonds.

Although the apex angles of diamonds must be matched to their surrounding geometrical counterparts, the diamond most usual in patchwork is the lozenge, one found as the space between rows of symmetrical hexagons. There are absorbing interrelationships between diamonds and star patterns. The lozenge related to the hexagon produces a six-point star, a complete hexagon resulting from the addition of six more lozenges occupying the interstices. By shortening one end of the lozenge and combining the spare triangles to form more contained shapes, the relationship of diamonds and hexagons becomes progressively complex. The long diamond related to the square produces an eight-point star, a complete square resulting from

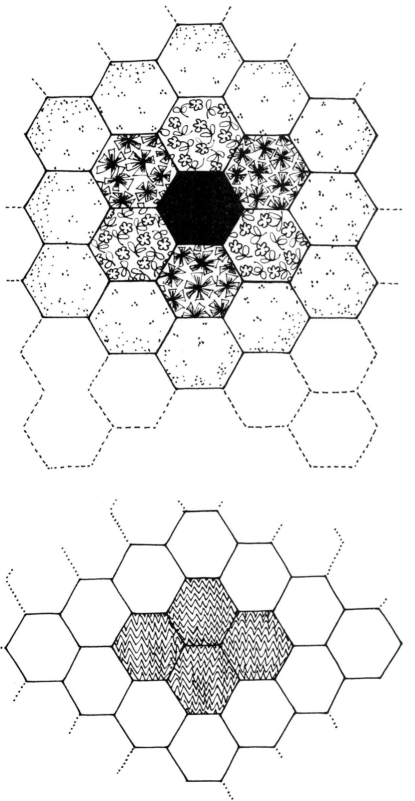

Grandmother's Flower Garden, French Bouquet, a regular hexagon constructed with compasses. By adding triangles of three hexagons the rosettes can be joined to make a continuous fabric

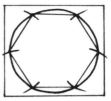

the addition of eight more small squares, four of them dissected and forming isosceles triangles. The lozenge and the square used alone with carefully chosen colours and tones produces the box pattern, or baby blocks, a favourite illusory arrangement.

Triangles make the popular chevron and dog's tooth patterns in alternating colours. A pyramid triangle occupies half the total area of a square and has an acute angle opposite its base. A long triangle with a right angle opposite its hypotenuse is formed by cutting diagonally across a square. Triangles are not easy to stitch together, since inevitably one or two sides must be cut on the bias of the fabric. Often a line of running stitches is needed beforehand to help retain the shape and match corners.

Squares and diamonds are usual in the simple strippy quilts (see *applied patchwork*) so typical of north-east England, and Amish quilts in America employ squares and rectangles almost exclusively. With those two exceptions, parallel-sided figures in patchwork are

Mosaic, honeycomb. An irregular hexagon folded from a square produces a 16-piece diamond. Alternating diamonds fit together

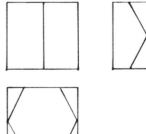

rare, because the visual impact is less exciting and because perfectly regular squares are difficult to make. Rhomboids and asymmetrical rectangles can be used to make undulating illusions of light and shade,

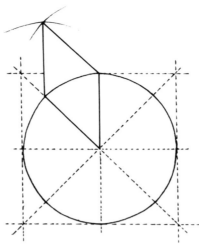

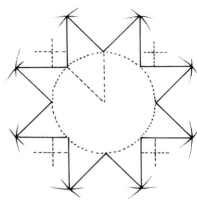

Flying Geese, Ocean Waves, Birds in the Air – a strippy pattern based on an isosceles triangle

Constructing and using a rhombus. Star of Lemoine, Blazing Star, Lone Star – the eight-pointed star has many variations. It

may be extended indefinitely with successive rings of diamonds. Isosceles triangles and squares complete a block

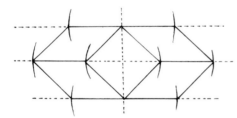

Patience Corners, Baby Blocks, squares and long diamonds

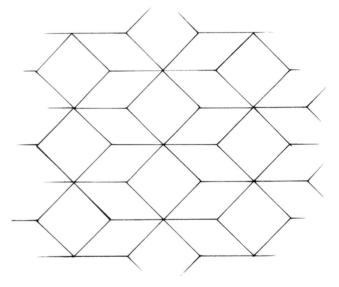

or simply to accommodate complex arrangements of stars and triangles.

Octagons can be used to construct a flat surface only in conjunction with squares or shapes forming a square. Twelve pentagons used exclusively will form a twelve-sided solid figure, popular in the nineteenth century for making ornaments and pincushions hung from ribbons. A pentagon which is not equilateral, with two opposing sides shortened, can be used to form six-pointed stars in combination with a hexagon and six lozenges.

A one-patch pattern is an all-over design using one unit such as squares or hexagons. Also in this category are single-unit medallion quilts which often have a repeating but variable border. Two-patch quilts are those where the patch is halved, with one half pieced and the other plain or appliquéd; they also include the alternating lengthwise strips such as

Flying Geese. Three-patch patterns, consisting of three various but basic shapes within one block, are unusual. Four-patch ones are very common, with the square equally divided or redivided into equal sub-squares. Five-patch involves 25 subdivisions usually organized on a counterchange basis like the Double Irish Chain, and seven-patch has 49 subdivisions. The most versatile and satisfying is probably the nine-patch.

Planning a piece, whether large or small, must be given careful

consideration. The usual criteria of scale, pattern, colour and texture apply, but there are additional valuations to be made. Accepting that a quilt or hanging will be the dominant feature of an interior, and even small pieces like cushions and pillows will need integrating, great care must be given to the choice of fabrics. Decisions must be made about the scale of the pattern or blocks in relationship to total size, and about any padding technique which may be employed. Working with full-size squares and strips of scrap paper at this stage is helpful. To avoid unsatisfactory compromise in design it is important to estimate accurately the amount of fabric needed in any one pattern or colour before cutting out begins. When working with scraps generous estimates must be made. The number of pieces plus turnings should be calculated across a width and then the required length measured in multiples.

Simple patterns should be attempted first. Those with curves and fine points are for the experienced worker.

The Coarse Woven Patch, a one-patch based on the rectangle

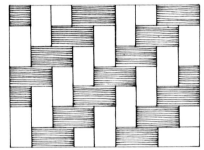

Broken Dishes, a four-patch – blocks joined with lattice strips interrupted by squares

Double Nine Patch alternating with plain blocks set as diamonds. Diagonals at quilt edges often have a contrasting sawtooth edge

It is usual to make a number of trial blocks using progressively exacting geometric shapes before a more ambitious piece such as a quilt is undertaken.

All new materials must be washed for shrinkage and fastness, and pressed completely free of creases. The most important consideration is that the weight of materials used in any one piece of work should be exactly similar. Cottons are still favourites because they can be precisely worked for geometric designs. Silks, satins, velvets and ribbons reflect the light more variably and their flatness is less important. Employing old fabrics together with new ones on the same piece is undesirable. Pins mark new fabrics, so they should be used only on the turnings, basting stitches made with a fine needle being used on the pieces where necessary.

Vinyls and plastics with woven backings are often easy to sew and simple to cut. A wider seam allowance is preferable, but pinning and tacking must be done inside the seam allowance, or tape or clips must be used to hold the right sides together. If seams must lie flat they can sometimes be lightly pressed with a warm iron or taped down. Fur and fur fabric must be planned on the wrong side and cut with a knife. As seams are made, the fur itself must be persuaded away from the stitching line. A small pen knife is excellent for this purpose. If seams are to be flat they can be catch-stitched to the leather or fabric on the wrong side. Most double-knit fabrics can be used providing they are not too stretchy, but they must be regarded as suitable only for machining with a narrow zigzag stitch.

The use of papers is not general in American work. In Britain pieces are turned and basted on to papers cut with the aid of a template, and then overcast; in America the template is outlined on the back of the pieces, so that they can be placed face to face and joined with a running stitch. Commercially produced templates are available in plastic and perspex. Home made ones must be precise, and those cut from card may need renewing several times during the working of a quilt. Pairs of window templates are intended for use where the actual patch or piece must be accurately placed on the fabric pattern. The cutting line is that indicated by the outside of the window template and the paper is cut using the second solid template. When papers are used, the pieces must be sufficiently stiff to support the fold of the fabric but not so thick that they become difficult to handle. Workers usually collect old documents, accounts and envelopes for this purpose. It is considered inappropriate to buy paper specially for patchwork.

Experts advise against drawing an outline round the template on to the paper, and favour direct cutting; but, since most workers do make an outline, a hard, sharp pencil is needed for this purpose. Papers or templates can now be organized on the fabrics. Corners and points must be kept particularly precise. Right-angled pieces must be cut with the weave of the material, and squat triangles must also conform, with one side on the true bias. All long triangles or diamonds must have the straight grain from point to mid-base or opposite apex. Each patch is cut individually allowing 1 cm ($\frac{3}{8}$ in.) all round. Precision is essential, and even small errors will be compounded over a large area of work. Where papers are used, each patch must be turned and tacked on to its paper, the seam allowance turned over the paper to fit snugly, and spare fabric at sharp points trimmed off. Convex curves need small running stitch gathers to distribute the excess of the turning evenly, and concave curves must be carefully and regularly snipped.

The Middle Eastern craftsman's habit of respecting Allah's perfection by hinting at man's imperfection appears in traditional quilts; whether for this reason or merely as a protective device against ill-luck, somewhere on the patchwork there must be a mistake in colour repeat.

Needles must be carefully chosen for the fabric. Most workers prefer betweens because they are shorter than sharps, and more suitable for the close, accurate stitchery needed for seaming. For very tiny patches both needles and pins must be scaled down. Care must be taken not to leave steel pins in work set aside for any length of time as they will make rust marks. Thread should be of a high quality and strong.

Working without papers, piecing or setting together consists of placing two opposing edges together right sides facing, and making close, regular running stitches along the marked line to join. These two edges will frequently have variable grains, and some skill and patience is required in stitching them successfully. When the patches have been tacked over paper templates they are placed right sides facing and overcast. It is quite permissible to begin each seam with a

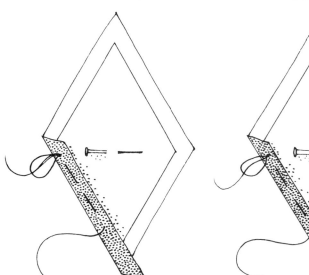
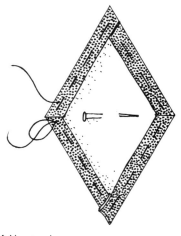

Making turnings over papers

knot. Corners must be given particular attention. Tacking stitches and papers can be cut and removed as the work grows, but it is quite common to remove papers only when the work is completed and save them to use again. The turnings on each piece are pressed, but not ironed, so that they both lie towards the darker patches.

Bibliography

Betterton; Carlisle; Colby 1958, 1965; Cundy and Rollett; Finley; Fitzrandolph; *Golden Hands*; Gonsalves; Hall and Kretsinger; Higgins; Holstein; Mahler; Marston; Newark; Osler; Proctor, R.M.; Safford and Bishop; Timmins; Webster

Collections

UK American Museum, Bath; Gawthorpe Hall, Burnley; Welsh Folk Museum, Cardiff; Cheltenham Museum; Victoria and Albert Museum, London; Beamish North of England Open Air Museum, Stanley; Ulster Folk and Transport Museum, Co. Down
USA Boston Museum of Fine Arts; Old Sturbridge Village, Massachusetts; Brooklyn Museum, New York; Newark Museum; Shelburne Museum, Vermont

PATTERN DARNING

See *Darning*

PEARLING

Little loops of thread at textile edges, often close and regular. Pearling is more usually just twisted and secured, or plaited, rather than knotted like picots.

PEARLS

Seed pearls have been used on precious textiles throughout the history of embroidery. Sometimes mounted into metal which could be stitched on, they are more usually perforated and sewn on like beads. Elizabethan garments weighted with many thousands of pearls feature on period portraits. Pearls from freshwater molluscs have been popular for embroidery at various periods. They tend towards pinks, greens and greys, and their baroque shapes appealed to textile workers. Artificial pearls have been in common use since glass beads were made in commercial quantities. In the Russian tradition pearls were especially favoured incorporated in netting as cauls and costume decoration. For working, they were threaded and wound round a viteika, a protective bobbin, so that the thread could be kept under tension without handling the pearls.

Bibliography

Edwards 1966

Collection

UK Nottingham Museum

PERFORATED CARD WORK (punctured card work)

Stitchery on thin card stamped mechanically with regular, close, tiny holes, which could be counted just like an evenweave ground. Belonging to the second half of the nineteenth century, it was used for bookmarks and for framed religious and cautionary mottoes. There was almost always some lettering together with floral sprays or borders, and the use of shaded wool or silk threads was quite common. It may be distantly related to *colifichets*.

PERSIAN OPENWORK

Throughout the Middle East, and in Iran particularly, *drawn thread* and *drawn fabric* grounds are expertly handled. On open weaves stitchery is often simple, bold expanses of opened ground occupying rich borders or forming pools of metallic texture amongst lavish and colourful surface stitchery. In embroidery manuals the terms Persian openwork, Russian drawn ground, and punch work are used variously, usually for open fillings where the diagonal working covers most of the yarn.

Bibliography

de Dillmont; Liley

Collection

UK Nottingham Museum

PESSANTE DARNING

See *Darning*

PETAL PATCHWORK

See *Star patchwork*

PETIT POINT

The term probably once distinguished all delicate white work from heavier stitchery, but came to mean almost any detailed counted work, as distinct from *gros point*. Tent stitch is sometimes referred to as petit point, especially when it is very fine.

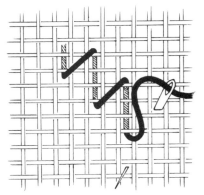

Petit point: tent stitch.
(a) the downward diagonal turning to return upwards

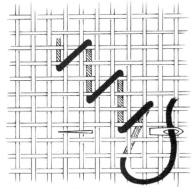

(b) with the needle horizontal, starting to return upwards

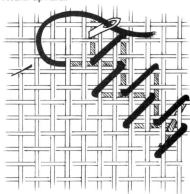

(c) making the turn for the second downward diagonal

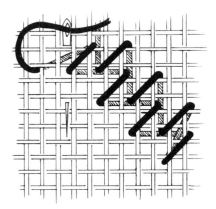

(d) with the needle vertical, starting to
return downwards

PHULKARI

Embroidery of the Punjab consisting
of damask *darning* in floss silks on
earth-red or indigo heavy cotton cloth,
the khaddar. Phulkari means flowered
work, and originally described the
everyday type for clothing on which
the design was distributed over the
ground in a loose ogee arrangement,
with a border panel to fold around the
face. The ceremonial bagh designs are
geometrically based and stitched to
cover most of the ground.

Although its influence can be seen
elsewhere on the Indian Continent,
phulkari is associated entirely with the
Punjab. Persian influence seems to
have been minimal, and it is perhaps
closest to the early medieval Ajanta
designs. It may represent the remnants
of the true Indian pre-Mughal
tradition of chequered and striped
patterning.

The bagh designs have varieties
such as Chand, Dhunia, Kakri and
Shalimar. Chevrons, squares and
diamonds form closely stitched borders
and solid central compartments. The
silk is almost always yellow and white,
with compact areas of other primaries.
Stitchery is done from the back, using
preliminary tacking lines as a guide,
and taking long stitches on the right
side and small picks on the side seen
by the worker. The reverse side of the
work is, therefore, a linear version of
the voided right side. The lack of
precise planning leads to discrepancies
and accommodations in the pattern

which add to its exciting qualities. The
silk is worked horizontally, vertically
or diagonally according to selected
sections of pattern, its lustre adding an
evanescence which can never be
achieved with woven techniques.

Phulkari work is laborious and time-
consuming. Attempts to form an
export market have been limited. It is
worked largely as a domestic art and
partly as an industry for the home
market. The birth of a child was
followed by a small ceremony at which
the grandmother initiated the
production of a bagh cloth. This
would eventually form part of the
child's marriage ceremony. The chope
was made by a girl's maternal
grandmother and her immediate
relatives. Double darning was used,
making it the same on both sides.
Baghs, chopes and khaddars are valued
as symbolic heirlooms rather than as
commodities. Designs are passed down
from mother to daughter and from
friend to friend.

Bibliography
Birdwood; Irwin and Hall 1973;
Dhamija; Dongerkery; Steel

Collections
UK Victoria and Albert Museum,
London
India Calico Museum of Textiles,
Ahmedabad; Jaipur Museum

PICOTS

Small loops, twists or knots of working
thread which decorate edges or bars.
They may be regularly spaced or
occupy strategic decorative positions;
they may be quite flat or raised as
textural features. Some are referred to
as *pinwork*. They are specific in their
type and distribution and strongly
characteristic in many forms of lace
and cutwork.

Bibliography
de Dillmont

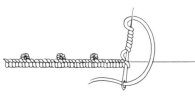

Bullion picots

Pin picots

Picots: detail of a collar, late nineteenth-
century. Carrickmacross guipure.
(*Embroiderers' Guild*)

Woven picots

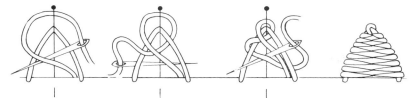

PIECED WORK

See *Patchwork*

PIÑA CLOTH EMBROIDERY

White or cream pineapple fibre cloth woven and embroidered in the Philippines. Strongly influenced by European tradition, the style was introduced by missionaries and settlers. It consists of a fine translucent ground with softly lustrous pineapple thread worked in flat satin stitch and wide outlines. Square-netted, cut, pulled and lace stitch fillings complete the simple, meandering, floral forms.

Pina cloth embroidery: Philippines, nineteenth-century veil, pineapple fibre. Detail 51 × 56 cm (29 × 22 in.). (*Nottingham Museum*)

The embroidery is fine, intricate and deftly worked, often on expansive stoles or shawls.

The availability of modern textile processes has prompted researchers in the Islands to investigate revitalization of the cottage industry. Mechanical retting, de-gumming and softening of the fibres, together with the introduction of minor proportions of synthetic yarn, is causing commercial interest. The cloth is starched and beetled before embroidery is begun.

PINEAPPLE PATCHWORK

See *Applied patchwork*

PINKING

Stamping out, pouncing, perforating or cutting decoratively a textile fabric or leather. The technique occurs in many forms wherever textiles are decorated. The Eskimos and Aleut were once expert at perforated, slit and threaded borders on leather and skins, as were a number of northerly hunting peoples. Cloth was cut with pinking irons and anvil blocks to make eyelets or serrated edges long before there were scissors for the purpose.

PINWORK

A specific kind of lace picot which occurs frequently as an edging to babies' caps from the eighteenth century. Pinwork is always buttonholed and always very tiny. Pin picots are simple loops made over a pin without buttonholing.

Tiny buttonholed spines

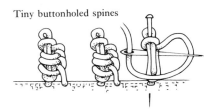

PIQUÉ EMBROIDERY

Marcella or piqué was a figured white cotton cloth woven with relief diapers like Marseilles quilts. In the nineteenth century it was made into household textiles and children's clothes and decorated with white cord or braid, sewn in interlaced or meandering outlines. Simple fillings were sometimes added in a primary colour, and knitted lace or crochet formed the edgings.

PLATERSQUE EMBROIDERY

That which resembles or intentionally copies the art of the goldsmith or silversmith, like the ecclesiastical Spanish work of the sixteenth and seventeenth centuries.

PLUSH WORK

See *Raised woolwork*

POUNCE

Fine powder used in *transferring designs* by the process known as prick and pounce, so that tiny points of it

outline the design on the fabric. Sometimes this outline alone is sufficient to the ensuing process, but sometimes the lines are painted and the pounce shaken away. White pounce is traditionally made of ground cuttlefish bone, and black from charcoal. Greys are obtained by admixtures. Substitutes such as talc are quite successful. The tool used to stipple the pounce powder through the pricked tracing, usually a hard roll of felt, is called a pouncer. *Pinking* may be confused with pouncing.

POWDERING

See *Seeding*

PRE-COLUMBIAN

The Peruvian cultures developed superb weaving, textile construction and embroidery techniques about 4000 years ago. Complete Paracas burial mantles survive from about the third century, loosely woven wool or cotton cloth darned with vital, multi-coloured figures and fantastic birds and animals. Stem stitch fillings are used integrally,

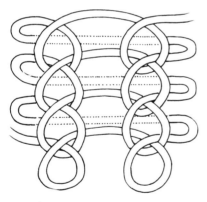

Pre-Columbian: knit stem stitch

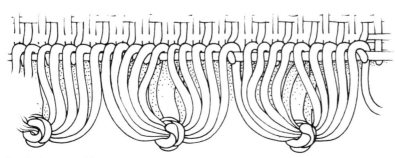

Bundled overcast fringe

lying along the ground yarn like soumak weaving.

Both Paracas and Nazca versions of the burial cloths are bordered in some instances with highly elaborate, robustly active figures and beasts reminiscent of both *stumpwork* and *bebilla* in that they are sophisticated techniques of lace-like construction. Braids, tabs and tubes are worked independent of a ground fabric in what is described as a knit-stem stitch. Successive buttonhole loops are taken up with the needle, precisely like knitting. New colours are introduced at frequent intervals, those not in use being taken inside the shapes for added bulk.

Bibliography
Bird and Bellinger; D'Harcourt; Stafford

Collections
UK British Museum, London
USA Boston Museum of Fine Arts; Art Institute of Chicago; Peabody Museum, Harvard University; Brooklyn Museum, New York; Metropolitan Museum of Art, New York; University Museum, Philadelphia
FRANCE Musée de l'Homme, Paris
PERU Museo Nacional de Anthropologia y Arqueologia, Lima

PRESSED QUILTS

See *Applied patchwork*

PRICK AND POUNCE

See *Transferring designs*

PRINTWORK PICTURES

See *Silk pictures*

PUFF PATCHWORK (stuffed work)

Small pillows or blocks of pieced fabric, each made separately and filled before being joined to form a continuous surface. It differs from *puff quilting* in that the squares are turned so that their seams are inside. The technique is very rich, but design possibilities are limited. Shapes other than squares present difficulties but are worthy of experiment. Research has revealed no historical equivalent; there are tenuous parallels with small containers of both functional and decorative value made by tribal societies, but, used to make a continuous, insulated surface, stuffed work seems to have developed late.

The choice of design and materials are governed in much the same way as ordinary *patchwork*. Cut two squares for each shape, the piece which is to form the top being considerably larger than that for the backing. The two squares must then be sewn together with flat seams on three sides to form a pocket. This can be done by machine. There are three accepted methods of taking up the extra fabric of the top piece: it can be gathered, tucked or pleated. Each pocket is then turned right side out and the batting or stuffing inserted according to the required density. The fourth side can be finished with a top stitch or a slip stitch. The pillows are joined by oversewing from the back or by simple *insertions*.

PUFF QUILTING

Closely resembling *puff patchwork*, the essential difference is that all the squares are sewn right-side out leaving raw edges of fabric all round. If the squares are raised by means of tucks it is called biscuit quilting, and the finished textile is quite different, having steep-sided pockets of wadding on the top and a flat backing. It is ideal for the machine.

Cut the squares from both top fabric and backing, leaving generous turnings. Taking one top and one backing square, place right sides out and sew three sides together. Stuff each pocket generously with dacron filling or well combed fleece, sufficient to lift it well but not so much as to make it difficult to sew. Tack and then stitch the puffs together in lines with right sides facing, so that all the raw edges are together on the backing side. These lines of stitching should be just inside the previous ones, so that the latter do not show on the top of the quilt. The whole piece is backed with a continuous lining and tied (see *stobbed quilts*) at all the puff corners. A substantial backing will accentuate the indentation of the ties and add warmth.

Puff quilting: biscuit construction

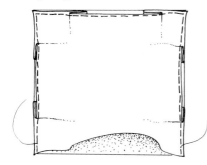

PULLED WORK

See *Drawn fabric*

PUNCH WORK (Rhodes embroidery)

There are several methods of working *drawn fabric* or *drawn thread* grounds which produce a simple network occupying an important role in the design of the textile. In embroidery manuals the terms *Persian openwork* and *Russian drawn ground* and punch work are used variously, usually for open fillings where the diagonal working covers most of the yarn. Flora Klickmann in *Girls' Own Paper* (about 1918) gives a version with needlewoven flowers interrupting the overcast ground and a castellated edge of buttonholing.

The term punchwork also refers to the coarse stitchery worked with a punch needle which forms close loops on hessian cloth.

Bibliography
Klickmann

Punch work: overcast ground

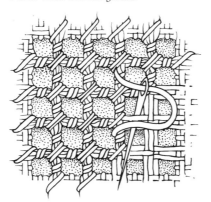

PUNTO IN ARIA

The ground fabric of *drawn thread* work became more and more open for elaborate reconstruction with stitchery and eventually was dispensed with altogether in favour of yarns laid over parchment. Thus the designer was freed from the strict verticals and horizontals imposed by weaving, and needlemade lace independent of a ground fabric became progressively more intricate and delicate, literally stitched in the air. Distinctive styles developed, the direct descendant in Italy being *reticella*.

PURLS

See *Metal threads* and *Metal thread work*

PYRAMID EDGING

See *Armenian needlepoint*

QUILLWORK AND HAIRWORK

A highly developed form of couching on skins, birch bark or woven cloth, using porcupine or feather quills, vegetable fibres or hair. Techniques, materials and designs for both quills and hair are inseparable, and indigenous to the American-Indian culture, where they are recognized as an art form. Skilled artists were celebrated and their work was much sought after. Symbolism and the expression of ancestral and religious associations was very important. *North American Indian beadwork* is closely related.

The first known decorative examples of quillwork are from a thirteenth-century site in Utah. The Indians used moose, reindeer, elk and seal hair at an early date, but these materials do not appear amongst Alaskan and Siberian peoples until the eighteenth century. White moosehair on birch bark or leather was a favourite, often dyed and enriched with pieces of quill. Being of necessity nomadic, Indian styles and influences are cross-fertilized, but tribal work can usually be distinguished.

Before the mid-seventeenth century the Ursuline nuns had set up a school in Quebec for Huron, Iroquois, Algonkians and Eskimo, teaching them to embroider with imported silk and

gilt. Local materials were soon substituted, and tribal flower subjects took on a European flavour, but were worked in hair or quills, using satin stitch, couched knotted work and French knots. Initial enthusiasm for producing ecclesiastical vestments and furnishings extended to commercial objects. Convent schools were started, where the daughters of the Colonists were taught this amalgam of styles and cultural influences known by the early eighteenth century as 'Indian curios'. It may be merely coincidental that about this time Europeans revived the use of human hair for embroidery in the form of *silk pictures*, and that

knotted work became popular. A particular interest in the goods of the Canadian Huron stimulated a flourishing and organized moccasin industry by the nineteenth century. Quillwork declined as the use of manufactured glass beads was substituted, but both hair and quillwork were still carried out on a non-commercial basis as late as the beginning of the twentieth century, and recent revival of interest has revealed latent skills.

Artifacts, containers and garments of a wide variety were decorated, knife-sheaths, tepee panels and boxes were made of birch bark, bags, pouches and

Quillwork and hairwork: Woodlands Indian birchbark case with encroaching stitches and knots, in softly dyed quills. 10 cm (4 in.) high. (*Bankfield Museum*)

gloves from cloth, shirts, dresses and moccasins from skins. Bark was prepared by trimming, soaking and steaming, and perforating a pattern to take the stitchery. Leather was soft and often thick, the embroidery penetrating only the surface.

Designs were sometimes drawn free-hand, but frequently a hide or bark template was used. The ground was marked with a bone point used either to make a depression or scratch mark, or dipped in a solution of ochre and blood binder.

Porcupine quills were graded according to size. The largest tail ones were used across broad surface areas

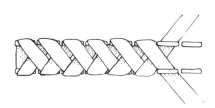

Quillwork and hairwork: three couching methods

or wide wrappings. General purpose ones came from the back and the neck, and the finest belly quills, which may often be mistaken for moosehair, were reserved for delicate couched borders. Long journeys were undertaken, not only to procure the quills and the animals, but to collect choice dye stuffs. The Cheyenne worked with grasses and husks. Rarely, bird quills were used, split and dyed. Hair of many kinds occurs according to availability. Moosehair was popular because it is elastic and versatile, the hairs from the front of the animal providing a good length of thread and a white basis for dye colour. Elk, bear, walrus and seal hair feature on Aleut

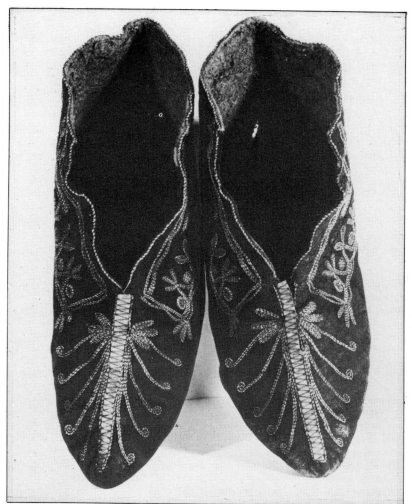

Quillwork and hairwork: moosehair and quill on birch-dyed black. Early nineteenth-century. Woodlands Indians. (*Leeds Museum*)

and Eskimo embroidery. The preparation of working sinew is described under *North American Indian beadwork*.

Some writers seem convinced that the surface of the skin was always prepared with awl perforations, others that the sinew itself was sufficiently stiff to penetrate the softer upper layers, and some suggest that fishbone needles were used. The basic stitch technique consists of couching down quill or hair in lines or lapped braidings, either alone or over a backing, either single or double. Several splicing devices accommodate the frequent joinings of the short quills. Weaving, cording, folding and binding techniques exploit the full potential within the limitations of the materials. The finished stitchery was

sometimes flattened with a smooth bone.

Bibliography
Birchbark; Gunther; Hawthorn; Orchard; Turner, Geoffrey

Collections
UK American Museum, Bath; Gawthorpe Hall, Burnley; Bankfield Museum, Halifax; British Museum, London; Horniman Museum, London; Pitt Rivers Museum, Oxford
USA Indian Service Museum, Browning, Montana; Denver Art

Museum; Museum of the American Indian, New York; University of Pennsylvania Museum in Philadelphia; Portland Art Museum, Seattle

QUILTING

See *Wadded quilting*

QUILTMAKING

The process of assembling and stitching together a large textile conventionally for use as a bed cover. A quilt may consist of *applied patchwork, applied work, wadded* or *corded quilting*, or *patchwork*, all of which are dealt with as separate entries. In America the term quiltmaking often means pieced work or patchwork, the stitching together of a quilt top.

Wadded bed *quilts* occur outside the American and European tradition, and survive from the sixteenth century onwards from both cool and equatorial countries. Ordinary household quilts had little elaborate pattern, but special ones were designed and often stitched by professional quilters. They travelled as itinerants in America as in Britain, and especially in Wales, the Mendips and the Isle of Man, carrying with them their own frames. Those who specialized in marking were paid separately, and those who stitched were paid by the spool length. Although Wales, Ireland, Cumbria and Northumberland are recognized as regional areas where quilting was a speciality, this may be simply because of their strong traditional vocabulary of distinctive Celtic patterns. Most farmhouses throughout Britain and America contained a quilting frame as part of the household furniture, and the process was a family occupation. Children threaded needles and cut pieces, and the men in the family assisted with sewing and pattern making and often devised and made templates. Quiltmaking was a necessary accomplishment for a young woman and several quilts were made before a wedding, including a special marriage quilt.

Quilting Bees were, and still are, community quilting parties. Groups of workers gathered socially in the house where the quilt was to be assembled, and if the accommodation was large and enough workers came, more than one could be stitched in the day. Two utilitarian quilts could be put in and taken out of one frame during a day's work, but time and care were devoted to special pieces. Although patchwork skill was admired and competitive, skill in quilting was considered a social necessity, and experts were guaranteed an invitation to these occasions.

The making of both machine and hand traditional quilts survives wherever there are small groups of enthusiasts. The Mountain Artisans, a craft cooperative in the Appalachians of West Virginia, are among the few groups who still work quilts commercially.

There are no rules concerning the relationship of the quilting pattern to the patchwork or appliqué shapes. Where the two processes are complementary the result is certainly more successful, especially where areas of rounded quilting enhance straight or angular pieces of work. Reference should be made to the entry dealing with the technique used on the quilt.

Frames resemble ordinary slate frames but on a large scale. They sometimes have ratchets so that the work can be wound on and stopped like a piece of weaving on a loom. The frame can be supported on the backs of chairs, on trestles, or even suspended by pulleys from the ceiling. Only that width of the quilt which can easily be reached from either side is stretched at any one time, the rest being taken up on the rollers. By stretching the backing and laying the batting and top over it without tension, the density of stitched texture will be accentuated.

The lining, cut a little larger than the required size of the quilt, is stitched carefully and evenly to the bars of the frame, taking great care that it is placed on the straight grain. With one edge rolled under to leave a suitable working portion, the lining is stretched and the frame secured. The wadding or batting is placed smoothly on top of that portion, paying special attention to the edges. If basting stitches help to hold it in place they must be very loose and held with vertical stabs of the needle. The top is placed smoothly over this and pinned or basted to the edge of the lining. That part of it not to be immediately worked is rolled and secured over the bar and protected with a soft cloth tacked around it. Holding stitches should be made wherever possible because pins hinder the quilting process and cause frequent finger injuries, increasing the chances of staining the work.

Some workers, especially when dealing with continuous sheets of wadding, prefer to combine the three layers over the whole quilt simultaneously before putting it in the frame. Because some tension on the lining is better than none at all, this can be done by pinning the edges of the lining as tightly as possible to a carpet. Those with a looped pile hold the pins best. With lining, wadding and top in place the whole can be pinned and then basted. Careful and time consuming work at this stage will avoid many problems later.

For reasons of convenience many quilters worked in the hand and on the lap, and a number of quite successful methods of doing this were devised. A full size quilt can be worked without a frame providing it has been carefully prepared first. Quilts with thin batting can be worked in a tambour hoop. Machine quilting can be done without a frame using the sewing foot or the darning foot. Blocks of patchwork can be individually quilted, with or without a small square frame; they can be finished separately and then in turn pieced to each other; or they can be stitched, right sides facing, and set onto a continuous backing, with a second batting for added warmth quilted in at the edges of the blocks or spot stitched at frequent intervals (see *stobbed quilts*).

With all stitching completed the quilt is removed from the frame and finished with a border, which makes up the required dimensions and becomes a frame for the main pattern. Wide borders or strips of edging may themselves be decorated with piecing or applied work, colours matching or contrasting. This is the part which takes most friction in use. There are several recognized methods.

Providing sufficient spare backing fabric remains the quilt can be finished without any addition. With the batting

Joining blocks with a strip and a lining

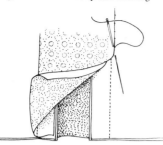

trimmed and the top turned over the edge of it and tacked, the backing is hemmed on to this and slip stitched along the edge. The width of the hem must be sufficient for *mitreing corners* neatly. An added hem or binding can also be achieved with a strip of fabric cut on the bias. This can be stitched first by machine to the edge of the top, and then turned and slip stitched to the backing. Corners can be gathered and eased rather than mitred. Many old pieces were completed with a line of quilting following the stitching, making a padded roll edging. Wide borders or bindings may themselves be decorated with piecing or applied work, colours matching or contrasting.

Sawtooth borders are made in two ways. Where diagonal blocks produce a toothed or indented edge to the main pattern of the quilt these can be turned and stitched on to a lining so that the complex edge is retained. Where a sawtooth edge is needed to decorate a straight one, squares of fabric are cut and stitched together in pairs by machine all the way round,

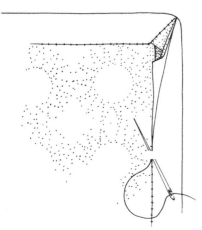

Border made with the backing

right sides facing. Each square is cut diagonally from corner to corner and the resulting triangles are turned right sides out. The triangles are tacked to the edge of the quilt top, making adjustments in spacing to accommodate the corners of the whole quilt, and machine stitched. The backing is then slip stitched behind them on the same line. The triangles can be attached separately by means of a facing if this proves more practical.

Quilts should always be signed.

Bibliography

Betterton; Colby 1965; Fitzrandolph 1954; Fitzrandolph and Fletcher 1968; Ickis; Laury; McKain; Osler; Peto; Safford; Webster; Wooster

QUILTS

The noun quilt is often used to refer to almost any bedcover whether it is quilted or not and whatever size it is. In the United States the term refers principally to *patchwork* and *applied patchwork*. The people who make them are called quilters. A patchwork quilt is more accurately a piece quilt, and an *applied work* one a patch quilt. A domestic quilt is a lined covering for a bed, a textile sandwich with two layers of fabric stitched together containing a filling. Comforters, coverlets, throws and puffs are all variations. The techniques of quilting, which often occur together on the same piece, are separately dealt with under *cord*, *corded*, *Italian*, *trapunto* and *wadded quilting*. *Quiltmaking* is also dealt with separately.

A language of symbols and superstitions grew up around quilts and the romantic story of their development. The flourishing trade in wool blankets exported to the New World was for barter with the Indians in exchange for beaver skins. Virtually no blankets were available to the Settlers, and the Pilgrim Fathers struggled for decades to import sheep and establish flocks. The earliest quilts, probably crudely pieced from every scrap of woven fabric available or embroidered with crewel wools and simple quilting patterns on homespun linen, did not survive, since of necessity they were used to destruction.

Large and small houses in Britain,

and the hastily built homes of the early American Settlers, were draughty, and needed well insulated sleeping accommodation. Bedrooms were often over-subscribed and much of the living area was also used at night. The large bed of the household, a four-poster or a built in bank, was a status symbol according to its width and degree of ornamental carving. Children and servants slept in pull-out beds, on settles or on the floor, and in the morning all the feather beds, pallets and bedding were accommodated under an enormous counterpane, often with high valances, on the large bed.

Quilts may be constructed of blocks, strips, all-over patterns or framed centre pieces, but it is often their purpose or motivation which describes them rather than their technique.

An Album or Presentation quilt is made in blocks by separate individuals and then stitched together, for presentation at some public ceremony or as a gift. Each block is usually signed by the worker in ink or stitchery.

Amish quilts have a particular beauty. The sect rejects decoration of any kind, but simple, non-representational patchwork is considered permissible, since a quilt is a utilitarian possession. Strips of dark colour combinations are relieved by touches of glowing, richer colours.

Autograph quilts display collections of signatures on separate pieces or applied blocks, written by groups of friends or celebrities. The signatures are usually in ink, but where the handwriting is large enough it can be stitched over.

Commemorative quilts make use of printed textiles produced to mark special national events and celebrations. Many were made at Independence and for later political triumphs.

Freedom quilts were the only kind made specially for men, to celebrate the end of an apprenticeship or coming of age.

Friendship quilts, still made from time to time, were constructed by groups of neighbours who each pieced a block then met at Quilting Bees to sew the blocks together. Embroidery or appliqué additions are common.

They were given at marriage, or to help a family in distress or about to leave the area.

Hospital quilts seem fairly late in the tradition. They consisted of alternate squares of red twill and white calico, the white ones having texts or scriptural pictures outlined in laundry ink.

A Marriage quilt or Wedding quilt was the last of the required collection a girl needed. It was the only one where heart motifs were permitted. By the 1750s it was considered bad luck for an engaged girl to work on her own marriage quilt and so her friends worked it for her, in the same community spirit which influenced the Friendship quilts.

The term Masterpiece quilt is still used by modern workers. This piece is considered the summit of the maker's technical ambitions, a prestigious display of skill. In the American West neat applied motifs were fit accomplishment, whilst in the East the perfect use of long diamond piecing was the ultimate achievement.

The Medallion quilt was popular in the eighteenth century and into the nineteenth. A central appliqué, embroidery or chintz picture is framed by a succession of radiating pieces, by more appliqué, or with whole cloth bearing secondary motifs. Sometimes the quilt has a narrative or commemorative interest.

The term Whole (or All-white) quilt is used in the American tradition to describe several different techniques, the common factor being a continuous ground, which was not always white. In early applied patchwork a single piece of fabric was used to form the ground for the whole quilt. *Caddow quilts*, cotton *candlewicking* and *Marseilles quilts* are included in this category.

Bibliography

Bishop; Brown; Carlisle; Finley; Pforr; Safford and Bishop; Webster

R

RAFFIA (rapphia, Madagascar straw)

All work using raffia as the principal stitching thread may be referred to as raffia work, whether it is done on a raffia ground or a coarse cloth. The fibre is grown largely in Madagascar. It has been used both decoratively and functionally throughout Africa and the West Indies and those countries which import it for craft work. *Bakuba* velvet is a specialized form of raffia work.

The fibre is soft, easily worked and accepts dyes well, though these are often fugitive. Modern plastic substitutes eliminate some difficulties,

Raffia work: purse, deep pink, blue and leaf-green with natural soft raffia on doubles canvas. 19 × 10 cm (7½ × 4 in.)

but they lack elasticity, and their bright colour and lustre give them quite different qualities. The use of raffia has undergone periodic minor revivals, but it still thrives on a commercial scale for export and tourist trades in many parts of the World.

Designs for working in raffia should be bold and simply stated. Materials like canvas, hessian, raffia cloth and linen are all suitable. The working thread is variable in thickness, but it can be doubled or split with ease, and used in short lengths. The scale of stitchery in relationship to the weave of the ground and the thickness of the working thread is crucial. Coarse stitchery used on harsh grounds has its own interest, but a good quality waxy raffia may be split quite fine, allowing the use of a flexible ground and producing a silky, softer finish. Closely worked surface stitches like satin, cretan and herringbone are usual, and on canvas, many of the accepted counted stitches may be used. A blunt needle with a large eye is necessary. Raffia is not as pliable as most spun threads, and so each stitch should be flattened with the thumb in working, for evenness and continuity. Much of the more traditional work has a back stitch outline defining filled areas of the design. Edges are folded over and overcast. Pressing the finished embroidery gently on the wrong side with a cool iron helps to stabilize the stitchery.

RAG RUGS (cloth rugs, scrap rugs, thrift rugs)

Coarse floor rugs or wall hangings, employing woven or felted cloth in strips or scraps, which are looped, pegged, or sewn into a stout, open ground. The technique is probably as old as weaving and the habit of making floor coverings, the final use for remnants of warm, hand-spun and hand-woven clothing. Belonging to ordinary agricultural and industrial households it has no written history, and only recently a few examples have been preserved to furnish period rooms in folk museums. *Bed ruggs* are a particular category. Traditional hooked or *needlemade rugs* are often dull because they were made from worn outer garments in muted colours, but vibrant or pastel colours can be used in just the same way, and fabrics of all kinds can be utilized as appropriate for individual pieces of work. Rejects from patchwork or applied work can be stitched to form loops or pile. Several techniques are common to those used in yarn stitched needlemade rugs, but the use of fabric strips leads generally to coarser work.

Designs should be bold and not excessively angular, and colour carefully controlled. *Transferring the design* can be a matter of simply drawing in the ground with a felt-tip pen. Experiments with grounds and cloth, strip widths and density of pile are advisable before a rug is begun. The ground fabric must be either loosely woven or open meshed if the cloth strips are to be sewn through it. Where the cloth is stitched with a thread the ground must be firm and strong, but sufficiently pliable to handle with reasonable ease. The cloth chosen for making strips to sew through the ground must be fairly closely woven, otherwise narrow bias-cut pieces will fray and break in working.

Cloths which are to be sewn on may be more loosely woven since they are less subject to friction in the working process. Short strips can be sewn together into working lengths before the rug is begun, or sewn as work progresses, changing colour as the design dictates. Strong linen thread with a good twist, preferably

Rag rugs: machined tufts, hand-stitched loops and flat stitches, blue on green. Sample, 15 cm (6 in.). Made by Christine Hall, Manchester Polytechnic

Rag rugs: ruched and gathered caterpillar braiding with fine fabrics in bright pinks and blues. Detail 18 × 23 cm (7 × 9 in.). Made by Gillian Longton, Manchester Polytechnic ▼

beeswaxed, is used for stitching. Some upholstery needles, particularly those with a wide shaft designed to part the weave of the ground, are ideal, but will not be large enough for coarse work. Large *needles* are not difficult to make.

A shirred strip rug is made by cutting bias or straight grain widths of cloths and stitching them down straight, gathered or pleated. This is sometimes known as caterpillar braiding or chenille stitchery. Using a running and occasional back stitch strips can be gathered down the centre, folded and gathered through the fold or at the meeting edges, or accordion pleated and stitched across the width. For simple patterns the use of the machine should be considered. Overcast firmly to the ground, each method provides variety of texture. Detail can be worked in tight curves, and ground fillings in horizontal or contour lines. A version known as pleated shirring employs the strips in regular small folds to form a pile, stitched to the ground across each folded width.

Button cloth rugs are made with small squares or rounds of cloth folded in four and stitched onto the ground through the fold, grouped in dense bunches of colour.

Rugs made with sewn-through strips employ the same stitches as *canvas work*. The simplest flat stitches are best, and ghiordes knot or turkey knot can be used to form a pile with closely woven fabrics or firm felt strips.

A looped running stitch, producing a texture almost exactly like that of hooking or punch work, can be used for needlemade rugs. After a little practice the loops can be made evenly without a gauge. If a cut pile is required they should be snipped as each succeeding row secures them.

The edges can be turned over and hemmed, finished with a binding, or buttonholed. Adding a lining always prolongs the life of a rug.

Bibliography
Bath 1979; *Bed Ruggs*

RAISED APPLIQUÉ

Areas of fabric or embroidered surfaces which are either stitched over

Rag rugs: Cornely tufting, Seminole applied patchwork and rug techniques. Greys, whites and silver on grey hessian. Made by Judy Barry

padding on the ground or padded before they are applied. Usually it is the stitchery which is supported, but there are some traditional techniques such as *stumpwork* where it is characteristic that both applied fabric and stitchery should be raised.

A padded area may be built up directly on the ground by applying one small piece of felt in a central position and a slightly larger one on top, oversewing each progressively until the final largest shape defines the extremities. The covering fabric can be turned under this final layer to avoid problems with raw edges or ridges.

With free machine stitchery in a tambour frame padding can be held down beneath a covering fabric while firm, close stitches are formed around it. The edges of the top fabric need hand-stitched finishing.

There are various forms of *applied patchwork* and *appliqué* in which shapes are padded or supported before they are stitched to the ground. Technical experiments with patchwork panels may involve the use of covered stiff supports which raise the surface in relief. These must be cut fractionally smaller and the covering fabric considerably larger, allowing for gathered, snipped and trimmed hems which are glued beneath.

Tags are separately made appendages applied to the edges or the body of a ground, supported by a lining and sometimes also by padding. Ideally, they are made by machine and incorporated into a hem or binding. Long ones cut on the bias and those with contrasting linings provide variation and three-dimensional interaction with other surfaces.

Shapes assembled before they are stitched all round to the ground must have a foundation stiffening appropriate to the eventual function of the textile. They may be raised in successive layers on top of the stiffening. The covering fabric is turned under and glued or laced before the shape is applied to the ground.

Bibliography

Frew; Swift

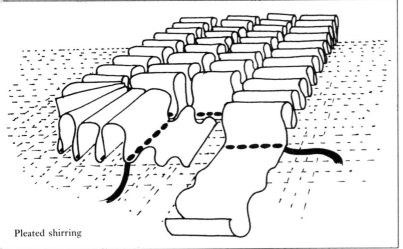

Pleated shirring

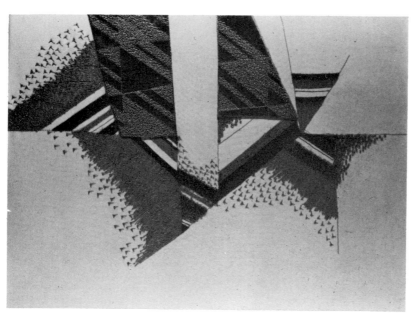

Raised appliqué: multiple Shiffli fabric on raised card. Machined darning in greys and pinks on smooth white cotton, with hand seeding. 38 × 25 cm (15 × 10 in.). (*Manchester Polytechnic*)

RAISED WOOLWORK (French raised work, plush work, raised Berlin work, sculpturing, velvet woolwork, worsted work on canvas)

Relief surfaces achieved by working pile stitchery which is then cut and sculptured. The technique was used on the eighteenth-century Savonnerie tapestries and copied by embroiderers throughout the nineteenth century, appearing on some of the more proficient and ambitious pieces of *Berlin woolwork*. The raised areas were normally complemented by flat canvas stitchery and confined to the main subject matter of the composition. They were made over a gauge with simple loops and glued on the back

Raised wool work: plush stitch

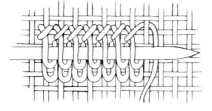

before they were cut, or, with a looped stitch like those used on *needlemade rugs*, worked over a gauge sufficiently closely for the stitches to support one another vertically. Purposeful choice of subject matter and careful shading of the colour and tone enhanced the sculptural qualities. The loops were subsequently cut and shaped, sometimes professionally.

Bibliography
Groves 1972

Collections
UK Bowes Museum, Barnard Castle; Industrial Museum, Leeds; Harris Museum and Art Gallery, Preston

RAISED WORK

A term applicable to all embroidery having three-dimensional qualities as distinct from that consisting wholly of flat stitchery closely combined with the ground fabric. The stitchery itself may be padded or supported by some foundation construction, applied fabrics may be wadded or stiffened, or the stitchery may be looped or cut into a raised pile. The term applies specifically to embroidery widely produced in *metal thread work* in the sixteenth and seventeenth centuries.

RAVELLINGS

Yarn removed from the ground fabric. It may be simply stripped away from the edge and discarded, leaving remaining yarn to form a fringe, or used to bunch, tie or tassel those yarns. In *drawn fabric* the yarn can be removed for use as a working thread. Traditional costume often features buttons formed from ravellings stitched over coiled paddings of the same material. In societies where

Raised work: canvas with wool and silk padding and plushwork. Mid-nineteenth-century. (*Embroiderers' Guild*)

Raised work: padded satin stitch circles and buttonholed edge on a child's muslin dress.

spinning was difficult, imported woven textiles were unravelled for the purpose of obtaining working thread. Ravellings can be grouped and used to pad raised stitchery. This is particularly suitable for close satin stitch by machine.

RENAISSANCE

Of the four main types of needlemade *lace*, Renaissance is that worked largely in buttonholing but without picots except on the outer edges. It may be worked entirely independently of a ground fabric or constructed over a ground which is later cut away with the remaining enclosures either decorated or left plain. It is always white or unbleached in colour, and has a floral basis with some arcading and scrolling.

Like most laces it has its origins in medieval drawn grounds and network. Period portraits offer a wealth of study, as do surviving early examples. The production of Renaissance survives only amongst small interested groups, having been replaced largely by machine-made copies.

Bibliography
de Dillmont

Collections
UK Gawthorpe Hall, Burnley; Nottingham Museum

RESCHT WORK (Persian work)

Plain coloured appliqué and reverse appliqué outlined with chain stitch, cord, or sometimes composite stitches, made in Rescht in Iran in the eighteenth and nineteenth centuries.

Bibliography
Caulfeild and Saward

Collection
UK Nottingham Museum

RETICELLA (radexela, radicelle, reticello, Greek point)

One of the main kinds of needlemade *lace* and claimed by some authorities to be the first, Reticella lies close to its drawn thread and filet origins, always set apart by the geometric basis of its design. The main bars are vertical and horizontal, fillings are conservative, and picots widely spaced. It may be worked entirely independent of a ground fabric as a lace or constructed over a frail framework of ground yarns

Rescht work: Pooshtee Reshtee cloth, *c.* 1850. Detail 43 × 48 cm (17 × 19 in.). Red and green predominate. (*Nottingham Museum*)

Reticella: early example. Ilké and Jacoby Collection. (*Textilmuseum, St Gallen*)

Reticella: sixteenth-century Italian cross stitch border, probably in imitation of Reticella. Silk on linen. 13 cm (5 in.) wide. (*Nottingham Museum*) ▼

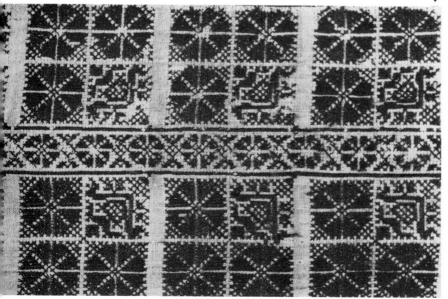

running in both directions. Those edgings and cutwork techniques which still retain the trellis-like warp and weft yarns, even if these are substitutes for a true ground, are categorized as Reticella. *Ruskin work* shares both design and technical characteristics on a coarser scale.

Bibliography
Caulfeild and Saward; de Dillmont

Collections
UK Victoria and Albert Museum, London; Nottingham Museum
USA Cooper Hewitt Museum, New York
Switzerland Textilmuseum, St Gallen

REVERSE APPLIQUÉ (Decoupé)

A method in which two or more layers of fabric are stacked one over the other, each layer being cut away in turn to reveal the one below. Each edge is turned and hemmed before the

Reticella: Italian 1610–25. 8 cm (3 in.) wide. (*Nottingham Museum*)

RIBBON WORK

In embroidery, the use of narrow ribbon in the needle for stitchery, or the application of ruched or gathered ribbons joining braids and rosettes. Ribbon is festive, ephemeral and quick and easy to do, and has enjoyed brief periods of popularity, Broderie de faveur, a favour being a token or knot of ribbon, was fashionable on eighteenth-century court dress. Shaded ribbon was particularly sought after. In Spain ribbon was simulated by cutting silk in strips from the piece, the edges frayed out into soft fringes, ruched and stitched at the fold in coils or outlines. The earliest use of silk ribbon work by the North American Indians was probably in the mid-eighteenth century. Complex borders of coloured overlays and lacings complemented skin and fur textures. Bindings and multi-coloured panels of stitched and flowing ribbons occur a great deal in European peasant costume from the early nineteenth century.

China ribbon, shaded across its narrow width from light to dark, appears liberally on nineteenth-century waistcoats and costume accessories, often used exquisitely in conjunction with *aerophane* or *fish scale embroidery*, or with silks and chenille and referred to as rococo work. It was surface stitched on *crazy patchwork*, and a feature of the sweetheart cards of World War One, with the ribbons dyed in patriotic colours. Between the Wars silk or satin souvenir squares with prints of architectural or seaside interest were decorated with ribbon work.

A wide colour range of very narrow double-faced satin ribbon is available. It is sufficiently strong and pliable to use as a working thread for simple embroidery stitches on loosely woven grounds. A resilient one with a strong edge will form a bubble with each stitch; a soft one will form a stitch more closely resembling that made with thread. Couching the ribbon with another thread offers further variation. Stitched down at intervals, the bunching or gathering of the ribbon

Ribbon work: woven ribbon strip sample in pastel colours. Made by Anne Stubbs

fabric below is cut. Design is restricted by the width of hems and so all linear work must be widely spaced. The technique occurs widely, from Eskimo and Aleut cultures around the Arctic Circle to the Jains in India. *San Blas appliqué* is often mistaken for reverse appliqué.

RHODES EMBROIDERY

See *Punch work*

RIBBON LACE

See *Tape lace*

Stars made from ribbon or binding. Fold the two ends alternately into the middle until the hexagon is complete, cut off, push in and fasten the corners

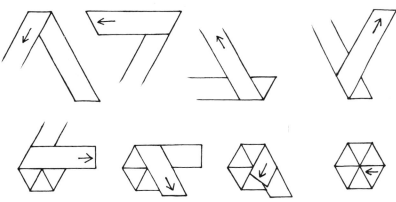

Ribbon work: wide shaded ribbons with a metal weft, orange, green and lilac with a metal braid edge, all worked on a tarlatan backing as an appliqué motif. 27 × 20 cm (10½ × 8 in.)

Ribbon work: bright lilac, cerise and scarlet ribbon, tonally shaded, couched on cream satin. The architecture is painted. Ground 41 cm (16 in.) square

Ribbon work: wide satin ribbon and woven strips joined by insertion stitches. Pastel colours. Made by Anne Stubbs

can make rich textures, particularly where opposing changes of direction are made. *Quillwork and hairwork* techniques are useful. Starting and finishing ends should be anchored to the back of previous or succeeding stitchery by means of a few overcasting stitches in a sewing thread.

RICE EMBROIDERY

Late nineteenth-century table linens, often all white or in limited soft colours, with fillings of rice grain running stitch and outlines of stem or cable stitch. Designs were often voided.

RICHELIEU

One of the main kinds of needlemade *lace*, consisting of floral scrollings, with an emphasis on bars with double picots, many of them radiating from woven wheels. It is still related to *filet* in construction, and the simpler forms are referred to as filet Richelieu. It is reputedly named after Cardinal Richelieu who served Henry IV of France.

Collections
UK Gawthorpe Hall, Burnley; Harris Museum and Art Gallery, Preston

ROCOCO WORK

The name given to a style of cutwork, not always white, in which the design outline was heavily worked with wide buttonholing and the ground trimmed away around the motifs. The china *ribbon work* of the late Victorian period, loosely rococo in character, was

also referred to by this name.

Bibliography
Caulfeild and Saward

ROSE BLANKETS (rose wheel blankets)

Imported blankets were stitched by the North American Indians with large, crude roundels of long darning and concentric cross stitches. The practice influenced the homespun versions of the Settlers, and simple designs began

Rice embroidery: blue chain and stem stitches on fine white linen, the acanthus leaves voided. 48 cm (18 in.) square

in Westmorland in 1880 with his housekeeper Marion Twelves, and there took up a friendship with John Ruskin living at Brantwood near Coniston. Together they developed an enthusiasm for the old home industries of hand spinning and weaving, ousted by the development of power looms. Elderly craftspeople were consulted and skilled carpenters enlisted, until in 1884 the first piece of hand-spun, hand-woven linen was produced. John Ruskin offered financial support through his Guild, and classes, social gatherings and an exhibition in Keswick encouraged the spread of skills throughout surrounding communities. By 1890 drawn lace work was being introduced, to the delight of tourists and retailers. Marion Twelves continued to teach and promote the industry for many years, and linen was hand-woven in the area until the 1930s. The embroidery is still vigorously continued through groups

Ruskin work: mat worked on linen spun and woven early in the twentieth century by Mrs Coward of Coniston and embroidered by Elizabeth Prickett

to incorporate the characteristics of Oriental prints. Floral sprays of coarse wool or silk stitchery survived until the end of the nineteenth century in the form of stencilled prints, usually of roses.

ROSETTES

See *Suffolk puffs*

RUSKIN WORK (Ruskin lace, Ruskin linen work, Greek lace)

A strong linen lace formed as drawn thread work or as an independent edging structure, characterized by geometrical bars crossing open squares, padded and overcast edgings, open hemstitching and regularly spaced picots and bullion knots. It is technically indistinguishable from traditional *Reticella* lace, but developed separately at the very end of the nineteenth century.

Albert Fleming moved to Elterwater

Ruskin work: border detail of mat spun, woven and stitched by Elizabeth Prickett

Leaving four ground yarns all round, one yarn is cut and drawn at each side, representing the new inner square. Then the middle four yarns at each side of the new square are found, and one ground yarn is cut and drawn to either side of them, isolating a symmetrical cross which bisects the square exactly. The single yarns are cut so that the surrounding four ground yarns remain intact.

The whole ground of one or more squares is now firmly tacked to a strong backing. The one used today is a firm vinyl upholstery material of a dark colour. The tacking or basting is

and schools, especially in the north-west of England, but it is now worked on machine-woven evenweave.

Ruskin lace is always designed within the strict geometry of a series of squares, usually closely related to the hem of the ground or sometimes independent from any ground. Most needlepoint lace fillings are appropriate. Modern evenweaves, closely matched with a similar working thread in two weights, adequately replace the traditional materials.

With the position of the hem and the mitred corners determined, the border is drawn as either a single or a double open hem, and the turning is slip stitched to the back of the work. The drawn border must have two or three sets of yarns drawn in pairs, and fours left between. A variation is one drawn, four left, two drawn, four left and one drawn. The ends of the yarns are clipped at the hem. The remaining central space must accommodate one or more typical drawn squares which will span up to 80 ground yarns each. The border is hemstitched on the right side with the heavier thread. Shaped buttonhole stitch is made over the cut yarns at each corner. This both secures them and emphasizes the shape, tending to push the ground fabric into curves rather than points. Alternatively, usually on a double hem, the corner may be overcast and decorated at its outer right angles with groups of bullion knots.

The area of linen inside the squares left for the cutwork is now prepared.

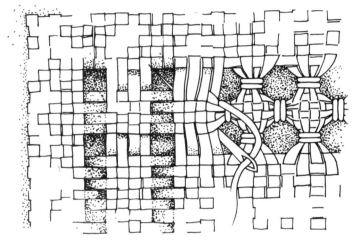

Single open hem

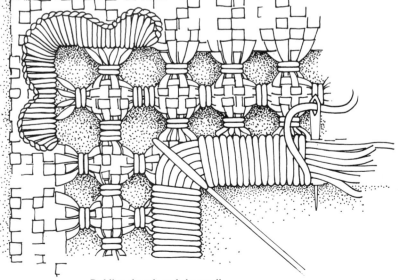

Padding threads and the scroll

made through the open hems. It must be firm, stretching the work slightly, but not disturbing the ground yarns. At this stage the inner squares of ground are cut away and the edges overcast, stitching through each hole of the open hem. This journey adds the two diagonal bars which will later bear the fillings. These may be single or double, depending on whether they are to be overcast or woven. Still using the heavier thread, the next stage is to work the characteristic padded roll over the overcasting. The padding consists of about four ravelled yarns from the linen, or four working threads. They are knotted together and held in position as the overcasting progresses around the inner square. The overcasting must be close, forming a raised roll which remains as straight as possible at the sides of the

Ruskin work: cut work, often called Greek lace, probably from Crete. (*Rachel Kay Shuttleworth Collection, Gawthorpe Hall*)

Ruskin work: sampler, Glenshee 29s, 50s linen thread. Detail, 46 cm (18 in.) wide. Made by Elizabeth Prickett ▼

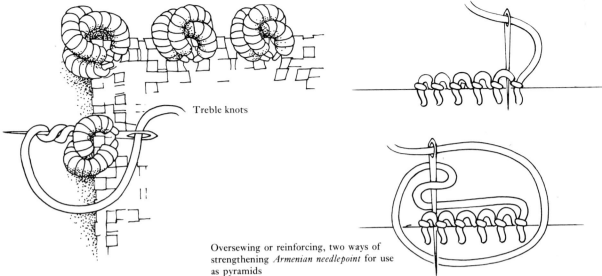

Treble knots

Oversewing or reinforcing, two ways of strengthening *Armenian needlepoint* for use as pyramids

squares and forms rounded corners. When the starting point is regained, both knot and padding threads are trimmed and the overcasting closed. If necessary, additional threads may be added to the crossing ground yarns and stitched diagonals at this stage.

A representative selection of lace fillings is given under *lace* and pyramids are under *Armenian needlepoint*. The patterns are worked with a round-eyed needle. Starting and finishing the working thread must be done beneath the overcast rolls. When all the fillings are completed the hemmed ground is finished with either a lace edge or with bullion knots. Lace edges must be measured and drawn on the backing cloth and worked while the ground is still attached to it. The bullion knots are worked in the hand. Single ones may be worked as surface stitches near the edge of the hem, but usually they are made along the fold of the edge itself. Worked either singly or as clusters of overlapping threes, they should be about 1 cm ($\frac{1}{3}$ in.) apart, stitched over two ground yarns.

Bibliography
Benjamin; Cave 1962; Petrakis; Raby

Collections
UK Gawthorpe Hall, Burnley; Ruskin Museum, Coniston

RUSSIAN DRAWN GROUND (first drawn ground, squared ground, Russian overcast filling)

A simple drawn open network on loosely woven linen, surrounding bold design features and usually worked in deep borders. The thread closely resembles the yarn of the ground.

There is dissension in instructions for the correct working method. Recent diagrams and pieces show that yarns are drawn only over the ground of the design and woven in behind voided areas. Examination of older examples from Russia reveals that the whole area to be worked is drawn both horizontally and vertically, ignoring the central features, and having two cut and two uncut yarns alternately. The extremities of the drawn ground are reinforced with a hemstitch which holds the loose ends firmly. The central features of the design are voided as part of the stitching process. The working thread journeys

diagonally, overcasting alternate bars and intersections in steps. With each journey, as the edge of the central design feature is reached, the working thread weaves across the voided area replacing the missing yarn, and resumes its overcasting role at the opposite edge. Thus the ground of the voided area is gradually rebuilt.

Where spinning and weaving took place in the same home or a nearby locality, matching working thread to ground yarn would be no problem. Ravellings from the edge of the fabric are almost as successful. Their twist can be encouraged by light waxing, and by turning the needle whilst stitching.

In embroidery manuals the terms *Persian openwork*, *punch work* and Russian drawn ground are used variously, usually for open fillings where the diagonal working thread covers most of the yarn.

Bibliography
Liley

are filled with couched gold. The solid metal is in the form of a strip spiralling a red silk core, and the resulting thread is extremely fine. It is very closely worked and remarkable not only for its minute couched patterns but for a specialized technique: many of the couching stitches interlace, whether deliberately or accidentally, with those of the previous row, so that although the ground has virtually disintegrated the gold is held intact.

Bibliography
Battiscombe; Christie 1938; Kendrick 1937

SAINT CUTHBERT'S VESTMENTS

These three important pieces of embroidery, a stole, maniple and girdle, belong to the early tenth century. Their inscriptions state that they were made at the command of Queen AElfflaed for Fridestan, who was Bishop of Winchester. They were presented to St Cuthbert's Shrine by King Athelstan soon after Fridestan's death, and are housed in Durham Cathedral. With the exception of fragments in Milan and Soestern they are the only surviving examples of Anglo-Saxon pure gold embroidery, and represent a highly developed and sophisticated skill.

Unlike the later medieval work (see *opus anglicanum*) there is no representation of light and dark or rounded features. The primitive, flat treatment of the figures and drapery is strong and successful. An openly woven white silk net of about 60 picks per 2.5 cm (1 in.) forms the ground, each fragment being about 6 cm (2⅜ in.) wide. They are worked in coloured silks and the background and haloes

Saint Cuthbert's vestments: the back of the couching. The shaded area represents the metal thread on the right side

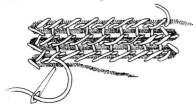

Collection
UK Durham Cathedral

SAMPLER (exampler, exempler, suamplarie, sam-cloth)

A piece of cloth bearing examples of stitchery and patterns of design for the purpose of recording these and for gaining experience in technique. Samplers are popularly associated with the nineteenth century, for it was during that period that children were

Sampler: Bosnia, sampler, pinks, lilacs and ochres. Silk on linen. Detail 28 × 20 cm (11 × 8 in.). (*Bankfield Museum*)

expected to make one as a matter of course, but by then samplers had lost their original purpose. There are Coptic and Mamluk samplers in Guildford Museum. Written references to samplers in Europe date from the beginning of the sixteenth century, when it is clear that they were worked in mixed techniques, but the earliest dated surviving sampler is a German one of 1618. Most of the designs were derived from pattern books, but these were rare and expensive, so the stitchery was necessary as a record for other workers and for posterity. Worked on bleached or unbleached linen, early samplers are long and narrow, about 18 cm (7 in.) wide, and sometimes longer than 92 cm (36 in.). The decoration is in bands of coloured silk stitchery and cut and drawn panels, white work and point lace, often mixed on the same piece. In some, the decoration consists of devices dispersed over the ground. Once pattern books became generally available samplers assumed two quite distinct forms; they were worked by the young and by beginners, or as verification for the purposes of securing commissioned work. Regional and fashionable exceptions occur such as the map samplers which were popular in Britain from about 1790 to 1810.

Bibliography
Ashton; Bolton and Coe; Christie 1920; Dreesman; Huish; Jones, M.E.; Jourdain 1910

Collections
UK Fitzwilliam Museum, Cambridge; Guildford Museum; Bankfield Museum, Halifax; Industrial Museum, Leeds; Nottingham Museum; Harris Museum and Art Gallery, Preston
USA Philadelphia Museum of Art
Germany Altona Museum, Hamburg

SAN BLAS APPLIQUÉ (Kuna Indian appliqué, mola work)

A form of cotton cloth appliqué constructed from stacked fabrics which are cut and turned to expose one another. Applied fabrics and ground are equally emphasized. Surface stitchery is of secondary importance, the interest being on the interplay of flat pattern and colour producing vibrant spatial cohesions. Designs are concerned with traditional body painting and ritual symbolism, sometimes interspersed with dynamic images from the Christian Church.

Until its recent wide exposure it was peculiar to the San Blas Kuna Indians who inhabit the Comarca de San Blas on the Atlantic Coast and coastal islands adjoining Panama. San Blas work has undergone a great deal of attention and appears in numerous forms outside its own cultural enclave. Since mola work became a profitable commercial enterprise in the tourist trade the Kuna have received some economic advantage. Because of a lack of understanding of the methods used by the Indians it has become associated with *reverse appliqué*.

Although the San Blas Indians had their own cotton cloth when the Spaniards arrived in the sixteenth-century there is no real evidence of the existence of molas until the early twentieth century. The molas are two similar, rectangular bodice panels back and front of a simple blouse, which, together with a wrap skirt, a head scarf and a mass of jewellery, form the Kuna woman's costume. They are made mainly of plain colours and the other garments of rich prints. Children wear them as dresses, and older molas sometimes extend to form skirt panels. Simple appliqués are of two or three colours but many are very complex and obey strict rules of procedure in their order of cutting and exposing of the layers. As pairs, pieces cut from one may appear incorporated in the pattern of the other. The addition of borders and bindings as the panels are made into a blouse adds to their richly colourful qualities.

The design of the mola is very dependent on the number of coloured layers incorporated. The rigidity of four or five layers can be softened by cutting and sewing blocks of slits or slashes through to the final layer. Starting with a small, two colour example is advisable, progressing to more layers only as each stage is mastered. Working fabrics should consist entirely of cottons or poplins of similar weight and clearly defined tone variation. Very dark or light colours together may show through one another.

There are two quite separate methods. The first is worked from the uppermost layer progressively downward, and from the outside of the design towards the inside. With this method the colour margins cannot be

San Blas appliqué: cut work cotton mola from San Blas in Panama. (*Photograph: Joss Graham Oriental Textiles, London*)

San Blas appliqué: two-colour mola with slits, contour running stitches and sawtooth border, from Ailigandi, Panama. (*Courtesy Herta Puls*)

narrow because of the restriction of each hem width, and therefore the number of layers used must be restricted to two or three. The second is worked from the base layer progressively upward, and from the inside of the design towards the outside. Colour margins can be narrow, since they can overlap previous seam allowances. This method can be worked with the first method as a basis, by working only base and one layer, and then adding consecutive layers above.

For the first, select several layers of fabric of the same size with a strong top colour. Straight grains must match. Allow a 6 cm ($2\frac{3}{8}$ in.) margin of

fabric around the whole design. As all the layers must be stitched through, the most expansive apertures are cut out first, working progressively down to the base. Pin a tracing to the layer to be cut and rough tack the layers together. Using small, regular tacking stitches follow the lines to be cut, together with their parallel turning allowances. Indicate corners and curves accurately. When tacking is completed remove the tracing by slicing through it with a long needle alongside each stitch, so that the paper can be removed intact and used again. This layer can now be cut and turned in short lengths, the tufts of tacking thread left beneath indicating the final line of the turned edge. Small, regular stitches through all layers complete this stage. As surplus shapes are entirely pared away they must be set aside, perhaps pinned to their

corresponding areas on the paper design, so that they can be incorporated later in a mola sharing similar design features. Successive layers are treated in exactly the same way, making continuous margins of colour. Symmetrical variations in the width of the margins or closures of peninsulas of colour may be dictated by the design.

The second working method is more complex, and examination of old molas would suggest that they were done on this principle. If layers are to be built up from the base, only that and the first layer must be tacked behind the tracing. For a two-colour appliqué the design should be linear, with lines at least 13 mm ($\frac{1}{2}$ in.) wide, balanced evenly over the whole rectangle without symmetrical repetition, and leaving a border of about 29 mm (1 in.). The fabric is simply turned and none is cut away. Both layers of cotton are basted together with the tracing, and all design lines are followed with precise tacking stitches. With the tracing sliced or torn away the cutting line is drawn in hard pencil equidistant between the basting lines. Snipping is done carefully through the top layer only, leaving some allowance at sharp corners. Turning and hemming leaves a 6 mm ($\frac{1}{4}$ in.) wide line.

A second sampler can be designed with wide lines, adding isolated spots of appliqué in the resulting fields of ground, or perhaps parallel slashes exposing the base layer. Slits are opened out and turned under with closely stitched V points.

For the three-colour mola the two-colour method is followed, this time allowing at least 29 mm (1 in.) for the width of the lines. The third layer is applied at a later stage. Snipping is done through the top layer only, and all edges are trimmed to their 6 mm ($\frac{1}{4}$ in.) seam allowance. Complete all hemming without removing the tackings, and baste the third layer over the whole appliqué. Turn the work over and draw lines immediately between the original bastings. Tack all three layers together with accurate small stitches along the drawn lines. Turn the work right way up once more and draw lines immediately between the new bastings and 13 mm ($\frac{1}{2}$ in.) outside the bordering one. Snip along these new drawn lines through the top layer only, trim the edges to their 6 mm ($\frac{1}{4}$ in.) seam allowance and complete all hemming. Release the frame of the top layer.

The four-colour mola employs the same method with an allowance of 42 mm ($1\frac{1}{2}$ in.) for the line width. Snipping through the top layer only all the edges are trimmed to 9 mm ($\frac{3}{8}$ in.) for their hem allowance. Follow the three-colour method for the third layer, cutting the hems to a 9 mm ($\frac{3}{8}$ in.) allowance once more. Remove the frame as before. With the fourth layer basted to the top, turn the work over and tack carefully over all the stitched lines on the wrong side with small, accurate stitches. Turning the work right way up once more, snip between the stitched lines through the top layer only, trimming the edges to their 6 mm ($\frac{1}{4}$ in.) seam allowance, and complete all

hemming. Unpick the bastings only when additions have been made. Where a final inside colour is to be applied it still conforms to the contours of previous layers. This is achieved by basting the final colour in one piece over the whole mola and locating the edges of the area of appliqué by touch. Bands of the final colour are worked over the whole mola wherever there is room to accommodate them on the base.

Variations emerge as molas are considered in sets or developments of a given theme. More than four colours can be built up by making wider allowances, and colour sequences can be reversed or broken by reserving layers in some areas in order to reveal them at a later stage. Grounds with pieces already applied may be added to spaces and treated as successive layers. Surface stitchery sometimes takes the form of running stitches conforming to the contours, not unlike *Hawaian quilting*. Selected sawtooth edges of hemmed triangles feature on most molas.

Machine-worked San Blas appliqué now appears on simple two-colour molas made for work clothing, and on imitative versions, but the necessary top stitching is not characteristic.

Bibliography
Auld; *Molas*; Puls

Collections
UK British Museum, London
USA Field Museum of Natural History, Chicago; Museum of the American Indian, New York

SATIN SKETCHES

See *Silk pictures*

SCOTCH SEWED MUSLIN

See *Ayrshire*

SEEDING (semé, speckling, powdering)

The texture obtained by making small regular stitches sprinkled over the ground. The stitches are distributed at variance with one another to make lighter or darker tone fillings. They are usually evenly spaced, but may be dense at one extremity of the field and widely dispersed at the other in the same way as *shading*.

The term powdering is used for a wider range of stitches, sometimes french knots or tête de boeuf, and for the distribution of isolated motifs over extensive grounds such as a sari or a veil. Separate slips scattered over a frontal or cope in the form of symbols or seraphim may also be described as powderings.

The machine can be used to make a wide variety of seeded textures, each group of stitches joined by the needle thread to a neighbouring group.

SEMINOLE PATCHWORK

Juxtaposed strip patchworks of tiny cotton or ribbon triangles, squares or lozenges in bright repeat borders, worn as gathered garments by the Seminole Indians. They were a form of *applied patchwork*, and closely resemble *Thai patchwork*.

SEQUINS (spangles, paillettes)

Small perforated metal, cellulose or plastic shapes for sewing to textiles. Sequins are usually shiny discs with a central hole, but there are many variations. Early precious metal ones were almost always referred to as laminae. The small metal eyelets used as dress decoration in the late sixteenth century were called oes or owes. The chekeen, a coin struck in Venice at the end of the eighteenth century, was used for trade purposes with the Far East. Some metal spangles have a split across their radius and appear to be burnished sections of turned metal shavings or pressed coils of wire.

Sequins: back stitched with purl

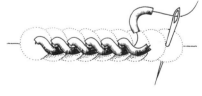

SHADING

A term frequently used in embroidery to denote changes in colour or tone associated with the description of form over an area of close stitchery. In gradual shading the colours are continuously modified with each succeeding line of stitchery, and

Seeding: waistcoat, eighteenth-century.
Multi-coloured sprigging. (*Rachel Kay
Shuttleworth Collection, Gawthorpe Hall*)

blendings require a detailed selection
of colours. In coarse shading strictly
limited tones are introduced, with
toothed edgings closely resembling the
hachures of tapestry, but free from its
horizontal confines.

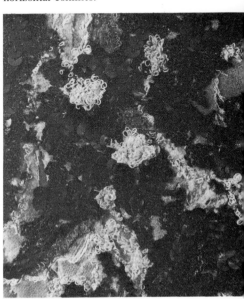

Sequins: black sequins and Cornely on
velvet. Made by Anne Stubbs

Sequins: gauntlets from a pair of gloves,
1600–25. Coloured silks, metal lace and
spangles. (*Nottingham Museum. Photograph:
Layland-Ross*)

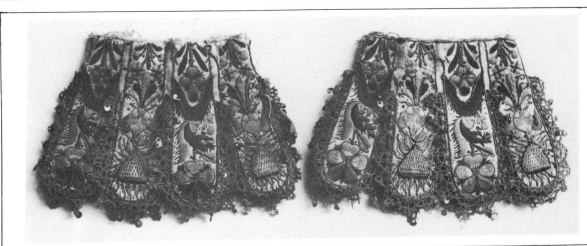

conservative. Small anemone-like flowers and paired leaves are worked in bands of herringbone on the reverse of organdie, producing an outline like back stitch on the right side. Colours are white or softly pastel. Designs are usually sprigged or powdered, or consist of small repeat motifs forming a border to a scalloped or pin-tucked edge.

A number of kinds of embroidery make full use of stitchery seen through the ground. Many *drawn fabric* fillings worked on sheer grounds are enriched by shadowed stitches. *Dresden work* achieved its graceful smoothness in this way, and *Chikan* has carefully considered thread journeys beneath the work which complement the delicate textures on the surface.

Bibliography
Liley; Thomas 1936

SHADOW QUILTING (ombre)

The use of coloured thread, fabric or wadding, stitched behind and showing through a translucent ground. It is applicable to all raised quilted techniques but more usually found in Italian quilting.

The stuffed areas in trapunto can be outlined individually and the stuffing added in individual compartments, starting in the middle of the work and progressing outwards.

Shadow quilting can be used as a flat technique, a means of applying delicate found objects and protecting them between layers of sheer transparent terylenes or chiffons. Pressed plant forms or scraps of fine printed fabric can be backed or bonded and stitched each in its own pocket between the layers. Using a tambour frame and the machine, pieces can be placed on the backing, held there by means of the top fabric, and secured with surrounding lines of stitchery. Surface stitching can be corded before or after the quilting.

SHADOW WORK

All those embroideries which feature stitchery, appliqué, or wadding showing beneath a translucent ground may be classed as shadow work. Traditionally, shadow work is very

Sequins: sprayed cream satin ground, raised gold kid, pailettes, beads and braids. Detail of a panel 18 × 15 cm (7 × 6 in.). Made by Di Bates

Shadow work: yellow crocus flowers mounted on iron-on backing, cut out and held in place with machine darning between layers of terylene ▼

Shadow work: white herringbone stitch on blue organdie. 18 × 13 cm (7 × 5 in.). Made by Christine Burke

SHIP PICTURES

Accurate crewel work representations of named sailing ships of the nineteenth century. By tradition they were worked by the sailors while aboard, using Berlin wools in long straight stitches, with the rigging superimposed in black thread.

Collection
UK Guildhall Museum, Rochester

SHISHA (abhla bharat, shisha dur, śīśadār, mirror glass)

Rounds cut from *mica* or thin mirror glass. Shisha cannot be pierced and so each piece must be sewn on with a mount, threads laid across it, or with a framework of stitchery. It is the main feature of *Kathiawar* work and associated in the West with exported Indian embroidery generally.

The tightly worked floral ornament liberally inlaid with tiny pieces of shisha in petal and leaf shapes has its origins among the Jats of Banni and the Lohanas of Khavada several centuries ago. The aba was heavily decorated at neck, sleeves and hem, with a horizontal panel at the front, and the salwar with a wide band across the lower legs. Birds and flowers in broad chain stitch and closely arranged rounds of shisha appeared on dark or red cotton grounds such as cadars and colīs. Cloths, wall hangings and friezes were all liberally decorated. Bolder chain stitch and interlacings with large shisha discs feature in Sindh, often worked on pieced, printed, or tie-dye cloth.

Mirror glass is still readily available in its crudely cut form, although there are metal and mounted substitutes. Of the several ways of attaching it the most time-consuming one is also the safest and the oldest. Secure the working thread on the point it is to occupy. Holding the piece in position between index finger and thumb, bring the thread through from the back, making two squares across the shisha, the second diagonally across the first, leaving an octagon in the middle. The tension of the working thread must hold the shisha firmly without distorting the fabric. Bringing the thread diagonally across the back a button-hole stitch is formed, embracing all adjacent holding threads. Then a small stitch is made through the fabric at the circumference, with the thread looped behind the needle. By repeating the buttonhole and the loop closely and alternately all round the shisha, a ridge of enclosing stitches is formed.

With care and dexterity, shisha can be stitched down using a free machine feather stitch. The needle must enter the fabric closely around the circumference, and the needle thread tension must be much tighter than the spool tension so that long loops are formed over the shisha.

Bibliography
Birdwood; Dongerkery; Dhamija; Irwin and Hall; Simpson 1978

Collections
UK Museum of Costume, Bath; Gawthorpe Hall, Burnley; Bankfield Museum, Halifax; Leeds Museum; Horniman Museum, London
India Calico Museum of Textiles, Ahmedabad

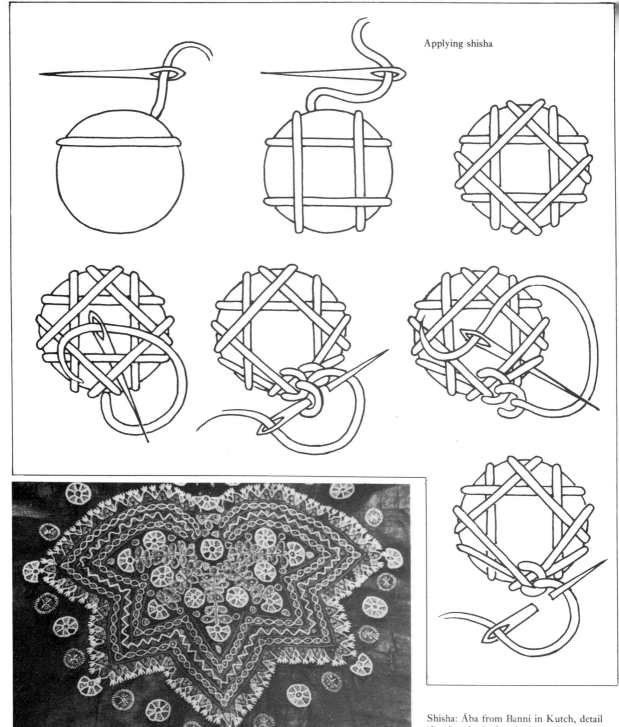

Applying shisha

Shisha: Ába from Banni in Kutch, detail showing the leaf at the base of the yoke. Chain stitch in primary colours, and tiny shisha roundels on black sateen. Leaf 18 cm (7 in.) wide. (*Bankfield Museum*)

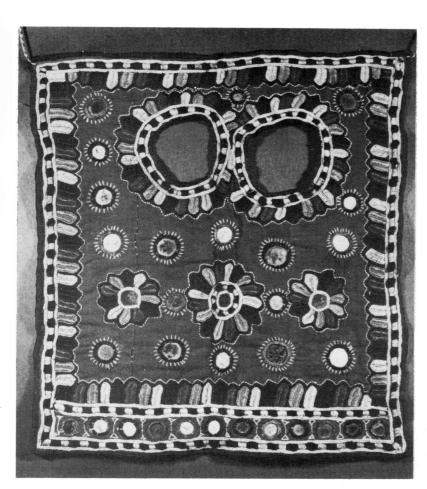

Shisha: North-western Indian, Gujarati horse's head cover. Shisha rounds on red cotton. (*Leeds Museum*)

SICILIAN WORK

A term applicable to several forms of embroidery.

It can refer to textiles which consist largely of applied coral beads, because this work was characteristic of the island.

It also applies to early examples of both cord and Italian quilting from Sicily, where they seem to have developed into an accomplished technique before they became common

Sicilian work: red silk in long-legged cross stitch on voided ground. Band 19 cm ($7\frac{1}{2}$ in.) wide

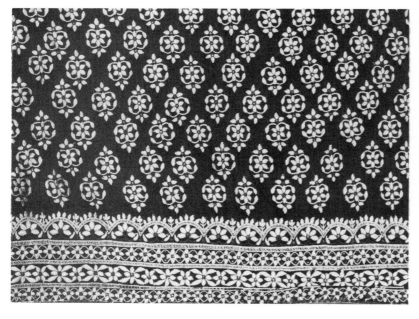

Shisha: dark blue fine silk sari, professional embroidery from Gujarat. Delicate red and white stitchery and minute shisha rounds. Detail 51 × 41 cm (20 × 16 in.). (*Leeds Museum*)

in the rest of Europe and the Mediterranean.

Much of the beautiful early drawn thread and drawn fabric work was Sicilian in origin. It seems to be grouped collectively under the heading of *Assisi*, perhaps because of the characteristically voided animal subjects and stitched grounds.

The diagonal overcast stitch commonly referred to as Sicilian drawn ground is merely one of the commoner stitches occurring on early embroideries from both Italy and Sicily.

SILK

Yarn, thread or fabric made from a continuous filament produced by the caterpillars of several species of moth to protect their pupae. References to sericulture suggest that silk was in use as a textile in China as early as 5000 BC. There are many records of the fascination and enjoyment of silk throughout ancient cultures, but the silkworm and the close secrets of its domestication did not leave China until the sixth century AD. Attempts to cultivate silk of quality outside China

have met with only limited success. Although the Chinese perfected the skills of silk weaving and embroidery so long ago, it is the Indians who excel in the ability to use silk in order to reflect shimmering light culminating in the bagh designs of the *Phulkari*.

Of all the insects which produced silk, few have real commercial value. It is the larvae of the mulberry silkworm, *Bombyx mori*, which extrude silk of the best quality. The inner layers of the cocoon are used without spinning. Shorter filaments are combed and

Silk: polychrome silk buttonholing on tablecloth. Detail 25 × 20 cm (10 × 8 in.). Made by P.M. Thornber

Silk: Chinese nineteenth-century dragon robe. Silks and couched gold on panels of sky blue silk with thunder symbols. (*Collection P.M. Thornber*)

carded for spun silk, and material left from that process is spun separately for silk noil. Wild silkworms produce Tussah and Eri, but the yellowish filament is considered inferior. Sometimes all second quality yarn is referred to as Tussah.

The finest even filaments are made into soft translucent fabrics with a lustre that only silk possesses. Even the most inferior slubby yarns have depth and glow when they are carefully dyed and expertly woven. Silk is strong and warm but not durable. It accepts dyes readily but does not absorb moisture. It combines with linen, wool and synthetics easily and usefully to provide versatile and functional textiles. Even on the heaviest weaves, silk is best lined for embroidery since it has no natural

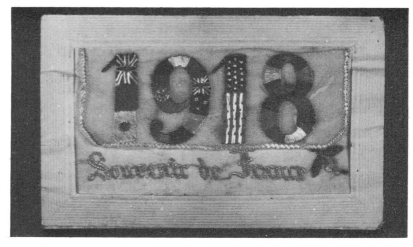

elasticity. Needles must be sharp and smooth, and working threads should not disturb the balance of the surrounding fabric. Apart from organzine and coin nets silk is rarely woven as a ground for counted stitchery.

Silk: floss silk on organdie. Whole card 14 × 9 cm (5½ × 3½ in.)

Bibliography
Stein

Silk: Chinese jacket, late nineteenth-century. Many bright colours on scarlet silk. (*Leeds Museum*)

Silk: Spanish, seventeenth-century, detail of a chasuble. Applied silk and laid metal thread on velvet. (*Embroiderers' Guild*)

SILK GROUNDS AND WORKING THREADS

Virtually all silk grounds, far too numerous to detail, are suitable for some form of embroidery. Fashions dictate manufacture, but the grounds most readily available are of plain weaves varying from the finest translucent soft colours to richly glowing heavy slubs. *Kimono* are worked on medium-weight pieces dyed and printed with great sophistication. Costume silks used to be weighted with metallic salts, and so deteriorated sadly when they were washed. Modern additives are more durable. Working threads in silk are not generally available and must be specially ordered. Mercerised six-ply cotton threads are sometimes referred to as embroidery silks.

Dacca silk or soie ovale was variously described as fine, twisted and stranded for working Berlin patterns. Medium was an untwisted floss. It was imported from Dacca in East Bengal during the eighteenth and nineteenth centuries.

Filoselle or bourre de soie is a glowing stranded silk of medium quality, coming from the coarser, outer fibres of the cocoon.

Filo floss or filo silk is thicker than filoselle with a slight twist but less gloss. It is usually two-ply.

Floss gives a beautiful lustre but it is not very strong. Its old names are sleave or slaided silk, in India it is hir, and its many thicknesses include bobbin, church and tram weights. Soft and without twist, it is difficult to work. It should be used for laid work and long stitches which display its sheen to best advantage.

Horsetail or Maltese is very fine and tightly twisted, designed for working metal threads. It should always be beeswaxed.

Mallard resembled horsetail but was slightly coarser, rather like buttonhole silk.

Mitorse had more twist than floss, like a heavy filo floss, of the kind which features richly on much Greek embroidery.

Purse silk and mallard seem to be synonymous.

Twist or etching silk, also called buttonhole, can still be found in its handspun form, but usually only in neutral colours.

Bibliography
Bellinger; Irwin and Hall

SILK MOSAIC

Pieced work in silk is common both archaeologically and on traditional costume in those countries which are historically associated with sericulture. In Western societies, mathematical precision and logic in the fine arts and the availability of plain-coloured silk fabrics have led to silk mosaic as a medium of expressive composition.

SILK PICTURES (hairwork pictures, print pictures, printwork pictures, satin sketches)

A variety of pictorial embroideries beginning during the Royalist period, associated because of their adaptation from paintings and engravings, and by the frequent use of hair as a working thread and paint for backgrounds and features.

The macabre use of human hair is

Silk pictures: hairwork, eighteenth-century. Carefully chosen tones of human hair in darning stitches. 15 × 13 cm (6 × 5 in.). (*Lancaster Museum*)

recorded surprisingly late in the history of Western textiles, but by the time of the Tudors it was being used in a more conventional way, associated with affection rather than conquest. Called point tresse, the hair, presumably of sentimental association, was spun around a silk or linen core and used for knitting purposes. The Stuarts exchanged embroidered gifts worked in hair and silks, with affectionate symbols and lovers' knots entwined. During the last year of his imprisonment Charles I sent hair to his devoted followers so that portrait miniatures of him could be completed with it.

Satin sketches, from about 1780 to 1800, were of fashionable ladies and then of landscapes and Biblical scenes. Tiny and delicate drawings were made in sepia ink, or printed onto cream satin or silk, with skies, faces and hands painted in water colours. Working threads were of silk, or silk and human hair, carefully selected for fineness and colour.

By the eighteenth century the techniques had extended to map samplers, classical and mythological themes and maritime landscapes. Features were sometimes painted separately and then applied to the ground, and stitchery could be defined

with overpainting. Working threads such as fine metal purls or chenille were incorporated.

Etching embroidery emerged in the late eighteenth century and enjoyed a revival during the Victorian period. On creamy slipper satin, distance was achieved with painted grounds and finely pencilled perspective. Stitchery was in silks and hair, delicately cross-hatched and graded to imitate contemporary etching techniques. Fine french knots were permissible to simulate stippling on trees and grass. Despite its limitations, etching work was probably the most sensitive style to emerge from the Victorian period.

A short revival in the 1930s consisted of kits of patriotic subjects coarsely printed on linen, to be worked with supplied black thread.

Bibliography
Caulfeild and Saward; Marshall

Collections
UK The Moravian Museum, Fulneck; Lancaster Museum

SLATE FRAME
See *frames*

Silk pictures: human hair used on a Chinese wall-hanging. Coarse floss on red flannel. 76 cm (30 in.) deep. Late nineteenth-century. (*Leeds Museum*)

SLIPS

Separately made motifs or figures applied to the ground after their stitchery has been completed. They were used on *opus anglicanum*, especially on difficult grounds like velvet, and occur frequently on ecclesiastical and ceremonial embroidery, where it is expedient to work intricate pieces before they are brought together on the ground. The Elizabethans used them liberally, working counted motifs on canvas which were cut out and firmly finished with rich outline stitchery.

Bibliography
Jourdain 1927

Collections
UK Traquair House, Innerleithen; Hardwick Hall, Mansfield; Nottingham Museum

SMOCKING

The gathering of fullness on garments which are constructed from the woven width of cloth rather than shaped or tailored. The area to be gathered is prepared by lines of gauging stitches. The term now refers to the embroidered decoration of these gathers, tubes or reeds which serves to hold them in place. Reverse, or *Italian smocking* is a variation. Historically, smocking seems to be a vernacular skill, occurring only rarely on fashionable or court dress. Traditional smocking in Spain is worked boldly in primary colours on heavy linen grounds with spiralling stitchery and deeply scalloped flounces. The main areas of decoration are amongst the folds rather than on the gathers. Smocks and smocking are well known in Britain because of their romantic rural association, and because they were durable and took their place in many museum collections.

There is some illustrative evidence to suggest that smocking was used on peasant clothes in the fourteenth century. Smock frocks or round smocks themselves were popular by the middle of the eighteenth century and declined towards the end of the nineteenth. They were probably only in daily use by those who had special need of them, like shepherds and drovers, but a general labourer would reserve his for high days and holidays.

Smocking: *c.* 1890. White linen, smocking on chest, back, shoulders and cuffs, and surface feather stitchery. (*Gloucester Folk Museum*)

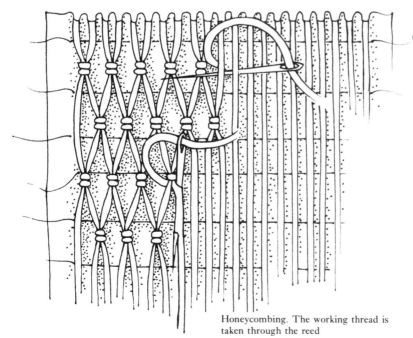

Honeycombing. The working thread is taken through the reed

Smocking: 1870. Heavy white linen with rope, chevron and backstitch, and surface feather stitching on panels and collar. Sleeve heads and cuffs smocked. (*Gloucester Folk Museum*)

According to their weight, weave and treatment they could be waterproof and windproof and indispensable for protecting other clothing. The fabric was plain linen, closely woven Barnsley duck or drabbet, in unbleached white, brown or sometimes blue. The stitchery was in white or unbleached linen thread at yoke, neck and cuffs.

Cunnington and Lucas state that 'There seems no evidence that there was any correspondence between the various designs and the wearer's job.' Nevertheless, there is verbal and written encouragement for an opposing viewpoint, however tentative. Itinerant specialist workers needed some visual identification at hiring fairs, and smocks bear embroidered tree symbols for foresters, wheels for carters, and

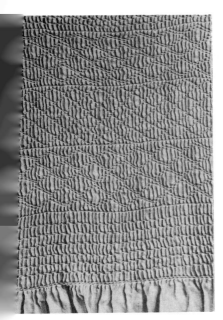

Smocking: early twentieth-century forester's smock from Dorset. Detail. (*Rachel Kay Shuttleworth Collection, Gawthorpe Hall*)

Smocking: Spanish, nineteenth-century. Madder-red floss silk on heavy linen, collar and one sleeve head. The smocked panel below the double-curve motifs opens out to form enriched lobes. (*Rachel Kay Shuttleworth Collection, Gawthorpe Hall*)

tups' horns for shepherds. Much of the decoration surrounds the smocked areas and is closely allied with the symbolism of *wadded quilting*.

The potential of the dense gathered ground is revealed only by stitchery. The traditional stem, wave, honeycomb and chevron stitches, used with due consideration for their spatial arrangements, expose conflicting distortions of the reeds and unlimited textural richness. Used informally, uneven gathers and random stitches offer scope of another kind, especially when worked on fabrics not usually associated with smocking.

Traditional work may be done on almost any firm ground. It requires approximately three times the width of the finished garment. Checked gingham is recommended for beginners, since the rows of regular gathering stitches can be made exactly at the junctions of the squared pattern without gauging or the use of a transfer, and the lines of stitches are

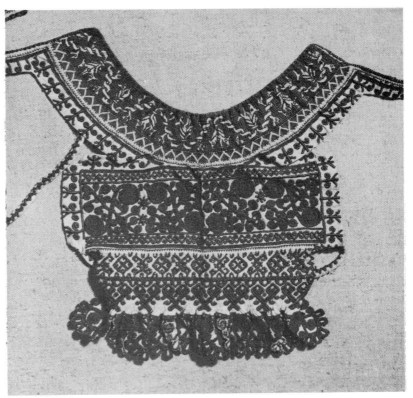

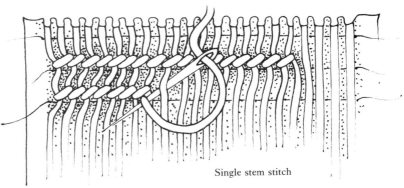

Single stem stitch

certain to be on the straight grain. Plain fabrics must be measured and marked in dots with a sharp, hard pencil on the wrong side, or a smocking transfer may be ironed on. Various spacings can be bought. The dots should describe an exact square grid over the whole area to be gathered. Beginning with a large knot on a strong thread a line of running stitches is made right across one row, piercing the fabric exactly at each dot. The other end of the thread is left loose. Each row is treated in the same

way. When all the gauging rows are stitched the threads are drawn up in small groups until the whole area is evenly gathered. To secure the gathers, the threads are tied together in pairs.

At this stage it is necessary to consider the final garment and allow for slight shaping in the nature of the gauging stitches and the final tension of the gathers. Lines of stem stitch will immediately stabilize the smocked area, and serve as a useful anchor near a seam when the garment is made up. At the base of the smocking an undulating line is preferable, avoiding a sharp distinction between gathering and fullness of fabric. Obviously, those stitches which produce an uneven line will allow more elasticity than those which make a straight one, and equally, any stitch following a deeply waved or steeply chevroned line will allow more softness in the gathers and more textural interest. The gauging stitches are removed only when all the work is completed.

Bibliography

Armes; Buck; Cave 1980; Cunnington and Lucas 1976; Durand; Knott; Liley; Stapley; Thom

Collections

UK Bowes Museum, Barnard Castle; Gawthorpe Hall, Burnley; Welsh Folk Museum, Cardiff; Cheltenham Museum; Gloucester Folk Museum; Guildford Museum; Hereford City Museum; Norwich Castle Museum; Museum of English Rural Life, Reading; Warwick Museum; Oxfordshire County Museum, Woodstock

SOL LACE

See *Tenerife lace*

SOUTACHE

See *Froggings*

SPANGLES

See *Sequins*

SPANISH WORK

See *Blackwork*

SPIDER'S WEB WORK

An all-over or chequered arrangement of counted squares, the edge of each sharing the same shed of the weave with its neighbour. Each square has a worked spider's web or woven wheel. Popular during the first half of the twentieth century, it was worked in mercerised cotton on linen, or a special soft canvas, and later on glass towelling. It bears close resemblance to parachute string work which was done over nails hammered vertically at measured intervals on a board, the intersecting threads decorated with webs, wheels or clipped pompons.

SQUARE NET EMBROIDERY

See *Filet*

SQUARING UP

See *Transferring designs*

STAMPS

Raised *metal thread work* for regalia is sometimes worked over wooden moulds or relief card shapes known as stamps. *Stumpwork* and stamp work are synonymous. Card ones were hollow-cast from pulp, and the gold was worked right over or through fine holes previously made with a stiletto.

STAR PATCHWORK

A form of *applied patchwork* consisting of separately folded tags of material lapped over one another like alternating roofing tiles. Each square of fabric is folded in half diagonally, and then each acute angle is folded in again to meet the right angle, so that the hypotenuse becomes a central diagonal fold and all corners meet at the base. These small squares are then arranged either concentrically or in parallel lines so that all their raw edges are concealed beneath succeeding squares.

Petal patchwork is similarly constructed, but the triangles are arranged into flower forms, their raw edges gathered and concealed beneath applied circles or clusters of beads. The gathering causes the petals to be raised. By using just four petals to each flower an all over pattern of diamonds or squares can be achieved.

STITCHES

Stitches are the embroiderer's vocabulary. Most of them are universal, the simpler ones occurring across broad cultural bands, sometimes remote from external influences. Recently, mixed media experiments and the manipulation of fabrics have overtaken them, adding richness and

Star patchwork: tags set on the foundation being prepared to make a box top. Size of square 15 cm (6 in.). Made by Ethel Mitchell

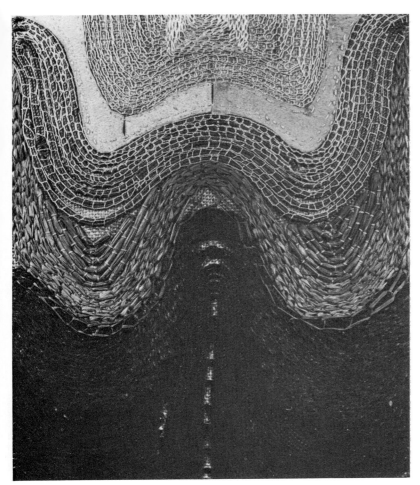

Stitches: string, raffia and chamois leather on hessian. Panel 86 × 61 cm (34 × 24 in.)

Stitches: Cretan stitch worked into radiating buttonhole. Mat of natural linen with ochre and green. Detail 46 cm (18 in.) wide

expression: but the importance of stitchery cannot be over-emphasized. An understanding of the pattern, virtuosity and variability of stitches, together with the skill in choosing and manipulating them, is crucial to the embroiderer.

Bibliography
Butler 1980; Caulfeild and Saward; Christie 1920; de Dillmont; Enthoven; *Good Housekeeping Sewing Crafts*; Gray; Howard 1979; John 1967; Karasz; Nichols; Pesel 1912, 1917; Petersen and Svennäs; Rhodes 1980; Snook 1963; Thomas 1934

STOBBED QUILTS (tied quilts)

Thick bed or cot coverings with ample batting which is held in place at spaced intervals rather than with a continuous quilting line. The top may be pieced or whole. Traditionally, the batting was cotton waste or combed wool, and each tie was decorated by a small tuft of thread.

The top is measured and marked in dots spaced appropriately to the scale of the quilt and the nature of the materials, and describing an exact square grid over the whole surface. All three layers are laid flat with the marked top uppermost. Using many large, sharp safety pins the layers are pinned together, starting at the edges and working from one side to the other towards the centre. A small stitch is made with a long needle at the position for each tie and secured with a strong knot and sufficient tension to make a considerable dimple. Through loose weaves and synthetic filling, very fine tape or ribbon can sometimes be substituted for thread. There is scope for surface stitching or applied work before the quilt is made up, and decorative treatment of the ties.

STRING QUILTING

See *Applied patchwork*

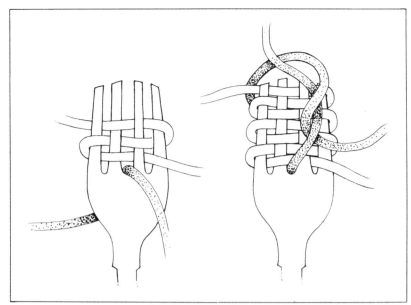

Stobbed quilts: making tufts to decorate the stitched points

STUFFED QUILTING

See *Trapunto* and *Corded quilting*

STUMPWORK (embroidery on the stamp)

Seventeenth-century embroidery, largely belonging to Britain, which consisted of richly decorative bas relief stitchery and appliqué worked on satin panels, mirror frames, cabinets and baskets.

Raised embroidery was practised widely on the Continent and especially in Germany as part of the Gothic striving towards realism. Metal thread stitchery was worked over high paddings of closely structured wadding or carved wooden blocks. Britain clung to the tradition of *opus anglicanum*, and relief work appeared only minimally during the early years of the reign of Henry VIII, in the form of canopies and enclosures decorating vestments. In the Mediterranean countries and in Britain needlemade lace and cutwork were becoming intricate and inventive, with figures and animals worked in detached buttonhole and padded overcastings. After the Reformation raised work became secular. Much maligned since its heyday, stumpwork is an apt reflection of Tudor well-

being and optimism. The Marshalls, writing in the late nineteenth century when stumpwork was so much despised, dared to say 'Infinite trouble and ingenuity were exercised upon the minutest of details of this very curious work, and the crudeness of the designs is atoned for by the extreme beauty of the technique.' Some authorities credit the nuns of Little Gidding with the invention of stumpwork, others state that it was they who practised it extensively.

These embroideries are certainly more than schoolgirl masterpieces, since much of the fine technique, however naïve in its presentation, is

Stumpwork: sixteenth-century sweet bag in fine silk tent stitch and lace-stitched metal thread, with a metal passementerie edge. 9 × 10 cm (3½ × 4 in.). (*Rachel Kay Shuttleworth Collection, Gawthorpe Hall*)

Stumpwork: seventeenth-century box top. Silk and metal threads on cream satin, seed baroque pearls, mica, knotting, purls, chenille, fine plate and raised lace-stitch petals. 36 × 30 cm (14 × 12 in.). (*Lancaster Museum*)

the result of more experienced finesse. The caskets vary in size, but all have a highly decorated lid and intricate interiors. Some of the surviving panels or pictures in stumpwork are probably lids which were never incorporated into cabinets or were preserved when the box was destroyed. The lid usually has a central canopy with figures, a castle with trees, birds and beasts on hummocks, and a deep floral border. A sloping frame around the lid bears another border, resting on decorative side panels. The lid opens to reveal a three-dimensional garden, which in turn lifts for access to silk quilted trays and tiny compartments. The double doors to the front of the cabinet open to display sets of drawers, each covered with laid silk floss couched in floral or geometric patterns. The subject matter is Royalist, Biblical, mythological and allegorical, often amusingly mixed. It is characteristic of raised work that no ground space should be left unfilled. This leads to delightful juxtapositions and a total lack of proportional scale, the motifs collected from pattern books being squeezed and adapted to fill all available space. Many pieces are alike. The caskets may have been sold in kit form, and most of the designs, materials and accessories were probably provided as progressive packages, being professionally made up afterwards.

The cream satin ground was always backed with linen. The design was either drawn direct with black ink or traced through some form of carbon from published patterns. Individual motifs and figures were probably selected from patterns and distributed by the embroiderer on the area to be worked. The stumps which formed the bas relief were constructed with hanks of wool or hair stitched over and over with couching thread until the required relief and detailed contouring was achieved. A silk or satin covering was applied, oversewn carefully around the edges to keep it quite smooth.

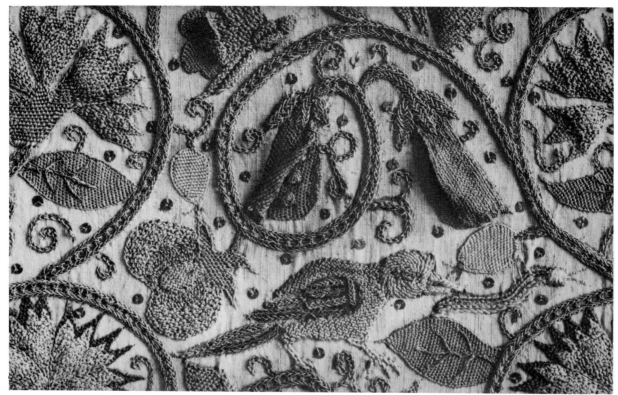

Stumpwork: early seventeenth-century panel detail. Silk and silver-gilt threads and sequins on white linen. (*Embroiderers' Guild*)

Often this appliqué had to be done in separate pieces to accommodate the moulding underneath. When figures were in high relief they were made beforehand like tiny dolls, and sometimes heads and hands were carved in wood and covered, the features delicately painted. Buttonholing and lace stitches were used extensively to cover moulds, to make detached petals, leaves and fruit, their edges rich in picots. The little tents or awnings which so often framed the figures were pre-embroidered. Everything was highly decorated with silks, pearls, beads and jewels, paper, chenilles, cord, guimp, purls and plate. Mica was used to represent window glass, silver plate for water, and iridescent feathers for birds. Late during the period whole panels and baskets were worked entirely in multi-coloured beads.

Bibliography
Marshall

Collections
UK Bowes Museum, Barnard Castle; Bankfield Museum, Halifax; Ipswich Museum; Lancaster City Museum; Temple Newsam Museum, Leeds; London Museum; Victoria and Albert Museum, London; Whitworth Art Gallery and Museum, Manchester; Strangers' Hall, Norwich
USA Museum of Fine Art, Boston; Metropolitan Museum of Art, New York

SUFFOLK PUFFS (yo-yos, powder puffs, rosettes)

Circles of fabric turned and gathered at their edges so that, in taking up the gathering thread, the circumference can be brought to the centre and smaller, folded circles formed. These small circles have textural and decorative qualities when they are grouped or sewn together in patterns. Traditionally they are placed together to form a continuous surface, and are often included in a *quiltmaking* method

Suffolk puffs: turning and gathering the circle

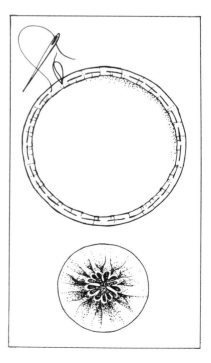

or as an *applied patchwork* method. Puffs were often completed with a small pompon.

Bibliography
Ickis *Complete Book of Needlework*;

SUN LACE

See *Tenerife embroidery*

SWEDISH DARNING

See *Darning*

SWISS WORK

See *Broderie anglaise*

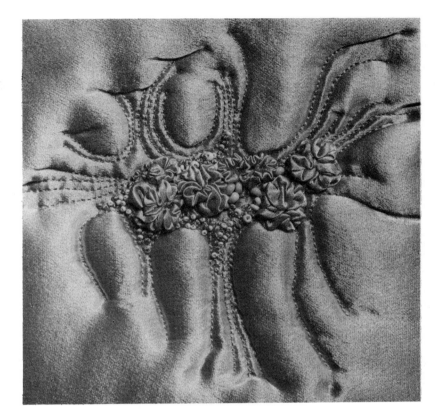

Suffolk puffs: cream quilting sample with crunched Suffolk puffs. Made by Estelle Liley. (*Photograph: Chris Locke*)

different kinds of work. Sets of sizes may be fitted into a common handle. The chain loop is guided on to the hook beneath the stretched fabric with the other hand, and workers employ a guard for the forefinger. Beginnings and endings of the working thread must be carefully secured.

The technique probably came from China, and was used extensively in India for centuries, particularly in Gudjerat and Sind where it is still practised. It was popular in Europe and America in the eighteenth and nineteenth centuries for waistcoats, bedcovers and portières. With the manufacture of fine muslin and bobbin net *Ayrshire, Limerick lace* and *Dresden work* all had tambouring incorporated into the design at some stage of their development. In some cases it eventually superseded all needle stitchery.

Beading on open fabrics and net can be done quickly with the tambour

Tambour work: Mochi work from Banni in Kutch. Green silk satin skirt with bright colours in regular chain. Detail 24 × 17 cm (9½ × 6½ in.). (*Bankfield Museum*)

TAGS

See *Raised appliqué*

TAMBOUR WORK

A chain stitch produced with a hook which draws the thread through from the back of the work and secures it with the succeeding chain. It is always worked in a frame. Tambour is distinguishable from ordinary needle-made *chain stitch* in that it is clearly done at speed, producing wide, open curves which are smooth and unhesitating, often abutting or overlapping. In scale it varies from very fine white work on hexagonal net for wedding veils or fichus, to coarse crewels on *namdhas*.

The ari, tambour hook or crochet needle is made in various sizes for

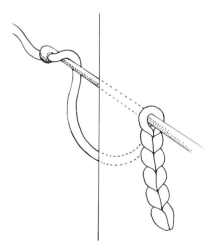

The action of the tambour hook

hook. The beads are accommodated on a continuous thread laid on the surface of the ground and the hook is used beneath, emerging regularly to catch the bead-bearing thread with a chain stitch. It is still used extensively in fashion and often juxtaposed with tamboured yarns, *Cornely* braiding or free stitchery.

Bibliography
Bath 1974, 1979; Caulfeild and Saward; Irwin and Hall 1973; Nicholson

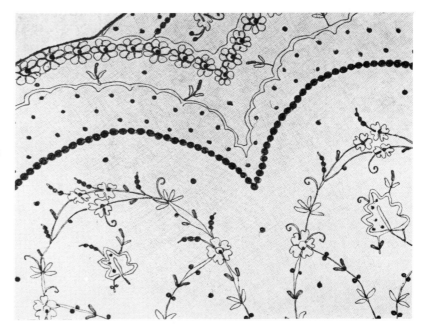

Tambour work: linen lace thread on cream silk net. Flounce, detail 36 × 30 cm (14 × 12 in.)

Tambour work: Moroccan curtain. Soft floss in pastel colours and white cotton tambour, on open, white muslin. Detail. (*Leeds Museum*)

Tambour work: boy's jacket from Ketchi. Thick unbleached cotton, multi-coloured ari work and herringbone stitching. (*Leeds Museum*)

TAPE LACE (Bohemian, dictal, ribbon lace)

Coarse needlepoint worked independently of a ground, based on a foundation of equidistant meanders formed with narrow bobbin tape, and featuring separately-made bound or buttonholed rings applied at intersections. The work was given a great deal of exposure in needlework articles and magazines around the end of the nineteenth century, when it

acquired several novelty names. Magazines promoted kits which contained all the patterns and materials needed for a given piece. Lustrous threads and creamy silk tape were used for shoulder wraps or headcoverings, and soft pure white cottons for household linens.

Tape lace is not to be confused with tape work, where lacet braid or straight narrow lengths of tape were joined at their edges with insertion stitches to form a continuous fabric. The technique known as cracklestitch mesh does, however, overlap. Sometimes it was presented as a method in its own right, but

Klickmann's instructions for the mesh suggest that it was an integral part of tape lace, with a more random and complex journey for the working thread.

Patterns were printed on paper or cloth and there is little evidence to suggest that workers ever made their own designs. The cloth patterns allowed the finished work to be starched and ironed before it was removed.

The tape is tacked carefully over the pattern and most spaces are filled by taking a thread across from one tape edge to the other like herringboning, fastening the thread each time with a knot. Long radiating crossings can be made in there-and-back journeys, twisting the thread over itself for stability. Buttonhole bars can fill very wide spaces, and close bars or even simple lace fillings can be accommodated in narrow spaces.

The buttonholed rings are made by winding a thread around a suitably sized stiletto or knitting needle, keeping the thread spiralling flat rather than winding on top of previous circuits. The thread is continued to form the buttonholing, which may have its looped edge at the circumference or at the top of the ring.

Bibliography
Bath 1974; Klickmann

TAPESTRY

Although true tapestry is woven on a loom warp, the shuttle travels only across the area of its own colour, to lock with the adjacent colour before returning to its other extremity. Many shuttles are in use at any given time. Some kinds of embroidery have for centuries imitated the design and function of tapestry, and for this reason *canvas work* and other forms of coloured, counted stitchery are often referred to as tapestry work. Some early forms of *needleweaving* were worked over reserved warp yarns, and supplementary weft brocading employs the same principle.

The use of surface stitchery techniques which imitate tapestry has caused some significant embroideries to remain uninvestigated under the

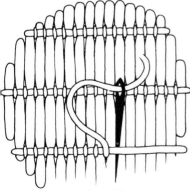

Tapestry: a laid version of Oriental stitch, which, like Bokhara, can be mistaken for woven texture

Tapestry: Guatemalan huipil from the Quiche Indians in Nebaj. Supplementary weft brocading. Panel of figures and horses in brilliant colours. 51 cm (20 in.) square. (*Leeds Museum*)

category of tapestry weaving. Gertie Wandel discusses the omission in the light of some Icelandic refill-saum textiles on which the ground is completely covered. Detail is achieved in added linen stitchery. They probably date from the early medieval period. One shows scenes from the life of Saint Martin and other scenes from the Life of the Virgin. Like earlier Danish archaeological finds, the Gerona Creation hanging, and the Bayeux tapestry, they are worked with a filling stitch which provided extraordinary durability.

Bibliography
de Dillmont; Hald; Wandel

Collections
UK   Victoria and Albert Museum, London
Denmark   Copenhagen National Museum
France   Bayeux Museum
Spain   Gerona Cathedral

TASSELS

Separately made bunches of yarn, ribbon or cord, each suspended by its head and applied as textile decoration. They may be used in identical groups or rows, clustered in small numbers at corners, or individually suspended from tags or cords. They vary from tiny modest ones applied to household linens or scarves to opulent ones which feature on heavy drapery, furnishings and banners. See pp. 206–7.

Bibliography
de Dillmont; Harvey

TEMPLATE (guide)

A specially made flat geometric shape of any material, or a household article adapted for the purpose, employed as a guide for repetitive pattern making. Some *patchwork* and *wadded quilting* templates have apertures which aid measured overlapping. Others have secondary windows or frames so that

Tassels: Yugoslavia, Njegushi clan, Montenegro. Knitted mitten with white glass beads. (*Bankfield Museum*)

Tassels: detail from a Macedonian shawl. Black silk on cotton with wrapped tassels. (*Embroiderers' Guild*)

◀ Tassels: Chinese shoulder wrap. Polychrome minute silk stitches on cream with appliqué, braiding, netting and tassels. (*Leeds Museum*)

each piece, its hem allowance, and its corresponding paper can be accurately assessed. Old ones were made of bone, ivory, bark, wood and metals. Modern templates are made of clear acrylic.

It is worth considering making simple transparent perspex or acetate templates. These are an advantage in placing the motifs on the quilt top. They can be cut from discarded packaging. A transparent ruler is also useful. Where pattern shapes overlap or intersect, the template can be marked at strategic points and so matched to previously stitched lines as the work progresses.

Bibliography
Whiting

Tassels: north-west Indian horse necklace. Rich colours with shisha on cotton, and metallic glass beads. 8 cm (3 in.) wide. (*Leeds Museum*)

TENERIFE EMBROIDERY (Canary Island embroidery, Calado, Taoro, La Palma, Mexican openwork, Mexican drawn work, de sols)

Linen ground drawn in large regular open squares with diagonal working threads across them, reinforced with wheels, rings and needleweaving. It is a white or unbleached *drawn thread* technique named after the capital of the Canary Islands. *Tenerife lace* and embroidery have a parallel and shared development, the two methods often being used together on the same piece, but the lace suns are worked quite differently, and independent of a ground fabric.

Rich Spanish laces were taken to the Colonies and developed as an offshoot after the Conquistadores. Missionaries introduced profitable textile industries to the Americas, where local symbolism and techniques were assimilated. The openwork bearing the sun and wheel motifs was both successful and profitable. Exported to Europe, it was taken up once more in

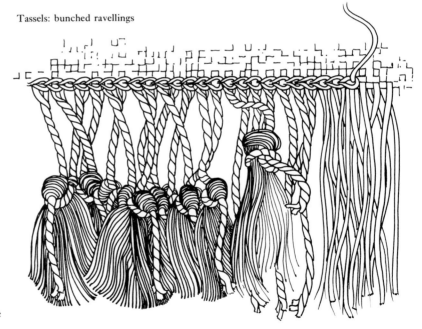

Tassels: bunched ravellings

Spain as a cottage industry, and both sources flourished until the early twentieth century.

Alternating blocks of yarn are cut over wide borders, leaving the same number of holes as those squares of yarn. The total weave remains on abutting squares, which are

strengthened and tightened by connecting loop stitches. A background lattice of overcasting loop stitches called punto espiritu strengthens the blocks of trailing ground threads and the open squares are transversely crossed and often decorated. This is usually in a slightly coarser thread

Tenerife lace: a Nanduti type from Paraguay, *c.* 1900. 18 cm (7 in.) wide. (*Nottingham Museum*)

Tenerife embroidery: Mexican drawn work with wheels and spider webs, white linen with a knitted border. Detail 28 × 22 cm (11 × 8½ in.)

than the ground to give a knobbly appearance. On older pieces the overcasting is so close as to form a stiff and sometimes protruding lattice.

Bibliography
de Dillmont; Lewis; Stapley; Stillwell; *Weldon's*

Collection
UK   Nottingham Museum

TENERIFE LACE (Brazilian, Bolivian, Paraguay, sol lace)

A form of needlewoven lace constructed with suns or medallions worked independently of one another and stitched together, often without being attached to any ground. It is a white technique and belongs to South America and the Canary Islands. *Tenerife embroidery* and lace have a parallel and shared development.

The suns are worked in linen or sometimes cotton thread, over small circular cushions or bobbins covered with blue cloth or over metal discs, with many pins set along the outer edge. Needles are very long, of a uniform thickness, and curved and flattened at the end, without a point. The working thread loops around opposing pins to form regular diameters, the threads all crossing at the centre. The needlewoven patterns are worked on this foundation. When one sun is completed it is covered with paper so that another can be made, until there are about 12 stacked on the cushion. These are removed and stitched together to form insertions, edgings, fichus and collars. Sometimes their circumferences are reinforced and decorated with scallops or lace points.

Bibliography
de Dillmont; Lewis; Stapley; Stillwell; *Weldon's*

Tenerife lace: coarse sols overstitched together, around a cut square of Mexican drawn work. 20 cm (8 in.) in diameter

Collections
UK   Gawthorpe Hall, Burnley; Nottingham Museum

TENT STITCH

See *Petit point*

THAI PATCHWORK

Delicate assemblies of fine silks in successively smaller layers used as bands and borders. *Applied patchwork* of this kind has a history of thousands of years in the Far East. It closely resembles Guatemalan and *Seminole patchwork*.

THREADING (drawn-in drawn thread)

This is a simple method for replacing the warp or weft of white ground linen with another thread. The one to be introduced is tied to a single warp or weft yarn and then pulled into the fabric in the same action as that which withdraws the yarn from the opposite

Threading: mercerised cotton on white linen. 13 cm (5 in.) square

edge. Characteristically, it is used to form simple borders in one or two soft primary colours in association with little clusters of sprigged bullion knot rosebuds. The style belongs to the early twentieth century.

Bibliography
Anchor Manual; Polkinghorne

THREADS

Commercial working threads for embroidery are made in a wide variety under a number of established brand names. Most are either wool or mercerised cotton. Linen, silk and metal threads will be found only at specialist retailers. Quilting thread, linen lace thread and Italian quilting wool are among those manufactured for a specific purpose. Weaving yarns often prove perfectly acceptable, and those which cannot be used in a needle can be couched. Weaving and knitting yarns are normally sold in quantities

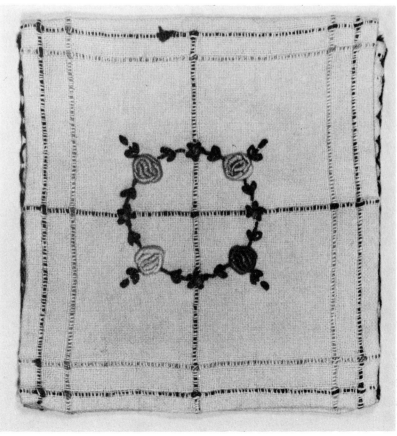

too large for the embroiderer, but weavers and knitters have oddments, yarns can be shared by groups, and reserves of stock build a wealth of readily available working threads. Experienced spinners may enjoy the challenge of making a yarn in imitation of that on historical embroidery, and dyeing experiments are always worthwhile. Many old drawn thread and drawn fabric pieces have ravellings from their own ground incorporated. Some modern furnishing rayons unravel to give a wealth of glowing, softly spun colours. Natural plant fibre and animal hair reward investigation. Strings, ties, packaging and gift wraps should be examined for anything which might be used.

Modern embroiderers often fail to appreciate that their work lacks the mellow qualities of old stitchery not simply because of the intervening years, but because of the difference between machine-made and hand-made materials. Whereas it may well be unrealistic to suggest weaving one's own grounds, it is worthwhile experimenting with yarn dyeing and random fading.

TIED QUILTS

See *Stobbed quilts*

TOILE CIRÉE

A fine soft tissue onto which the design was traced or the design transfer ironed, to be tacked behind translucent fabrics. The embroidery was stitched through the ground only, the toile being removed when the work was finished. It was used for fine white work and for many laces.

TRACING

See *Transferring designs*

TRAMMING

Preparation of the ground by means of long threads stitched parallel to each weft yarn or group of yarns. Canvas work or *Berlin woolwork* grounds were available already trammed in colours appropriate to areas of the design, so that the pattern could be accurately followed. Trammed stitchery covered the ground completely and produced a raised texture.

TRANSFERRING DESIGNS

There is controversy about the process of transferring designs from paper to fabric, and it is misleading to insist upon a correct method for each particular material or technique. Ambitious pieces require proper consideration beforehand, and the process must be allocated a large proportion of the total work time.

Medieval embroideries were drawn direct on the ground in pen or brush by professional artists, but these were all instances where the stitchery would adequately cover the design lines. Wooden blocks for stamping repetitive patterns onto grounds were in use by Tudor times. Most of the commercial white work techniques were worked over printed or blocked designs. The refreshingly naïve quality of many historical embroideries arose in part because the embroiderer working without an artist's assistance was obliged to enlarge material from illustrations and make individual judgements.

All grounds should be taped or pinned taut to a flat surface before any method is attempted. Centre lines can be marked by folding or tacking. Very large expanses can be worked in sections weighted at the edges over a table, or pinned to a carpet or floor with board or card beneath the main body of the fabric.

Many designs, drawings or photographs for embroidery need enlarging to the intended size, or very occasionally reducing.

There are instances where the design can be drawn direct on the fabric from a smaller drawing, particularly where the ground is to be completely covered with stitchery, like canvas work or rugs. Both design and ground are measured out in the same number of grid squares and then the main design lines are free drawn on to the ground, using the measured lines as a guide. Drawing is done with wax crayon or waterproof ink or felt tip. Avoid using a soft pencil, since the lead dust will soil any stitching done later. Alternatively, working from a design on squared paper, the grid can be counted out on the ground in running stitches of a contrasting colour, the stitches themselves

performing a regular counting function. The embroidery is then worked direct from the squared paper design and needs no transferred lines.

Large embroideries can be designed full size. Where motifs or shapes are to be repeated their outlines can be cut from thin card so that, by distributing them across paper representing the ground full size, their proper spacing can be estimated, using progressively firmer outlines until the final arrangement is decided.

With both design and ground squared up, a full size cartoon overlay of the design can be cut up, following the main drawing lines. Each component can be pinned to the ground and drawn round. Shapes and motifs must be numbered and recorded on the original design. Positions can be constantly cross checked by referring to the grid lines.

The use of a photographic transparency to project an enlarged image has possibilities. The ground fabric replaces the projector screen, and considerable detail can be drawn out in this way. It must be remembered that the transparency will be damaged by overheating if left in the projector for too long.

When large embroideries cover more than a full loom width of the ground, the selvedges must be turned and basted to each other before the design is transferred, and unstitched before the work is begun. As the embroidery stitches approach the edge of each width they must be abandoned as loose ends and taken up again for completion across the join when the ground widths are reunited.

For free machine stitchery it is important that any transferring method leaves only a rudimentary guide. The machine must be allowed its role as an independent drawing medium.

Dressmaker's carbon is useful wherever design lines can be completely obliterated by stitching or appliqué. Washing will not remove them, and in any instance, washing a piece of work should never be considered as a finishing process, only as an ultimate expediency after much use. Laces and white work are exceptions. Where there will be majority or total ground cover as in canvas work, the line may be strong and clear. Using a hard pencil with a blunt point, or a ball-point pen, or any other instrument which proves appropriate to the mark required on the fabric, begin to follow the design lines with firm pressure. Lift the corner of the design paper and the carbon to check that the line is visible without being unnecessarily heavy. Modifications must be made for intended stitchery technique and coverage of the ground.

Tailor's chalk can be disastrous on linens and fine white fabrics, leaving waxy lines impossible to remove. Blackboard chalk is far safer, or fine brush strokes, or dots of similarly coloured poster paint, process white, or typewriter correcting fluid. China clay pencils may be used where lines are certain, if, for instance, they are traced through direct from a design behind a translucent ground.

Specially manufactured carbon pencils to make hot iron transfers are available. The design is drawn out on tracing paper and redrawn on the back of the paper with the sharpened carbon pencil, lightly and accurately. (If the original design drawing is made on a translucent paper the carbon drawing can be made direct from the back of it, avoiding repetitive tracing.) The transfer is taped in place with the carbon side facing the ground fabric. A moderately hot iron is pressed regularly but briefly over the paper, lifting and pressing without smoothing. Leaving the iron too long in one place will cause the lines to spread. Experiment and caution are recommended. The carbon lines will fade considerably after a few weeks.

The hot-iron method used with sugar solution is successful for light or delicate fabrics. Make a syrup with two parts sugar and one part water. The sugar must be quite dissolved, but if it is boiled for any length of time it will thicken too quickly to be workable. A small amount of gouache or designers' colour should be mixed with the water in the first instance, but adjustment to the depth can be made at any stage. The final mixture should produce a clear but unobtrusive guide line on the fabric, perhaps very similar in colour but slightly darker. With the tracing firmly taped wrong side up to a smooth surface the solution can be painted on sparingly with a fine line following the traced lines on the right side. When the tracing is dry it can be ironed on using the same precautions as for the hot transfer method. If the sugar is liable to crackle and split away from the tracing it may be advisable to leave the paper taped down and secure the ground over it, ironing the wrong side of the ground instead.

Knitted fabrics, and sometimes velvets, can be marked from the back with running stitches through a backing material which also helps to stabilize the yarns. The design must be traced onto the finest muslin, chiffon or terylene using a hard pencil. On very light fabrics there is a slight possibility that the lead from the pencil will emerge with the stitchery, in which case tailor's chalk may be preferable. Pin the transparent fabric to the back of the knitting to be embroidered, taking care not to cause any stretching. Tack over the design lines so that small stitches are visible on the right side of the knitting. If the colour of the tacking thread is carefully chosen it may not be necessary to remove it when embroidery has been completed.

Where open pulled or drawn grounds are the main feature of the work, consideration should be given to the possibility of transferring the design on to the wrong side and defining it with a running stitch which shows on the right side. Alternatively, using a tracing on tissue or other brittle, translucent paper behind the fabric, the design can be tacked through direct on to the ground and the paper torn away. For free machine stitchery the tissue should be removed once main design lines are completed.

A tracing taken on very open, stiff tarlatan can be taped on the ground and worked over with a drawing medium which gives a suitably broken line. Some experiment is necessary.

The simplest way to make a direct tracing is to make the cartoon drawing on translucent paper and use the ground fabric like a tracing, with both drawing and fabric taped to a window. The design is then drawn through with poster paint or a hard pencil. This is practical only on sheer fabrics.

Scratching, or marking with the needle as work progresses, is the method sometimes employed by workers in traditional wadded quilting. The *template* is matched to previously measured marks and scored round with the needle, providing a line which lasts just long enough to stitch. Marking straight lines is done by holding a chalked cord taut immediately above the top, and then snapping it.

Another simple but useful method, particularly on fine open lines, is to cut the main design shapes from thin, clear acrylic sheet or packaging and place them on the ground, tacking round each as the arrangement is decided.

The prick and pounce method is at its most appropriate for metal thread work. Sheet brass templates are pricked for ceremonial embroidery and regalia where hundreds of repeats may be needed. A mixture of carbonated chalk and gum is pushed through the template with a stencil brush, leaving dense dots which crack away as the stitching progresses. These templates can also be used to mark card backings or felt raising shapes cut out for subsequent purling. It is important that any transfer medium should not in any way affect the life of the metal threads. For commercial quilting an oiled paper or parchment template is used, and the pounce is in powder form, since only a very temporary line is required. Prickings to be used only a few times may be made on tracing paper, and pounced through with powder which is followed by painted lines. Experiments must first be made on a spare piece of ground fabric so that the weight of the pounce dots, the consistency of the paint and the width of the line are right. Tape strong tracing paper on top of the design and draw through, using a sheet larger than the exposed area of ground fabric so that the pounce powder is controlled on the paper. Marked centre lines must not be pricked. Register marks at each corner are useful; these must be pricked but not painted. Place the tracing over layers of light coloured blanket, or soft white cloth covering underfelt, and use the pricker to make fine holes at regular intervals along all the design lines. The spacing is determined by the detail required. Pricking from the back of the design makes minimally smaller dots of pounce than pricking from the front. Tape the pricked tracing on the material over a firm surface. Using the pouncer, with regular and gentle round movements apply powder to pricked lines evenly. Lift the paper vertically. Mix gum arabic with a water-based paint very close in colour to the ground fabric and minutely paint over the pounced lines. Poster paint and display colours of a creamy consistency work equally well without the gum, but most acrylics will set too hard. For pile or brushed fabrics use diluted oil-based paint. The pounce powder can be shaken away afterwards.

Another method uses spirit to fix the pounce. It follows the previous method, but the ground fabric is sprayed first with methylated spirits or petrol. After the pouncing is completed the tracing is removed and the ground sprayed again to fix the pounce powder dots to the fabric.

A commercial variation of prick and pounce consists of using paint direct through the pricked lines. It obviates the pouncing stage, but must be used with great care and only after proper trials. It is particularly good on velvets. Prepare strong brown paper larger than the ground fabric by scumbling it sparingly with a good, oil-based undercoat. Allow it to dry thoroughly. Using a tracing, make a full-size cartoon of the design on this painted surface. Place the cartoon over a blanket, and prick fine holes at regular intervals. Place the framed ground on a firm surface and the pricked cartoon on the ground. Mix oil-based paint and turpentine to a consistency previously determined by trials, where it will cause just visible dots of paint to penetrate the perforations without flooding or clogging. Apply this very evenly over all the design lines in circular movements with a hog-hair brush. Remove the paper vertically as soon as the application is finished. Allow the dots of paint to dry thoroughly before any more handling is attempted. The cartoon must be cleaned with turpentine immediately and can be used repeatedly.

TRAPUNTO QUILTING (stuffed quilting, Italian quilting, matelassé)

Embossed areas of padding outlined with stitchery which holds together two layers of fabric, usually white or unbleached in colour. The stuffing is introduced from behind into the completely enclosed islands on an otherwise flat ground. *Italian quilting* and *cord quilting* were often used with trapunto, and it was frequently combined with surface stitchery and drawn grounds. Both trapunto and cord quilting are referred to as stuffed work, and often the word trapunto is used also for the cord variety. Since most early examples are Sicilian both techniques were once regarded as Italian in origin. On some pieces the backing is cut to introduce the stuffing and then repaired, but on others the stuffing has been forced through holes, parting the yarns of the backing. Traditionally the ground was linen and occasionally silk, then later, when closely woven white cotton fabric became available in the American South, the technique was used for *corded quilting*. Early Indian quilting, technically trapunto since it is only partially wadded, has rich grounds of surface stitchery between the padded areas. The subject matter is patterned and pictorial.

Trapunto has a particularly opulent appearance, with the raised areas complementing the flat spaces which pucker and sag slightly around the stitchery. Although most traditional design was floral, there are no special technical limitations to design possibilities. Variety in the size of padded shapes is important, with the smaller ones strategically spaced or arranged in clusters. The shapes are normally rounded ones which make less disturbance to the flat areas, but the use of straight lines or sharp corners can become a feature of a less traditional design. It is clear from historical examples that the scale of the design in relationship to the total size is important, and that, although the drawing may be complex, the initial composition must be simple. On quilts the main area of padding is normally central, avoiding undue weight at the vertical sides.

Any reasonably closely woven material that will contain the stuffing adequately can be used. Soft fabrics with a nap or pile are dense and give gentle shadows, while lustrous fabrics crinkle at the stitch lines and produce intricate shadows. Loose synthetic wadding has now replaced wool or cotton. Carded fleece is more satisfying to work with. The backing must also retain the stuffing. If it is not to be cut it must be sufficiently loosely woven to part for the stuffing holes; if it is to be cut it must be sufficiently closely woven for subsequent repair. Suitability of thread to fabric is just as important in quilting as in any other form of embroidery. Tudor petticoats were stitched with linen, formal garments with yellow or pale blue silk, American quilts with fine cotton, and modern workers often utilise synthetic threads. A quilting cotton is still made specially for the purpose. A stiletto or knitting needle is used for stuffing, and if slits are to be cut, small embroidery scissors with very sharp points are needed.

Most large scale quilting is done in a frame. The usual method of *framing up* applies. The top fabric should be held firmly in place with radiating tacking stitches. The most common stitch in use is running stitch. Sometimes an occasional back stitch is introduced at intervals on difficult curves or to stabilize a long line, but it must not be pulled very tight. Starting and finishing ends are run under the line to be worked, leaving a tail of thread and going through the backing. At the point where the quilting stitch is to begin, the needle is turned and the thread locked in by the subsequent running stitch. With practice this will hold the end very firmly. The tail can be trimmed later. Never use a double thread or a knotted one.

With stitching completed the basting is pulled out, the work removed from the frame, and the stuffing is done from the wrong side. If slitting is necessary it should be only large enough to distribute small amounts of wadding evenly. Slits must be made with great care so that the fabric on the right side is not penetrated, and they must not approach the stitched lines. If slitting is unnecessary the stiletto holes must be made with equal care so that both fabrics remain undamaged and the holes can be persuaded gently back into place. Too much wadding will result in a hard surface and exaggerated puckering, too little will soon appear mean and flatten with wear. All repair work to the backing is completed with herringbone stitch, which may overlap and criss-cross but will remain neat and functional if the tension is right.

Collection

USA Daughters of the American Revolution Museum, Washington DC

TULLE EMBROIDERY

See *Net embroidery*

TURKEY WORK

See *Needlemade rugs*

U

UNDERSIDE COUCHING
(couché rentré, point couché rentré et retiré)

Carrying a loop of gold down through the same hole in the fabric made by each couching stitch. In this way the couching thread is not visible on the surface and the gold appears on the back of the work as tiny loops close to the linen. The soft play of light on the surface is very beautiful, and the texture of the fabric remains pliable.

It is not known where underside couching began or how it came to be so important in English ecclesiastical embroidery. It is found in some Continental medieval textiles, but the earliest surviving English examples are those from the tomb of Bishop William de Blois in Worcester Cathedral. The technique dominated the use of *metal threads* during the *opus anglicanum* period and was one of the main features in its success. It was

used for fillings and grounds, and the stitches were often organized into chevron and diaper patterns. Most of these were worked by counting the yarn of the ground, but where the geometric devices were complex or where representational figures patterned a ground the couching covered a drawn design.

Bibliography
Christie 1938; Kendrick 1937; Johnstone 1967

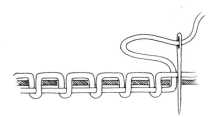

The principle of underside couching. The shaded area represents the ground

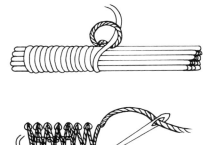

The front and back of a padded gold line

VANISHING MUSLIN

An openly woven fine scrim ground
used in the manufacture of machine-
made lace. The lace is made on the
muslin as a means of support, and
then immersed in a solvent which
dissolves the ground and leaves the
stitchery intact. It can be used equally
well for individually made textiles.
One version is heat soluble and can
therefore be burnt away with a

moderately hot iron. Stitchery must be
self-supporting and appliqué must be
joined by stitchery which will hold it
in position.

VELVET WORK

See *Raised woolwork*

VENETIAN (Gros point de Venise)

Of the main types of needlemade *lace*,
Venetian seems generally recognized as
that characterized by dominant padded
outlines on floral scrollings, often
highly raised with further motifs
worked above. There is a clear

Vanishing muslin: pink, turquoise and blue
batik on silk, worked on vanishing muslin,
with machine lurex darning and chain
stitch. 15 × 18 cm (6 × 7 in.). Made by
Christine Hall, Manchester Polytechnic

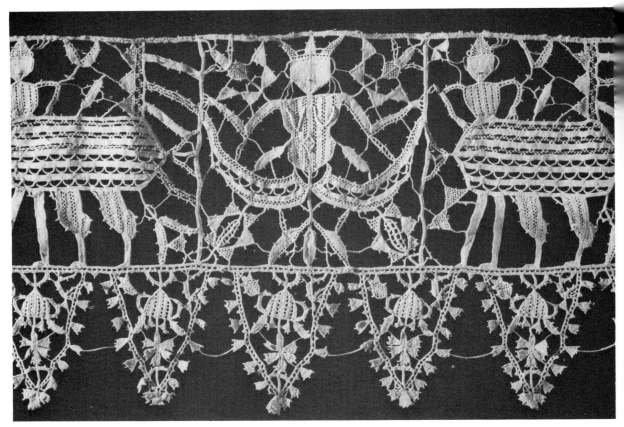

Venetian: early example. (*Ilké and Jacoby* ▲
Collection, Textilmuseum, St Gallen)

distinction between the closely worked buttonhole fillings and the widely spaced connecting bars. The fillings have a simple diamond arrangement of tiny interstices like *Hollie point*, and the bars may be sparsely dotted with picots or stars. It is finely worked but bold.

Pattern books for flat Venetian and *Reticella* were published from 1525 onwards, and the earliest designs seem to have developed from *filet*. Formal and open, it had a complex edge of points and scallops. It was fashionable for stiffened Tudor accessories and later for the falling collars and ruffs of the Stuarts and Cromwellians. Gros point, or scolpito in relievo, was much favoured by Renaissance fashion and particularly by the dignitaries of the Church. The variation known as Rose Point became highly padded and raised, and shares some characteristics with *Casalguidi* and *stumpwork*.

Bibliography
de Dillmont; Lovesey

VIRÁGOZÁS

The Hungarian furriers' and leather workers' embroidery, meaning flowering. The formal decoration was crowded into selected areas of the garment and worked largely in bold satin stitch with silk. Styles, colour and ornament were characterized by regions and by the individual design strictures of master families. The skins, complete with fleece, were carefully selected and prepared. Any repeating motifs were stencilled and the whole pattern was drawn with pen and ink, often with the aid of templates. Taking a pinch of leather between the fingers for each stitch, the skin was lifted so that the needle travelled through it without picking up the fleece beneath, leaving it undisturbed. On rounded forms the satin stitch radiates, and on leaves and scrolling it changes direction to reflect the light. This embroidery is still maintained for special occasions. The suba, a sleeveless Hungarian cloak consisting of about 14 radiating sheepskins forming a complete circle, was the main garment for virágozás embroidery.

Bibliography
Fél

VOIDING

An expedient of design frequent on textiles, where subject or outline is treated in reserve, the ground fabric assuming the main role whilst the background bears the heavier stitch decoration. Many embroideries with open grounds, such as the needlemade laces, drawn fabric work and cutwork are based on voiding, and it is a strong characteristic of *Assisi*. There are instances in Eastern and Indian styles where both subject and ground are filled, usually with flat satin stitch or darning and the outlines are left voided. Nineteenth-century Oriental embroidery in the West copied the convention.

Voiding: pale green floss on corded rayon. Cushion cover 38 cm (15 in.) square

Venetian: late nineteenth-century point d'Espagne. Partly worked on blue gloving leather drawn in ink. Border 9 cm ($3\frac{1}{2}$ in.) wide. (*Bankfield Museum*)

WADDED QUILTING (English quilting, pourpointing, padded quilting)

The stitching together, by means of evenly distributed lines, of several layers of material to afford warmth, protection and decoration. The filling is continuous throughout the whole piece, unlike cord, Italian and trapunto, which are only partially filled. Stobbed quilts have a continuous layer of filling but it is held in place by single knots rather than by lines of stitchery. Biscuit and puff quilting closely resemble wadded quilting in appearance but their divisions are separately stuffed before construction, as are those on raised appliqué.

The term English quilting is misleading. It probably arose at the time of the early colonial settlers, to distinguish wadded quilting from those forms more characteristic of the Mediterranean and the Middle East. Wadded quilting was almost certainly indigenous to all northerly peasant communities where woven fabric was a precious commodity. For the purposes of definition English quilting must include Welsh, Irish, Northumbrian and Durham, and all those forms which flourish in the United States, and so the term wadded quilting is more appropriate. In America the term quilter means someone who makes patchwork or pieced work.

Wadded quilting is a very ancient craft in China. There is ample evidence that it was used extensively as part of outdoor clothing and body

armour thousands of years ago. It is probable that the technique came to Europe with the Crusaders, but more likely that their travels merely influenced already existing designs and helped to make quilting decorative as well as functional. Many traditional quilting patterns probably have their origins in heraldry and in Islam. The finest quilting of the Middle Ages is attributable to Persia, to Spain and to Holland.

Before tapestries were imported heavy textiles provided insulation at doorways and over expanses of cold stone wall. It is quite likely that resourceful folk of limited means pieced and layered, utilizing every scrap of woven textile that was of no further use for any other purpose. Similarly, the peasant population would certainly emulate the intricately quilted silk and fine linen garments of the wealthy with their own substitutes in order to make warm clothing.

There have been references since the sixteenth century to Indian bedcovers and canopies quilted and surface stitched with yellow silk and metal threads and finished with fringing and tassels. Described as Colcha embroideries, they were often commissioned by the Portuguese and influenced by both cultures. White cotton fabric is still pieced and layered by the Kantha peoples in designs closely resembling their wall paintings. Darned grounds, surface stitchery and appliqué are combined with concentric rounds of quilted running stitches.

The Earl of Northumberland attended the siege of Turwin in 1513 provided with white satin arming doublets quilted in a lozenge pattern, and crimson satin ones 'French styched' with arming partlets of quilted white satin lined with linen.

The Tudors favoured the use of yellow silk thread as can be seen in their portraits. Personal and domestic linens in unbleached colours combined

Wadded quilting: jacket, 1580–90. White linen padded over horn discs. (*Nottingham Museum. Photograph: Layland-Ross*)

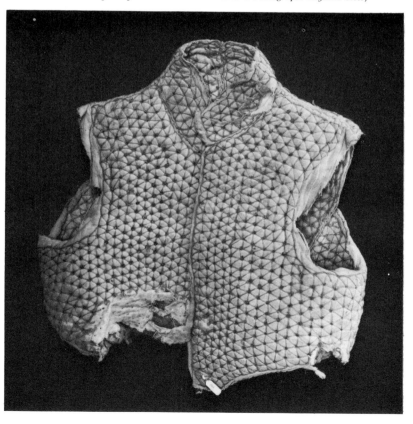

most successfully the techniques of pulled work, pattern darning and quilting. It seems that some of the quilted ground may have been imported.

Dutch ladies of the eighteenth century were renowned for their quilted petticoats of grosgrain camlet or satin, padded with high quality wool. The preference for a stout figure led them to wear between four and nine at any one time. The fashion for quilted petticoats in Britain extended into the nineteenth century in the form of burial garments. In poorer communities the beautifully worked soft brown or black petticoats were owned by the village, and used only for laying out, to be removed before burial, and so some examples have survived in good condition, never subject to domestic use.

Regency fashion relegated decorative quilting to ordinary homes where it flourished in its own right. Working people still needed to quilt, and there was comparatively inexpensive imported cotton cloth and wadding. Traditional patterns could be explored on pieces that were creatively satisfying, and the art of quilting progressed alongside the production of recycled everyday domestic textiles. The most exciting quilts are those which combine several techniques.

Wool blankets were exported to the New World in vast quantities, but trade was confined to barter with the Indians in exchange for beaver skins. Virtually no blankets were available to the Settlers, and while the Pilgrim Fathers struggled to import sheep against the regulations, their efforts to keep warm were the origins of the great American quilting tradition. Later, in America as in Britain (and especially in Wales and the Isle of Man), there were professional itinerants, carrying their own frames, who earned money as freelance quilters and markers. Those who specialized in marking were separately paid for, and those who stitched were paid by the spool. Stamped patterns used repeatedly in a locality can sometimes positively identify the work of a marker. The main areas of quilting in Britain were Ireland, the Mendips, Northumberland, Durham and Wales.

Recently, particularly since the soft

sculpture of the '50s and '60s, quilting has enjoyed a renewed phase as an expressive medium in its own right without needing to be functional. Used with patchwork and appliqué, and with fabric painting, printing and dyeing it has expanded to encompass painting and sculpture.

There are many regional elaborations on the standard patterns of traditional wadded quilting. The most functional, and probably the earliest, is that of simple diagonal lines, which hold the wadding against the grain of the top and the lining and show to best advantage the natural texture of the fabric. On this one theme alone many variations in the grouping of lines, and then the crossing of them to form squares and lozenges, can be developed. Wavy lines, Celtic interlacings, the universal

Wadded quilting: silk backstitch on cream silk, synthetic batting. Detail from the back of a waistcoat. Each iris about 15 cm (6 in.) wide. Made by June Irons

shell and pineapple, feather, fan and rope patterns are all familiar. Pieced quilt tops are sometimes stitched by following the edges of the pieces with the lines, but there are many quilts where the patchwork pattern has been partially or entirely ignored by the quilter. Stitchery on printed cottons often simply followed the outline of the print.

It is characteristic of quilting patterns that the runs of stitchery should be sufficiently long to avoid thread wastage. Straight runs on the grain always produce uneven stretch of the top which is in its own way typical. Where straight runs are

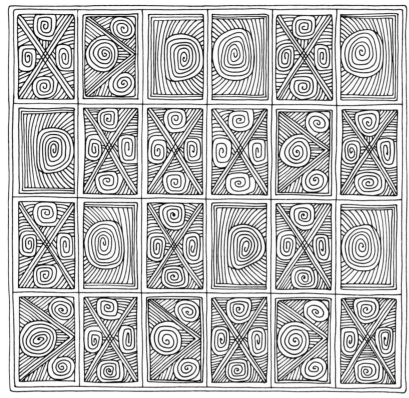

Whole Welsh quilt pattern

required and the stretching is not, this can be avoided by placing the top fabric with grain running diagonally. Lines or stitchery placed too close compress the filling and give a not so attractive flatness with less warmth. However, where thin blankets were utilized as filling, or where speed of stitchery was a priority, traditional quilts were often fairly flat with little attention given to the play of light or the need for warmth.

The idiosyncracies of individual pieces of quilting are directly related to the materials used. It is the wadded shapes rather than the quilted lines which form the pattern. Soft and pliable top fabrics will produce exaggerated raised areas between the lines of stitchery, closely woven and harder fabrics will crush the wadding and make less distinction. Non-reflective fabrics will produce soft shadows, whilst lustrous ones will cause light and dark contrasts to dominate the stitchery, often with characteristic puckering and complex indentations. The materials, and especially the top, must be absolutely smooth before working. Silk, satin, firm cotton and finely woven linen are all suitable to traditional work. Linen quilting is the hardest wearing and the least raised. Knitted materials offer luxurious softness but are difficult to quilt on the machine; some allow tufts of wadding to pull through with the stitching. Leather is most satisfying to quilt, particularly suede and the fine soft finishes.

Attention should be given at this stage to the two forms of stitches used on quilting, the stabbing vertical movement or the slipping of several stitches horizontally, both of them making a running stitch. The horizontal stitch can be done evenly only through thin batting where both top and backing are sufficiently pliable.

The traditional wadding material was carded fleece or woven pieces saved from worn wool. When the American Colonists eventually had enough cotton left over from their export crops to satisfy the domestic market, cotton batting was preferred,

North Country patterns. (a) Weardale Wheel; (b) Paisley Pear; (c) Flat Iron; (d) Heart

Some ways of quilting patchwork squares

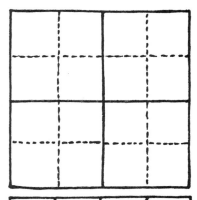

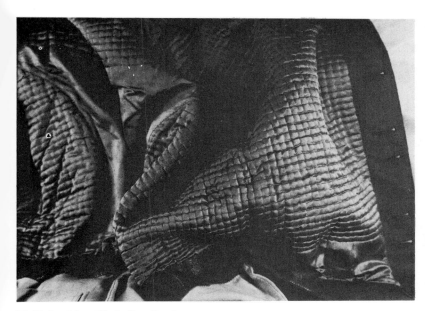

Wadded quilting: King's Own Royal
Lancaster Regiment, dress jacket lining
detail. Deep oyster satin, red cloth and
scarlet leather. (*Lancaster Museum*)

and its use soon became frequent in
Britain. Its springy elasticity
accentuated the lines of stitchery, but
it did not have the long lasting
stability of woven wool. For delicate,
light quilting, domette is the most
suitable wadding. Synthetics have
brought a wide range of choice. They
are retailed in several thicknesses and
the layers can be pulled apart.

The backing should be appropriate
in weight to the purpose of the
finished piece, firm and sufficiently
closely woven to confine the interlining
or wadding but easy to stitch through.

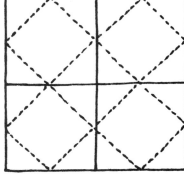

The directions used in quilting will
influence the final texture

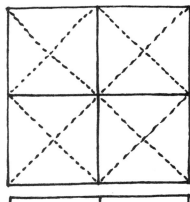

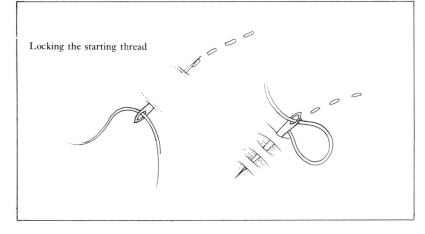

Locking the starting thread

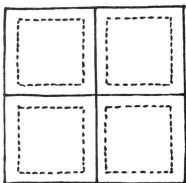

Wadded quilting: painted silk ground with machine quilting. Made by Lynda Colt

Traditional choices are white or unbleached cotton muslin and calico or fine linen, or printed cotton. Pre-washing will remove dressing and allow for shrinkage.

Suitability of thread to fabric is just as important to the quilter as in any other form of embroidery. Tudor petticoats were stitched with linen, formal garments with yellow or pale blue silk, and American quilts with cotton. A quilting cotton is still made specially for the purpose. For thick quilting a tailor's buttonhole silk or linen is best, well beeswaxed.

Quilting needles are usually short sharps. Some workers renew bent needles whilst others cherish a well worn favourite. Long pins are needed, glass headed ones being best since it is easy to lose ordinary ones in the wadding. Workers should preferably become used to using two thimbles, each placed appropriately on either hand over and beneath the frame. For

planning designs graph paper is useful, and plenty of cheap paper is necessary for organizing and laying out.

There are several methods of *transferring designs* all of which must leave minimal marks and be completely invisible once the stitchery is done. Dotted lines are just as easy to follow on smooth fabrics as continuous ones. Where marking is to be applied to limited areas as stitchery proceeds it

need only be very temporary. Experiments must be made to find the best process for the top fabric, the worker, and the working method.

Most large-scale quilting is done in a frame. By stretching the lining and laying the batting and top over it without tension, the density of texture is accentuated when the completed piece is eventually removed from the frame. Where the whole piece is lap quilted and both top and backing are similar in weight, the raised texture will be alike on both sides and both will shrink equally in the working. The usual method of *framing up* applies. The back rail is rolled when the backing has been sewn to it, leaving about 61 cm (24 in.) between it and the front rail. On this is laid the padding and then the top, both with surplus folded and protected away from the working area. Once stitching is completed on this section it is rolled up from the front and more is exposed from the back for marking and stitching.

The most common stitch in use is running stitch. Sometimes an occasional back stitch is introduced at intervals. Traditionally, back stitch appears from time to time on pieces that were intended for regular wear and tear, and later, chain stitch was used, with great difficulty, in imitation of that produced by machine. Starting and finishing ends are run under the line to be worked, leaving a trail and without going through the backing. At the point where the quilting stitch is to begin, the needle is turned and the thread locked in by the subsequent running stitch. With practice this will

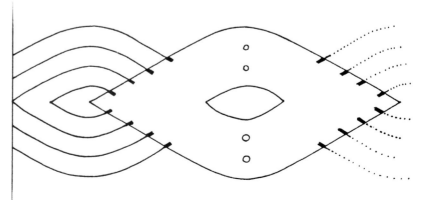

Using marked templates

hold the end very firmly. The tail can be trimmed later. Never use a double thread or a knotted one.

Types of *quilts* and methods of *quiltmaking* are discussed under those headings. The back, which is usually white, is often just as beautiful as the top. When the fashion for white bedspreads came, most quilts had their linings rather than their tops on display.

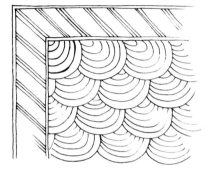

Two versions of Sea Waves

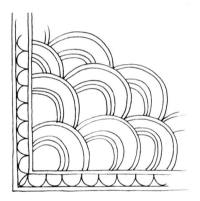

Cloud pattern

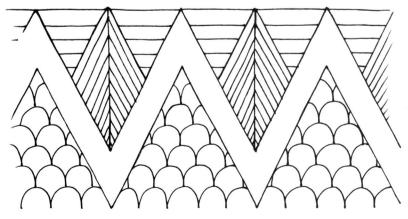

Wadded quilting: screen-printed silk with hand satin stitch. Made by Lynda Colt

Bibliography
Brown; Cunnington and Lucas 1972; Fitzrandolph; Hake; Irwin and Hall 1973; McNeill 1975; Thomas 1936; Short 1974; Svennås; Webster

Collections
UK American Museum, Bath; Gawthorpe Hall, Burnley; Welsh Folk Museum, Cardiff; Traquair House, Innerleithen; Levens Hall, Kendal; Lancaster Museum; London Museum; Victoria and Albert Museum, London;

Platt Hall, Manchester; Nottingham Museum; Harris Museum and Art Gallery, Preston; Beamish Museum, Stanley
India Calico Museum of Textiles, Ahmedabad

WESSEX EMBROIDERY
(Anglo-Saxon embroidery)

A form of softly coloured counted stitchery on linen borders, braids and bands. The stitches are mainly of simple darning and darned fillings derived from old British, Angle and Danish origins.

Bibliography
S.N.E.

WHITE WORK

All embroidery which is colourless and worked with white or unbleached cotton or linen thread. The term is more narrowly applied to fine pure

True Lovers' knot 15 cm (6 in.) in diameter, Scotch diamonds ground and basket ground, Fancy Shells border

Allendale feather 43 cm (17 in.) long, Northumberland chain, Fan, Wineglass

white stitchery on sheer fabrics or net.

Ireland is one of the numerous countries or districts which had been famed for their white embroidery for centuries before textile manufacture became mechanized. Skilled professional and peasant work was supported by home spinning and weaving, and financed and sheltered by private patronage, religious organizations and commercial agencies. Knotted and quilted counterpanes and other household textiles flourished alongside cutwork and early laces. The introduction of powered machinery in factories destroyed domestic textile making, and the Irish turned to the *Flowerin'*. Throughout much of the nineteenth century there was a ready market for most forms of white embroidery, laces, hemstitching and crochet, at all of which the Irish excelled. The extreme poverty and starvation experienced by a large proportion of the population at several periods was only marginally alleviated by the setting up of the embroidery industry, sometimes with training grants and charitable intentions, sometimes simply for commercial gain. Grounds of linen cambric and muslin came already stamped from Scotland, each piece marked with the subsistence

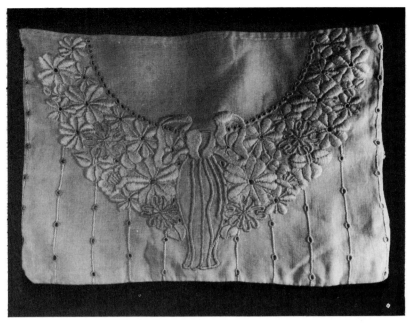

White work: Irish. Fine cotton on sheer white muslin. Bodice panel 33 × 23 cm (13 × 9 in.)

price it was to command when perfectly completed and returned to join the flood of *Ayrshire* work on the market. There were schools and workshops for Mountmellick, Carrickmacross and Limerick, and needlepoint Youghal lace and several rich and fine forms of crochet flourished.

Bibliography
Boyle; Pethebridge; Wardle

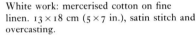

White work: mercerised cotton on fine linen. 13 × 18 cm (5 × 7 in.), satin stitch and overcasting.

WOOL

Yarn, fabric or thread made from soft animal hair. Many animals produce fibre which can be woven into pliable fabrics. Some of the softest comes from alpaca, goats, camels and angora rabbits. Sheeps' wool is very variable, even that from different parts of the same animal. Wool is categorized and sorted extensively according to purpose. The finest fibres make textiles which are luxurious against the human skin, and the coarsest are woven into carpets.

Hair and wool consist of filaments covered with tiny scales. Where these scales are numerous and tightly packed the spinning process locks them together, holding the twist and strengthening the yarn. For embroidery purposes, wool with a long staple is worsted spun, with all the filaments and scales lying in the same direction, making a lustrous thread resilient to friction. Until long staple was bred on sheep and worsted spinning became practical, embroidery wool was frequently of goat or camel.

Plain fabrics made of pure wool which are suitable for embroidery are becoming increasingly rare. Evenweave seems to be available in 7 counts per centimetre (18 counts per inch). Some flannel can be counted, and nuns' veiling is countable and very beautiful, but also difficult to find.

Best quality fine carpet yarn called Brussels thrums is left over from weaving ends and sold for making rugs by hand. By the eighteenth century it was accepted that good stitching wool came from Germany or Saxony. The fine zephyr merino used for Berlin woolwork was also from Saxony.

Tapestry wool is finer but still quite bulky. It is usually four-ply. Crewel wool is a two-ply worsted

manufactured in very large colour ranges. The plys of some crewels can be separated for finer work, or several threads can be worked together in the needle where different thicknesses are required for varying stitches on the same piece of work. Crewels should be threaded so that the smooth grain of the fibre runs from the needle to the working end. Where two threads are needed these should be threaded in the same way, not one thread looped through the needle with the fibres travelling in opposition.

Paternay, or Persian wool is made of lustrous fibres with a long filament.

There are many sources of *threads*

other than those spun specifically for embroidery. Blends of wool and synthetic fibres made for knitting or weaving purposes are often most successful.

Bibliography
Stenton

Collections
USA   Textile Museum, Washington D.C.
Peru   Museo Nacional de Anthropologia y Arqueologia, Lima

Wrapping: north-west Indian bullock forehead cover. Detail. Edge 20 cm (8 in.) deep. Soft rich colours. (*Leeds Museum*)

WRAPPING

There are several instances where wrapping rather than stitchery techniques feature as part of embroideries.

Coarse laces, of the kind which formed stiff ruffs and high headwear, were sometimes constructed by wrapping metal threads around shapes of cartisane or vellum. The shapes were joined by bars across open spaces and edged with picots of metal twist.

Quillwork and hairwork of the North American Indians includes wrapped yarns, threads and bundles, sometimes incorporated into the weaving like rows of bullion knots (see *false embroidery*).

Renewed interest in hand loom weaving has caused several techniques like wrapping to be assimilated by embroidery and jewellery. Glowing silks or mercerised cottons coil smoothly around groups of yarns, often with startling colour changes.

There are several working threads which are wrapped, particularly the metal ones like jap and passing. In tenntradsbroderi, an ancient form of stitchery among the Lapps, tin filaments are wrapped on a core of sinew and couched in geometric patterns.

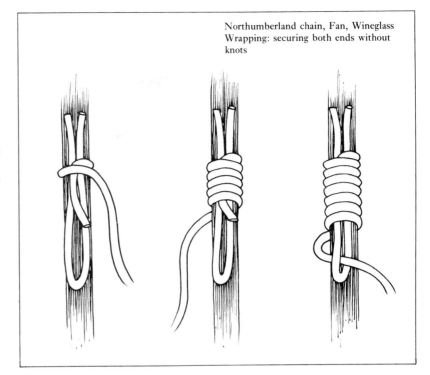

Northumberland chain, Fan, Wineglass
Wrapping: securing both ends without knots

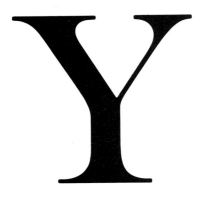

YARN-SEWN RUGS

See *Bed ruggs* and *Rag rugs*

YO YO

See *Suffolk puffs*

Bibliography

Aber, Ita, *The Art of Judaic Needlework*, Bell and Hyman 1980

Agutter, Margaret, *Cross Stitch Patterns*, Pitman 1952

Alford, Lady M., *Needlework as Art*, Sampson Low 1886

Ambuter, Carolyn, *Carolyn Ambuter's Complete Book of Needlepoint*, Crowell 1977

Anchor Manual of Needlework, Batsford 1971

Andrew, H.E.L., *Batsford Encyclopaedia of Crafts*, Batsford 1978, paperback 1982

Armes, *English Smocks*, Dryad Press c. 1926

The Art of Drawn Work, Butterick Publishing Company 1896

Ashley, Clifford W., *The Ashley Book of Knots*, Doubleday & Co. 1944

Ashton, Leigh, *Samplers*, The Medici Society 1926

Auld, Rhoda L., *Molas*, Van Nostrand Reinhold 1977

Bain, George, *Celtic Art: the methods of construction*, William Maclellan 1961

Baker, M.L., *A Handbook of American Crewel Embroidery*, Rutland & Tuttle 1966

Baker, Muriel, *Stumpwork: the art of raised embroidery*, Bell & Hyman 1980

Baker, M., and Lunt, M., *Blue and White: the Cotton Embroideries of Rural China*, Sidgwick & Jackson 1981

Barker, June, *Making Plaits and Braids*, Batsford 1973

Barnes, Charles, and Blake, David P., *Bargello and Related Stitchery*, Hearthside Press 1971

Bath, Virginia Churchill, *Embroidery Masterworks*, Henry Regnery 1972

Bath, Virginia Churchill, *Lace*, Henry Regnery 1974

Bath, Virginia Churchill, *Needlework in America*, Mills & Boon 1979

Battiscombe, C.F., ed., *The Relics of St Cuthbert*, Oxford 1956

Beaney, Jan, *Embroidery: new approaches*, Pelham 1980

Beck, H.C., 'Classification and Nomenclature of Beads and Pendants' in *Archaeologia*, Vol. 77, 1928

Beeton's Book of Needlework, Ward, Locke & Tyler 1870

Bed Ruggs, Wadsworth Atheneum, exhibition catalogue, Hartford, Connecticut 1972

Bellinger, Louisa, *Textile Analysis*, Washington D.C. 1950

Bengtsson, Gerda, *Cross Stitch Embroidery*, Haandarbeidets Fremmes Forlag 1958

Benjamin, Frederick A., *Ruskin Linen Industry of Keswick*, Michael Moon, Cumbria 1974

Benson, D., *Singer Machine Embroidery* 1946

Benson, D., *Your Machine Embroidery*, Sylvan Press 1952

Betterton, Sheila, *Quilts and Coverlets*, The American Museum at Bath 1978

Binchette, Dorothy, *Needlework Blocking and Finishing*, Scribners 1974

Birchbark, 'Quill and Beadwork' in *Denver Art Museum Quarterly*, Spring 1950

Bird, J., and Bellinger, L., *Paracas Fabrics and Nazca Needlework*, The Textile Museum, Washington D.C.

Birdwood, George, *Industrial Arts of India*, 1880

Bishop, Robert, *New Discoveries in American Quilts*, Dulton 1975

Blunt, W., *The Art of Botanical Illustration*, Collins 1950

Blunt, W., and Raphael, S., *The Illustrated Herbal*, Weidenfeld & Nicolson 1979

Bolton, Ethel Stanwood, and Stone Coe, Eva John, *American Samplers*, Boston Massachusetts Society of the Colonial Dames of America 1921

Borssuck, *1001 Designs for Needlepoint and Cross Stitch*, Prentice Hall International 1980

Boyle, Elizabeth, *The Irish Flowerers*, Ulster Folk Museum and the Institute of Irish Studies, Belfast 1971

Bridgeman, H., and Drury, E., *Needlework: an Illustrated History*, Paddington Press 1978

Bright, Sigrid, *Hardanger Embroidery*, Constable 1979

British Needles, British Needle Company Limited, Redditch

Broderie Religieuse de Style Byzantin, École des Hautes Études, Paris 1947

Brown, Elsa, *Creative Quilting*, Pitman 1975

Buck, Anne, 'The Countryman's Smock' in *Folk Life*, Vol. i, 1963

Butler, Anne, *Machine Stitches*, Batsford 1976

Butler, Anne, *The Batsford Encyclopaedia of Embroidery Stitches*, Batsford 1980, paperback 1983

Cabot, Nancy Graves, 'The Fishing Lady and Boston Common' in *Antiques*, December 1941

Cabot, N.G., *Pattern Sources of Scriptural Subjects in Tudor and Stuart Embroideries*, Needle and Bobbin Club, Vol. 30 No. 1, 1946

Campbell, Etta, *Linen Embroidery*, Batsford 1958

Carità, *Lacis*, Sampson Low 1909

Carlisle, Lillian Baker, *Pieced Work and Appliqué Quilts at the Shelbourne Museum, Vermont*, Shelbourne Museum Publications 1957

Carter Howard, 'Embroidery and its Probable Evolution' in *Embroidery*, Vol., 1 No. 1, 1932

Caulfield, S.F.A., and Saward, B.C., *Encyclopedia of Victorian Needlework*, Cowan 1882, Dover reprint 1972

Cave, OEnone, *Cutwork*, Vista 1962

Cave, OEnone, 'Linen Cutwork' in *Embroidery*, Vol. 15 No. 1, 1964

Cave, OEnone, *Traditional Smocks and Smocking*, Mills and Boon 1980

Child, Heather and Colles, Dorothy, *Christian Symbols Ancient and Modern*, Bell

Christensen, Jo Ippolito and Ashner, Sonie Shapiro, *Bargello Stitchery*, Sterling 1972

Christie, A., *Samplers and Stitches*, Batsford 1920

Christie, A.G.I., *Embroidery and Tapestry Weaving*, John Hogg, Pitman 1928

Christie, A.G.I., *English Medieval Embroidery*, Oxford 1938

Chung, Young Yang, *The Origins and Development of the Embroidery of China, Japan and Korea* 1977

Chung, Young Yang, *The Art of Oriental Embroidery*, Bell & Hyman 1980

Clabburn, Pamela, *The Needleworker's Dictionary*, MacMillan 1976

Clucas, Joy, *Your Machine for Embroidery*, Bell 1973

Coats Sewing Group, *The Bargello Embroidery Book* 1975

Colby, Averil, *Patchwork*, Batsford 1958, paperback 1982

Colby, Averil, *Samplers*, Batsford 1964

Colby, Averil, *Patchwork Quilts*, Batsford 1965

Colby, Averil, *Quilting*, Batsford 1972, paperback 1983

Cole, Alan S., *A Renascence of the Irish Art of Lace Making*, Chapman & Hall 1888

Coleman, Anne, *The Creative Sewing Machine*, Batsford 1980

Collector, A., 'English Stumpwork' in *Antiques*, Vol. 4 No. 1, 1981

Collier, Anne, *Lace – History and Identification*, Kingsclere Publications, Reading 1978

Complete Book of Needlework, Ward Lock and Co 1962

Cooper, Grace Rodgers, 'The Invention of the Sewing Machine' in *Smithsonian Institution Bulletin* 254, Washington, D.C.

Cornelius, R., Doffek, P., and Hardy, S, *Exploring Assisi*, Sinbad 1976

Crompton, Rebecca, *Modern Design in Embroidery*, Batsford 1936

Cundy, H.M., and Rollett, A.P., *Mathematical Models*, Clarendon Press 1951

Cunnington, Phyllis and Lucas, Catherine, *Costume for Births, Marriages and Deaths*, Black 1972

Cunnington, Phyllis and Lucas, Catherine, *Occupational Costume in England*, Black 1976

Currey, 'Chevening' in *Embroidery*, Autumn 1951

Cutts, E.L., *Dictionary of the Church of England* 1896

Dance, Peter, *The Art of Natural History: Animal Illustrators and their Work*, Country Life Books 1978

Daniels, M.H., *Early Pattern Books for Lace and Embroidery*, Needle and Bobbin Club, No. 17, 1933

Davenport, Cyril, *English Embroidered Bookbindings*, Kegan Paul, Trench, Trubner 1899

Davis, Mildred, J., *Crewel Embroidery*, Thomas Nelson 1962

Dawson, Barbara, *Metal Thread Embroidery*, Batsford 1968, paperback 1982

Day, Lewis, F., *Art in Needlework*, Batsford 1926

Dean, Beryl, *Creative Appliqué*, Studio Vista 1970

Dean, Beryl, *Ecclesiastical Embroidery*, Batsford 1958

Dean, Beryl, *Ideas for Church Embroidery*, Batsford 1968

Dean, Beryl, *Embroidery in Religion and Ceremonial*, Batsford 1981

de Dillmont, Thérèse, *Encyclopedia of Needlework*, D.M.C. Library from about 1886

de Dillmont, Thérèse, ed., *Motifs pour Broderies*, Ire Series, Mulhouse

De Farcy, L., 'Colifichets' in *Needle and Thread*, July 1914

Delamote, F., *Embroiderers' Book of Design*, Crosby Lockwood 1877

Dendel, Esther Warner, *Finger Weaving*, Nelson 1974

Dhamija, J., *The Survey of Embroidery Traditions*, Marg, Bombay, March 1964

D'Harcourt, Raoul, *Textiles of Ancient Peru and their Techniques*, University of Washington Press 1962

D.M.C., *Drawn Thread Work*; *Tenerife Lace Work*; *French Network (filet)*; *The Net Work (filet)*; *Net Work Embroidery (filet)*; *Hardanger Embroideries*; *Embroidery on Tulle*; *Needlemade Laces*

Dirsztay, Patricia, *Church Furnishings*, Routledge, Kegan & Paul 1978

Dolby, Anastasia, *Church Embroidery*, Chapman & Hall 1867

Dongerkery, Kamala, S., *The Romance of Indian Embroidery*, Thacker, Bombay 1951

Douglas, Frederick H., *Main Types of Sewn Beadwork*, Denver Art Museum, May 1953

'Drawn Thread Work' in *Needlecraft Practical Journals* 18, 25, 38, 53, 73, Needlecraft Limited

Dreesmann, Cécile, *Samplers for Today*, Van Nostrand Reinhold 1972

Drysdale, Rosemary, *The Art of Blackwork Embroidery*, Mills and Boon 1975

Drysdale, Rosemary, *Pulled Work on Canvas and Linen*, Bell & Hyman

Durand, Dianne, *Smocking Technique, Projects and Designs*, Dover 1980

Dyer, Anne, and Duthoit, Valerie, *Canvas Work from the Start*, Bell 1972

Earnshaw, P., *The Identification of Lace*, Shire Publications 1980

Edwards, J. *Bead Embroidery*, Batsford 1966

Edwards, J., *Church Kneelers*, Batsford 1967

Edwards, J., *Crewel Embroidery in England*, Batsford 1975

Ellwood, P.W., *Saints, Signs and Symbols*, S.P.C.K. 1966

Enthoven, Jacqueline, *The Stitches of Creative Embroidery*, Reinhold 1964

Ernst, Henri, ed., *Broderies Chinoises*, Ernst 1922

Fairholt, F.W., *Costume in England*, George Bell 1846

Fangel, Esther, *Haanarbejdets Fremmes Haandbøger*, Copenhagen 1958

Fawdry, Marguerite, and Brown, Deborah, *The Book of Samplers*, Lutterworth 1980

Feeley, Helen Howard, *The Complete Book of Rug Braiding*, Coward McCann 1957

Fél, E., *Hungarian Peasant Linen Embroideries*, Corvina 1976, Batsford 1979

Felcher, Cécilia, *The Needlepoint Workbook of Traditional Designs*, Hale 1975

Finch, Karen, and Putnam, Greta, *Caring for Textiles*, Watson Guptill 1977

Finley, R.E., *Old Patchwork Quilts and the Women who Made Them*, Lippincott 1929

Fischer, Pauline, and Lasker, Arrabel, *Bargello Magic*, Dent 1972

Fisher, Eivor, *Swedish Embroidery*, Batsford 1953

Fisher, Joan, *The Creative Art of Needlepoint Tapestry*, Hamlyn 1972

Fitzrandolph, Mavis, *Traditional Quilting*, Batsford 1954

Fitzrandolph, Mavis and Fletcher, Florence, *Quilting: Traditional Methods and Design*, Dryad 1968

Fitzwilliam, A.W., and Hands, A.F., *Jacobean Embroidery*, Kegan Paul, Trench, Trubner 1935

Fowke, Frank Rede, *The Bayeux Tapestry*, George Bell 1918

Freehof, Lillian S, and King, Bucky, *Embroideries and Fabrics for Synagogue and Home*, Hearthside Press 1966

Freeman, B. *The St Martin Embroideries*, Metropolitan Museum of Art, New York 1968

Freherr, Alfred von Henneberg, *The Art and Craft of Old Lace*, Batsford 1931

Frew, Hannah, *Three Dimensional Embroidery*, Van Nostrand Reinhold 1975

Gahran, Robert A, *Hawaiian Quilting on Kauai Lihue*, Kauai Museum 1973

Ganguli, K.K., 'Chamba Rumal' in *Journal of the Indian Society of Oriental Art*, Vol. XI 1943

Geddes, E., and McNeill, M., *Blackwork Embroidery*, Mills & Boon 1965

Gierl, Irmgard, *Cross Stitch Patterns*, Batsford 1977

Glover, Elizabeth, *The Gold and Silver Wyre-drawers*, Phillimore, Chichester 1979

Golden Hands Encyclopaedia of Embroidery, Collins 1973

Golden Hands: Bargello and Florentine Embroidery, Reinhold

Gonsalves, Alison S., *Quilting and Patchwork*, Sunset Books 1973

Good Housekeeping Sewing Crafts, Ebury Press 1979

Gostelow, Mary, *A World of Embroidery*, Mills and Boon 1975

Gostelow, Mary, *Blackwork*, Batsford 1976

Gostelow, Mary, *Embroidery*, Marshall Cavendish Editions 1977

Gostelow, Mary, *The Coats Book of Embroidery*, David & Charles 1978

Gostelow, Mary, *Art of Embroidery*, Weidenfeld & Nicolson 1979

Goubard, Mme, *Book of Guipure D'Art*, Ward Locke 1869

Graumont, Raoul and Hensel, John, *Square Knot Tatting, Fringe and Needlework*, Cornell Maritime Press 1943

Gray, Jennifer, *Canvas Work and Design*, Batsford 1960

Gray, Jennifer, *Machine Embroidery, Technique and Design*, Batsford 1973

Groves, S., 'French Raised Work' in *Embroidery*, Vol, XXIII No. 1, 1972

Groves, S., *The History of Needlework Tools and Accessories*, Hamlyn 1966

Gunther, E., *Art in the Life of the North West Coast Indians*, Portland Art Museum, Seattle, Superior Publishing 1966

Gutcheon, Beth, *The Perfect Patchwork Primer*, Penguin 1973

Hackenbrock, Y., *English and Other Needlework Tapestries and Textiles in the Irwin Untermeyer Collection*, Thames & Hudson 1961

Hake, Elizabeth, *English Quilting Old and New*, Batsford 1937

Hald, M., *Olddanske Texstiler*, Nordiske Fortidsminder, V.

Hall, C.A., and Kretsinger, R., *The Romance of the Patchwork Quilt in America*, Caxton 1935

Hall, Nancy and Riley, Jean, *Bargello Borders*, Edwards 1974

Hanley, Hope, *Needlepoint*, Scribners 1966

Harbeson, G.B., *American Needlework*, Crown Publishers 1938

Harding, Valerie, *Textures in Embroidery*, Batsford 1977

Harding, Valerie, *Faces and Figures in Embroidery*, Batsford 1979

Harrison, C.C., *Woman's Handwork in Modern Homes*, 1881

Harvey, Lula M., *The Priscilla Irish Crochet Book*

Hawthorn, A., *Art of the Kwakiutl Indians*, University of British Columbia 1968

Heathcote, David, 'Some Hausa Lizard Designs' in *Embroidery* Vol. XXIII No. 4

Heathcote, David, 'A Shabka mai yanka from Zaria' in *Embroidery* No. 2 Vol. 27

Hedhind, Catherine, *A Primer of New England Crewel Embroidery*, Massachusetts 1977

Henderson, M., and Wilkinson, E., *Cassells Compendium of Victorian Crafts*, Cassell 1978

Henze, Anton, and Filthaut, Theodor, *Contemporary Church Art*, Sheed and Ward 1956

Higgin, L., *Handbook of Embroidery*, Sampson Low, Marston 1880

Higgins, Muriel, *Machine Patchwork*, Batsford 1980

Hodges, *Artifacts, Early Materials and Technology*, Baker

Holme, Charles, ed., *Peasant Art in Italy*, Studio 1923

Holme, Geoffrey, ed., *A Book of Old Embroidery*, Studio 1921

Holstein, Jonathan, *The Pieced Quilt*, Graphic Society 1973

Houck, Carter and Miller, Myron, *American Quilts and Coverlets*, Pelham 1975

Howard, Constance, *Design for Embroidery*, Batsford 1956

Howard, Constance, *Inspiration for Embroidery*, Batsford 1966

Howard, Constance, *Embroidery and Colour*, Batsford 1976

Howard, Constance, *Constance Howard's Book of Stitches*, Batsford 1979

Howard, Constance, *Twentieth-Century Embroidery in Great Britain to 1939*, Batsford 1981

Howard, Constance, *Twentieth-Century Embroidery in Great Britain 1940 to 1963*, Batsford 1983

Hughes, Therle, *English Domestic Needlework*, Lutterworth Press 1966

Huish, Marcus Bourne, *Samplers and Tapestry Embroideries*, Fine Art Society 1900, Dover 1970

Hulbert, Anne, *Victorian Crafts Revived*, Batsford 1978

Hulton, Helen, *The Technique of Collage*, Batsford 1968

Humbert, Claude, *Ornamental Design*, Thames & Hudson 1970

Hunt, W.B., and Burshears, J.F., *American Indian Beadwork*, Bruce Publishing 1951

Hurburt, Regina, *Left-handed Needlepoint*, Reinhold 1972

Ickis, Margaret, *The Standard Book of Quiltmaking and Collecting*, Dover 1959

Ionides, H.E., 'Bebilla' in *Embroidery*, June 1936, Autumn 1955, Winter 1956

Ireys, Katherine, *Finishing and Mounting Your Needlepoint Pieces*, Crowell 1973

Irwin, John, *Indian Embroideries*, Victoria and Albert Museum large picture book No. 7, 1951

Irwin, John, 'Indo European Embroidery' in *Embroidery*, Spring 1959

Irwin, John, *The Kashmir Shawl*, H.M.S.O. 1973

Irwin, John, and Hall, J., *Indian Embroideries*, Calico Museum of Textiles 1973

Ives, Suzy, *Ideas for Patchwork*, Batsford 1974

Ives, Suzy, *Patterns for Patchwork Quilts and Cushions*, Batsford 1977

Iverson, M.D., 'The Bed Rug in Colonial America' in *Antiques*, January 1964

Jaray, Madeleine, *The Carpets of the Manufacture de la Savonnerie*, Lewis Publishers 1966

John, Edith, *Creative Stitches*, Batsford 1967

John, Edith, *Filling Stitches*, Batsford 1967

John, Edith, *Needleweaving*, Batsford 1970

John, Edith, *Experimental Embroidery*, Batsford 1976

Johnsen, E, *Gamla Danska Korsstingsmotiver fra Amager*, Copenhagen, Host & Sons

Johnson, Beryl, *Advanced Embroidery Techniques*, Batsford 1983

Johnstone, Pauline, *Greek Island Embroidery*, Tiranti 1961

Johnstone, Pauline, *The Byzantine Tradition in Church Embroidery*, Tiranti 1967

Jones, Stella M., *Hawaiian Quilts*, Honolulu Academy of Arts 1930

Jones, Mary Eirwen, *British Samplers*, Pen in Hand, 1948

Jones, Mary Eirwen, *English Crewel Designs*, Macdonald 1974

Jourdain, M.A., *The History of English Secular Embroidery*, Kegan Paul, Trench & Trubner 1910

Jourdain, Margaret, 'Needlework at Hardwick' in *Country Life* LXI, February 1927

Kaestner, Dorothy, *Four Way Bargello*, Scribners 1973

Kaestner, Dorothy, *Needlepoint Bargello*, Scribners 1974

Karasz, Mariska, *Adventures in Stitches*, Funk & Wagnalls 1949

Kaufmann, Ruth, *The New American Tapestry*, Van Nostrand Reinhold 1968

Kay Shuttleworth, R.B., 'Carrickmacross' in *Embroidery*, Winter 1960

Kendrick, A.F., *English Embroidery*, Batsford 1904

Kendrick, A.F., *Catalogue of Textiles from the Burying Grounds in Egypt*, Victoria and Albert Museum 1920

Kendrick, A.F., *A Book of Old Embroidery*, The Studio Limited 1921

Kendrick, A.F., *English Needlework*, A. & C. Black 1937

Kiewe, H.E., *History of Folk Cross Stitch*, Sebaldus Verlag, Nuremberg 1950

Kiewe, H.E., 'Holbein's influence on Elizabethan Embroidery' in *Embroidery*, Autumn 1956

Kiewe, H.E., 'Jacobean Nostalgia' in *Embroidery*, Summer 1957

Kimmins, Nancy, 'The World of Textile Conservation' in *Embroidery*, Autumn 1976

King, D., 'Boxers' in *Embroidery*, Winter 1961

King, D., *Catalogue of an Exhibition of Opus Anglicanum*, Arts Council and Victoria and Albert Museum 1963

Kinmond, Jean, *Embroidery for the Home*, Batsford 1970

Kinmond, Jean, *The Coats Book of Lacecrafts*, Batsford 19—

Klickmann, Flora, *The Stitchery Annual*, 1913

Klickmann, Flora, ed., 'The Cult of the Needle' in *The Girl's Own Paper*

Klickmann, Flora, *Dictionary of Needlework*

Klimova, N.T., *Folk Embroidery of the U.S.S.R.*, Van Nostrand Reinhold 1981

Knight, Pauline, *The Technique of Filet Lace*, Batsford 1980

Knott, Grace L., *English Smocking*, Fredrick Muller Limited 1962

Knox Arthur, Anne, *The Embroidery Book*, A. & C. Black Limited 1920

Krishna, M., 'Designs from Burmese Kalangas' in *Embroidery*, Autumn 1963

Ladbury, Anne, *The Batsford Book of Sewing*, Batsford 1967

Laliberté, Norman, and McIlhany, Sterling, *Banners and Hangings*, Van Nostrand Reinhold 1966

Lambert, Miss, *The Handbook of Needlework*, John Murray 1843

Lane, Maggie, *Needlepoint by Design*, Charles Scribners 1970

Lane, Rose Wilder, *Woman's Day Book of American Needlework*, Simon & Schuster 1963

Lantz, Sherlee, and Lane, Maggie, *A Pageant of Pattern for Needlepoint Canvas*, André Deutsch 1973

Lantz, Sherlee, *Trianglepoint*, Viking 1976

Laury, Jean Ray, *Quilts and Coverlets*, Van Nostrand Reinhold 1970

Lawson, C.P., *A History of the Uniforms of the British Army*, Kaye 1961

Leach, and Cartwright, R.S., *Mountmellick Embroidery*, Mrs Leach's Complete Books. c. 1895

Leach, M. Agnes, *Drawn Fabric Embroidery*, Hulton 1959

Lefébure, Ernest, *Embroidery and Lace*, H. Grevel 1888

Lemon, Jane, *Embroidered Boxes and other Construction Techniques*, Faber 1980

Lewis, May Florence, *Hispanic Lace and Lace Making*, The Hispanic Society of America 1939

Liley, Alison, *The Craft of Embroidery*, Mills & Boon 1961

Lofthouse, Kate, S., *A Complete Guide to Drawn Fabric*, Pitman 1951

Lovelock, B., 'Embroidery of Tsu Hsi' in *Embroidery*, Vol. 3 No. 1

Lovesey, Nenia, *The Technique of Needlepoint Lace*, Batsford 1980

Lubell, Cecil, *Textile Collections of the World*, Vol. 1, Studio Vista 1976

Lyford, C.A., *Quill and Beadwork of the Western Sioux*, Haskell Institute, Kansas 1940

Macbeth, Ann, *The Countrywoman's Rug Book*, Dryad Press 1929

Macquoid, Percy, *English Furniture, Tapestry and Needlework*, The Leverhulme Art Collections III, Batsford 1928

Mahler, Celine, *Once upon a quilt*, Van Nostrand Reinhold 1973

Mailey, Jean, *Embroidery of Imperial China*, 1978

Mann, Kathleen, *Appliqué Design and Method*, Black 1937

Marein, Shirley, *Stitchery, Needlepoint, Appliqué and Patchwork*, Viking 1974

Markrich, Lilo, and Kiewe, H.E., *Victorian Fancywork*, Pitman 1975

Marks, S.S., ed., *Fairchild's Dictionary of Textiles*, London 1959

Marshall, F. and H., *Old English Embroidery, its Technic and Symbolism*, Horace Cox 1894

Marston, D.E., *Patchwork Today*, Bell 1968

Marston, Doris, *Exploring Patchwork*, Bell 1972

Masters, Ellen T., *The Book of Stitches*, James Bowden 1889

Matthews, S.I., *Needlemade Rugs*, Mills & Boon and Hearthside Press 1966

McCalls Needlework, Hamlyn 1964

McNeill, Moyra, *Pulled Thread*, Mills & Boon 1971

McNeill, Moyra, *Quilting for Today*, Mills & Boon 1975

McRoberts, D., 'The Fetternear Banner' in *Innes Review*, Vol. VII 1956

Melen, Lisa, *Drawn Thread Work*, Van Nostrand Reinhold 1972

Melen, Lisa, *Knotting and Netting*, Van Nostrand Reinhold 1972

Mera, H.P., *Pueblo Indian Embroidery*, Laboratory of Anthropology, Santa Fe 1943

Meulenbelt-Nieuwberg, Alberta, *Embroidery Motifs from Dutch Samplers*, Batsford 1974

Messent, Jan, *Embroidery and Nature*, Batsford 1980

Meyer, Ann, *Pulled Thread on Canvas*, Leisure Arts 1976

Miller, Irene Preston, and Lubell, Winifred, *The Stitchery Book*, Odhams

Minter, David C., *Modern Needlecraft*, Blackie 1932

Molas: Art of the Cuna Indians, The Textile Museum, Washington D.C. 1973

Moore, M., 'Coggeshall Embroidery' in *Embroidery* Vol. 7, No. 2

Morris, Barbara, *Victorian Embroidery*, Barrie and Jenkins 1965

Morris, James A., *The Art of Ayrshire White Needlework*, Glasgow School of Art and Glasgow Herald 1916

Morris, May, *Decorative Needlework*, Joseph Hughes 1893

Needlecraft Monthly Magazine, 1907

Needlecraft Practical Journals: Nos. 9 *Net Darning*; 16 *Point Lace*; 18 *Drawn Thread Work*; 22 *Ribbon Work*; 25 *Drawn Thread Work*; 28 *Carrickmacross lace*; 31 *Limerick Lace*; 35 *Tenerife Lace*; 38 *Drawn Thread Work*; 42 *Smocking*; 47 *Hardanger*; 52 *Danish Hedebo Embroidery*; 53 *Drawn Thread Work*; 55 *Embroidery Shading*; 63 *Ribbon Work*; 66 *Filet Lace*; 73 *Drawn Thread Work*; 74 *Raffia Work*; 92 *Bead Bags and Purses*; 108 *Mountmellick Embroidery*; 111 *Drawn Thread Work*

Needlecraft Artistic and Practical, Butterick Publishing 1889

Neild, Dorothea, *Adventures in Patchwork*, Mills & Boon 1975

Nevinson, J.L., 'Peter Stent and John Overton, publishers of embroidery designs' in *Apollo* XXIV, November 1936

Nevinson, J.L., *Catalogue of English Domestic Embroidery of the 16th and 17th centuries*, Victoria and Albert Museum 1938

Nevinson, J.L., *English Domestic Embroidery Patterns of the 16th and 17th centuries*, Walpole Society 1940

Newark Museum, *Quilts and Counterpanes in the Newark Museum*, New Jersey 1948

New Encyclopaedia of Textiles, Editors of *American Fabrics and Fashions* magazine, Prentice Hall

Newland, Mary and Walkin, Carol, *Printing and Embroidery*, Batsford 1977

Nichols, M., *Encyclopaedia of Embroidery Stitches*, Dover 1973

Nicholson, M., 'Embroidery in Fashion' in *Embroidery* Vol. 18 No. 2

Nielsen, Edith, *Scandinavian Embroidery, Past and Present*, Scribners/Bell 1978

Norbury, James, *Counted Thread Embroidery*, Brockhampton Press, Leicester 1955

Nordfors, Jill Denny, *Needle Lace and Needleweaving*, Van Nostrand Reinhold 1974

Norris, Herbert, *Church Vestments, Origin and Development*, J.M. Dent 1949

Nye, Thelma M., ed., *Cross Stitch Patterns*, Batsford 1969

Nylander, Jane C. Giffen, 'Some Print Sources of New England Schoolgirl Art' in *Antiques*, August 1976

Odhams' Encyclopaedia of Needlecraft, Odhams Press

Orchard, William C., *Beads and Beadwork of the American Indians*, Museum of the American Indian, New York 1929

Orchard, William C., *The Technique of Porcupine Quill Decoration amongst the Indians of North America*, Heye Foundation, New York

Osler, Dorothy, *Machine Patchwork*, Batsford 1980

Overton, John, *The second part of Fower-footed creatures*, London, n.d., 17th century

Overton, John, *A new and perfect book of beasts, flowers, fruits, butterflies and other vermine*, London 1674

Overton, John, *A new book of flowers and fishes*, London 1671

Owen, Mrs Henry, *The Illuminated Ladies Book of Needlework*, 1847

Pakula, Marion Broome, *New Ideas for Needlepointers*, Crown 1976

Palliser, B., *A History of Lace*, Sampson Low, Marston, 1902; revised by Jourdain and Dryden

Parker, K., 'Leek Embroidery Society' in *Studio*, Vol. 1

Pass, Olive, *Dorset Feather Stitchery*, Mills and Boon 1957

Paulsen-Townsend, W.G., *Embroidery or the Craft of the Needle*, Truelove, Hanson and Comba 1899

Paulsen-Townsend, W.G., *Modern Decorative Art in England*, Batsford 1922

Penelope Jacobean Embroidery, Briggs

Pesel, Louisa F., *Practical Canvas Embroidery*, Batsford 1929

Pesel, Louisa F., *Stitches from Eastern Embroideries*, Percy Lund, Humphries 1912

Pesel, Louisa F., *Stitches from Old English Embroideries*, Percy Lund, Humphries 1912

Pesel, Louisa F., *Stitches from Western Embroideries*, Percy Lund, Humphries 1917

Pesel, Louisa F., 'Knotted Work' in *Embroideress* No. 16

Pesel, Louisa F., *Double Running or Back Stitch*, Batsford 1931

Pesel, Louisa F., *Cross Stitch*, Batsford 1931

Petersen, Grete, and Svennås, Elsie, *Handbook of Stitches*, Reinhold 1970

Pethebridge, J.E., *A Manual of Lace*, Cassell 1947

Peto, Florence, *Historic Quilts*, The American Historical Company 1939

Peto, Florence, *American Quilts and Coverlets*, Parrish 1949

Petrakis, Joan, *The Needle Arts of Greece*, Scribners 1977

Pfannschmidt, E.E., *Twentieth Century Lace*, Mills & Boon 1975

Pforr, Effie Chalmers, *Award Winning Quilts*, Birmingham, Alabama/Oxmoor House 1974

Pickup, J., and Field, P., 'Ideas in Suffolk Puffs' in *Embroidery* Vol. 25 No. 1

Polkinghorne, R.K. and M.I.R., *The Art of Needlecraft*, Associated Newspapers

Poyntz, *New and singular patterns and workes of linnen*, London 1591

Pranda, Adam, 'Slovak Paper Cuts' in *Embroidery*, Spring 1961

Priscilla Hardanger Book, 1909

Priscilla Drawn Work Book, 1909

Priscilla French Eyelet and Shadow Embroidery Book

Priscilla Book on Mexican Drawn Work

Priscilla Cross Stitch Book, ed. H.E. Wilkie, 1899

Proctor, Molly G., *Victorian Canvas Work, Berlin Woolwork*, Batsford 1972

Proctor, Richard M., *The Principles of Pattern*, Van Nostrand Reinhold 1969

Proud, Nora, *Simple Textile Dyeing and Printing*, Batsford 1974

Puls, Herta, *The Art of Cutwork and Appliqué*, Batsford 1978

Putnam, Greta, 'The Textile Conservation Centre' in *Embroidery* Vol. 32 No. 4

Raby, W.L., 'Greek lace, Ruskin linen work' in *Embroidery* Vol. 9 No. 3

Ramazanoglu, G., *Turkish Embroidery*, Van Nostrand Reinhold 1976

Ramsey, Gloria, *Couching: Decorative Laid Thread Embroidery*, Batsford 1976

Remmington, Preston, *English Domestic Needlework of the XVI, XVII and XVIII centuries*, Metropolitan Museum of Art, New York 1945

Rhodes, Helen, *Cross Stitch*, Hulton 1969

Rhodes, Mary, *Ideas for Canvas Work*, Batsford 1970

Rhodes, Mary, *Needlepoint: the art of canvas embroidery*, Octopus 1975

Rhodes, Mary, *Dictionary of Canvas Work Stitches*, Batsford 1980

Rhodes, Mary, *The Batsford Book of Canvas Work*, Batsford 1983

Ricci, Elisa, 'Italian Pattern Books of the 16th century' in *The Collector*, September 1930

Ring, Betty, 'Memorial Embroideries by American Schoolgirls' in *Antiques*, October 1971

Risley, Christine, *Creative Embroidery*, Studio Vista 1969

Risley, Christine, *Machine Embroidery*, Studio Vista 1973

Rock, D., *Textile Fabrics*, c. 1890

Roeder, Helen, *Saints and their Attributes*, Longman Green & Co. 1955

Rolleston, *Embroideress* No. 19

Rollins, J.G., *The Early Victorian Needlemakers, 1830–1860*, Early Victorian Costume Society 1969

Rome, Carol Cheyney, *A New Look at Bargello*, Crown 1973

Rosen, Ilke, *Modern Embroidery*, Batsford 1972

Rosensteil, Helene von, *American Rugs and Carpets*, Barrie & Jenkins 1978

Roth, Ann, *Needlepoint Designs from the Mosaics of Ravenna*, Barrie & Jenkins 1975

Rubi, Christian, *Cut Paper Silhouettes and Stencils*, Kaye & Ward 1970

Rumania: Folk Art, Rumanian Institute for Cultural Relations with Foreign Countries 1955

Rumania: Folk Costumes, Woven Textiles and Embroideries, State Publishing House 1958

Russell, Pat, *Lettering for Embroidery*, Batsford 1971

Safford, Carleton L., and Bishop, Robert, *America's Quilts and Coverlets*, Studio Vista 1973

Schuester, C., and Whymant, N., *Embroidery*, 1935

Schuette, M., and Muller-Christensen, S., *A Pictorial History of Embroidery*, Praeger 1963

Schuette, M., and Muller-Christensen, S., *The Art of Embroidery*, Thames & Hudson 1964

Schwab, D.E., *The Story of Lace and Embroidery*, 1957

Scobey, J., and McGrath, L.P., *Do-It-All-Yourself Needlepoint*, Simon & Schuster 1971

Scoular, Marion, *Blackwork*, Leisure Arts 1976

Sebba, Anne, *Samplers*, Weidenfeld & Nicholson 1979

Seligman and Hughes, *Domestic Needlework*, Country Life 1926

Sexton, Carlie, *Old Fashioned Quilts*

Seyd, Mary, *Designing with String*, Batsford 1967

Sherman, Vera, *Wall Hangings of Today*, Mills & Boon 1972

Shorleyker, Richard, *A schole-howse for the needle*, 1624

Short, Eirian, *Embroidery and Fabric Collage*, Isaac Pitman 1967

Short, Eirian, *Introducing Quilting*, Batsford 1974

Short, Eirian, *Quilting: Technique and Design*, Batsford 1974

Silverstein, Mira, *Fun with Bargello*, Scribners 1971

Simeon, Margaret, *The History of Lace*, Stainer & Bell 1980

Simpson, Jean, *Shisha Embroidery*, Van Nostrand Reinhold 1978

Simpson, Stephen, *History of the Firm of Stephen Simpson, 1829–1929*

Smith, Jerome Irving, 'Dressed Pictures' in *Antiques*, December 1963

S.N.E. 'Wessex Stitchery' in *Embroidery*, Vol. 2 No. 3

Snook, Barbara, *English Historical Embroidery*, Batsford 1960

Snook, Barbara, *Embroidery Stitches*, Batsford 1963

Snook, Barbara, *Creative Art of Embroidery*, Hamlyn 1972

Snook, Barbara, *English Embroidery*, Mills & Boon 1974

Spence, Anne, *Creative Embroidery*, Nelson 1975

Springall, Diana, *Canvas Embroidery*, Batsford 1980

Stafford, Cora E., *Paracas Embroideries*, J.J. Augustin 1941

Stapley, Mildred, *Popular Weaving and Embroidery in Spain*, Batsford 1974

Start, L.E., 'The Durham Collection of Garments and Embroideries from Albania and Yugoslavia' in *Bankfield Museum Notes* No. 4

Stearns, M.G., *Homespun and Blue*, Scribners 1963

Steel, F.A., 'Phulkari Work in the Punjab' in *Journal of Indian Art*, Vol. II No. 24 London 1888

Stein, Sir Marc Aurel, *Serindia*, Oxford University Press 1921

Stent, Peter, *A Booke of Beastes, Birds, Flowers, Fruits, Flies, and Wormes*, n.d.

Stent, Peter, *A New booke of Flowers, Fruicts, Beastes, Birds and Flies*, 1661

Stent, Peter, *Flora, Flowers, Fruicts, Beastes, Birds and Flies exactly drawne*, n.d.

Stent, Peter, *A Book of Slips*, n.d.

Stenton, Sir Frank, *The Bayeux Tapestry*, Phaidon 1957

Stevens, Gigs, *Freeform Bargello*, Scribners 1977

Stillwell, Alexandra, The Technique of Teneriffe Lace, Batsford 1980

Svennås, Elsie, Advanced Quilting, Evans 1980

Swain, M.H., *The Flowerers*, Chambers, Edinburgh 1955

Swain, M.H., 'Colifichets' in *Embroidery*, Vol. 18 No. 2, 1967

Swain, M.H., *Historical Needlework*, Barrie & Jenkins 1970

Swain, M.H., *The Needlework of Mary Queen of Scots*, Van Nostrand Reinhold 1973

Swain, M.H., 'Moose hair embroidery on birch bark' in *Antiques* 1975

Swain, M.H., *Figures on Fabric*, A. & C. Black 1980

Swan, S.B., *Plain and Fancy: American Women and their Needlework, 1700–1850*, Holt, Reinhart & Winston 1977

Swanson, Margaret and Macbeth, Ann, *Educational Needlecraft*, Longman Green, 1918

Swanson, Margaret and Macbeth, Ann, *Needlecraft for Older Girls*, Longman Green 1920

Swift, Gay, *Machine Stitchery*, Batsford 1974

Symonds, M., and Preece, *Needlework in Religion*, Pitman 1924

Symonds, M., and Preece, *Needlework Through the Ages* 1928

Taylor, John, *The Needle's Excellency*, James Boler 1640

Thom, Margaret, *Smocking in Embroidery*, Batsford 1972

Thomas, Mary, *A Dictionary of Embroidery Stitches*, Hodder 1934

Thomas, Mary, *Mary Thomas's Embroidery Book*, Hodder & Stoughton 1936

Tilke, M., *East European Costumes*, Ernest Benn

Timmins, Alice, *Introducing Patchwork*, Batsford 1968

Townsend, Mrs, *Art Needlework*, Collins 1910

Turmo, Isabel, *Bordados y Bordadores Sevillanos, Siglos XVI a XVIII*, Laboratorio de Arte, Universidad de Sevilla 1955

Turner, Miss, *Crewel and Silk Embroidery*, 1877

Turner, Geoffrey, *Hair Embroidery in Siberia and North America*, Oxford University Press 1955

Undi, Maria, *Hungarian Fancy Needlework*

Untermeyer, Irwin, *English and other Needlework, Tapestries and Textiles*, Cambridge University Press 1960

Vaclavik, A., and Orel, J., *Textile Folk Art in Czechoslovakia*, 1957

Varju-Ember, Maria, *Hungarian Domestic Embroidery*, Athenaeum Printing House, Budapest 1963

Vear, Rose, *A Textbook of Needlework, Knitting and Cutting-out with Methods of Teaching*, Macmillan 1894

Vinciolo, F., *Renaissance Patterns for Lace and Embroidery*, Dover reprint 1971 (1587)

Volkskunst in Europa, Verlag Ernst Wasmuth, Berlin

Wace, A.G.B., *Mediterranean and Near Eastern Embroidery*, Halton 1935

Waller, Irene, *Knots and Netting*, Studio Vista 1976

Walpole Society, 'English Domestic Embroidery Patterns of the 16th and 17th centuries' in Vol. XXVIII 1940

Wandel, Gertie, 'Icelandic Origin of Two Embroideries' in *Embroidery* Vol. 15, No. 3

Ward, 'Quilting in the North of England' in *Folk Life*, Vol. 4

Wardle, Patricia, *Guide to English Embroidery*, 1970

Wark, E., *Drawn Fabric Embroidery*, Batsford 1979

Warren, Geoffrey, *A Stitch in Time*, David and Charles 1976

Wasley, Ruth, and Harris, Edith, *Bead Design*, Allen & Unwin 1970

Watt, Sir George, *Indian Art at Delhi*, Calcutta 1904

Webster, M.D., *Quilts, Their Story and How to make Them*, Doubleday Page 1915, Tudor 1948

Weiss, Rita, ed., *Victorian Alphabets: monograms and names for needleworkers*, Dover 1974

Weldon's Practical Needlework, 1900

Wheeler, Candace, *The Development of Embroidery in America*, Harpers 1921

White, M.E., 'American Patchwork Quilts' in *Embroidery*, Autumn 1956

Whiting, Gertrude, *Old Time Tools and Toys of Needlework*, Dover reprint 1971 (1928)

Whyte, Kathleen, *Design in Embroidery*, Batsford, new edition 1982

Willcox, Donald, J., *New Designs for Stitchery*, Van Nostrand Reinhold 1970

Wild, J.P., *Textile Manufacture in the Northern Roman Provinces*, Cambridge University Press 1970

Wilder-Lane, Rose, *American Needlework*, Batsford 1963

Wilkie, Harriet Cushmann, ed., *The Priscilla Cross Stitch Book*

Wilkinson, M.E., *Embroidery Stitches*, Herbert Jenkins 1912

Williams, Elsa S., *Creative Canvas Work*, Van Nostrand Reinhold 1972

Williams, Elsa S., *Bargello, Florentine Canvas Work*, Van Nostrand Reinhold 1967

Williams, Elsa S., *Heritage Embroidery*, Van Nostrand Reinhold

Williams, Janice, *Lettering in Embroidery*, Batsford 1982

Williams, Violet M., *Pearson's Embroidery Book*, Pearson

Wilton, the Countess of, *The Art of Needlework*, 1840

Wingfield Digby, *Connoisseur*, IXXXII 1928

Wingfield Digby, *Connoisseur*, May 1960

Wingfield Digby, George, *Elizabethan Embroidery*, Faber & Faber 1963

Wooster, Ann-Sargent, *Quiltmaking*, Drake 1972, Studio Vista 1974

Worsley, Marie, *Embroidered Church Kneelers*, Mills & Boon 1967

Yarwood, Doreen, *The Encyclopaedia of World Costume*, Batsford 1978

Zimmerman, Jane, *Techniques of Metal Thread Embroidery*, Zimmerman 1977

Zulueta, F. de, *Embroideries by Mary Stuart and Elizabeth Talbot at Oxburgh Hall, Norfolk*, Oxford 1923

Collections

It would be impossible to give the names of all museums and galleries where embroidery can be seen. The following list is intended only as an introduction to some of the more important collections. Under the country headings, institutions are listed in alphabetical order according to location.

United Kingdom

Aston Hall, Trinity Road, Aston, Birmingham

The Bowes Museum, Barnard Castle, County Durham

The American Museum in Britain, Claverton Manor, Bath, Avon

The Museum of Costume, Assembly Rooms, Bath, Avon

Bolton Central Museum and Art Gallery, Le Mans Crescent, Bolton, Lancashire

Gawthorpe Hall, Padiham, Near Burnley, Lancashire

Fitzwilliam Museum, Trumpington Street, Cambridge

Cheltenham Museum, Clarence Street, Cheltenham, Gloucestershire

Colchester and Essex Museum, The Castle, Colchester, Essex

Ruskin Museum, Coniston, Cumbria

Clandon Park, Polesdon Lacey, Dorking, Surrey

Dorset County Museum, Dorchester

Durham Cathedral, County Durham

National Museum of Antiquities of Scotland, Queen Street, Edinburgh

The Embroiderers' Guild, Hampton Court Palace, East Molesey, Surrey

Glasgow Museums and Art Galleries, Camphill Museum, Pollokshaws Road, Glasgow

Gloucester Folk Museum, Westgate Street, Gloucester

Hauteville House, Guernsey

Guildford Museum, Castle Arch, Guildford, Surrey

Bankfield Museum and Art Gallery, Akroyd Park, Halifax, Yorkshire

Hardwick Hall, Derbyshire

Hereford City Museum and Art Gallery, Broad Street, Hereford

Ulster Folk and Transport Museum, Cultra Manor, Holywood, Co. Down

Traquair House, Innerleithen, Peeblesshire

Ipswich Museums, Civic Centre, Civic Drive, Ipswich, Suffolk

Levens Hall, Kendal, Cumbria

Lancaster City Council Museum, Market Square, Lancaster

Leeds City Museum, Municipal Buildings, Leeds

The Industrial Museum, Armley Mill, Canal Road, Leeds

The Moravian Museum, Fulneck, Pudsey, Leeds

Temple Newsam House, Leeds

Leek Art Gallery, Leek, Staffordshire

The Lady Lever Art Gallery, Port Sunlight Village, Birkenhead, Liverpool

The British Museum, Museum of Mankind, Great Russell Street, London

The Horniman Museum, London Road, Forest Hill, London

The Museum of London, London Wall, London

National Army Museum, Royal Hospital Road, Chelsea, London

National Portrait Gallery, St Martin's Place, London

Victoria and Albert Museum, South Kensington, London

Whitbread & Co. Ltd., The Brewery, Chiswell Street, London

William Morris Gallery, Walthamstowe, London

Luton Museum and Art Gallery, Wardown Park, Luton

The Gallery of English Costume, Platt Hall, Platt Fields, Rusholme, Manchester

Whitworth Art Gallery, Oxford Road, Manchester

Castle Museum, Norwich, Norfolk

Strangers' Hall, Charing Cross, Norwich

Nottingham Museum of Costume and Textiles, Castle Gate, Nottingham

Ashmolean Museum, Beaumont Street, Oxford

Pitt Rivers Museum, Parks Road, Oxford

The Harris Museum and Art Gallery, Market Square, Preston, Lancashire

Museum of English Rural Life, Whiteknights, Reading, Berkshire

Welsh Folk Museum, St Fagan's, South Glamorgan, Cymru

Cotehele House, St Dominick, Saltash, Cornwall

Beamish North of England Open Air Museum, Stanley, County Durham

Warwickshire Museum, Market Hall, Warwick

Oxfordshire County Museum, Fletcher's House, Woodstock

Wightwick Manor, Wolverhampton, Staffordshire

Castle Museum, York

Yorkshire Museum, York

USA

Museum of Fine Arts, Boston, Massachusetts

Indian Service Museum, Browning, Montana

Art Institute of Chicago, Illinois

Field Museum of Natural History, Chicago, Illinois

Memorial Hall Museum, Deerfield, Massachusetts

Denver Art Museum, Colorado

Peabody Museum of Archaeology and Ethnology, Harvard University, Massachusetts

William Penn Memorial Museum, Harrisburg, Pennsylvania

Newark Museum, New Jersey

Vivian Beck Ertelle Museum, New Jersey

Museum of the American Indian, New York

Brooklyn Museum, New York

Cooper-Hewitt Museum, Smithsonian Institution, New York

Metropolitan Museum of Art, New York

University of Pennsylvania Museum in Philadelphia

Valentine Museum, Richmond, Virginia

Museum of International Folk Art, Santa Fe, New Mexico

Shelburne Museum, Shelburne, Vermont

Old Sturbridge Village, Massachusetts

The Textile Museum, Washington, DC

Daughters of the American Revolution Museum, Washington DC

Williamsburg Museum, Virginia

Winterthur Museum, Wilmington, Delaware

Austria

Imperial Schatzkammer, Vienna

Museum für Volkerkunde, Vienna

Canada

Royal Ontario Museum, Toronto

Hudson's Bay Company Museum, Winnipeg

China

National Museum of History, Taipei

National Palace Museum, Taipei

Denmark

Copenhagen National Museum

Kunstindustrimuseet, Copenhagen

Eire

National Folk Museum of Ireland, Dublin

France

Bayeux Museum, Normandy

Cluny Museum, Paris

Musée de l'Homme, Paris

Germany

Altona Museum, Hamburg

National Museum, Munich

Greece

Benaki Museum, Athens

Museum of Greek Folk Art, Athens

Hungary

Ethnographical Museum, Budapest

India

Calico Museum of Textiles, Ahmedabad

Jaipur Museum

Italy

Industrie Femminili Italiano, Florence

Museo delle Opere del Duomo, Florence

Peru

Museo Nacional de Anthropologia y Arqueologia in Lima

Spain

Gerona Cathedral, Catalonia

Sweden

Ethnographic Museum, Göteborg

Switzerland

Basel Museum

Textilmuseum St Gallen

Appendix: Quotations

Decorated textiles are of an ephemeral and perishable nature, and so contemporary descriptions of them, their use and their making are even more tantalizing to those of us fascinated by them.

The Phrygian Queen to her rich wardrobe went,
Where treasured odours breathed a costly scent.
There lay the vestures of no vulgar art,
Sidonian maids embroidered every part,
Whom from soft Sidon youthful Paris bore,
With Helen touching on the Tyrian shore.
Here as the Queen revolv'd with careful eyes
The various textures and the various dyes,
She chose a veil that shone superior far,
And glow'd refulgent as the morning star.

> Homer, *The Iliad*, VI

And they did beat the gold into thin plates, and cut it into wires, to work it in the blue, and in the purple, and in the scarlet, and in the fine linen, with cunning work.
They made shoulderpieces for it, to couple it together: by the two edges was it coupled together.
And the curious girdle of his ephod, that was upon it, was of the same, according to the work thereof; of gold, blue, and purple, and scarlet, and fine twisted linen; as the Lord commanded Moses. . . .
And there was an hole in the midst of the robe, as the hole of a habergeon, with a band round about the hole, that it should not rend.
And they made upon the hems of the robe pomegranates of blue, and purple, and scarlet, and twined linen.
And they made bells of pure gold, and put the bells between the pomegranates upon the hem of the robe, round about between the pomegranates;
A bell and a pomegranate, a bell and a pomegranate, round about the hem of the robe to minister in; as the Lord commanded Moses.

> Exodus XXXIX

Gentle Reader, I would have you know that the Diversitie of Examples which you will find in the Scole-Howse for the Needle are only but patterns which serve but to helpe and inlarge your invention. But for the disposing of them into forme and order of Workes that I leave to your own skill and understanding. Whose ingenious and well practiced wits will soe readily (I doubt not) compose them into such beautiful formes as will be able to give content, both to the worker and the wearers of them.

> Shorleyker, *A Schole-Howse for the needle*, 1624

Flowers, plants and fishes, beasts, birds, flies, and bees,
Hills, dales, plains, pastures, skies, seas, rivers, trees,
There's nothing near at hand or farthest sought
But with the needle may be shaped and wrought.
                    Taylor, *The Needles Excellency*, 1634

I found plenty of slender-lipped, satin-clad maidens, wearing wondrous gold
fringes in the . . . rampart abounding in fair, sleek hounds.
                                        Oh'Uiginn, *Tadhg Dall*

The Company of Embroiderers can make appear by their worthy and famous
Pieces of Art, that they have been of ancient Ufe and Eminence, as may be feen
in divers Places at this Day. But as to the matter of their Incorporation, it hath
Relation to the 4th of Q Eliz.. Their Enfigns Armorial are Paly of fix Argent and
Sable, on a Fefs Gules between three Lions of England, two Broches Sattirewife
between as many Trundles, Or.

                                    Mr Guillim's Heraldry

. . . . no special studio need be devoted to its use, for most work can be done in
any well-lighted room, which indeed will be rendered more attractive by the
presence of an embroidery frame, for this is in itself a characteristic and dainty
piece of furniture. It need but seldom interfere with one of our pleasant
traditions, genial converse with, and about, our neighbours, for it is a distinctly
sociable occupation. Work of this kind can be put down and taken up at leisure;
the necessary outlay in materials need not be extravagant, and so on.
                                    Mrs Archibald Christie, 1928

HEREWARD COLLEGE OF FURTHER EDUCATION
BRAMSTON CRESCENT
COVENTRY
CV4 9SW